Advanced Information and Knowledge Processing

Also in this series

Gregoris Mentzas, Dimitris Apostolou, Andreas Abecker and Ron Young
Knowledge Asset Management
1-85233-583-1

Michalis Vazirgiannis, Maria Halkidi and Dimitrios Gunopulos
Uncertainty Handling and Quality Assessment in Data Mining
1-85233-655-2

Asunción Gómez-Pérez,
Mariano Fernández-López and
Oscar Corcho

Ontological Engineering

with examples from the areas of Knowledge Management, e-Commerce and the Semantic Web

With 159 Figures

 Springer

Asunción Gómez-Pérez, PhD, MSc, MBA
Mariano Fernández-López, PhD, MSc
Oscar Corcho, MSc
Facultad de Informatica, Universidad Politécnica de Madrid,
Campus de Montegancedo sn., Boadilla del Monte, 28660 Madrid, Spain

Series Editors
Xindong Wu
Lakhmi Jain

British Library Cataloguing in Publication Data
A catalogue record for this book is available from the British Library

Library of Congress Cataloging-in-Publication Data
Gómez-Pérez, Asunción, 1967-
 Ontological engineering : with examples from the areas of knowledge management,
 e-commerce and the semantic web / Asunción Gómez-Pérez, Mariano Fernández-López,
 and Oscar Corcho.
  p. cm.—(Advanced information and knowledge processing)
 Includes bibliographical references and index.
 ISBN 1-85233-551-3 (alk. paper)
  1. Expert systems (Computer science) 2. Knowledge management. 3. Semantic Web. I.
Fernández-López, Mariano, 1971- II. Corcho, Oscar, 1976- III. Title. IV. Series.
QA76.76.E95G65 2003
006.3'3—dc22

                                                                    2003058516

AI&KP ISSN 1610-3947

ISBN 1-85233-551-3 Springer-Verlag London Berlin Heidelberg
Springer-Verlag is a part of Springer Science+Business Media
springeronline.com

© Springer-Verlag London Limited 2004
2nd printing, 2004
3rd printing, 2004
4th printing, 2005

Typesetting: Electronic text files prepared by authors
Printed and bound in the United States of America
34/3830-5432 Printed on acid-free paper SPIN 11367574

Preface

Ontological Engineering refers to the set of activities that concern the ontology development process, the ontology life cycle, the methods and methodologies for building ontologies, and the tool suites and languages that support them.

During the last decade, increasing attention has been focused on ontologies and Ontological Engineering. Ontologies are now widely used in Knowledge Engineering, Artificial Intelligence and Computer Science; in applications related to knowledge management, natural language processing, e-commerce, intelligent integration information, information retrieval, integration of databases, bio-informatics, and education; and in new emerging fields like the Semantic Web.

Primary goals of this book are to acquaint students, researchers and developers of information systems with the basic concepts and major issues of Ontological Engineering, as well as to make ontologies more understandable to those computer science engineers that integrate ontologies into their information systems. We have paid special attention to the influence that ontologies have on the Semantic Web. Pointers to the Semantic Web appear in all the chapters, but specially in the chapter on ontology languages and tools.

Many different methods, tools and languages, as well as the most outstanding ontologies, are presented to illustrate a diversity of approaches, but no single technique receives special attention. Each individual may choose to emphasize particular techniques depending on his/her own circumstances and interests. So, the book is designed to operate at two levels. First, as a simple introduction to the major areas of Ontological Engineering, and second, as a reference book. The emerging areas and the most up-to-date standards have also been considered.

The layout of the text is divided into five chapters: theoretical foundations, the most outstanding ontologies, methodologies, languages, and tools for developing ontologies. In every chapter (except the chapter that describes the most outstanding ontologies) we have used examples taken from the traveling domain. This provides a focal point for the book and allows readers to practise and compare different modeling techniques, different and similar methods and methodologies for building ontologies, and learn about ontology languages and different types of tools. We also include comparative studies of methodologies, tools and languages to advise ontologists on their use.

The first chapter contains the **theoretical foundations** of the ontology field. Here we explain what an ontology is, the main types of ontologies, the main modeling components of ontologies based on frames or description logic, the design criteria for building ontologies as well as the relationships with other modeling techniques that are widely used on software engineering and databases.

Chapter 2 is devoted to **the most outstanding ontologies**. We present different types of ontologies: knowledge representation ontologies of traditional (i.e., Ontolingua and OKBC) and ontology mark-up languages (i.e., RDF(S), OIL, DAML+OIL, and OWL), top level ontologies, linguistic ontologies, and domain ontologies in the areas of e-commerce, medicine, engineering, enterprise, chemistry and knowledge management.

In Chapter 3 we explore different **methods and methodologies for ontology construction**. We present in detail the ontology development process and the methods and methodologies that support the ontology construction from scratch. We also discuss particular methods that allow specific activities. Special attention is given to the ontology learning methods that reduce the effort during the knowledge acquisition process; the merging of ontologies that generates a unique ontology from several ontologies; the ontology alignment that establishes different types of mapping between ontologies (hence preserving the original ones); and the ontology evaluation for evaluating the ontology content. For each methodology and method, we give an example taken from the traveling domain.

Chapter 4 deals with the process of selecting the **ontology language** (or set of languages) in which the ontology will be implemented. We describe how to implement ontologies in classical languages (Ontolingua, KIF, OCML and FLogic), the OKBC protocol, and web-based ontology languages (SHOE, XOL, RDF(S), OIL, DAML+OIL and OWL) that have laid the foundations of the Semantic Web. Some of them, like RDF(S) and OWL, are still in a development phase. As we have implemented an ontology of the traveling domain in all these languages, we compare their expressiveness and the reasoning mechanisms of each language.

Finally, Chapter 5 is concerned with several types of the **tools** and platforms used to build ontologies and tools that allow the use of ontologies for the Semantic Web. As in the previous chapters, we provide examples of ontologies with the tools of the traveling domain.

We hope that in the near future we will be able to support this text with a web site and give updates and slides for undergraduate and PhD courses.

For further information or comments contact *OE@delicias.dia.fi.upm.es*.

Asunción Gómez-Pérez
Mariano Fernández-López
Oscar Corcho

Facultad de Informática, UPM
May 2003

Acknowledgements

During the evolution of this book we have accumulated many debts, only a small proportion of which we have space to acknowledge here. We are particularly indebted to Rosario Plaza Arteche for her valuable help in checking and reviewing the grammar and spelling of the manuscript and improving clarity and style. Her sound, conscientious advice has been continuous while writing the whole book. We must also thank José Ángel Ramos Gargantilla who has helped us with the editing of the book and also for his valuable assistance with the creation of the text.

We are very grateful to the reviewers of some sections and chapters (Trevor Bench-Capon, John Domingue, Aldo Gangemi, Nicola Guarino, Boris Motik, Natasha Noy, Juan Pazos, York Sure, Valentina Tamma). They found time in their busy schedules to read the text and provide valuable suggestions for its improvement. We also give thanks to Manuel Lama Penín who reviewed the whole manuscript and contributed to the medical ontologies, and to Socorro Bernardos Galindo who made significant contributions to the linguistic ontologies.

We are also indebted to the Ontological Engineering community, whose ideas, methodologies, tools and languages are reported here. We have attempted to acknowledge their contributions where possible. Some of them are the results of interesting discussions with participants of OntoWeb (IST-2000-29243), MKBEEM (IST-1999-10589) and Esperonto (IST-2001-34373).

The following members of the Ontology Group at UPM made specially valuable suggestions and comments: Raquel Arpírez, Jesús Barrasa, José Cebrián, Miguel Esteban, Rafael González-Cabero, Antonio Pareja-Lora, Vanessa López, Ángel López-Cima, Adolfo Lozano-Tello, David Manzano, Rafael Núñez, José Ángel Ramos Gargantilla, Nuria Sánchez, María del Carmen Suárez-Figueroa, and Esther Úbeda-Portugués.

We are deeply beholden to the people at Springer-Verlag for their encouragement and belief in the value of this enterprise.

Finally, we owe very much to our families for their love and support without which we could not have finished this book.

All the errors and omissions which undoubtedly remain are entirely our own responsibility.

Contents

Chapter 1

Theoretical Foundations of Ontologies

Ontologies are widely used in Knowledge Engineering, Artificial Intelligence and Computer Science, in applications related to knowledge management, natural language processing, e-commerce, intelligent integration information, information retrieval, database design and integration, bio-informatics, education, and in new emerging fields like the Semantic Web.

In 1991, the DARPA Knowledge Sharing Effort (Neches et al., 1991, page 37) envisioned a new way to build intelligent systems. They proposed the following:

Building knowledge-based systems today usually entails constructing new knowledge bases from scratch. It could be instead done by assembling reusable components. System developers would then only need to worry about creating the specialized knowledge and reasoners new to the specific task of their system. This new system would interoperate with existing systems, using them to perform some of its reasoning. In this way, declarative knowledge, problem-solving techniques and reasoning services would all be shared among systems. This approach would facilitate building bigger and better systems and cheaply...

Declarative knowledge is modeled by means of ontologies while problem solving methods specify generic reasoning mechanisms. Both types of components can be viewed as complementary entities that can be used to configure new knowledge-based systems from existing reusable components. Nicola Guarino (1998) pointed out the main benefits of using ontologies at design time since

It enables the developer to practice a 'higher' level of reuse than is usually the case in software engineering (i.e. knowledge reuse instead of software reuse). Moreover, it enables the developer to reuse and share application domain knowledge using a common vocabulary

1

across heterogeneous software platforms. It also enables the developer
to concentrate on the structure on the domain and the task at hand and
protects him from being bothered too much by implementation details.

At the time of the presentation of DARPAs idea, several projects were being carried out on methodologies to develop knowledge-based systems. Although these projects did not all deal directly with ontologies, they laid the foundation of these notions in the Knowledge Engineering community. These projects included Task Structures (Chandrasekaran et al., 1992), Role-Limiting Methods (McDermott, 1988), CommonKADS (Schreiber et al., 1994), Protégé (Musen, 1993), MIKE (Angele et al., 1998), IDEAL (Gómez-Pérez et al., 1997), Components of Expertise (Steels, 1990), EXPECT (Swartout and Gil, 1995), GDM (Terpstra et al., 1993) and VITAL (Domingue et al., 1993).

Since then considerable progress has been made to develop the conceptual bases to build technology that allows reusing and sharing knowledge-components. Ontologies and Problem Solving Methods (PSMs) have been created to share and reuse knowledge and reasoning behavior across domains and tasks. Ontologies are concerned with static domain knowledge while PSMs deal with modeling reasoning processes. A PSM defines (Benjamins and Gómez-Pérez, 1999) a way of achieving the goal of a task. It has inputs and outputs and may decompose a task into subtasks, and tasks into methods. In addition, a PSM specifies the data flow between its subtasks. An important PSM component is its method ontology because it describes the concepts used by the method on the reasoning process as well as the relationships between such concepts.

The integration of ontologies and PSMs is a possible solution to the interaction problem (Bylander and Chandrasekaran, 1988) which states that

Representing knowledge for the purpose of solving some problem is
strongly affected by the nature of the problem and the inference
strategy to be applied to the problem.

Through ontologies and PSMs, this interaction can be made explicit in the notion of mappings between the ontology of the domain and the method ontology. Currently, there is an interesting study on the integration of ontologies and PSMs, for instance (Park et al., 1998).

The emergence of the Semantic Web has marked another stage in the evolution of ontologies (and PSMs). According to Berners-Lee (1999), the Semantic Web is an extension of the current Web in which information is given well-defined meaning, better enabling computers and people to work in cooperation. This cooperation can be achieved by using shared knowledge-components, and so ontologies and PSMs have become key instruments in developing the Semantic Web. Ontologies represent static domain knowledge and PSMs will be used inside Semantic Web Services that model reasoning processes and deal with that domain knowledge.

In this section, we will present the fundamental concepts about ontologies, and at the end of this chapter, the reader will be able to answer questions such as: what is an ontology?; what are the main types of ontologies?; what are their main components?; what design criteria should be followed to build ontologies?; what are the main differences between ontologies and databases?; what are the main differences between modeling a domain with ontologies and with software engineering modeling techniques?; and finally, how are ontologies and knowledge bases related?

1.1 From Ontology Towards Ontological Engineering

What are things? What is the *essence*[1] that remains inside things even when they change (changes in their color, changes in their size, etc.)? Do concepts (*book, tree, table*, etc.) exist outside our mind? How can the entities of the world be classified? These are some of the questions that Ontology, the philosophy of being[2], has tried to answer for thousands of years. In Ontology, we can distinguish between essence and existence. The essence of something is what this something *is* (Gambra, 1999). However, an existence is *to be* present among things in the real world. For instance, a centaur is half a man and half a horse, so it has essence though it does not exist.

Ancient Greeks were concerned about the difficulties encountered when they tried to find the essence of things through the changes. For example, a seed first gets rotten and then it becomes a tree. In this case, when the seed is not a seed any longer and the tree begins to be a tree, what does remain in the essence of that seed? Many different answers to this question were proposed by Greek philosophers, from Parmenides of Elea (5th and 4th centuries BC), the precursor of Ontology, to Aristotle, author of the *MetaPhysics* (a work that might as well have been called Ontology). But it was Parmenides, who assuming the independence of the essence of things with regard to our senses, provided a surprising answer to this question. There are no changes, because something that *is* cannot begin to be nor can end to be. That is, the seed is not transformed into a tree, but it is our senses that first perceive the seed and later perceive the tree. It is as if both the seed and the tree were in the same movie reel and, when placed in the light, we could only observe the seed or the tree. In terms of current information systems, it is as if both the seed and the tree were in the same database, but accessible through different views.

With regard to Aristotle's answer to the question "what does it remain in the essence of the seed?", he would say that the seed is a tree not completely fulfilled. Thus, according to Aristotle, it is not the case that something which is not a tree becomes a tree, but that the tree changes its mode of being, from not completely fulfilled (tree in potency) into completely fulfilled (tree in act). Aristotle also distinguished different modes of being to establish a system of categories (*substance, quality, quantity, relation, action, passion, place* and *time*) to classify anything that may be *predicated* (said) about anything in the world. For example,

---

[1] Rigorously speaking, we should not have used the word "essence" in some places of this section but different ones ("being", "to be", etc.). However, since this book is mainly addressed to non-experts in philosophy, we think that the word "essence" seems more natural and intuitive.
[2] *ontos* = being, *logos* = treatise

when we say "this computer *is* on the table" we are assuming a different mode of being to when we say "this computer *is* grey". The first statement is classified inside the category of *place*, while the second is inside the category of *quality*. The categorization proposed by Aristotle was widely accepted until Kant's.

Let us now move from the ancient Greek to the Middle Ages. In that period, one of the key issues in Ontology was *universals* (Marías, 2001). The counterparts of universals in knowledge modeling are classes or concepts (e.g., man, book, computer) in contrast with individuals (e.g., John, this book, my computer). A key question here is: are universals actual things? If the answer is yes, we assume *realism*. If the answer is that universals are only words used to refer to things, we assume *nominalism*. This was the prevailing tendency at the end of the Middle Ages. According to William of Ockam (14th century), universals are only signs (symbols). For instance, the universal *book* is just a symbol used to refer to all the books. This is the starting point of modern Physics, which handles symbols that represent different features of Nature (velocity, size, etc.). Modern Computer Science has also inherited this symbolic approach, especially in the symbolic paradigm, which considers intelligence as symbol management. However, if we had to question ourselves: "Where are universals in an information system?" We should answer that they are in the definition of its class frames, knowledge base, database tables, etc.

In the Modern Age, Emmanuel Kant (1724-1804) provoked a *Copernican turn*. The essence of things is not only determined by the things themselves, but also by the contribution of whoever perceives and understands them. According to Kant, a key question is "what structures does our mind use to capture the reality?". The answer to this question leads to Kant's categorization. Kant's framework is organized into four classes, each of which presents a triadic pattern: *quantity* (*unity*, *plurality*, *totality*), *quality* (*reality*, *negation*, *limitation*), *relation* (*inherence*, *causality*, *community*) and *modality* (*possibility*, *existence*, *necessity*). Therefore, our mind classifies the object John as unique, real, existing, etc.

Kant obtained these categories starting from the logic classification of judgments. Thus, for instance, *unity* matches singular judgments ("John is mortal"), *plurality* matches particular judgments ("some English are rich"), and *totality* matches universal judgments ("all men are mortal"), etc. To capture reality, a person puts its sensations in order: first, in space and time, and then, according to the categories. For example, when a person sees John, first, (s)he situates John as something which is here and now, and then, (s)he establishes that John is unique, real, existing, etc. Information systems do not work exactly in the same way as the processes of perception and understanding proposed by Kant. However, this new approach can be applied to the current information systems. In fact, in an information system, an object of a domain does not depend only on reality, but also on the information system design. For instance, John has a name and an age inside a system because the system has created John as an instance of the class Person, which was created at design time, and which has two attributes called name and age. Another key concept in Kant's philosophy is "experience". In fact, the reality in a subject is also conditioned by his experience. In the case of computers, their experience is in their memory.

José Ortega y Gasset (1883-1955) went one step further than Kant. He stated that the world strongly depends on the person who perceives it. And then we could add that this is not valid only for persons but for information systems. In fact, each system may represent the world in different ways, and it may even perceive different features of the same world. Furthermore, according to the *pragmatism* proposed by William James (1842-1910), truth is what each person considers to have the best consequences. Information systems also follow this theory, in the sense that their data structures and knowledge bases are designed not to represent the world faithfully but to work more efficiently for the purpose they have been designed.

At the end of the 20th century and the beginning of the 21st, ontologies have emerged as an important research area in Computer Science. One of the philosophical areas that provides theoretical foundations is Formal Ontology, a branch of the ontological research begun by Husserl, who followed Kant's line of thought evolved through the years. According to Nino Cocchiarella (1991), Formal Ontology is the systematic, formal, axiomatic development of the logic of all forms and modes of being. It studies the formal properties and the classification of the entities of the world (physical objects, events, etc.), and of the categories that model the world (concept, property, etc.).

Until now, a large number of ontologies have been developed by different groups, under different approaches, and with different methods and techniques. **Ontological Engineering** refers to the set of activities that concern the ontology development process, the ontology life cycle, and the methodologies, tools and languages for building ontologies. The progress in building ontologies, which have to model agreed views of the reality, are many. Nevertheless, consensus has its own limits. As Ortega y Gasset (1939, page 91) said: *"una realidad que vista desde cualquier punto resultase siempre idéntica es un concepto absurdo"*[3]. Therefore, ontologies must make unity compatible with variety. So we return to the essence of the Greek philosophy, which tried to make unity compatible with variety, although in a different context.

To finish, we would like to pose a question. According to Julián Marías (2001), from the ancient Greeks until approximately Galileo's times, learned people were concerned about what things are, what remains inside things even when they change, etc. That is, they were interested in extracting the essence of things. However, the pre-eminent position of nominalism at the end of the Middle Ages led to a new science, which was much more concerned in how to codify characteristics of things (size, speed, etc.) using symbols. But currently, Ontological Engineering originates in the context of the new science that codifies features of things, and on the other hand, ontologists are devoted to extract the essence of things. Furthermore, the more the essence of things is captured, the more possible it is for the ontology to be shared. Therefore, is not Ontological Engineering a synthesis of old and new science?

---

[3] It is nonsense to have a real thing which is always the same independently from where it is perceived.

1.2 What is an Ontology?

As was seen in the previous section, the word ontology was taken from Philosophy, where it means a systematic explanation of being. In the last decade, this word has become relevant for the Knowledge Engineering community. Guarino and Giaretta (1995) propose to use the words 'Ontology' (with capital 'o') and 'ontology' to refer to the philosophical and Knowledge Engineering senses respectively. We have read many definitions about what an ontology is and have also observed how such definitions have changed and evolved over the years. In this section, we will review these definitions and explain the relationships between them.

One of the first definitions was given by Neches and colleagues (1991, page 40), who defined an ontology as follows:

An ontology defines the basic terms and relations comprising the vocabulary of a topic area as well as the rules for combining terms and relations to define extensions to the vocabulary.

This descriptive definition tells us what to do to build an ontology, and gives us some vague guidelines: this definition identifies basic terms and relations between terms, identifies rules to combine terms, and provides the definitions of such terms and relations. Note that, according to Neches' definition, an ontology includes not only the terms that are explicitly defined in it, but also the knowledge that can be inferred from it.

A few years later, Gruber (1993a, page 199) defined an ontology as follows:

An ontology is an explicit specification of a conceptualization.

This definition became the most quoted in literature and by the ontology community. Based on Gruber's definition, many definitions of what an ontology is were proposed. Borst (1997, page 12) modified slightly Gruber's definition as follows:

Ontologies are defined as a formal specification of a shared conceptualization.

Gruber's and Borst's definitions have been merged and explained by Studer and colleagues (1998, page 185) as follows:

An ontology is a formal, explicit specification of a shared conceptualization. Conceptualization refers to an abstract model of some phenomenon in the world by having identified the relevant concepts of that phenomenon. Explicit means that the type of concepts used, and the constraints on their use are explicitly defined. Formal refers to the fact that the ontology should be machine-readable. Shared reflects the notion that an ontology captures consensual knowledge, that is, it is not private of some individual, but accepted by a group.

In 1995, Guarino and Giaretta (1995) collected and analyzed the following seven definitions:

1. *Ontology as a philosophical discipline.*
2. *Ontology as an informal conceptual system.*
3. *Ontology as a formal semantic account.*
4. *Ontology as a specification of a conceptualization.*
5. *Ontology as a representation of a conceptual system via a logical theory*
   5.1. *characterized by specific formal properties.*
   5.2. *characterized only by its specific purposes.*
6. *Ontology as the vocabulary used by a logical theory.*
7. *Ontology as a (meta-level) specification of a logical theory.*

On that paper, Guarino and Giaretta proposed to consider an ontology as:

> *A logical theory which gives an explicit, partial account of a conceptualization.*

where a conceptualization is basically the idea of the world that a person or a group of people can have. Though on the surface the notion of conceptualization is quite similar to Studer and colleagues' notion (1998), we can say that Guarino and Giaretta (1995) went a step further because they formalized the notion of conceptualization and established how to build the ontology by making a logical theory. Hence, strictly speaking, this definition would be only applicable to ontologies developed in logic. Guarino and Giaretta's work has been further refined (Guarino, 1998, page 4), and they provide the following definition:

> *A set of logical axioms designed to account for the intended meaning of a vocabulary.*

There is another group of definitions based on the process followed to build the ontology. These definitions also include some highlights about the relationship between ontologies and knowledge bases. For example, the definition given by Bernaras and colleagues (1996, page 298) in the framework of the KACTUS project (Schreiber et al., 1995) is:

> *It [an ontology] provides the means for describing explicitly the conceptualization behind the knowledge represented in a knowledge base.*

Note that this definition proposes "extracting" the ontology from a knowledge base, which reflects the approach the authors use to build ontologies. In this approach, the ontology is built, following a bottom-up strategy, on the basis of an application knowledge base by means of an abstraction process. As more applications are built, the ontology becomes more general, and, therefore, it moves further away from what would be a knowledge base.

Another strategy for building ontologies is to reuse large ontologies like SENSUS (Swartout et al., 1997, page 138) (with more than 70,000 nodes) to create domain specific ontologies and knowledge bases:

> *An ontology is a hierarchically structured set of terms for describing a domain that can be used as a skeletal foundation for a knowledge base.*

According to this definition, the same ontology can be used for building several knowledge bases, which would share the same skeleton or taxonomy. Extensions of the skeleton should be possible at the low level by adding domain-specific subconcepts, or at the high level by adding intermediate or upper level concepts that cover new areas. If systems are built with the same ontology, they share a common underlying structure, therefore, merging and sharing their knowledge bases and inference mechanisms will become easier.

Sometimes the notion of ontology is diluted, in the sense that taxonomies are considered full ontologies (Studer et al., 1998). For instance, UNSPSC[4], e-cl@ss[5], and RosettaNet[6], proposals for standards on the e-commerce domain, and the Yahoo! Directory, a taxonomy for searching the Web, are also considered ontologies (Lassila and McGuinness, 2001) because they provide a consensual conceptualization of a given domain. The ontology community distinguishes ontologies that are mainly taxonomies from ontologies that model the domain in a deeper way and provide *more restrictions* on domain semantics. The community calls them *lightweight* and *heavyweight ontologies* respectively. On the one hand, lightweight ontologies include concepts, concept taxonomies, relationships between concepts, and properties that describe concepts. On the other hand, heavyweight ontologies add axioms and constraints to lightweight ontologies. Axioms and constraints clarify the intended meaning of the terms gathered on the ontology.

Since ontologies are widely used for different purposes (natural language processing, knowledge management, e-commerce, intelligent integration of information, the Semantic Web, etc.) in different communities (i.e., knowledge engineering, databases and software engineering), Uschold and Jasper (1999, page 11-2) provided a new definition of the word ontology to popularize it in other disciplines. Note that the database community as well as the object oriented design community also build domain models using concepts, relations, properties, etc., but most of the times both communities impose less semantic constraints than those imposed in heavyweight ontologies. Uschold and Jasper defined an ontology as:

> *An ontology may take a variety of forms, but it will necessarily include a vocabulary of terms and some specification of their meaning. This includes definitions and an indication of how concepts are inter-related which collectively impose a structure on the domain and constrain the possible interpretations of terms.*

In this section we have collected the most relevant definitions of the word ontology, though other definitions of this word can be found in Artificial Intelligence literature. However, we can say that as there is consensus among the ontology community, no one can get confused about its usage. Different definitions provide different and complementary points of view of the same reality. Some authors provide definitions that are independent of the processes followed to build the ontology and of its use in applications, while other definitions are influenced by its development process. As a main conclusion to this section, we can say that ontologies aim to capture *consensual* knowledge in a generic way, and that they may

---

[4] http://www.unspsc.org/
[5] http://www.eclass.org/
[6] http://www.rosettanet.org/

be reused and shared across software applications and by groups of people. They are usually built cooperatively by different groups of people in different locations.

1.3 Which are the Main Components of an Ontology?

Heavyweight and lightweight ontologies can be modeled with different knowledge modeling techniques and they can be implemented in various kinds of languages (Uschold and Grüninger, 1996). Ontologies can be *highly informal* if they are expressed in natural language; *semi-informal* if expressed in a restricted and structured form of natural language; *semi-formal* if expressed in an artificial and formally defined language (i.e., Ontolingua (Farquhar et al., 1997), OWL (Dean and Schreiber, 2003)); and *rigorously formal* if they provide meticulously defined terms with formal semantics, theorems and proofs of properties such as soundness[7] and completeness. Note that according to the definition of Studer and colleagues (1998), a highly informal ontology would not be an ontology since it is not machine-readable. Figure 1.1 presents the template used to build the class `Research-Topic` in the ontology of the (KA)[2] initiative (Benjamins et al., 1999) in a semi-informal language, and its implementation in the Ontolingua language.

At the beginning of the 1990s, ontologies were built using mainly AI modeling techniques based on frames and first-order logic (i.e., Cyc ontology (Lenat and Guha, 1990), Ontolingua ontologies[8]). In the last few years, other knowledge representation techniques based on description logics (Baader et al., 2003) have been used to build ontologies and new description logics languages like OIL (Horrocks et al., 2000), DAML+OIL (Horrocks and van Harmelen, 2001) and OWL (Dean and Schreiber, 2003) have appeared in the context of the Semantic Web.

It is important to mention here that there are important connections and implications between the knowledge modeling components (concepts, roles, etc.) used to build an ontology, the knowledge representation paradigms (frames, description logics, logic) used to represent formally such components, and the languages used to implement the ontologies under a given knowledge representation paradigm. That is, an ontology built with frames or description logics can be implemented in several frames or description logics languages, as we will explain in Chapter 4.

Other techniques widely used in software engineering and databases for modeling concepts, relationships between concepts, and concept attributes could also be appropriate for building lightweight ontologies because these techniques impose a structure to the domain knowledge and constrain the interpretations of terms. However, it is important to remark that the model can only be considered an ontology if it is a shared and consensual knowledge model agreed by a community.

---

[7] Inspired by classical first order logic terminology (Hermes, 1973) (Lloyd, 1993), we say that an ontology is sound if and only if it does not allow deducing invalid conclusions. We say that an ontology is complete if and only if it allows deducing all the possible valid conclusions starting from the ontology vocabulary and applying the deduction rules permitted.

[8] http://ontolingua.stanford.edu/

```
Class: Research-Topic
 Attributes:
    Name: <string>
    Description: <text>
    Approaches: <set-of keyword>
    Research-groups: <set-of research-group>
    Researchers: <set-of researcher>
    Related-topics: <set-of research-topic>
    Sub-topics: <set-of research-topic>
    Events: <set-of events>
    Journals: <set-of journal>
    Projects: <set-of project>
    Application-areas: <text>
    Products: <set-of product>
    Bibliographies: <set-of HTML-link>
    Mailing-lists: <set-of mailing-list>
    Webpages: <set-of HTML-link>
    International-funding-agencies: <funding-agency>
    National-funding-agencies: <funding-agency>
    Author-of-ontology: <set-of researcher>
    Date-of-last-modification: <date>
```

a) Template used to build the class `Research-Topic` ontology of the (KA)² ontology.

```
(define-class Research-Topic (?X)
   ""
:def
 (and (name ?X String) (description ?X String) (approaches ?X String)
      (research-groups ?X Research-Group) (researchers ?X Researcher)
      (related-topics ?X Research-Topic) (sub-topics ?X Research-Topic)
      (events ?X Event) (journals ?X Journal) (projects ?X Project)
      (application-areas ?X String) (products ?X Product)
      (bibliographies ?X URL) (mailing-lists ?X EMail) (webpages ?X URL)
      (international-funding-agencies ?X Funding-Agency)
      (national-funding-agencies ?X Funding-Agency)
      (author-of-ontology ?X Researcher)
      (date-of-last-modification ?X Date))
:axiom-def
 (and (Template-Facet-Value Cardinality name Research-Topic 1)
      (Template-Facet-Value Minimum-Cardinality description Research-Topic 1)
      (Template-Facet-Value Minimum-Cardinality researchers Research-Topic 1)
      (Template-Facet-Value Minimum-Cardinality related-topics Research-Topic 1)
      (Template-Facet-Value Minimum-Cardinality bibliographies Research-Topic 1)
      (Template-Facet-Value Minimum-Cardinality author-of-ontology Research-Topic 1)
      (Template-Facet-Value Cardinality date-of-last-modification Research-Topic 1)))
```

b) The class `Research-Topic` implemented in Ontolingua.

Figure 1.1: Semi-informal and semi-formal implementation of the class `Research-Topic`.

In this section we present different techniques that could be applied to model ontologies, although not all of them can represent the same knowledge with the same degree of formality and granularity. We show how heavyweight ontologies can be modeled taking AI-based approaches that combine frames and first order logic or use description logics. We also present how other approaches based on software engineering (UML) and databases (Entity/Relationship diagram) only allow the representation of lightweight ontologies. In this section we are comparing the models obtained with AI-based techniques and software engineering and database techniques, and we conclude that ontologies built using AI techniques constrain the possible interpretations of terms much more than ontologies built with software engineering and database techniques.

1.3.1 Modeling heavyweight ontologies using frames and first order logic

Gruber (1993a) proposed to model ontologies using frames and first order logic. He identified five kinds of components: classes, relations, functions, formal axioms and instances. In this section we present such components with an example in the traveling domain.

Classes represent concepts, which are taken in a broad sense. For instance, in the traveling domain, concepts are: locations (cities, villages, etc.), lodgings (hotels, camping, etc.) and means of transport (planes, trains, cars, ferries, motorbikes and ships). Classes in the ontology are usually organized in taxonomies through which inheritance mechanisms can be applied. We can represent a taxonomy of entertainment places (theater, cinema, concert, etc.) or travel packages (economy travel, business travel, etc.). The following example illustrates the class Travel in Ontolingua, where ?travel is a variable. The sentences inside the :axiom-def keyword are KIF[9] sentences that state that a flight is a kind of travel and establish constraints on the cardinalities of its attributes. The sentence following the :def keyword states a necessary condition over the argument. This definition expresses that all travels have a unique departure date and an arrival date, a company name and at most one price for a single fare with the company.

```
(define-class Travel (?travel)
   "A journey from place to place"
:axiom-def
 (and (Superclass-Of Travel Flight)
      (Template-Facet-Value Cardinality
            arrivalDate Travel 1)
      (Template-Facet-Value Cardinality
            departureDate Travel 1)
      (Template-Facet-Value Maximum-Cardinality
            singleFare Travel 1))
```

[9] KIF (Genesereth and Fikes, 1992) provides a Lisp-like notation for writing the axioms in Ontolingua definitions. It is a case-insensitive, prefix syntax for predicate calculus with functional terms and equality. It is described in detail in Chapter 4.

```
:def
  (and (arrivalDate ?travel Date)
       (departureDate ?travel Date)
       (singleFare ?travel Number)
       (companyName ?travel String)))
```

Classes can represent abstract concepts[10] (intentions, beliefs, feelings, etc.) or specific concepts (people, computers, tables, etc.). For instance, we can model the class Location as a kind of SpatialPoint as follows:

```
(define-class Location (?location)
  "A location is a spatial point, identified by a name"
:def
  (SpatialPoint ?location)
:axiom-def
  (Template-Facet-Value Cardinality
          locationName Location 1))
```

In the frame-based KR paradigm, metaclasses can also be defined. Metaclasses are classes whose instances are classes. They usually allow for gradations of meaning, since they establish different layers of classes in the ontology where they are defined. In Chapters 4 and 5 we will see how to use them to model ontologies.

Relations represent a type of association between concepts of the domain. They are formally defined as any subset of a product of n sets, that is: $R \subset C1 \times C2 \times ... \times Cn$. Ontologies usually contain binary relations. The first argument is known as the domain of the relation, and the second argument is the range. For instance, the binary relation *Subclass-Of* is used for building the class taxonomy. Examples of classifications are: a Four-Star-Hotel is a subclass of a Hotel, a Hotel is a subclass of a Lodging, and a Flight is a subclass of Travel, which is identified by the flightNumber.

```
(define-class Flight (?flight)
  "A journey by plane"
:axiom-def
  (and (Subclass-Of Flight Travel)
       (Template-Facet-Value Cardinality
            flightNumber Flight 1))
:class-slots
  ((transportMeans "plane")))
```

Binary relations are also used to connect different taxonomies. For instance, we can use a binary relation arrivalPlace to state that the arrival place of a Travel is a Location.

---

[10] For a formal definition of abstract entities, see WonderWeb Deliverable D1.7, at http://wonderweb.semanticweb.org/

```
(define-relation arrivalPlace (?travel ?arrPlace)
   "A journey ends at a location"
:def
  (and (Travel ?travel)
       (Location ?arrPlace)))
```

Relations can be instantiated with knowledge from the domain. For example, to express that the flight AA7462-Feb-08-2002 arrives in Seattle we must write: (arrivalPlace AA7462-Feb-08-2002 Seattle)

Binary relations are sometimes used to express concept attributes (aka slots). Attributes are usually distinguished from relations because their range is a datatype, such as *string*, *number*, etc., while the range of relations is a concept. The following code defines the attribute flightNumber, which is a *string*.

```
(define-relation flightNumber (?flight ?flightNumber)
   "It identifies the flight company and the number"
:def
  (and (Flight ?flight)
       (String ?flightNumber)))
```

We can also express relations of higher arity, such as "a road connects two different cities". In Ontolingua this relation is defined as follows:

```
(define-relation connects (?city1 ?city2 ?road)
   "A road connects two different cities"
:def
 (and
  (Location ?city1)(Location ?city2)(RoadSection ?road)
  (not (part-of ?city1 ?city2))
  (not (part-of ?city2 ?city1))
  (or (and  (start ?road ?city1)(end ?road ?city2))
      (and  (start ?road ?city2)(end ?road ?city1)))))
```

Functions are a special case of relations in which the *n-th* element of the relation is unique for the *n-1* preceding elements. This is usually expressed as: F: C1 x C2 x ... x Cn-1 $\rightarrow$ Cn. An example of a function is Pays, which obtains the price of a room after applying a discount. The *lambda-body* expression on the definition is written in KIF and denotes the value of the function in terms of its arguments.

```
(define-function Pays (?room ?discount) :-> ?finalPrice
   "Price of the room after applying the discount"
:def (and (Room ?room) (Number ?discount)
          (Number ?finalPrice)
          (Price ?room ?price))
:lambda-body
          (- ?price (/ (* ?price ?discount) 100)))
```

According to Gruber, ***formal axioms*** serve to model sentences that are always true. They are normally used to represent knowledge that cannot be formally defined by the other components. In addition, formal axioms are used to verify the consistency of the ontology itself or the consistency of the knowledge stored in a knowledge base. Formal axioms are very useful to infer new knowledge. An axiom in the traveling domain would be that it is not possible to travel from the USA to Europe by train.

```
(define-axiom No-Train-from-USA-to-Europe
   "It is not possible to travel from the USA to Europe
    by train"
:= (forall (?travel)
    (forall (?city1)
     (forall (?city2)
       (=> (and (Travel ?travel)
                (arrivalPlace ?travel ?city1)
                (departurePlace ?travel ?city2)
                (EuropeanLocation ?city1)
                (USALocation ?city2))
           (not (TrainTravel ?travel)))))))
```

We also know that we cannot travel by train from Europe to the USA. We can modify the previous axiom and represent such knowledge as follows:

```
(define-axiom No-Train-between-USA-and-Europe
   "It is not possible to travel by train between the
    USA and Europe"
:= (forall (?travel)
    (forall (?city1)
     (forall (?city2)
       (=> (and (Travel ?travel)
                (arrivalPlace ?travel ?city1)
                (departurePlace ?travel ?city2)
                (or (and (EuropeanLocation ?city1)
                         (USALocation ?city2))
                    (and (EuropeanLocation ?city2)
                         (USALocation ?city1))))
           (not (TrainTravel ?travel)))))))
```

Formal axioms can also be domain independent. We are now going to redefine the relation `connects` in a domain independent way. We can model a connection as a link between a source and a target by means of an edge. Note that in this definition, we define the source and target of the connection as a `SpatialPoint`. Besides, we formally define its properties (symmetry, irreflexivity, etc.) with axioms. For a complete definition of the relation `connects` we refer to Borst (1997) and for a unified framework for spatial representation we refer to Casati and Varzi (1999).

```
(define-relation connects (?edge ?source ?target)
   "This relation links a source and a target by an
edge. The source and destination are considered as
spatial points. The relation has the following
properties: symmetry and irreflexivity."
:def (and (SpatialPoint ?source)
          (SpatialPoint ?target)
          (Edge ?edge))
:axiom-def
((=> (connects ?edge ?source ?target)
     (connects ?edge ?target ?source)) ;symmetry
  (=> (connects ?edge ?source ?target)
     (not (or (part-of ?source ?target) ;irreflexivity
              (part-of ?target ?source)))))))
```

We can specialize the previous relation for the travel domain and express the connection between two cities as a specialization of the relation `connects`. We call it `roadConnectsCities`. Note that in this case we define `?city1` and `?city2` as a kind of `Location`, which was already defined as a subclass of `SpatialPoint`.

```
(define-relation roadConnectsCities (?city1 ?city2)
   "A road connects two different cities"
:def (and (Location ?city1)
          (Location ?city2))
:iff-def
   (exist ?road
       (and (RoadSection ?road)
            (connects ?road ?city1 ?city2))))
```

Instances are used to represent elements or individuals in an ontology. An example of instance of the concept AA7462 is the flight AA7462 that arrives at Seattle on February 8, 2002 and costs 300 (US Dollars, Euros, or any other currency).

```
(define-instance AA7462-Feb-08-2002 (AA7462)
:def ((singleFare AA7462-Feb-08-2002 300)
      (departureDate AA7462-Feb-08-2002 Feb8-2002)
      (arrivalPlace AA7462-Feb-08-2002 Seattle)))
```

There are ontology platforms for modeling ontologies using frames and logic. These platforms are described in detail in Chapter 5. Figures 1.2 and 1.3 present a screenshot of a travel ontology in the platform WebODE (Arpírez et al., 2003) and in the ontology editor Protégé-2000 (Noy et al., 2000). WebODE represents axioms in first order logic with WAB (WebODE Axiom Builder language) (Corcho et al., 2002), and Protégé on the Protégé Axiom Language, also known as PAL[11].

---

[11] http://protege.stanford.edu/plugins/paltabs/PAL_tabs.html

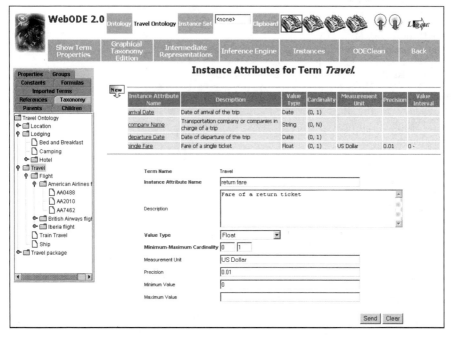

Figure 1.2: Screenshot of a travel ontology in WebODE.

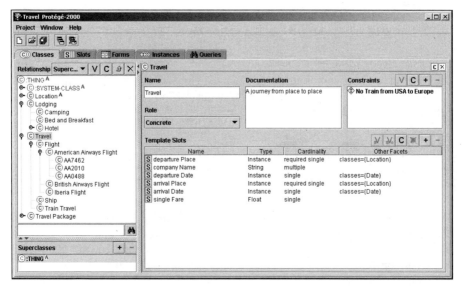

Figure 1.3: Screenshot of a travel ontology in Protégé-2000.

1.3.2 Modeling heavyweight ontologies using description logics

Description Logics[12] (DL) is a logical formalism whose first implementation languages and systems were: KL-ONE (Brachman and Schmolze, 1985), Krypton (Brachman et al., 1983), Classic (Borgida et al., 1989), LOOM (MacGregor, 1991) and Kris (Baader and Hollunder, 1991). A Description Logics theory is divided into two parts: the TBox and the ABox. The TBox contains intensional (terminological) knowledge in the form of a terminology and is built through declarations that describe general properties of concepts. The ABox contains extensional (assertional) knowledge, which is specific to the individuals of the discourse domain (Baader et al., 2003). In other words, the TBox contains the definitions of concepts and roles, while the ABox contains the definitions of individuals (instances).

Basically, DL systems allow the representation of ontologies with three kinds of components: concepts, roles and individuals. *Concepts* in DL have the same meaning as in the frame paradigm: they represent classes of objects. *Roles* describe binary relations between concepts, hence they also allow the description of properties of concepts. Higher arity relations among concepts are also allowed in some DL languages and systems. Finally, *individuals* represent instances of classes.

Table 1.1: Common DL constructors and their correspondence with language names[13].

Construct	Syntax	Language			
Concept	A				
Role name	R	FL_0			
Intersection	$C \cap D$				
Value restriction	$\forall R.C$		FL^-		
Limited existential quantification	$\exists R$			AL	
Top or Universal	⊺N				S^{14}
Bottom	$\perp$				
Atomic negation	$\neg A$				
Negation[15]	$\neg C$		C		
Union	$C \cup D$		U		
Existential restriction	$\exists R.C$		E		
Number restrictions	$(\geq n\,R)\ (\leq n\,R)$		N		
Nominals	$\{a_1 \ldots a_n\}$		O		
Role hierarchy	$R \subseteq S$		H		
Inverse role	R^-		I		
Qualified number restriction	$(\geq n\,R.C)\ (\leq n\,R.C)$		Q		

---

[12] Names previously used for Description Logics were: terminological knowledge representation languages, concept languages, term subsumption languages, and KL-ONE-based knowledge representation languages.

[13] In this table, we use A to refer to atomic concepts (concepts that are the basis for building other concepts), C and D to any concept definition, R to atomic roles and S to role definitions. FL is used for structural DL languages and AL for attributive languages (Baader et al., 2003).

[14] S is the name used for the language ALC_{R+}, which is composed of ALC plus transitive roles.

[15] ALC and ALCUE are equivalent languages, since union (U) and existential restriction (E) can be represented using negation (C).

Concepts and roles are both described with terminological descriptions, which are built from pre-existing terms and with a set of constructors (conjunction, disjunction, negation, value restriction, existential quantification, existential restriction, qualified number restriction, etc.). The choice and combination of the different constructors permit designing different DL languages, as shown in Table 1.1. For example, a SHIQ language is a language that combines (ALC_{R+}) intersection, value restriction, limited existential quantification, the concepts *top* and *bottom*, atomic negation, negation, union, existential restriction, and transitive roles; with (H) role hierarchies; (I) inverse roles; and (Q) qualified number restrictions. The different combinations of constructors give different expressiveness/reasoning tradeoffs to the corresponding language.

Concepts in DL can be *primitive* (if they are defined specifying necessary conditions for the individuals of that concept) or *defined* (if they are defined specifying both necessary and sufficient conditions that must be satisfied by individuals of the concept). Suppose that in our example the concept Travel is primitive (it defines necessary conditions for an individual that belongs to this concept), while the concept Flight is defined (it defines necessary and sufficient conditions for an individual to belong to that concept). These definitions are presented in LOOM:

```
(defconcept Travel
   "A journey from place to place"
:is-primitive
  (:and
     (:all arrivalDate Date) (:exactly 1 arrivalDate)
     (:all departureDate Date) (:exactly 1 departureDate)
     (:all companyName String)
     (:all singleFare Number) (:at-most singleFare 1)))

(defconcept Flight
   "A journey by plane"
:is (:and
      Travel
      (:all flightNumber Number) (:exactly 1 flightNumber)
      (:filled-by transportMeans "plane")))
```

Roles in DL can be either primitive or defined (also called derived). Many DL systems do not permit defining derived roles, because of their reasoning disadvantages, though they do permit the creation of role hierarchies. Examples of role definitions are presented below. The first piece of code contains a primitive definition while the second corresponds to a derived definition, which is also a ternary relation.

```
(defrelation arrivalPlace
   "A journey ends at a location"
:domain Travel
:range Location)
```

```
(defrelation connects
  "A road connects two different cities"
:arity 3
:domains (Location Location)
:range RoadSection
:predicate
  ((?city1 ?city2 ?road)
   (:not (part-of ?city1 ?city2))
   (:not (part-of ?city2 ?city1))
   (:or (:and (start ?road ?city1)(end ?road ?city2))
        (:and (start ?road ?city2)(end ?road ?city1)))))
```

Some DL systems do not permit defining n-ary roles, but only binary ones. In that case, the role `connects` should be described as a concept with three binary roles and each role is attached to each of the concepts that appear in that definition according to the following order: `City`, `City` and `RoadSection`.

Functions can also be created in some DL systems as a special kind of relation. A function returns a value following an expression that is present in its description. The definition below shows the function `Pays`:

```
(defrelation Pays
:is
 (:function (?room ?Discount)
  (- (Price ?room) (/(*(Price ?room) ?Discount) 100)))
:domains (Room Number)
:range Number)
```

Formal axioms in DL use a subset of the constructs of first order logic. They are usually embedded in concept or role definitions, as in the previous examples. Below we have modeled in LOOM the axiom about the non-availability of trains from the USA to Europe. This axiom is included in the `TrainTravel` concept definition:

```
(defconcept TrainTravel
:is (:and Travel
          (:satisfies ?x (:for-all ?y (:for-all ?z
           (:not (:and (arrivalPlace ?x ?y)
                       (EuropeanLocation ?y)
                       (departurePlace ?x ?z)
                       (USALocation ?z)))))))))
```

Reasoning in DL is mostly based on the subsumption test among concepts. For instance, we can explicitly say that the following two classes are disjoint: the class `TrainTravel`, and the class that is a `Travel`, whose `arrivalPlace` is a `EuropeanLocation` and whose `departurePlace` is a `USALocation`. From the disjointness of these two classes, we can infer that travels by train between Europe and the USA are not possible. As this knowledge cannot be represented in LOOM we represent it in OIL, another DL language:

```
disjoint
  TrainTravel
  (Travel and (slot-constraint arrivalPlace
                      value-type EuropeanLocation)
       and (slot-constraint departurePlace
                      value-type USALocation))
```

Individuals represent instances of concepts and the values of their roles (properties). DL systems usually separate individuals from concepts and roles descriptions. The former are included in the ABox (assertional knowledge) while the latter are included in the TBox (terminological knowledge). We present the LOOM definition for the instance of the flight AA7462 that departs on February 8, 2002, arriving in Seattle and costing 300:

```
(tellm (AA7462 AA7462-08-Feb-2002)
       (singleFare AA7462-08-Feb-2002 300)
       (departureDate AA7462-08-Feb-2002 Feb8-2002)
       (arrivalPlace AA7462-08-Feb-2002 Seattle))
```

In some DL systems, the ABox also contains rules that allow inferring information. There have been some discussions about the most convenient place for rules, and we think rules should be placed in the TBox, as they really define intensional rather than assertional knowledge. Figure 1.4 presents a screenshot of our travel ontology in a DL tool named OilEd (Bechhofer et al., 2001a).

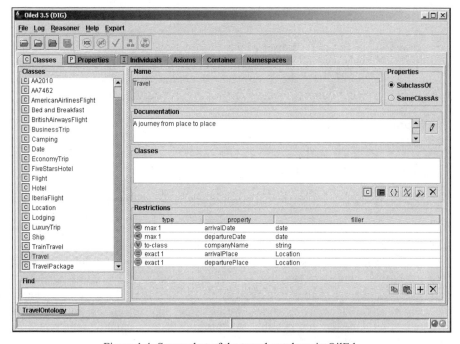

Figure 1.4: Screenshot of the travel ontology in OilEd.

Our last comment about DL is on the reasoning capabilities of this paradigm. As we have already said, the decision about which constructs to use in a DL language has strong effects not only on its expressiveness, but also on its reasoning power. Reasoning in DL is mainly based on concept subsumption, for which DL systems provide efficient automatic classifiers. From these subsumption tests, DL systems derive concept satisfiability and consistency in the models represented. These classifiers are commonly built by means of tableaux calculus and constraint systems.

1.3.3 Modeling ontologies with software engineering techniques

UML (Unified Modeling Language) (Rumbaugh et al., 1998) might be used as a technique for modeling ontologies. Some of the reasons to use this language in ontology construction are: UML is easy to understand and use for people outside the AI community; there is a standard graphical representation for UML models; and many CASE tools are available.

Cranefield and Purvis (1999), Baclawski and colleagues (2001) and Kogut and colleagues (2002) have shown how to use UML to represent lightweight ontologies[16], and how to enrich UML models by adding OCL[17] (OMG, 1997; Warmer and Kleppe, 1998) expressions to these specifications. According to their proposal, UML class diagrams will be used for representing concepts (and their attributes), relations between concepts (both taxonomic relationships and ad hoc ones) and axioms in OCL. UML object diagrams will be used for representing instances.

Figure 1.5 shows part of the class and object diagrams of our travel ontology, with the concepts Travel, Location, Flight and Road Section. It also shows two instances (AA7642 08 Feb 2002 and Seattle), and the relations between the concepts (arrival Place, departure Place and connects).

In a UML diagram, *classes* are represented with boxes divided into three parts: the name, the attributes and the operations of the class. Operations are not used for representing ontologies. In UML there is no difference between class and instance attributes. Types of attributes are included in the attribute description, and their values and default values might also be expressed there. Cardinalities of the attributes must be defined using OCL and these OCL expressions are attached to concepts as notes. Class instances are represented with objects linked to the concept they belong to by means of dashed arrows.

Concept taxonomies are created through generalization relationships between classes. Figure 1.5 shows that the concept Flight is a subclass of the concept Travel, using a generalization path (a solid line from Flight to Travel that ends with a large hollow triangle). No disjoint nor exhaustive knowledge can be created without OCL. Aggregation of classes can also be specified (which is equivalent to the *Part-Of* relationship used in some other systems).

---

[16] See also the draft proposal in *http://www.swi.psy.uva.nl/usr/Schreiber/docs/owl-uml/owl-uml.html* to represent OWL Lite ontologies in UML.
[17] Object Constraint Language.

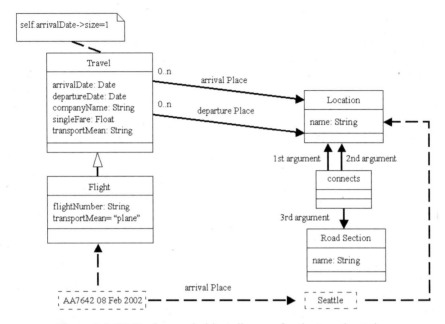

Figure 1.5: UML class and object diagram for the travel ontology.

Binary *relations* are expressed in UML as associations (solid arrows) between classes, where we can restrict the cardinalities, as presented in Figure 1.5 for the relations `arrival Place` and `departure Place`. However, higher arity relations cannot be represented directly in UML, though we can represent them by creating a class. This class is associated with other classes that represent the relation arguments, as shown in the ternary relation `connects`.

Formal axioms must be represented in OCL, though there is no standard support for this language in common CASE tools. UML models lack formal semantics, although efforts are being made to solve this deficiency[18]. Consequently, expressions in OCL cannot be evaluated.

Finally, packages and modules are used to represent the way terms are imported in UML.

UML has been used for ontology modeling in several projects. In the UBOT project[19] (UML Based Ontology Tool-set), transformations from UML to DAML+OIL are under study and extensions to UML are being proposed for a better modeling of ontologies. The CODIP[20] project (Components for Ontology Driven Information Push) is building a tool called DUET as a Rational Rose[21] add-in.

---

[18] http://www.puml.org/
[19] http://ubot.lockheedmartin.com/
[20] http://codip.grci.com/
[21] http://www.rational.com/

Sandpiper Software[22] has developed an add-in for Rational Rose that supports ontology development by means of a frame-based approach. Protégé-2000 and WebODE export and import ontologies in UML format.

1.3.4 Modeling ontologies with database technology

In this section we will explore the relationship between what an ontology is and what a database is. We have modeled the previous example in the traveling domain using an Entity/Relationship (ER) diagram (Chen, 1976), with the common extension of generalization relationships between entities.

As we can observe in Figure 1.6, the ER notation allows modeling:

* *Classes* through ER-entities. In the figure the concepts Travel, Flight, Location and Road Section are modeled. Classes can be organized in class taxonomies with the generalization relationship between ER-entities. In the same figure the concept Flight is defined as a subclass of the concept Travel.
* *Attributes* through ER-attributes. The ER notation also allows representing the value types of attributes. For instance, for the class Travel we have defined the attributes arrivalDate, departureDate, companyName, singleFare and transportMeans, whose value types are Date, Date, String, Float and String respectively.
* *Ad hoc relations* between ontology classes through ER-relations between ER-entities. These relations can have any arity. In the figure we have represented the binary relations arrival Place and departure Place, and the ternary relation connects. The ER notation permits modeling relation cardinalities. For example, we have defined that a Travel has at least one arrival Place and only one. An interesting feature of the ER notation is that it allows representing relation attributes. For example, we could define connectionLength as an attribute of the relation connects, as shown in Figure 1.6.

There are many other extensions of ER diagrams. HERM (higher-order entity-relationship model) (Thalheim, 2000), for example, adds complex attribute types based on the basic types (string, integer, real, etc.), key constraints, functional dependencies, relationship roles, generalization and specialization relationships, and generalized cardinality constraints for relations. Ontologies can also be modeled with other types of databases, such as object oriented database models or deductive database models.

Formal axioms can be represented as integrity constraints using some of these extensions, or using complementary notations, such as first order logic, production rules, etc.

---

[22] http://www.sandsoft.com/

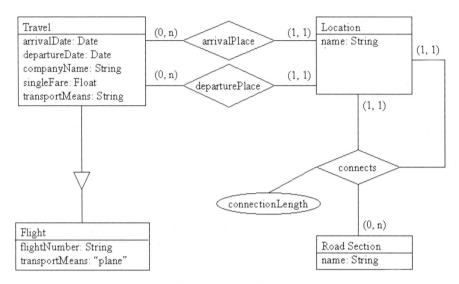

Figure 1.6: Extended entity-relationship diagram for the travel example.

Therefore, it is not possible to model heavyweight ontologies with the extended ER diagrams commonly used. But other extended ER notations or complementary notations would be needed to build a heavyweight ontology from a consensual ER diagram. In both cases, only those ER diagrams that have been agreed upon could be considered ontologies.

Another important feature pointed out in the definition of Studer and colleagues (1998) is that ontologies should be machine-readable. An ER diagram can be processed and translated into SQL (Structured Query Language), and many CASE tools, like Rational Rose or PowerDesigner[23], are used for this purpose.

SQL allows creating **instances** through the sentence *insert*. However, SQL is not appropriate to represent formal constraints in a declarative way, since consistency rules must be specified using procedural triggers. On the other hand, SQL views are useful to represent inferences from the database tables. Every SQL version permits, at least, defining views using query expressions as expressive as those written in Datalog (Ullman, 1988) except for recursive expressions. Datalog is the Prolog's counterpart for databases, and it is used to build databases from a logic view point.

According to the former paragraphs, database technology can be used to build ontologies, although such a technology is not always the most appropriate one for heavyweight ontology construction. In the linear continuum from lightweight to heavyweight ontologies, the domain model expressed in an ER diagram is the lightest one, the one expressed in SQL is heavier and the one expressed in Datalog is the heaviest one. We do not claim that the domain model expressed in SQL or

---

[23] http://www.sybase.com/products/enterprisemodeling/powerdesigner

Datalog is a heavyweight ontology, what we do claim is that the domain model in Datalog is "heavier" than the one expressed in SQL, and that the one expressed in SQL is "heavier" than the one expressed in an ER diagram.

1.3.5 Conclusions

As a conclusion of this section, we can say that both the formalisms used to model the domain knowledge and the languages that implement these techniques limit the kind of knowledge that can be modeled and implemented.

On the one hand, every representation formalism described in this section can represent classes, organized in class taxonomies, attributes, and binary relations. Therefore, with approaches based on AI, software engineering, and databases we are able to represent the basic skeleton of an ontology.

On the other hand, only AI formalisms are specially prepared to model formal axioms either as independent components in the ontology or embedded in other components. For example, neither with the most commonly used ER diagrams nor with UML class diagrams easily we can restrict that a city and its parts cannot be related to each other through the relation `connects`, since we cannot easily express the formal axiom that imposes this restriction.

Another important conclusion to this section is that a domain model is not necessarily an ontology only because it is written in Ontolingua or OWL, for the same reasons that we cannot say that a program is a knowledge-based system because it is written in Prolog.

Moreover, AI-based languages (Ontolingua, LOOM, OCML, FLogic, etc.) and ontology markup languages (RDF(S), DAML+OIL, OWL, etc.) are better candidates for representing and implementing ontologies than other non AI approaches such as UML, ER diagrams, or SQL scripts. However, a domain model implemented in SQL could be considered a lightweight ontology if and only if it expresses agreed knowledge. The same could be applied to UML models and their implementations.

1.4 Types of Ontologies

One of the main purposes of this section is to provide a general understanding of the vocabulary used to classify ontologies. Here we present the most common types of ontologies and a unified vocabulary to classify them. In Chapter 2 you will find the ontologies most recognized, and in this Section 1.4 we give examples of representative ontologies that could be classified under these types.

Finally, we will describe how different types of ontologies could be combined into an ontology library.

1.4.1 Categorization of ontologies

Some of the works on the categorization of ontologies that will be presented in short detail are: Mizoguchi and colleagues (1995), van Heijst and colleagues (1997), Guarino (1998) and Lassila and McGuinness (2001).

Initially, Mizoguchi and colleagues (1995) proposed four kinds of ontologies, shown in Figure 1.7:
1. Content ontologies for reusing knowledge. These ontologies include other subcategories: task ontologies, domain ontologies and general or common ontologies.
2. Communication (tell & ask) ontologies for sharing knowledge.
3. Indexing ontologies for case retrieval.
4. Meta-ontologies (for Mizoguchi) are equivalent to what other authors refer to as a knowledge representation ontology.

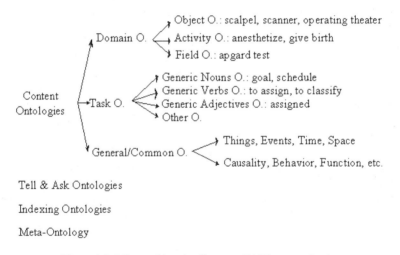

Figure 1.7: Mizoguchi and colleagues (1995) categorization.

Van Heijst and colleagues (1997) classified ontologies according to two orthogonal dimensions, as Figure 1.8 illustrates: *the amount and type of structure of the conceptualization* and *the subject of the conceptualization*. In the first dimension, they distinguish three categories: terminological ontologies such as lexicons, information ontologies such as database schemata, and knowledge modeling ontologies that specify conceptualizations of the knowledge. In the second dimension, they identify four categories: representation, generic, domain and application ontologies.

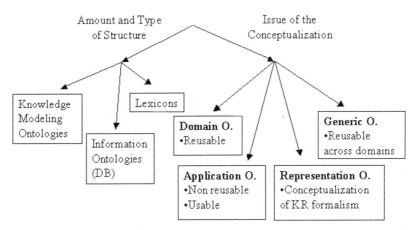

Figure 1.8: Van Heijst and colleagues (1997) categorization.

Later on, Guarino (1998) classified types of ontologies according to their level of dependence on a particular task or point of view. Guarino distinguished the following: top-level, domain, task, and application ontologies, as we can see in Figure 1.9.

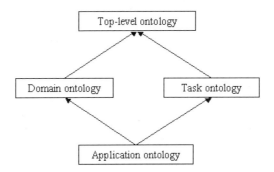

Figure 1.9: Guarino (1998) categorization.

Finally, Lassila and McGuinness (2001) classified ontologies according to the information the ontology needs to express and the richness of its internal structure. They point out the following categories: controlled vocabularies, glossaries, thesauri, informal is-a hierarchies, formal is-a hierarchies, formal instances, frames, value restriction, and general logical constraints, as Figure 1.10 illustrates.

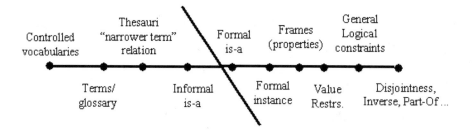

Figure 1.10: Lassila and McGuinness (2001) categorization.

This section presents different types of ontologies that combine the previous approaches. We have classified them according to the richness of their internal structure and also to the subject of the conceptualization. The first group is described following Lassila and McGuinness (2001) classification, shown in Figure 1.10, and the second one extends Van Heijst and colleagues (1997) classification, shown in Figure 1.8, with other kind of ontologies already identified on the literature, such as upper-level ontologies, and task, domain-task and method ontologies.

1.4.1.1 Types of ontologies based on the richness of their internal structure
Lassila and McGuinness (2001) classified different types of lightweight and heavyweight ontologies in a continuous line, as presented in Figure 1.10. The main categories and their meanings are:

- Controlled vocabularies, i.e., a finite list of terms. A typical example of this category is a catalogue.
- Glossaries, that is, a list of terms with their meanings specified as natural language statements.
- Thesauri, which provide some additional semantics between terms. They give information such as synonym relationships, but do not supply an explicit hierarchy. For instance `traveler` and `passenger` could be considered as synonyms on our travel example.
- Informal is-a hierarchies, taken from specifications of term hierarchies like Yahoo's. Such hierarchy is not a strict subclass or "is-a" hierarchy. For instance, the terms `car rental` and `hotel` are not kinds of travel but they could be modeled in informal is-a hierarchies below the concept `travel`, because they are key components of the travel and allow the user to select either a car rental for the trip or an accommodation.
- Formal is-a hierarchies. In these systems, if B is a subclass of A and an object is an instance of B, then the object is an instance of A. Strict subclass hierarchies are necessary to exploit inheritance. In our example, subclasses of the concept `travel` could be: `flight`, `train travel`, etc.
- Formal is-a hierarchies that include instances of the domain. In this case, we would include instances of flights: the flight AA7462 arrives in Seattle, departs on February 8, and costs 300$.

- Frames. The ontology includes classes and their properties, which can be inherited by classes of the lower levels of the formal is-a taxonomy. In our example, a travel has a unique departure date and an arrival date, a company name and at most one price for a single fare with the company. All these attributes are inherited by the subclasses of the concept `travel`.

- Ontologies that express value restriction. These are ontologies that may place restrictions on the values that can fill a property. For instance, the type of the property `arrival date` is a `date`.

- Ontologies that express general logical constraints. These are the most expressive. Ontologists can specify first-order logic constraints between terms using expressive ontology languages (see Chapter 4 for their description). A logical constraint in our traveling domain is that it is not possible to travel from the USA to Europe by train.

1.4.1.2 Types of ontologies based on the subject of the conceptualization
Let us see now some of the different types of ontologies identified in the literature, based on the subject of their conceptualization.

Knowledge Representation (KR) ontologies (van Heijst et al., 1997) capture the representation primitives used to formalize knowledge under a given KR paradigm.

The most representative examples are the *Frame Ontology* (Gruber, 1993a) and the *OKBC Ontology*, both available in the Ontolingua Server. They provide formal definitions of the representation primitives used mainly in frame-based languages (i.e., classes, subclasses, attributes, values, relations and axioms). They permit building other ontologies by means of frame-based conventions. Figures 1.11 and 1.12 show the vocabulary gathered in both ontologies. Figure 1.11 also shows the definition of the relation *Subclass-Of* formalized in the Ontolingua language. In Figure 1.12 we can see the definition of the function *All-Instances* formalized in the Ontolingua language. Both definitions show some logical expressions written in KIF.

In addition to the *Frame Ontology* and the *OKBC Ontology*, in Chapter 2 we will review other KR ontologies (*RDF KR Ontology*, *RDF Schema KR Ontology*, *OIL KR Ontology*, *DAML+OIL KR Ontology* and *OWL KR Ontology*).

General (van Heijst et al., 1997) or **common ontologies** (Mizoguchi et al., 1995) are used to represent common sense knowledge reusable across domains. These ontologies include vocabulary related to things, events, time, space, causality, behavior, function, mereology, etc.

The *Mereology Ontology* (Borst, 1997) is one of the most classical examples of a general ontology. It defines the *Part-Of* relation and its properties. With the *Part-Of* relation we can state that devices are formed by components, each of which might also be decomposed into subcomponents. This ontology defines the properties that any decomposition should have. The following code (page 32) presents an excerpt from the *Mereology Ontology*.

Class hierarchy (8 classes defined):

```
Facet
Individual
Slot
Thing
    Class
        Primitive
    Frame
    Stub-Frame
```

36 relations defined:

```
Cardinality
Collection-Type
Documentation-In-Frame
Domain
Facet-Of
Instance-Of
Inverse-In-Frame
Maximum-Cardinality
Minimum-Cardinality
Not-Same-Values
Numeric-Maximum
Numeric-Minimum
Range
Same-Values
Slot-Cardinality
Slot-Chain-Value
Slot-Collection-Type
Slot-Maximum-Cardinality
Slot-Minimum-Cardinality
Slot-Not-Same-Values
Slot-Numeric-Maximum
Slot-Numeric-Minimum
Slot-Of
Slot-Same-Values
Slot-Some-Values
Slot-Subset-Of-Values
Some-Values
Subclass-Of
Subset-Of-Values
Superclass-Of
Template-Facet-Of
Template-Facet-Value
Template-Slot-Of
Template-Slot-Value
Type-Of
Value-Type
```

3 functions defined:

```
Handle
Inverse
Pretty-Name
```

```
(define-relation SUBCLASS-OF (?child-class ?parent-class)
  "Class C is a subclass of parent class P if only if every
instance of C is also an instance of P. A class may have
multiple superclasses and subclasses. Subclass-of is
transitive: if (subclass-of C1 C2) and (subclass-of C2 C3)
then (subclass-of C1 C3).
  Object-centered systems sometimes distinguish between a
subclass-of relationship that is asserted and one that is
inferred. For example, (subclass-of C1 C3) might be
inferred from asserting (subclass-of C1 C2) and
(subclass-of C2 C3).
  The functional interfaces to such systems might call the
asserted form something like 'parents' and the inferred
form 'ancestors'. However, both are logically identical to
subclass-of; distinctions based on inference procedures
and the current state of the knowledge base are not
captured in this ontology."

  :iff-def
    (forall ?instance
      (=> (instance-of ?instance ?child-class)
          (instance-of ?instance ?parent-class)))
  :axiom-constraints
    (Transitive-Relation Subclass-Of)

  :issues
  ((:see-also direct-subclass-of)
   (:see-also
     "In CycL, subclass-of is called #%allGenls because it is
from a collection to all of generalizations
(superclasses)."
     "In the KL-ONE literature, subclass relationships are
also called subsumption relationships and ISA is sometimes
used for subclass-of"
     ("Why is it called Subclass-of instead of subclass or
superclass?"
      "Because the latter are ambiguous about the order of
their arguments. We are following the naming convention
that a binary relationship is read as an English sentence
'Domain-element Relation-name Range-value'. Thus, person
subclass-of animal rather 'person superclass animal'.")))
```

Figure 1.11: An example of a KR ontology: The OKBC Ontology.

Class hierarchy (23 classes defined):

```
Binary-Relation
    Antisymmetric-Relation
        Asymmetric-Relation
        Partial-Order-Relation
            Total-Order-Relation
    Irreflexive-Relation
        Asymmetric-Relation
    Many-To-Many-Relation
    Many-To-One-Relation
    One-To-Many-Relation
    Reflexive-Relation
        Equivalence-Relation
        Partial-Order-Relation ...
    Symmetric-Relation
        Equivalence-Relation
    Transitive-Relation
        Equivalence-Relation
        Partial-Order-Relation ...
    Weak-Transitive-Relation
Class
    Root_Class
Class-Partition
Function
    Many-To-One-Relation
Individual-Thing
Named-Axiom
One-To-One-Relation
Relation
Unary-Relation
```

31 relations defined:

```
Alias
Composition-Of
Default-Facet-Value
Default-Slot-Value
Default-Template-Facet-Value
Default-Template-Slot-Value
Disjoint-Decomposition
Documentation
Domain-Of
Exhaustive-Decomposition
Has-Author
Has-Instance
Has-Source
Has-Subdefinition
Has-Subrelation
Inherited-Facet-Value
Inherited-Slot-Value
Nth-Argument-Name
Nth-Domain
Nth-Domain-Subclass-Of
Obsolete-Same-Values
Obsolete-Value-Type
Onto
Partition
Range-Of
Range-Subclass-Of
Related-Axioms
Single-Valued-Slot
Slot-Documentation
Subrelation-Of
Total-On
```

13 functions defined:

```
All-Instances ─────────────────➤
All-Values
Arity
Compose
Domain-Name
Exact-Domain
Exact-Range
Function-Arity
Obsolete-Slot-Cardinality
Projection
Range-Name
Relation-Universe
Subdefinition-Of
```

```
(define-function ALL-INSTANCES (?class) :-> ?set-of-instances
  "The instances of some classes may be specified extensionally. That
is, one can list all of the instances of the class by definition. For
this case we say (= (all-instances C)(setof V_1 V_2...V_n)), where C is
a class and the V_i are its instances.
  ALL-INSTANCES imposes a monotonic constraint. Any subclass of C
cannot have any instances outside of the ALL-INSTANCES of C.
  Note that this is not indexical or modal: whether something is in
all-instances is a property of the modeled world and does not depend on
the facts currently stored in some knowledge base."

  :iff-def
  (and (Class ?class)
    (Set ?set-of-instances)
    (forall ?instance
      (<=> (member ?instance ?set-of-instances)
           (instance-of ?instance ?class)))))
  :issues
  (("Is all-instances the inverse of instance-of?"
    "No. Instances-of maps individual instances to classes, whereas
all-instances maps classes to sets of instances.")
    "the name all-instances is borrowed from Cyc."
    (:example (all-instances truth-values (setof true false)))))
```

Figure 1.12: An example of a KR ontology: The Frame Ontology.

```
1. define-theory mereology
2. define-class m-individual (x)
a.   m-individual (x) <-> equal (x,x)
3. define-relation proper-part-of (x,y)
a.   proper-part-of (x,y) -> not proper-part-of (y,x)
b.   proper-part-of (x,y) and
     proper-part-of (y,z) -> proper-part-of (x,z)
4. define-relation direct-part-of (x,y)
a.   direct-part-of (x,y) <-> proper-part-of (x,y) and
     not exists z: proper-part-of (z,y) and
     proper-part-of (x,z)
5. define-relation disjoint (x,y)
a.   disjoint (x,y) <-> not (equal (x,y) or
     exists z: proper-part-of (z,x) and
     proper-part-of (z,y))
6. define-class simple-m-individual (x)
a.   simple-m-individual (x) <-> m-individual (x) and
     not exist y: proper-part-of (y,x)
```

Another example of a generic ontology is the *Standard-Units Ontology*, which includes definitions about units of measure (i.e., Minute and Second-of-Time).

```
(define-frame Minute
:own-slots
  ((Documentation "Time unit")
   (Instance-Of Unit-Of-Measure))
:axiom-def
  ((Quantity.Dimension Minute Time-Dimension)))
```

```
(define-frame Second-Of-Time
:own-slots
  ((Documentation "The SI standard unit of time")
   (Instance-Of Si-Unit Unit-Of-Measure)
   (Quantity.Dimension Time-Dimension))
:axiom-def
  ((= Minute (* 60 Second-Of-Time))))
```

Top-level Ontologies or **Upper-level Ontologies** describe very general concepts and provide general notions under which all root terms in existing ontologies should be linked. The main problem here is that there are several top-level ontologies and they differ on the criteria followed to classify the most general concepts of the taxonomy. Figure 1.13 illustrates different top-level ontologies. To solve the heterogeneity in the classification (which is intrinsic or inherent to the philosophical problem), the IEEE Standard Upper Ontology[24] (SUO) Working Group is trying to specify an upper ontology. Concepts specific to given domains will not be included

---

[24] http://suo.ieee.org/

in SUO. This standard however will give a structure and a set of general concepts from which domain ontologies (e.g., medical, financial, legal, engineering, etc.) could be constructed.

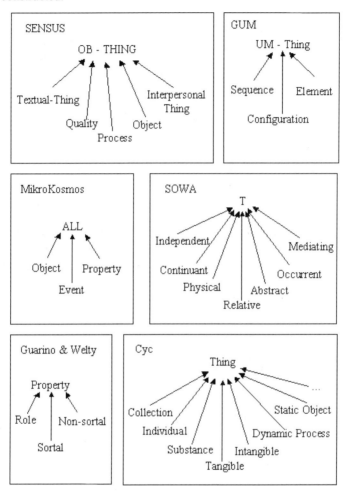

Figure 1.13: Examples of Top Level ontologies.

Domain ontologies (Mizoguchi et al., 1995) (van Heijst et al., 1997) are reusable in a given specific domain (medical, pharmaceutical, engineering, law, enterprise, automobile, etc.). These ontologies provide vocabularies about concepts within a domain and their relationships, about the activities taking place in that domain, and about the theories and elementary principles governing that domain. There is a clean boundary between domain and upper-level ontologies. The concepts in domain ontologies are usually specializations of concepts already defined in top-level ontologies, and the same might occur with the relations. For instance, the term `City` in a domain ontology is a specialization of a more generic concept `Location`, which is a specialization of the term `SpatialPoint` that may be defined on the upper-level ontology. Similarly, the relation `connects` defined in an upper-level ontology can be specialized to express that a road connects two cities (`roadConnectsCities`) in a domain ontology.

Task ontologies (Mizoguchi et al., 1995; Guarino, 1998) describe the vocabulary related to a generic task or activity (like diagnosing, scheduling, selling, etc.) by specializing the terms in the top-level ontologies. Task ontologies provide a systematic vocabulary of the terms used to solve problems associated with tasks that may or may not belong to the same domain. For instance, the *Scheduling Task Ontology* presented by Mizoguchi and colleagues (1995) includes generic names, generic verbs, generic adjectives, etc., as presented in Figure 1.7.

Domain-Task ontologies are task ontologies reusable in a given domain, but not across domains. They are application-independent. A domain-task ontology concerning trip schedules would include the following terms: `next city`, `previous city`, etc.

Method ontologies give definitions of the relevant concepts and relations applied to specify a reasoning process so as to achieve a particular task (Tijerino and Mizoguchi, 1993). An ontology about scheduling by means of task decomposition would belong to this category.

Application ontologies (van Heijst et al., 1997) are application-dependent. They contain all the definitions needed to model the knowledge required for a particular application. Application ontologies often extend and specialize the vocabulary of the domain and of task ontologies for a given application. For instance, we could create an application ontology for Spanish travel agencies specialized in North American destinations.

1.4.2 Ontologies and ontology library systems

Some of the most famous ontology libraries are: DAML ontology library[25], Ontolingua ontology library[26], Protégé ontology library[27], SHOE ontology library[28], WebODE ontology library[29], WebOnto ontology library[30], and (KA)^2 ontology library[31]. Only the first one is associated with an ontology language. The other libraries mentioned are attached to ontology tools.

The reusability-usability trade-off problem (Klinker et al., 1991) applied to the ontology field states that the more reusable an ontology is, the less usable it becomes, and vice versa (see Figure 1.14). Upper-level, general, and domain ontologies capture knowledge in a problem-solving independent way, whereas

---

[25] http://www.daml.org/ontologies/
[26] http://ontolingua.stanford.edu/
[27] http://protege.stanford.edu/ontologies.html
[28] http://www.cs.umd.edu/projects/plus/SHOE/onts/index.html
[29] http://webode.dia.fi.upm.es/
[30] http://webonto.open.ac.uk/
[31] http://ka2portal.aifb.uni-karlsruhe.de/

method, task, and domain-task ontologies are concerned with problem solving knowledge. All these types of ontologies can be taken from the same or different libraries and combined to build a new one. Figure 1.15 presents a screenshot of the DAML ontology library.

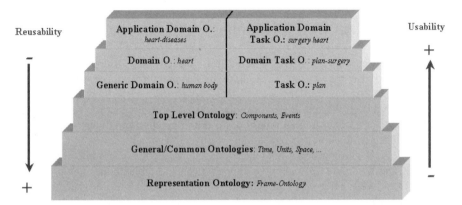

Figure 1.14: The reusability-usability trade-off problem.

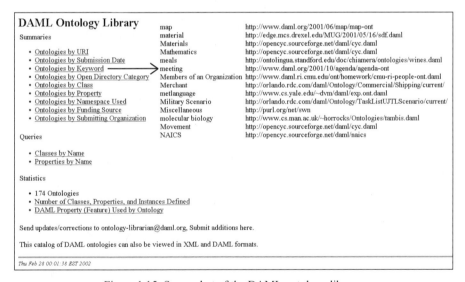

Figure 1.15: Screenshot of the DAML ontology library.

However, it is not trivial to combine ontologies from a library. Most of the ontologies are built incrementally reusing other ontologies already available. Thus one of the first decisions to make by the ontologist is which KR paradigm to use in order to formalize the ontology that will then be committed to a KR ontology. Once the KR ontology is selected, the following step is to decide to what extent general or common ontologies and top-level ontologies are needed. If they are required, new common ontologies are built and entered in the library. Then, domain knowledge and problem-solving knowledge can be modeled in parallel. When generic domain ontologies and domain ontologies are modeled, the ontologists should select first the top-level ontologies to be reused. And then the application domain ontologies are built on top of them. The same process is applied to task ontologies.

1.5 Ontological Commitments

Ontological commitments were defined by Gruber and Olsen (1994) as the agreements to use the shared vocabulary in a coherent and consistent manner. Guarino (1998) formalized the ontological commitment definition based on the connection between the ontology vocabulary and the meaning of the terms of such vocabulary. Thus, according to Guarino, an ontological commitment is a function that links terms of the ontology vocabulary with a conceptualization.

Ontological commitments guarantee consistency, but not completeness of an ontology, and this involves making as few claims as possible about the world being modeled, as well as giving the parties committed freedom to specialize and instantiate the ontology as required.

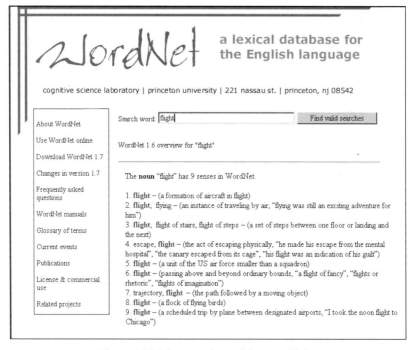

Figure 1.16: Nine meanings of the term flight.

In this section we will present in an intuitive way what an ontological commitment is. When building ontologies, we use natural language terms in a given language (usually English) to describe the conceptualization of a given domain.

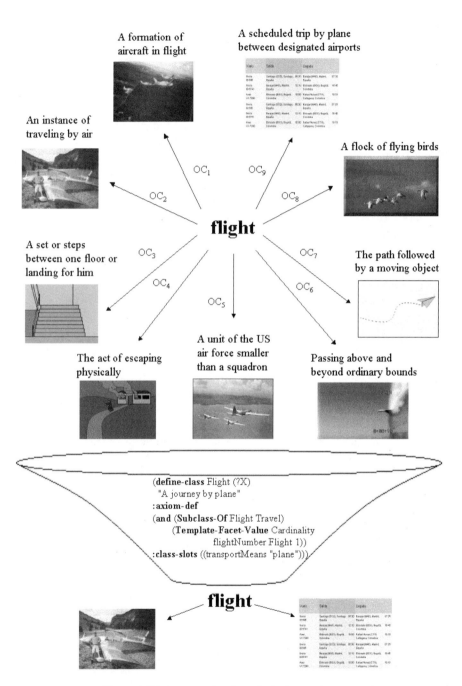

A formation of
aircraft in flight

A scheduled trip by plane
between designated airports

An instance of
traveling by air

A flock of flying birds

OC_1

OC_9

OC_2

OC_8

flight

A set or steps
between one floor or
landing for him

OC_3

OC_7

The path followed
by a moving object

OC_4

OC_6

OC_5

The act of escaping
physically

A unit of the US
air force smaller
than a squadron

Passing above and
beyond ordinary bounds

(**define-class** Flight (?X)
"A journey by plane"
:axiom-def
(**and** (**Subclass-Of** Flight Travel)
(**Template-Facet-Value** Cardinality
flightNumber Flight 1))
:class-slots ((transportMeans "plane")))

flight

Figure 1.17: An example of ontological commitment.

Most of the time the terms used in natural language have several meanings, and in the ontology we constraint the semantic interpretation of these terms and provide their formal definitions. Thus the ontological commitment could be seen, first, as a kind of mapping between the ontology terms and their intended meanings. Therefore one role of the ontological commitment is to determine precisely what meaning the term has.

In our traveling example, we have selected the term `flight`. If we look up what `flight` means in WordNet[32], we find the nine senses shown in Figure 1.16. For instance, only definitions two and nine could be used in our traveling domain. In our ontology the ontological commitment determines the mapping between a term in natural language and one of its meanings (for instance the meanings corresponding to OC2 and OC9 in Figure 1.17). Since the ontology should constrain the semantics of the terms in the domain according to the ontological commitment already chosen, we need a formal definition to filter the right (or the intended) meanings, represented in Figure 1.17 as a bottleneck. Such formal definition is a definition in the ontology and, as any other definition, we can extend it or specialize it as required, but the new definitions must always be consistent with the ontological commitment.

In general, ontological commitments involve more than a mapping between natural language terms and their senses, since they also include general choices such as the structure of time, space, events, etc.

1.6 Principles for the Design of Ontologies

This section summarizes some design criteria and a set of principles that have been proven useful in the development of ontologies. As Gruber (1993b) stated on his paper, design principles are objective criteria for guiding and evaluating ontology designs. He identified the following five principles for designing ontologies to be used in knowledge sharing: clarity, coherence, extendibility, minimal encoding bias and minimal ontological commitment. In this section, we will explain these principles using an example of the traveling domain to clarify the criteria.

Let us take as an example the following definition:

```
(define-class Travel (?travel)
   "A journey from place to place"
:axiom-def
 (and (Superclass-Of Travel Flight)
      (Subclass-Of Travel Thing)
      (Template-Facet-Value Cardinality
          arrivalDate Travel 1)
      (Template-Facet-Value Cardinality
          departureDate Travel 1)
      (Template-Facet-Value Maximum-Cardinality
          singleFare Travel 1))
```

---

[32] http://www.cogsci.princeton.edu/cgi-bin/webwn/

```
:def
  (and (arrivalDate ?travel Date)
       (departureDate ?travel Date)
       (singleFare ?travel Number)
       (companyName ?travel String)))
```

An important principle is **clarity**. Gruber (1993b) defined clarity in the following terms:

> *An ontology should communicate effectively the intended meaning of defined terms. Definitions should be objective. Definitions can be stated on formal axioms, and a complete definition (defined by necessary and sufficient conditions) is preferred over a partial definition (defined by only necessary or sufficient conditions). All definitions should be documented with natural language.*

Looking at the aforementioned Travel definition, the sentence after the *:def* keyword is a KIF sentence that states logical constraints over the arguments. A more complete and precise definition would state that the necessary and sufficient conditions for being a trip occurs when it has a unique departure and arrival date, and we keep the company name and the single fare as necessary conditions. The new definition is:

```
(define-class Travel (?travel)
  "A journey from place to place"
:axiom-def
  (and (Superclass-Of Travel Flight)
       (Subclass-Of Travel Thing)
       (Template-Facet-Value Cardinality
           arrivalDate Travel 1)
       (Template-Facet-Value Cardinality
           departureDate Travel 1)
       (Template-Facet-Value Maximum-Cardinality
           singleFare Travel 1))
:iff-def
  (and (arrivalDate ?travel Date)
       (departureDate ?travel Date))
:def
  (and (singleFare ?travel Number)
       (companyName ?travel String)))
```

However, this definition does not follow the **minimal encoding bias** (Gruber, 1993b) criterion. Minimal encoding bias means that:

> *The conceptualization should be specified at the knowledge level without depending on a particular symbol-level encoding.*

Encoding bias should be minimized for knowledge sharing because agents that share knowledge may be implemented in different ways. For instance, if we translate the definition of the concept Travel into the OIL language, we would not be able to model the attribute `singleFare` because the type `Number` does not exist in OIL. We should define it as an `integer`. In any case, this problem often comes up when we have defined amounts that are associated with units of measure. For instance, in the previous example, we define the attribute `singleFare` using types of values of the symbolic level rather than at the knowledge level (Newell, 1982). In fact, a single fare is a number followed by a currency (for instance, the single fare could be 6 Euros, which could be almost equivalent to 6 US Dollars, now in 2003).

   Gruber's proposal to solve such a problem and, consequently, to minimize the encoding bias, is to perform an engineering analysis where physical quantities are modeled by equation variables with numbers as values. He also describes amounts by physical-quantities as physical-dimensions. Time, length, mass, and energy are examples of physical-dimensions. Quantities are described in terms of reference quantities called units-of-measure. A `Meter` is an example of a `Unit-of-Measure` for quantities of the `physical-dimension` concerning length. Comparability is inherently tied to the concept of quantities.

   Figure 1.18 presents the relationships between the ontologies *Standard-Units*, *Physical-Quantities* and *Standard-Dimensions*. Three classes are defined on the ontology *Physical-Quantities*: `Unit-Of-Measure`, `System-of-Units`, and `Physical-Dimension`.

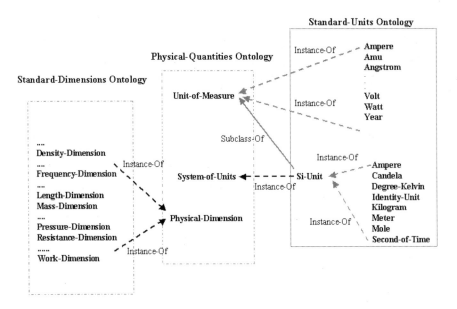

Figure 1.18: Relationships between the ontologies *Standard-Units*, *Physical-Quantities* and *Standard-Dimensions*.

The *Standard-Units Ontology* includes:
*   All the units of measure (meter, centimeter, gram, etc.) that are instances of the class `Unit-of-Measure` defined in the ontology *Physical-Quantities*. All the

units have a property that indicates the dimension of the aforesaid unit. These dimensions are defined in the *Standard-Dimensions Ontology*.

- The class `Si-Unit`, which groups all the SI units (Ampere, Candela, Degree-Kelvin, Kilogram, Meter, Mole and Second). Additionally this class is defined as an instance of the class `System-of-Units`. There could be other systems grouping other series of units, which would also be instances of `Unit-of-Measure`.

The *Standard-Dimensions Ontology* contains instances of the fundamental dimensions (i.e., `Density-Dimension`, `Length-Dimension`, `Frequency-Dimension`, `Mass-Dimension`, etc.)

Let us go back to our example in the traveling domain; to satisfy the minimal encoding bias criterion, the sentence:

```
(singleFare ?travel Number)
```

should be substituted by:

```
(singleFare ?travel CurrencyQuantity)
```

This sentence states that the attribute `singleFare` of the concept `Travel` is filled with a value type `CurrencyQuantity`, whose unit of measure could be `Euro`, `US Dollar`, `Yen`, etc.

Once our definition satisfies the minimal encoding bias, we should extend the *Standard-Units Ontology* with the new units, in that case, the currencies (Euro, US Dollar, Yen, etc.), and we should also include in the *Standard-Dimensions Ontology* the class `CurrencyQuantity`. The **extendibility** (Gruber, 1993b) criterion says that:

> *One should be able to define new terms for special uses based on the existing vocabulary, in a way that does not require the revision of the existing definitions.*

As Gruber (1993b) states, the ontologies *Standard-Units*, *Physical-Quantities* and *Standard-Dimensions* were built with that criterion in mind. The following terms can be added to the ontologies without revising existing definitions:

- The class `CurrencyDimension` to the *Standard-Dimensions Ontology*.
- All the currencies (US Dollar, Euro, Yen, etc.) are defined in the *Standard-Units ontology* as instances of the class `Unit-of-Measure`.
- We can also define relationships between currencies of the *Standard-Units ontology* with expressions like:

```
(define-individual Euro (Unit-of-Measure)
  "An Euro is the currency on the European Union"
:= (* 0,96 USDollar)
```

```
:axiom-def
  (= (Quantity.dimension Euro) CurrencyDimension))
```

Although the previous criteria are related to how we express knowledge in the ontology, there is a criterion that concerns inferences and is called **coherence** (Gruber, 1993b). Coherence is defined as follows:

> *An ontology should be coherent: that is, it should sanction inferences that are consistent with the definitions. [...] If a sentence that can be inferred from the axioms contradicts a definition or example given informally, then the ontology is incoherent.*

For example, let us take the previous formal axiom of the traveling domain that states that it is not possible to travel between the USA and Europe by train. And suppose now that in your ontology you have defined that Madrid and New York are instances of cities in Europe and the USA, respectively. The previous axiom forbids instances of travel by train between Madrid and New York.

Formal axioms are also used for detecting inconsistencies. For example, if you explicitly define that there is a train that goes from Madrid to New York, the axiom, using the fact that Madrid and New York are European and American cities, would infer that traveling by train between both cities is impossible. Consequently, there would be an inconsistency between the knowledge inferred and the knowledge explicitly stated in the ontology.

The last, but not less important criterion to support knowledge sharing is **minimal ontological commitments** (Gruber, 1993b).

> *Since ontological commitment is based on the consistent use of the vocabulary, ontological commitment can be minimized by specifying the weakest theory and defining only those terms that are essential to the communication of knowledge consistent with the theory.*

In our travel example we defined the attribute `arrivalDate` as a `Date`.

```
(arrivalDate ?travel Date)
```

But the main question is: what is a date? Is it an absolute date? Is it a relative date (i.e., tomorrow, the day after tomorrow)? Could the date be an interval (i.e., in summer)? Is the date defined by a month and a year? Is it defined by a day, a month and a year? To minimize the ontological commitments, we can define date as an absolute date that is defined by its day, month and year. At this point, we should not go into details as to specify if we are going to use the American English format for the dates (mm/dd/yyyy) or the Spanish format (dd/mm/yyyy). In this way, the ontology definitions can be reusable on different systems. For a detailed description of how to represent time and how to minimize the encoding bias, we refer to (Gruber, 1993b).

Some other criteria that have proven useful for building ontologies and did not appear in (Gruber 1993b) are: the representation of disjoint and exhaustive knowledge; the minimization of the syntactic distance between sibling concepts; and the standardization of names.

The representation of disjoint and exhaustive knowledge (Arpírez et al., 1998). If the set of subclasses of a concept are disjoint, we can define a disjoint decomposition. For instance, the concepts `AA7462`, `AA2010` and `AA0488` form a disjoint decomposition of the concept `AmericanAirlinesFlight`, since they are subclasses of `AmericanAirlinesFlight`, and `AA7462`, `AA2010` and `AA0488` cannot have common instances. The decomposition is exhaustive if it defines the superconcept completely. For instance, the concept `Location` can be decomposed exhaustively into the concepts `EuropeanLocation`, `AsianLocation`, `AfricanLocation`, `NorthAmericanLocation`, `SouthAmericanLocation`, `AustralianLocation`, and `AntarcticLocation`. There are no instances of the concept `Location` that are not instances of one of these concepts.

To improve the understandability and reusability of the ontology, we should implement the ontology trying **to minimize the syntactic distance between sibling concepts** (Arpírez et al., 1998), and this means that sibling concepts should be represented using the same primitives. For example, the SI base unit of measure called `Ampere` was defined at the *Standard-Units Ontology* in Ontolingua as follows:

```
(define-frame Ampere
:own-slots
  ((Documentation "SI electrical current unit")
   (Instance-Of Unit-of-Measure)
   (Quantity.Dimension Electrical-Current-Dimension))
:axioms
  ((= (Quantity.Dimension Ampere)
      Electrical-Current-Dimension)))
```

However, the following instance definition was used to define `Meter`, which is another SI base unit:

```
(define-instance Meter (Unit-of-Measure)
  "SI length unit. …"
:axiom-def
  (and (= (Quantity.Dimension Meter) Length-Dimension)
       (Si-Unit Meter)))
```

It is advisable to use the same pattern for making sibling definitions. For example, using in both definitions either the primitive *define-frame* or the primitive *define-instance*. Thus the understanding of the ontology would gain in clarity and the inclusion of new definitions would be carried out easily. All this would also improve the readability of the ontology and its monotonic extendibility.

The standardization of names (Arpírez et al., 1998). To ease the understanding of the ontology the same naming conventions should be used to name related terms. For example, `USALocation` and `LocationInEurope` do not follow the same naming conventions.

1.7 Bibliographical Notes and Further Reading

In this chapter, we have pointed out the most important publications and resources about ontologies that can be found in the literature. Apart from those already cited, we strongly recommend the paper written by Chandrasekaran and colleagues (1999) and the slides presented by Tom Gruber in the Bio-Ontologies 2000 workshop (*http://www.cs.man.ac.uk/~stevensr/workshop/gruber.zip*). The paper deals with ontologies in general, and the slides answer questions such as "what is an ontology?", "what is not an ontology?", "why should we create ontologies?", "which criteria should we follow to build ontologies?", etc. Another good resource where we can find a description of what an ontology is can be found at the URL *http://www-ksl.stanford.edu/kst/what-is-an-ontology.html*, which is maintained by the Knowledge Systems Laboratory (KSL) at Stanford University.

Concerning formal ontologies and ontological commitments, we recommend, from a philosophical perspective, Quine (1961) and Church (1958), and from an ontological engineering point of view, Guarino and colleagues (1994) and Guarino (1998). If you are interested in a more formal or philosophical approach, you can consult the *Metaphysics* of Aristotle to understand the origin of the Ontology as a philosophical discipline. To learn about current works of different philosophers about Formal Ontology, we recommend *http://www.formalontology.it/*. An interesting paper that relates Ontology to Logic is from Cocchiarella (2001).

Several Web portals provide general updated information about the ontology field: ontologies, tools, methodologies, applications, ongoing and past projects, researchers, etc. We recommend the following:
- The OntoRoadMap application, which has been created inside OntoWeb (*http://babage.dia.fi.upm.es/ontoweb/wp1/OntoRoadMap/index.html*), lets researchers consult and update the information on existing ontologies, ontology building methodologies, ontology tools, ontology-based applications, etc.
- The Web page maintained by Peter Clark, which can be accessed at *http://www.cs.utexas.edu/users/mfkb/related.html*.
- The ontology portal maintained by John Bateman, which can be accessed at: *http://www.fb10.uni-bremen.de/anglistik/langpro/webspace/jb/info-pages/ontology/ ontology-root.htm*
- The Ontology Page (TOP) (*http://www.kr.org/top/*).
- The OntoResearch portal (*http://www.ontoresearch.org/*) provides information about ontologies, ontology engineering, knowledge management and data mining to the academic research community.

Finally, to be updated in events, published books, and other news, we recommend the Knowledge Acquisition/Modeling/Management (KAW) mailing list (*http://www.swi.psy.uva.nl/mailing-lists/kaw/home.html*).

Chapter 2

The Most Outstanding Ontologies

This chapter is devoted to presenting the most outstanding ontologies. In this survey, we have considered different types of ontologies: knowledge representation ontologies (Section 2.1), top-level ontologies (Section 2.2), linguistic ontologies (Section 2.3) and domain ontologies (Section 2.4). In this last section, we will deal with ontologies from the following domains: e-commerce, medicine, engineering, enterprise, chemistry, and knowledge management.

At present, there is a huge number of ontologies; we have chosen those that are outstanding because of their use in important projects, their theoretical contributions, or their use as experimental bases to establish design criteria, to elaborate methodologies, etc.

After reading this chapter, you will be able to decide whether the ontologies presented here can be reused in your application, and you will know which applications are already using them.

2.1 Knowledge Representation Ontologies

A knowledge representation (KR) ontology (van Heijst et al., 1997) gathers the modeling primitives used to formalize knowledge in a KR paradigm. Examples of such primitives are *classes*, *relations*, *attributes*, etc.

The most representative KR ontology is the Frame Ontology (Gruber, 1993a), built for capturing KR conventions under a frame-based approach in Ontolingua. The Frame Ontology (FO) was modified in 1997 and some of its primitives were moved to the OKBC Ontology. The reason behind this change was the creation of OKBC (Chaudhri et al., 1998), a frame-based protocol for accessing knowledge bases stored in different languages: Ontolingua (Farquhar et al., 1997), LOOM (MacGregor, 1991), CycL (Lenat and Guha, 1990), etc.

Other ontology languages such as CycL (Lenat and Guha, 1990) and OCML (Motta, 1999) have also their own KR ontologies. In both cases, the foundations of such KR ontologies are similar to the Frame Ontology, since both languages are based on a combination of frames and first order logic. These and other languages will be described in depth in Chapter 4.

More recently, ontology markup languages have been created in the context of the Semantic Web: RDF (Lassila and Swick, 1999) and RDF Schema (Brickley and Guha, 2003), OIL (Horrocks et al., 2000), DAML+OIL (Horrocks and van Harmelen, 2001) and OWL (Dean and Schreiber, 2003). All these languages have also their corresponding KR ontologies. In this section we present these KR ontologies with their current primitives, as in April 2003[1].

2.1.1 The Frame Ontology and the OKBC Ontology

The Frame Ontology (Gruber, 1993a) was developed in KIF (Genesereth and Fikes, 1992) by the Knowledge Systems Laboratory at Stanford University. The Frame Ontology (FO) collects common knowledge-organization conventions used in frame-based representations. Its goal is to unify the semantics of the primitives most commonly used in the frame paradigm and to enable ontology developers to build ontologies with a frame-based approach.

The first version of the FO contained an axiomatization of classes and instances, slots and slot constraints, class and relation specialization primitives, relation inverses, relation composition, and class partitions. The FO was described by a set of ontological commitments that restricted the semantics of the FO primitives. Some examples of these ontological commitments are: relations are sets of tuples, functions are a special case of relations, classes are unary relations, etc.

The FO was modified in 1997 and some of its primitives were shifted to the OKBC Ontology. The reason for this change was the creation of a frame-based protocol to access knowledge bases stored in different languages: Ontolingua (Gruber, 1993a), LOOM (MacGregor, 1991), CycL (Lenat and Guha, 1990), etc., and the result was that the OKBC Ontology (Chaudhri et al., 1998) replaced some of the fundamental definitions of the original FO. At present the FO includes the OKBC Ontology and only provides formal definitions of the primitives not included in the latter. Such inclusion reflects that ontologies built with the FO primitives are more expressive than those built with the OKBC primitives. For instance, concept taxonomies built using OKBC primitives are based only on the *Subclass-Of* relation. However, concept taxonomies built using the FO may contain knowledge with exhaustive and disjoint partitions. Besides, the OKBC primitives are mainly concerned with frames, classes, and slots, while the FO includes more complex primitives for representing functions, relations, and axioms.

Both, the FO and the OKBC ontologies are available in the Ontolingua Server's ontology library[2]. Figures 1.11 and 1.12 presented the vocabulary provided by both

---

[1] Some ontology markup languages, such as RDF(S) and OWL, are not fully stable yet. Their specification together with their KR primitives may undergo small changes in the future.
[2] http://ontolingua.stanford.edu

KR ontologies. The FO contains 23 classes, 31 relations, and 13 functions; the OKBC Ontology contains eight classes, 36 relations, and three functions. We will not present all the primitives contained in these two ontologies, but only the most representative.

When building a concept taxonomy using the FO and the OKBC Ontology, the following primitives can be used:

Classes, class partitions and instances
In the frame-based KR paradigm, two types of frames can be represented: classes and instances. On the one hand, classes (aka concepts) represent collections or stereotypes of objects. On the other hand, instances represent individuals belonging to one or to several of those classes. The latter are called *individuals* in the OKBC Ontology. Two of the primitives, related to classes and instances, identified in the FO and the OKBC Ontology are:

- *Class (?Class)*. This primitive defines the class *?Class* as a collection of individuals. It is the only primitive appearing in both ontologies.
- *Individual (?Individual)*. This primitive defines an individual or instance.

Class taxonomies
Taxonomies are used to organize classes and instances in the ontology. The most important relations here are *Subclass-Of* (which means that a class is a specialization of another class) and *Instance-Of* (which states that an individual is an element of a class). Both primitives and some more specific ones for creating taxonomies are described below.

- *Subclass-Of (?Child-Class ?Parent-Class)*, which states that the class *?Child-Class* is a subclass of the class *?Parent-Class*.
- *Superclass-Of (?Parent-Class ?Child-Class)*, which states that the class *?Parent-Class* is a superclass of the class *?Child-Class*. This relation is the inverse relation of the *Subclass-Of* relation.
- *Disjoint-Decomposition (?Class ?Class-Set)*, which defines the set of disjoint classes *?Class-Set* as subclasses of the class *?Class*. This classification does not necessarily have to be complete, that is, there may be instances of *?Class* that are not instances of any of the classes of *?Class-Set*.
- *Exhaustive-Decomposition (?Class ?Class-Set)*, which defines the set of classes *?Class-Set* as subclasses of the class *?Class*. This classification is complete, that is, there are no instances of *?Class* that are not instances of any of the classes of *?Class-Set*. However, the classes in the set *?Class-Set* are not necessarily disjoint, as with the previous primitive.
- *Partition (?Class ?Class-Set)*, which defines the set of disjoint classes *?Class-Set* as subclasses of the class *?Class*. This classification is complete, that is, the class *?Class* is the union of all the classes that belong to *?Class-Set*.
- *Instance-Of (?Individual ?Class)*, where the instance *?Individual* is an instance of the class *?Class*.

Figure 2.1 shows examples where we use some of these primitives for creating class taxonomies. The class `AmericanAirlinesFlight` is a subclass of the class `Flight`. Hence, the class `Flight` is a superclass of the class

`AmericanAirlinesFlight`. The classes `AA7462`, `AA2010` and `AA0488` form a disjoint decomposition of the class `AmericanAirlinesFlight` (that is, there are no flights operated by American Airlines that have two flight numbers from the set AA7462, AA2010 and AA0488, but there are also other kinds of flights operated by American Airlines). The classes `EuropeanLocation`, `AsianLocation`, `AfricanLocation`, `AustralianLocation`, `AntarcticLocation`, `NorthAmericanLocation`, and `SouthAmericanLocation` form a partition of the class `Location` (any location belongs to one, and only one, of the seven continents). Finally, `NewYorkCity` is an instance of the class `NorthAmericanLocation`.

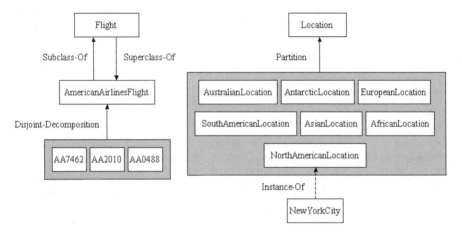

Figure 2.1: Examples of taxonomies with the FO and the OKBC Ontology primitives.

Relations and their properties

A relation represents the dependency between concepts in the domain. In Mathematics, relations are formally defined as sets of tuples of individuals. Relations in an ontology can be organized in relation taxonomies according to a specialization relationship, called *Subrelation-Of*. Several mathematical properties of a relation can also be determined: reflexive, irreflexive, symmetric, etc. Some of the primitives for defining relations identified in the FO are:

- *Relation (?Rel)*, which defines a relation *?Rel* in the domain. The classes to which the relation applies are defined as the domain and range of the relation respectively.
- *Subrelation-Of (?Child-Rel ?Parent-Rel)*. A relation *?Child-Rel* is a subrelation of the relation *?Parent-Rel* if, viewed as sets, *?Child-Rel* is a subset of *?Parent-Rel*. In other words, every tuple of *?Child-Rel* is also a tuple of *?Parent-Rel*, that is, if *?Child-Rel* holds for some arguments *arg_1*, *arg_2*, ...*arg_n*, then *?Parent-Rel* holds for the same arguments. Thus a relation and its subrelation must have the same arity, which could be undefined.
- *Reflexive-Relation (?Rel)*. Relation *?Rel* is reflexive if *?Rel(x,x)* holds for all *x* in the domain and range of *?Rel*.

- *Irreflexive-Relation (?Rel)*. Relation *?Rel* is irreflexive if *?Rel(x,x)* never holds for all *x* in the domain and range of *?Rel*.
- *Symmetric-Relation (?Rel)*. Relation *?Rel* is symmetric if *?Rel(x,y)* implies *?Rel(y,x)* for all *x* and *y* in the domain and range of *?Rel*.
- *Antisymmetric-Relation (?Rel)*. Relation *?Rel* is antisymmetric if *?Rel(x,y)* implies *not ?Rel(y,x)* when *x≠y*, for all *x* and *y* in the domain and range of *?Rel*.
- *Asymmetric-Relation (?Rel)*. Relation *?Rel* is asymmetric if it is antisymmetric and irreflexive over its exact domain. The exact domain of *?Rel* is the set elements of the *?Rel* domain linked to some element of the *?Rel* range through this relation; that is, the exact domain only keeps the domain elements that participate in the relation.
- *Transitive-Relation (?Rel)*. Relation *?Rel* is transitive if *?Rel(x,y)* and *?Rel(y,z)* implies *?Rel(x,z)*, for all *x* and *z* in the domain and range of *?Rel* respectively, and for all *y* in the domain and range of *?Rel*.
- *Equivalence-Relation (?Rel)*. Relation *?Rel* is an equivalence relation if it is reflexive, symmetric, and transitive.
- *Partial-Order-Relation (?Rel)*. Relation *?Rel* is a partial-order relation if it is reflexive, antisymmetric, and transitive.
- *Total-Order-Relation (?Rel)*. Relation *?Rel* is a total-order relation if it is a partial-order relation for which either *?Rel(x,y)* or *?Rel(y,x)* holds for every *x* or *y* in its exact domain.

As shown in Figure 1.12, these primitives for defining relations have been represented in the FO as classes, and they are organized in a class taxonomy. For example, the class *Asymmetric-Relation*, which represents the collection of relations that are asymmetric, is a subclass of the classes *Antisymmetric-Relation* and *Irreflexive-Relation*. This specialization relationship can be extracted from the definition of what an asymmetric relation is, as described above.

Slots
A slot (aka attribute) defines a characteristic of a class, which is also inherited by its subclasses. Attributes can be defined with the following two primitives of the OKBC Ontology:
- *Template-Slot-Of (?Slot ?Class)*, which states that *?Slot* is a slot of *?Class*. The slot *?Slot* can take different values in the different instances of *?Class*.
- *Slot-Of (?Slot ?Frame)*, which states that *?Slot* is a slot of *?Frame*. *?Frame* can be either a *class* or an *individual*.

Facets and types of facets
A facet is a slot property. In the FO facets are defined as ternary relations that hold between a frame (which can be either a *class* or an *individual*), a slot, and the facet. Common facets in the frame-based KR paradigm are, for example, those that define the cardinality of a slot, the type of a slot, and default values. Some of the primitives related to facets that are identified in the OKBC Ontology are:
- *Facet-Of (?Facet ?Slot ?Frame)*, where *?Facet* is facet of the slot *?Slot* in the frame *?Frame*.

- *Minimum-Cardinality (?Slot ?Frame ?Number),* which expresses that *?Number* is the minimum cardinality of the slot *?Slot* in the frame *?Frame.*
- *Maximum-Cardinality (?Slot ?Frame ?Number),* which expresses that *?Number* is the maximum cardinality of the slot *?Slot* in the frame *?Frame.*

Chapter 4 shows how to build ontologies with the FO and with the OKBC primitives in Ontolingua.

2.1.2 RDF and RDF Schema knowledge representation ontologies

RDF (Lassila and Swick, 1999) stands for *Resource Description Framework.* It is a recommendation of the W3C (the World Wide Web Consortium), developed for describing Web resources with metadata.

The RDF data model is equivalent to the semantic network KR paradigm, as explained by Staab and colleagues (2000), and by Conen and Klapsing (2001). A semantic network is a directed labeled graph composed of a set of nodes and a set of unidirectional edges, and each has a name. Nodes represent concepts, instances of concepts and property values. Edges represent properties of concepts or relationships between concepts. The semantics of the network depends on the node and edge names. The semantic network KR paradigm has less expressiveness than the frame-based KR paradigm, since it does not allow representing, for instance, default values and cardinality constraints on attributes.

The RDF data model consists of three components:
- *Resources,* which are any type of data described by RDF. Resources are described with RDF expressions and are referred to as URIs (*Uniform Resource Identifiers*) plus optional anchor identifiers.
- *Properties* (aka predicates), which define attributes or relations used to describe a resource.
- *Statements,* which assign a value to a property in a specific resource. Just as an English sentence usually comprises a subject, a verb and objects, RDF statements consist of subjects, properties and objects. For instance, in the sentence *"John bought a ticket"*, John is the subject, bought is the verb, and ticket is the object. If we represent this sentence in RDF, John and ticket are resources, denoted graphically by nodes, while bought is a property, denoted graphically by an edge.

Not only can resources be the objects of a RDF statement, but RDF statements can also be objects themselves. For example, in the sentence *"John said that Peter bought a ticket"*, John is the subject, said is the property and Peter bought a ticket is the object, which can also be decomposed, as we did before. This is known as reification in RDF.

It is important to note that the RDF data model does not make any assumption about the structure of a document containing RDF information. That is, the statements can appear in any order in a RDF ontology.

The RDF KR ontology[3] is written in RDFS (which will be presented later in this section) and contains the following modeling primitives[4] (seven classes, seven properties, and one instance):

- Class *rdf:Statement*. As we have commented, it defines the class of triples containing a subject, a property and an object.
- Class *rdf:Property*. It defines the class of properties.
- Classes *rdf:Bag*, *rdf:Seq* and *rdf:Alt*. They define the classes of collections (aka containers), and these can be unordered, ordered and alternative respectively. While it is clear what we mean by unordered and ordered collections, alternative collections may not be so. An alternative collection contains a set of resources from which we must select one for the single value of a property. For example, an alternative collection could be used to represent the values "*single*", "*double*" or "*triple*" for the attribute occupancy of a RoomReservation.
- Class *rdf:List*, properties *rdf:first* and *rdf:rest*, and instance *rdf:nil*. The class *rdf:List* defines the class of RDF lists. It is used with the properties *rdf:first* and *rdf:rest*, which represent the relationship between a list and its first item, and between the list and the rest of the list, respectively. The primitive *rdf:nil* is an instance of *rdf:List* that represents the empty list.
- Class *rdf:XMLLiteral*. It is a datatype that defines the class of well-formed XML literal values.
- Properties *rdf:predicate*, *rdf:subject* and *rdf:object*. They define the property, subject resource, and object resource of a statement respectively.
- Property *rdf:type*. It defines the class to which a resource belongs.
- Property *rdf:value*. It defines the value of a property, usually a string, when the value is a structured resource (another RDF statement).

The RDF data model does not provide modeling primitives for defining the relationships between properties and resources. For instance, in RDF we cannot define that the relation arrivalPlace can only hold between instances of the classes Travel and Location. This limitation is solved by the RDF Vocabulary Description Language (Brickley and Guha, 2003), also known as RDF Schema or RDFS. RDFS is a working draft of the W3C that extends RDF with frame-based primitives. The combination of RDF and RDF Schema is usually known as RDF(S).

The RDFS KR ontology[5] is written in RDFS. It contains 16 new modeling primitives (six classes and nine properties) added to the RDF modeling primitives. Figure 2.2 shows the class taxonomy of the RDF(S) KR ontology. As we can see, there are 13 classes in this KR ontology. The top concept in the class taxonomy is

---

[3] http://www.w3.org/1999/02/22-rdf-syntax-ns. At the time this description was written, the RDF KR ontology available at this URL was not yet compliant with the specification of RDF given by Lassila and Swick (1999) and extended by Brickley and Guha (2003). We have described this KR ontology based on the last document instead of the implemented KR ontology.

[4] In this section, we will use the prefix *rdf* to refer to RDF primitives and *rdfs* to refer to RDF Schema primitives.

[5] http://www.w3.org/2000/01/rdf-schema. As in the case of the RDF KR ontology, the ontology available at this URL is not yet compliant with the specification of RDF Schema given by Brickley and Guha (2003). We have described this KR ontology based on the document instead of the implemented KR ontology.

rdfs:Resource (which means that RDF statements, RDFS containers, RDFS classes, RDF properties, and RDFS literals are RDFS resources). The classes *rdf:Bag*, *rdf:Seq* and *rdf:Alt* are subclasses of *rdfs:Container*. The class *rdfs:Datatype* is a subclass of *rdfs:Class*, and the class *rdf:List* is defined apart in the class taxonomy.

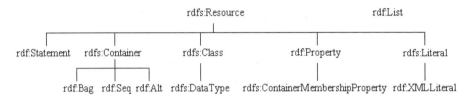

Figure 2.2: Class taxonomy of the RDF(S) KR ontology.

Table 2.1 summarizes the main features of the properties of the RDF(S) KR ontology. As we can see in this table, there are 16 properties defined in this KR ontology. In this table, we specify their domain and range, that is, the classes between which these properties can hold.

Table 2.1: Property descriptions of the RDF(S) KR ontology.

Property name	domain	range
rdf:type	rdfs:Resource	rdfs:Class
rdf:subject	rdf:Statement	rdfs:Resource
rdf:predicate	rdf:Statement	rdf:Property
rdf:object	rdf:Statement	rdfs:Resource
rdf:value	rdfs:Resource	rdfs:Resource
rdf:first	rdf:List	rdfs:Resource
rdf:rest	rdf:List	rdf:List
rdfs:subClassOf	rdfs:Class	rdfs:Class
rdfs:subPropertyOf	rdf:Property	rdf:Property
rdfs:comment	rdfs:Resource	rdfs:Literal
rdfs:label	rdfs:Resource	rdfs:Literal
rdfs:seeAlso	rdfs:Resource	rdfs:Resource
rdfs:isDefinedBy	rdfs:Resource	rdfs:Resource
rdfs:member	rdfs:Resource	rdfs:Resource
rdfs:domain	rdf:Property	rdfs:Class
rdfs:range	rdf:Property	rdfs:Class

In addition to these classes and properties, RDF also uses the properties *rdf:_1*, *rdf:_2*, *rdf:_3*, etc., each of which is both a subproperty of the property *rdfs:member* and an instance of the class *rdfs:ContainerMembershipProperty*. These properties (*rdf:_1*, *rdf:_2*, *rdf:_3*, etc.) are used to specify the members of collections such as sequences, bags and alternatives, which were previously mentioned. A more simple syntax for these properties consists in using *rdf:li* instead, which is equivalent to them. All these properties are not included in the RDF nor in the RDFS KR ontologies.

The RDFS primitives are grouped into core classes and properties, container classes and properties, collections, reification vocabulary, and utility properties.

- **Core classes** (*rdfs:Resource*, *rdfs:Literal*, *rdf:XMLLiteral*, *rdfs:Class*, *rdf:Property*, and *rdfs:Datatype*). The class *rdfs:Resource* is the most general class and defines any Web resource that can be described by RDF. The classes *rdfs:Literal* and *rdf:XMLLiteral* represent the class of untyped literal values (such as strings and integers) and well-formed XML string values respectively. The class *rdfs:Class* defines the class of all classes. The class *rdf:Property* defines the class of properties. The class *rdfs:Datatype* represents resources that are RDF datatypes.

- **Core properties** (*rdf:type*, *rdfs:subClassOf*, *rdfs:subPropertyOf*, *rdfs:domain*, *rdfs:range*, *rdfs:label*, and *rdfs:comment*). The property *rdf:type* states that a resource is an instance of a class. The properties *rdfs:subClassOf* and *rdfs:subPropertyOf* are used to define class taxonomies and property taxonomies respectively. The properties *rdfs:domain* and *rdfs:range* define the domain and range of the property they are applied to. Finally, the properties *rdfs:label* and *rdfs:comment*, which were previously classified as documentation primitives, are used for describing resources in natural language. The property *rdfs:comment* is mainly for long descriptions while *rdfs:label* is for defining alternative short labels of the resource to which it is applied.

- **Container classes and properties** (*rdfs:Container*, *rdf:Bag*, *rdf:Seq*, *rdf:Alt*, *rdfs:ContainerMembershipProperty*, and *rdfs:member*). The class *rdfs:Container* defines the class of resource collections, which can be a bag (*rdf:Bag*), a sequence (*rdf:Seq*), or an alternative (*rdf:Alt*). These containers were described above. The class *rdfs:ContainerMembershipProperty* defines the relationship between a resource and a container. The property *rdfs:member* is used to specify the members of a container. As we explained above, the properties *rdf:_1*, *rdf:_2*, *rdf:_3*, etc., are subproperties of this property, and *rdf:li* can also be used to express them.

- **Collections** (*rdf:List*, *rdf:first*, *rdf:rest*, and *rdf:nil*). The class *rdf:List* is used to describe lists. The properties *rdf:first* and *rdf:rest* are used to manage lists, and *rdf:nil* is an instance of *rdf:List* that represents the empty list.

- **Reification vocabulary** (*rdf:Statement*, *rdf:predicate*, *rdf:subject*, and *rdf:object*). This class and these properties were described when we referred to the RDF KR ontology. As we said, the class *rdf:Statement* defines the class of triples that can be described in RDF(S), and the properties *rdf:predicate*, *rdf:subject*, and *rdf:object* define the property, subject resource, and object resource of a statement, respectively.

- **Utility properties** (*rdfs:seeAlso*, *rdfs:isDefinedBy*, and *rdf:value*). The property *rdfs:seeAlso* defines a resource that might give additional information about the resource being described. The property *rdfs:isDefinedBy* provides the namespace where the resource is defined and is a subproperty of *rdfs:seeAlso*. The property *rdf:value* was described when we referred to the RDF KR ontology. It defines the value of a property when that value is a structured resource.

In Chapter 4 we will describe in detail how to use all these KR primitives to implement our ontologies in RDF(S), but now we want to show an example of how to use primitives of the RDF and RDFS KR ontologies. Below we present the definitions of the class `Flight` and of the relation `arrivalPlace`. In these definitions, primitives of the RDFS KR ontology (such as *rdfs:Class*, *rdfs:comment*, *rdfs:subClassOf*, *rdfs:domain* and *rdfs:range*) are combined with primitives of the RDF KR ontology (such as *rdf:Property*). The properties *rdf:ID* and *rdf:resource* are also used. However, they should not be considered as KR primitives since they are only used to identify RDF resources. We will describe their differences in Chapter 4. Please note that *rdf:resource*, which is used to refer to a RDF resource, should not be mistaken for *rdfs:Resource*, which is the class of RDF resources.

```
<rdfs:Class rdf:ID="Flight">
   <rdfs:comment>A journey by plane</rdfs:comment>
   <rdfs:subClassOf rdf:resource="#Travel"/>
</rdfs:Class>

<rdf:Property rdf:ID="arrivalPlace">
  <rdfs:domain rdf:resource="#Travel"/>
  <rdfs:range rdf:resource="#Location"/>
</rdf:Property>
```

2.1.3 OIL knowledge representation ontology

OIL (Horrocks et al., 2000) stands for *Ontology Inference Layer*. This language has been built as an extension of RDF(S) by adding it more frame-based KR primitives and avoiding the RDF reification mechanism. OIL uses description logics to give clear semantics to its modeling primitives.

OIL was developed using a layered approach, as shown in Figure 2.3. Each new layer is built on top of the existing ones and adds new functionality and complexity to the lower layer. *Core OIL* groups the OIL primitives that have a direct mapping to RDF(S) primitives, though it does not allow RDF(S) reification, as shown in the figure. *Standard OIL* adds frame-based primitives. Its relationship with *Core OIL*

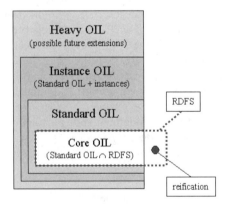

Figure 2.3: Layers of OIL.

was explained in depth by Broekstra and colleagues (2001). *Instance OIL* permits defining instances of concepts and roles and includes a full-fledged database capability. Finally, *Heavy OIL* is reserved for future extensions (such as rules, metaclasses, etc.). *Standard OIL* and *Instance OIL* share the same KR ontology. We must add that the *Heavy OIL* KR ontology has not been developed yet at the time this section was written.

Here we will only present the *Standard OIL* KR ontology[6]. This ontology consists of 37 classes and 19 properties. It is mostly written in RDF(S), except for two classes (*oil:Top* and *oil:Bottom*) written in OIL.

Figure 2.4 shows the class hierarchy of the OIL KR ontology in which we can see how this KR ontology extends the RDF(S) KR ontology. There are six groups of primitives that are classes:

- **Classes for defining concrete type expressions** (*oil:Equal*, *oil:Min*, *oil:Max*, *oil:GreaterThan*, *oil:LessThan*, and *oil:Range*). These primitives are subclasses of the primitive *oil:ConcreteTypeExpression*, which in its turn is subclass of *oil:Expression*. They allow defining numeric expressions for the numbers that are equal, greater or equal than, less or equal than, greater than and less than a number, as well as numeric ranges, respectively.
- **Classes for defining class expressions**. These primitives are defined as subclasses of the class *oil:ClassExpression*, which in its turn is subclass of *oil:Expression*. In OIL, classes can be primitive (*oil:PrimitiveClass*) or defined (*oil:DefinedClass*), and they specialize *rdfs:Class*. The difference between them was explained in Section 1.3.2, where we described how to model ontologies with description logic. Class expressions can also be formed with boolean expressions, property restrictions and enumerated expressions.
    - With regard to **Boolean expressions** (primitives that are subclasses of *oil:BooleanExpression*), we can use three primitives: *oil:And*, *oil:Or*, and *oil:Not*. They express conjunction, disjunction, and negation of classes respectively.
    - In relation to **property restrictions** (primitives that are subclasses of *oil:PropertyRestriction*), we can express qualified number restrictions[7] with the primitives that are subclasses of *oil:CardinalityRestriction* (*oil:MinCardinality*, *oil:Cardinality* and *oil:MaxCardinality*). We can also express value restriction[8] (*oil:ValueType*), existential restriction[9] (*oil:HasValue*) and role fillers to deal with individuals (*oil:HasFiller*).

---

[6] http://www.ontoknowledge.org/oil/rdf-schema/2000/11/10-oil-standard

[7] A qualified number restriction defines a cardinality restriction for a role when it is applied to instances of a specific class. For example, we know that a person always has two parents, of which one is a man and the other is a woman. This is represented as a qualified number restriction of the role hasParent, which has cardinality 1 when it is applied to Man and cardinality 1 when it is applied to Woman.

[8] Value restrictions are used to express that a role may have any number of values, and that these values must always be instances of the class specified in the restriction. For instance, a person can be married or not to somebody, but must always be married to a person (not to an animal).

[9] Existential restrictions are used to express that a role must have at least one value that is an instance of the class specified in the restriction. For instance, we can define a friendly person as a person who must have at least one friend, which is another person. However, he/she can also have other friends that are not persons (such as an animal).

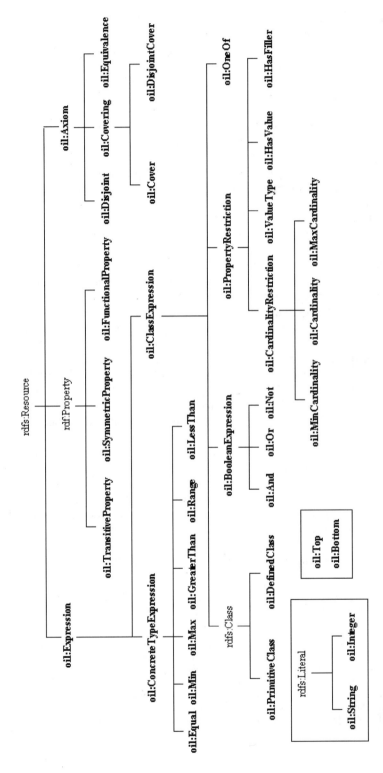

Figure 2.4: Class taxonomy of the Standard OIL KR ontology defined as an extension of RDF(S).

- Regarding **enumerated expressions**, we can use the class *oil:OneOf*. These primitives configure OIL as a SHIQ language[10], according to the DL terminology explained in Section 1.3.2.
- **Classes for defining mathematical characteristics of properties** (*oil:TransitiveProperty*, *oil:FunctionalProperty* and *oil:SymmetricProperty*). They express that the property is transitive, that it can only have one value for each instance in its domain and that it is symmetric respectively. All of them specialize *rdf:Property*.
- **Classes for defining axioms** (primitives that are subclasses of *oil:Axiom*). These primitives are used to define disjoint and exhaustive knowledge in class taxonomies (*oil:Disjoint* and the subclasses of *oil:Covering*, which are *oil:Cover* and *oil:DisjointCover*, respectively), as well as equivalence between classes (*oil:Equivalence*). The primitive *oil:Disjoint* defines a set of classes that are disjoint, that is, that cannot have common instances. The primitive *oil:Cover* expresses that a class is the union of a set of classes, that is, that there are no instances of the class that are not instances of at least one of the classes in the set. The primitive *oil:DisjointCover* expresses that a class is the union of a disjoint set of classes.
- **Classes for defining datatypes** (*oil:String* and *oil:Integer*). They specialize the primitive *rdfs:Literal*, and define the datatype of strings and the datatype of integers respectively.
- **Predefined classes** (*oil:Top* and *oil:Bottom*). The class *oil:Top* is the most general class and subsumes every other class. The class *oil:Bottom* is the empty class and is subsumed by every other class.

There are also several primitives in the Standard OIL KR ontology that are properties. Table 2.2 summarizes the main features of these 19 properties, specifying their domain and range, that is, the classes between which these properties can hold. We will first describe these properties and later present the table.

- The properties *oil:subClassOf*, *oil:domain* and *oil:range*. They replace the corresponding primitives in RDF(S).
- The property *oil:hasOperand*. It connects a Boolean expression with the operands. It is used with the primitives *oil:And*, *oil:Or* and *oil:Not*, described above.
- The property *oil:individual*. It connects an *oil:OneOf* expression with its individuals.
- The properties *oil:hasPropertyRestriction*, *oil:onProperty*, *oil:toClass* and *oil:toConcreteType*. They are used to express the property restrictions of a class. The primitive *oil:toClass* is used with properties whose range is another class, and the primitive *oil:toConcreteType* are used with properties that are concrete types.
- The properties *oil:stringValue* and *oil:integerValue*. They connect a concrete type expression with a string value or an integer value respectively.

---

[10] In Horrocks (2000) OIL appears as SHIQ(d), which means that it is a SHIQ language extended with concrete data types.

- The properties *oil:individualFiller*, *oil:integerFiller* and *oil:stringFiller*. They represent property values.
- The property *oil:number*. Used to express the number of a cardinality restriction.
- The property *oil:inverseRelationOf*. Used to define the inverse of a property.
- The properties *oil:hasObject*, *oil:hasSubject* and *oil:isCoveredBy*. They represent disjoint and exhaustive knowledge in class taxonomies.

Table 2.2: Property descriptions of the Standard OIL KR ontology.

Property name	domain	range
oil:subClassOf	rdfs:Class	oil:ClassExpression
oil:domain	rdf:Property	oil:ClassExpression
oil:range	rdf:Property	oil:ClassExpression
oil:hasOperand	oil:BooleanExpression	oil:Expression
oil:individual	oil:OneOf	rdfs:Resource
oil:hasPropertyRestriction	rdfs:Class	oil:PropertyRestriction
oil:onProperty	oil:PropertyRestriction	rdf:Property
oil:toClass	oil:PropertyRestriction	oil:ClassExpression
oil:toConcreteType	oil:PropertyRestriction	oil:ConcreteTypeExpression
oil:stringValue	oil:ConcreteTypeExpression	oil:String
oil:integerValue	oil:ConcreteTypeExpression	oil:Integer
oil:individualFiller	oil:HasFiller	rdfs:Resource
oil:stringFiller	oil:HasFiller	oil:String
oil:integerFiller	oil:HasFiller	oil:Integer
oil:number	oil:CardinalityRestriction	oil:Integer
oil:inverseRelationOf	rdf:Property	rdf:Property
oil:hasObject	oil:Axiom	oil:ClassExpression
oil:hasSubject	oil:Covering	oil:ClassExpression
oil:isCoveredBy	oil:Covering	oil:ClassExpression

In Chapter 4 we will describe in detail how to use these primitives to implement ontologies in OIL and we will use OILs plain text syntax. We now show a small example of how to use primitives of the OIL KR ontology with the XML syntax to get its flavor. Below we present the definition of the defined class `Flight`, which was described in Section 1.3.2. This class is a subclass of the class `Travel` that has exactly one value for the attribute `flightNumber`, whose type is `integer`, and that has a filler for the attribute `transportMeans` with value "plane".

```
<oil:DefinedClass rdf:ID="Flight">
  <rdfs:comment>A journey by plane</rdfs:comment>
  <oil:subClassOf>
   <oil:And>
     <oil:hasOperand rdf:resource="#Travel"/>
     <oil:hasOperand>
      <oil:Cardinality oil:number="1">
        <oil:onProperty rdf:resource="#flightNumber"/>
        <oil:toClass rdf:resource="&oil;Integer"/>
      </oil:Cardinality>
```

```
    </oil:hasOperand>
    <oil:hasOperand>
     <oil:HasFiller oil:stringFiller="plane">
       <oil:onProperty rdf:resource="#transportMeans"/>
     </oil:HasFiller>
    </oil:hasOperand>
   </oil:And>
  </oil:subClassOf>
</oil:DefinedClass>
```

2.1.4 DAML+OIL knowledge representation ontology

Like OIL, DAML+OIL (Horrocks and van Harmelen, 2001) was developed as an extension of RDF(S). However, this language is not divided into different layers: it provides DL extensions of RDF(S) directly. DAML+OIL is a SHIQ language extended with datatypes and nominals[11].

The DAML+OIL KR ontology[12] is written in DAML+OIL and contains 53 modeling primitives (14 classes, 38 properties and one instance). Two of the classes (*daml:Literal* and *daml:Property*) and 10 of the properties (*daml:subPropertyOf, daml:type, daml:value, daml:subClassOf, daml:domain, daml:range, daml:label, daml:comment, daml:seeAlso* and *daml:isDefinedBy*) are equivalent to their corresponding classes and properties in RDF(S).

Figure 2.5 shows the class taxonomy of the DAML+OIL KR ontology, and how this KR ontology extends the RDF(S) KR ontology. The following groups of primitives that are classes are defined in the DAML+OIL KR ontology:

- **Classes for defining classes, restrictions and datatypes** (*daml:Class, daml:Restriction* and *daml:DataType*). All these primitives specialize *rdfs:Class*. The primitive *daml:Class* is used to define classes. The primitive *daml:Restriction* is used to define property restrictions for classes (number restrictions, existential restrictions, qualified number restrictions, etc.). And the primitive *daml:DataType* is used to create datatypes. XML Schema datatypes (Biron and Malhotra, 2001) are permitted in DAML+OIL, and are considered subclasses of *daml:DataType*.

- **Classes for defining properties** (*daml:UnambiguousProperty, daml:TransitiveProperty, daml:ObjectProperty*, and *daml:DatatypeProperty*). They are used to define properties, so they specialize the class *daml:Property* (which is equivalent to *rdf:Property*, as stated above). The primitive *daml:ObjectProperty* is used to define properties that connect a class with another class. It is specialized in the primitives *daml:TransitiveProperty* and *daml:UnambiguousProperty*, which refer to properties that are transitive and injective[13] respectively. The primitive *daml:DatatypeProperty* is used to define properties that connect a class with a datatype. Finally, the primitive

---

[11] Also known as SHOIQ(d).
[12] http://www.daml.org/2001/03/daml+oil. There is another version of this ontology available at http://www.w3.org/2001/10/daml+oil, but the DAML+OIL developers recommend using the first one.
[13] If the relation *R* is injective, and *R(x,y)* and *R(z,y)* hold, then *x=z*.

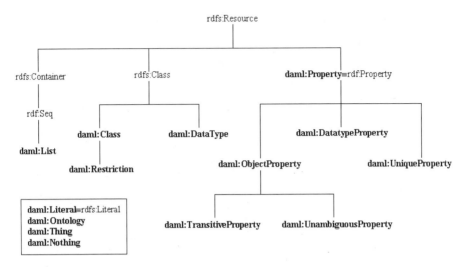

Figure 2.5: Class taxonomy of the DAML+OIL KR ontology defined as an extension of RDF(S).

daml:UniqueProperty can be used to define both kinds of relations (between classes and between a class and a datatype) provided that they are functional[14].

- **Classes for defining containers** (*daml:List*). DAML+OIL lists are special types of RDF sequences; hence *daml:List* is a subclass of *rdf:Seq*. Although lists are now defined in the RDF(S) KR ontology, they were not when the DAML+OIL KR ontology was created. This is why this primitive is included here.

- **Predefined classes** (*daml:Thing* and *daml:Nothing*). They represent the most and the least general class respectively.

- **Classes for defining literal values** (*daml:Literal*). This class represents untyped literal values (that is, strings and integers). It is equivalent to *rdfs:Literal*.

- **Classes for describing ontologies** (*daml:Ontology*). This primitive is used as the root element of a DAML+OIL ontology, containing all its definitions.

DAML+OIL class expressions are built with KR primitives that are properties[15]. These DAML+OIL primitives allow expressing:

- Conjunction (*daml:intersectionOf*), disjunction (*daml:unionOf*), and negation (*daml:complementOf*).

- Collection of individuals (*daml:oneOf*).

- Property restrictions. They are created with the class *daml:Restriction*, as described above. These restrictions are defined with two elements:

---

[14] This primitive is equivalent to the primitive *oil:FunctionalProperty*. If the relation R is functional, and $R(x,y)$ and $R(x,z)$ hold, then $y=z$.

[15] Let us remember that OIL class expressions were built with KR primitives that are classes, such as *oil:And*, *oil:Or*, *oil:MinCardinality*, etc.

daml:onProperty (which refers to the property name) and another element that expresses:

- Value restriction (*daml:toClass*).
- Role fillers (*daml:hasValue*).
- Existential restriction (*daml:hasClass*) and number restriction (*daml:cardinality*, *daml:maxCardinality*, and *daml:minCardinality*).
- Qualified number restriction (with the primitive *daml:hasClassQ* plus one of the following primitives: *daml:maxCardinalityQ*, *daml:minCardinalityQ* and *daml:cardinalityQ*).

Properties are not only used to create class expressions, but also to define other relationships between ontology components. The following properties are also defined in the DAML+OIL KR ontology:

- The primitive *daml:inverseOf*. It defines the inverse of a role.
- The primitives *daml:equivalentTo*, *daml:sameClassAs*, *daml:samePropertyAs*, and *daml:sameIndividualAs*. They define equivalences between resources, classes, properties and instances, respectively.
- The primitive *daml:differentIndividualFrom*. It defines that two instances are different.
- The primitives *daml:disjointWith* and *daml:disjointUnionOf*. They express disjoint and exhaustive knowledge between classes in the class taxonomy respectively.
- The primitives *daml:versionInfo* and *daml:imports*. They give information about the ontology version and the ontologies imported by the current ontology. There are no restrictions on the contents of the *daml:versionInfo* primitive.
- The primitives *daml:first*, *daml:rest* and *daml:item*. They are used for managing lists.

Finally, the primitive *daml:nil* is an instance of the class *daml:List*. It represents the empty list.

Table 2.3 summarizes the main features of the DAML+OIL KR ontology properties that are not a redefinition of the RDF(S) KR ontology primitives. As we can see in the table, there are 28 properties defined in this KR ontology, apart from 10 properties that are equivalent to the corresponding RDF(S) properties, as described at the beginning of this section. In this table we specify their domain and range, that is, the classes between which these properties can hold. If the value for the range is "not specified", then the property can take any value which is not restricted to a specific class of the DAML+OIL KR ontology. The *xsd* prefix used in the range of the cardinality restriction properties (*xsd:nonNegativeInteger*) refers to the XML Schema datatype namespace[16].

---

[16] http://www.w3.org/2000/10/XMLSchema. As we will see later, this namespace is not used any more to refer to XML Schema. However, DAML+OIL still uses it.

Table 2.3: Property descriptions of the DAML+OIL KR ontology.

Property name	domain	range
daml:intersectionOf	daml:Class	daml:List
daml:unionOf	daml:Class	daml:List
daml:complementOf	daml:Class	daml:Class
daml:oneOf	daml:Class	daml:List
daml:onProperty	daml:Restriction	rdf:Property
daml:toClass	daml:Restriction	rdfs:Class
daml:hasValue	daml:Restriction	*not specified*
daml:hasClass	daml:Restriction	rdfs:Class
daml:minCardinality	daml:Restriction	xsd:nonNegativeInteger
daml:maxCardinality	daml:Restriction	xsd:nonNegativeInteger
daml:cardinality	daml:Restriction	xsd:nonNegativeInteger
daml:hasClassQ	daml:Restriction	rdfs:Class
daml:minCardinalityQ	daml:Restriction	xsd:nonNegativeInteger
daml:maxCardinalityQ	daml:Restriction	xsd:nonNegativeInteger
daml:cardinalityQ	daml:Restriction	xsd:nonNegativeInteger
daml:inverseOf	daml:ObjectProperty	daml:ObjectProperty
daml:equivalentTo	*not specified*	*not specified*
daml:sameClassAs	daml:Class	daml:Class
daml:samePropertyAs	rdf:Property	rdf:Property
daml:sameIndividualAs	daml:Thing	daml:Thing
daml:differentIndividualFrom	daml:Thing	daml:Thing
daml:disjointWith	daml:Class	daml:Class
daml:disjointUnionOf	daml:Class	daml:List
daml:versionInfo	*not specified*	*not specified*
daml:imports	*not specified*	*not specified*
daml:first	daml:List	*not specified*
daml:rest	daml:List	daml:List
daml:item	daml:List	*not specified*

In Chapter 4 we will describe in detail how to use these primitives to implement ontologies in DAML+OIL. We will now show a small example of how to use them to define the class Flight exactly as the class Travel that has exactly one value for the attribute flightNumber, whose type is integer, and that has a filler for the attribute transportMeans with value "plane".

```
<daml:Class rdf:ID="Flight">
  <rdfs:comment>A journey by plane</rdfs:comment>
  <daml:intersectionOf rdf:parseType="daml:collection">
    <daml:Class rdf:about="#Travel"/>
    <daml:Restriction daml:cardinality="1">
      <daml:onProperty rdf:resource="#flightNumber"/>
      <daml:toClass rdf:resource="&xsd;integer"/>
    </daml:Restriction>
    <daml:Restriction>
      <daml:onProperty rdf:resource="#transportMeans"/>
      <daml:hasValue>
```

```
        <xsd:string rdf:value="plane"/>
      </daml:hasValue>
    </daml:Restriction>
  </daml:intersectionOf>
</daml:Class>
```

2.1.5 OWL knowledge representation ontology

The OWL language (Dean and Schreiber, 2003) has been created by the W3C Web Ontology (WebOnt) Working Group. It is derived from the DAML+OIL language, and it builds upon RDF(S). At the time of writing this section, the OWL specification is a W3C Working Draft, though both the language and its KR ontology[17] (which is implemented in OWL) are already in a stable state.

Like OIL, OWL is divided in layers: OWL Lite, OWL DL, and OWL Full. OWL Lite extends RDF(S) and gathers the most common features of OWL, so it is intended for users that only need to create class taxonomies and simple constraints. OWL DL includes the complete OWL vocabulary, which is described in this section. Finally, OWL Full provides more flexibility to represent ontologies than OWL DL does. We refer to Dean and Schreiber (2003) for a detailed description of this layer.

There are 40 primitives in the OWL DL KR ontology (16 classes and 24 properties). Figure 2.6 shows the KR primitives used in OWL Lite and OWL DL. In the figure, we can see that some RDF(S) primitives can be used in all the versions of OWL (OWL Lite and OWL DL), and that OWL Lite primitives can be used in OWL DL. OWL Full KR primitives are the same as the OWL DL ones, as explained above.

In the figure we also present in parentheses the corresponding primitive in the DAML+OIL KR ontology, in case there is a correspondance with a DAML+OIL KR primitive. For instance, *owl:allValuesFrom (daml:toClass)* means that the primitive *owl:allValuesFrom* corresponds to the primitive *daml:toClass* from the DAML+OIL KR ontology.

Figure 2.7 shows the class taxonomy of the primitives that are classes in the OWL KR ontology. All belong to OWL Lite. Hence, they also belong to OWL DL and OWL Full. These primitives can be grouped as follows:
- **Classes for defining classes and restrictions** (*owl:Class* and *owl:Restriction*). The primitive *owl:Class* specializes *rdfs:Class* and is used to define classes. The primitive *owl:Restriction* specializes *owl:Class* and is used to define property restrictions for classes (number restrictions, existential restrictions, universal restrictions, etc.).
- **Classes for defining properties** (*owl:ObjectProperty*, *owl:DatatypeProperty*, *owl:TransitiveProperty*, *owl:SymmetricProperty*, *owl:FunctionalProperty*, *owl:InverseFunctionalProperty*, and *owl:AnnotationProperty*). They are used to define properties, hence they specialize the class *rdf:Property*. The primitive

---

[17] http://www.w3.org/2002/07/owl

OWL DL

Class expressions allowed in: rdfs:domain, rdfs:range, rdfs:subClassOf
                                      owl:intersectionOf, owl:equivalentClass, owl:allValuesFrom, owl:someValuesFrom
Values are not restricted (0..N) in: owl:minCardinality, owl:maxCardinality, owl:cardinality

owl:DataRange, rdf:List, rdf:first, rdf:rest, rdf:nil

owl:hasValue (*daml:hasValue*)
owl:oneOf (*daml:oneOf*)
owl:unionOf (*daml:unionOf*), owl:complementOf (*daml:complementOf*)
owl:disjointWith (*daml:disjointWith*)

> **OWL Lite**
> owl:Ontology (*daml:Ontology*),
> owl:versionInfo (*daml:versionInfo*),
> owl:imports (*daml:imports*),
> owl:backwardCompatibleWith,
> owl:incompatibleWith, owl:priorVersion,
> owl:DeprecatedClass,
> owl:DeprecatedProperty
>
> owl:Class (*daml:Class*),
> owl:Restriction (*daml:Restriction*),
> owl:onProperty (*daml:onProperty*),
> owl:allValuesFrom (*daml:toClass*) (only with class identifiers and named datatypes),
> owl:someValuesFrom (*daml:hasClass*) (only with class identifiers and named datatypes),
> owl:minCardinality (*daml:minCardinality*; restricted to {0,1}),
> owl:maxCardinality (*daml:maxCardinality*; restricted to {0,1}),
> owl:cardinality (*daml:cardinality*; restricted to {0,1})
>
> owl:intersectionOf (only with class identifiers and property restrictions)
>
> owl:ObjectProperty (*daml:ObjectProperty*),
> owl:DatatypeProperty (*daml:DatatypeProperty*),
> owl:TransitiveProperty (*daml:TransitiveProperty*),
> owl:SymmetricProperty,
> owl:FunctionalProperty (*daml:UniqueProperty*),
> owl:InverseFunctionalProperty (*daml:UnambiguousProperty*),
> owl:AnnotationProperty
>
> owl:Thing (*daml:Thing*)
> owl:Nothing (*daml:Nothing*)
>
> owl:inverseOf (*daml:inverseOf*),
> owl:equivalentClass (*daml:sameClassAs*) (only with class identifiers and property restrictions),
> owl:equivalentProperty (*daml:samePropertyAs*),
> owl:sameAs (*daml:equivalentTo*),
> owl:sameIndividualAs,
> owl:differentFrom (*daml:differentIndividualFrom*),
> owl:AllDifferent, owl:distinctMembers
>
> > **RDF(S)**
> > rdf:Property
> > rdfs:subPropertyOf
> > rdfs:domain
> > rdfs:range (only with class identifiers and named datatypes)
> > rdfs:comment, rdfs:label, rdfs:seeAlso, rdfs:isDefinedBy
> > rdfs:subClassOf (only with class identifiers and property restrictions)

Figure 2.6: OWL Lite and OWL DL KR primitives.

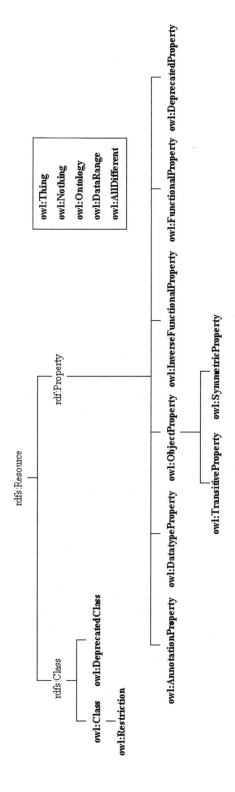

Figure 2.7: Class taxonomy of the OWL KR ontology defined as an extension of RDF(S).

owl:ObjectProperty serves to define properties that connect a class with another class, and the primitive *owl:DatatypeProperty* is used to define properties that connect a class with a datatype. The primitives *owl:TransitiveProperty* and *owl:SymmetricProperty* serve to define logical characteristics of properties. The primitives *owl:FunctionalProperty* and *owl:InverseFunctionalProperty* are used to define global cardinality restrictions of properties. In OWL Lite and OWL DL, *owl:InverseFunctionalProperty* is defined as a subclass of *owl:ObjectProperty*. In OWL Full, *owl:InverseFunctionalProperty* can be also an *owl:DatatypeProperty*. Hence, this primitive is defined as a subclass of *rdf:Property*, as shown in Figure 2.7. The primitive *owl:AnnotationProperty* is used to define properties that have no logical consequences on an OWL ontology, but just give information about its classes, properties, individuals or the whole ontology.

- **Classes for stating inequality among individuals** (*owl:AllDifferent*). This is to specify that several instances are different to each other. This is sometimes needed because OWL does not assume the unique names assumption in its ontologies. This means that two individual definitions with different identifiers could refer to the same individual.
- **Classes for describing enumerations of datatypes** (*owl:DataRange*). This is to create enumerated datatypes, that is, datatypes with a set of predefined values.
- **Predefined classes** (*owl:Thing* and *owl:Nothing*). They represent the most general and the least general class respectively.
- **Classes for describing ontologies** (*owl:Ontology*). This primitive is used as the root element of an OWL ontology, containing all its definitions.
- **Classes for describing ontology versioning** (*owl:DeprecatedClass and owl:DeprecatedProperty*). They specify, respectively, that a class or a property have been deprecated in the current version of the ontology. As occurs with *owl:AnnotationProperty*, these primitives have no logical consequences on an OWL ontology. They are only used for ontology versioning purposes.

Like in DAML+OIL, OWL class expressions are built with KR primitives that are properties. These will be organized in two groups: the one with primitives defined for OWL Lite (which can be used in OWL Lite, OWL DL and OWL Full) and the one with primitives defined for OWL DL (which can be used in OWL DL and OWL Full).

- **Properties for defining class expressions in OWL Lite**:
  - Conjunction (*owl:intersectionOf*). The range of this property is restricted in OWL Lite to class identifiers and property restrictions.
  - Property restrictions. They are defined with the class *owl:Restriction*, described above. Restrictions are defined with two elements: *owl:onProperty* (which refers to the property name) and another element that expresses:
    - Value restriction (*owl:allValuesFrom*).
    - Existential restriction (*owl:someValuesFrom*).

- Number restriction (*owl:cardinality*, *owl:maxCardinality*, and *owl:minCardinality*). The values of these properties are restricted to 0 and 1. This permits the user to indicate "at least one", "no more than one", and "exactly one".
- **Properties for defining class expressions in OWL DL**:
  - Conjunction (*owl:intersectionOf*), disjunction (*owl:unionOf*), and negation (*owl:complementOf*). Unlike in OWL Lite, there are no restrictions for the range of these properties.
  - Collection of individuals (*owl:oneOf*).
  - Property restrictions. As in OWL Lite, they are defined with the class *owl:Restriction*, decomposed in *owl:onProperty* and another element that expresses:
    - Role fillers (*owl:hasValue*).
    - Number restriction (*owl:cardinality*, *owl:maxCardinality*, and *owl:minCardinality*). The values of these properties are not restricted as in OWL Lite provided that they are positive integer values, including 0.

Other properties defined in OWL Lite and OWL DL are the following:
- **Other OWL Lite properties**:
  - The primitives *owl:versionInfo*, *owl:priorVersion*, *owl:incompatibleWith*, *owl:backwardCompatibleWith*, and *owl:imports*. The primitive *owl:versionInfo* gives information on the current ontology version. The primitives *owl:priorVersion*, *owl:incompatibleWith*, and *owl:backwardCompatibleWith* point to another OWL ontology, defining that the current ontology has a previous version, or is incompatible or compatible with another ontology respectively. Finally, *owl:imports* refers to another OWL ontology, which the current ontology imports.
  - The primitive *owl:inverseOf*. It defines the inverse of a property.
  - The primitives *owl:sameAs*, *owl:equivalentClass*, *owl:equivalentProperty*, and *owl:sameIndividualAs*. They define equivalences between resources, classes, properties, and instances respectively.
  - The primitive *owl:differentFrom*. It defines that two individuals are different.
  - The primitive *owl:distinctMembers*. It is used together with *owl:AllDifferent*, to define a list of instances that are different from each other.
- **Other OWL DL properties**:
  - The primitive *owl:disjointWith*. It expresses disjoint knowledge between classes in the class taxonomy.

Table 2.4 summarizes the main features of the properties of the OWL KR ontology, specifying their domain and range. If the value for the range is "not specified", we mean that the property can take any value which is not restricted to a specific class of the OWL KR ontology. As we can see in the table, there are 24 properties defined in this KR ontology. Besides, in OWL we can use the properties *rdfs:subClassOf*, *rdfs:subPropertyOf*, *rdfs:domain*, *rdfs:range*, *rdfs:comment*, *rdfs:label*, *rdfs:seeAlso*, and *rdfs:isDefinedBy* from the RDF(S) KR ontology.

As described in the table, the OWL KR ontology does not specify any domain or range for *owl:versionInfo*.

Table 2.4: Property descriptions of the OWL KR ontology.

Property name	domain	range
owl:intersectionOf	owl:Class	rdf:List
owl:unionOf	owl:Class	rdf:List
owl:complementOf	owl:Class	owl:Class
owl:oneOf	owl:Class	rdf:List
owl:onProperty	owl:Restriction	rdf:Property
owl:allValuesFrom	owl:Restriction	rdfs:Class
owl:hasValue	owl:Restriction	*not specified*
owl:someValuesFrom	owl:Restriction	rdfs:Class
owl:minCardinality	owl:Restriction	xsd:nonNegativeInteger OWL Lite: {0,1} OWL DL/Full: {0,..,N}
owl:maxCardinality	owl:Restriction	xsd:nonNegativeInteger OWL Lite: {0,1} OWL DL/Full: {0,..,N}
owl:cardinality	owl:Restriction	xsd:nonNegativeInteger OWL Lite: {0,1} OWL DL/Full: {0,..,N}
owl:inverseOf	owl:ObjectProperty	owl:ObjectProperty
owl:sameAs	owl:Thing	owl:Thing
owl:equivalentClass	owl:Class	owl:Class
owl:equivalentProperty	rdf:Property	rdf:Property
owl:sameIndividualAs	owl:Thing	owl:Thing
owl:differentFrom	owl:Thing	owl:Thing
owl:disjointWith	owl:Class	owl:Class
owl:distinctMembers	owl:AllDifferent	rdf:List
owl:versionInfo	*not specified*	*not specified*
owl:priorVersion	owl:Ontology	owl:Ontology
owl:incompatibleWith	owl:Ontology	owl:Ontology
owl:backwardCompatibleWith	owl:Ontology	owl:Ontology
owl:imports	owl:Ontology	owl:Ontology

To sum up, we can say that there are not many differences between the OWL KR ontology and the DAML+OIL one. In fact, most of the changes imply changing the names of the original DAML+OIL KR primitives, since they were not always easy to understand by non-experts. Two other important changes are the removal of qualified number restrictions (OWL is a SHIN language, according to the DL terminology) and the inclusion of symmetry as a characteristic of properties. The primitives for managing lists that were defined in the DAML+OIL KR ontology have not been included in this ontology, since OWL allows the use of the recent RDF(S) primitives for managing lists.

In Chapter 4 we will describe in detail how to use these primitives to implement ontologies in OWL. We now present a small example of how to use them to define the class `Flight` as the class `Travel` that has exactly one value for the attribute `flightNumber`, whose type is `integer`, and that has a filler for the attribute `transportMeans` with value "plane".

```
<owl:Class rdf:ID="Flight">
  <rdfs:comment>A journey by plane</rdfs:comment>
  <owl:intersectionOf rdf:parseType="Collection">
    <owl:Class rdf:about="#Travel"/>
    <owl:Restriction owl:cardinality="1">
      <owl:onProperty rdf:resource="#flightNumber"/>
      <owl:allValuesFrom rdf:resource="&xsd;integer"/>
    </owl:Restriction>
    <owl:Restriction>
      <owl:onProperty rdf:resource="#transportMeans"/>
      <owl:hasValue rdf:datatype="&xsd;string">
          plane
      </owl:hasValue>
    </owl:Restriction>
  </owl:intersectionOf>
</owl:Class>
```

2.2 Top-level Ontologies

Top-level ontologies (aka upper-level ontologies) describe very general concepts that are common across the domains and give general notions under which all the terms in existing ontologies should be linked to. Sometimes top-level ontologies are used to build domain ontologies, but often these are built first and then linked to upper-level ontologies.

On the framework of the Cyc project, the following characteristics are identified as desirable in a top-level ontology[18]:

a)   It should be "universal": every concept imagined in a specific ontology can be correctly linked to the upper-level ontology in appropriate places, no matter how general or specific the concept is, and no matter what the background of the ontology builder is (nationality, age, native language, epoch, childhood experiences, current goals, etc.). For example, a top-level ontology that just classifies entities in *physical objects* and *mental objects* is not universal, since *processes* and *situations* are not considered.

b)   It should be "articulate": on the one hand, there is a justification for every concept of the top-level ontology. On the other hand, there are enough concepts to enable and support knowledge sharing, natural language disambiguation, database cleaning and integration, and other kinds of applications. For example, a top-level ontology that classifies entities in *mortal entities* and *immortal entities* could be (in the best case) useful for theology, but not for other fields.

---

[18] http://www.cyc.com/cyc-2-1/cover.html

In the next subsections, we will present the following top-level ontologies: the top-level ontologies of universals and particulars, built by Guarino and colleagues, Sowa's top-level ontology, Cyc's Upper Ontology, and one of the Standard Upper Ontology working group. The top-level ontologies of universals and particulars are available in WebODE, Cyc's Upper Ontology is available in CycL and DAML+OIL, the Standard Upper Ontology is available in KIF and DAML+OIL. We do not know of any implementation of Sowa's top-level ontology.

2.2.1 Top-level ontologies of universals and particulars

Guarino and colleagues have built two top-level ontologies, as shown in Figure 2.8: one of universals, and another of particulars. A universal is a concept[19], like car or traveler, while a particular is an individual like my car or John Smith. Therefore, the terms car and traveler in a domain ontology can be linked to the top-level of particulars through the relation *Subclass-Of*, and they can be linked to the top-level of universals through the relation *Instance-Of*. Both top-level ontologies are presented in this section.

The *top-level ontology of universals* (Guarino and Welty, 2000) contains concepts whose instances are universals. This ontology has been obtained

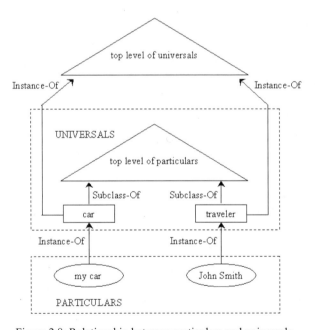

Figure 2.8: Relationship between particulars and universals.

---

[19] This is a simplified definition, but it is enough for the purpose of this book. For a complete definition consult Guarino and Welty (2000).

considering the philosophical notions of *rigidity*, *identity* and *dependency*[20]. Let us examine these notions (Gangemi et al., 2001), which will be explained in the context of the Ontoclean method in Chapter 3:

- *Rigidity*. This notion is defined according to the idea of essence. A property is essential to an instance if and only if it is necessary for this instance. Thus, a property is rigid (+R) if and only if it is necessarily essential to all its instances; a property is anti-rigid (~R) if and only if it is not essential for all its instances; and a property is non-rigid (-R) if and only if it is not essential for some of its instances. For example, the concept `person` is usually considered rigid, since every person is essentially such. The concept `traveler` is considered anti-rigid, since every traveler can possibly be a non-traveler once the journey has finished. Finally, the concept `red` is non-rigid, since there are instances that are essentially red (e.g., `drop of blood`), and instances that are not essentially red (`my pullover`).

- *Identity*. A property *carries* an identity criterion (+I) if and only if all its instances can be (re)identified by means of a suitable "sameness" relation. A property *supplies* an identity criterion (+O) if and only if such criterion is not inherited by any subsuming property. For example, if we take the DNA as an identity criterion, we can say that `person` not only carries the identity criterion, but also supplies it. Besides, if `traveler` is a subclass of `person`, then `traveler` only inherits the identity criterion of `person`, without supplying any further identity criteria.

- *Dependency*. An individual x is constantly dependent on the individual y if and only if, at any time, x cannot be present unless y is fully present, and y is not part of x. For example, a hole in a wall is constantly dependent on the wall. The hole cannot be present if the wall is not present. A property P is constantly dependent (+D) if and only if, for all its instances, there exists something on which the instances are constantly dependent. Otherwise, the property P is not constantly dependent (-D). For instance, the concept `hole` is constantly dependent because every instance of `hole` is constantly dependent. Note that the constant dependence of a property is defined according to the constant dependence of individuals.

Every concept of the top-level ontology of universals has four attributes: *rigidity*, *supplies identity*, *carries identity*, and *dependency*. This ontology has been built considering several combinations of values of these attributes (Welty and Guarino, 2001). For instance, the concept *type* is rigid, supplies identity, and carries identity (nothing is explicitly stated about its dependency). This means that the concepts that are instances of the concept *type* will be rigid and will supply and carry identity. Every concept of a specific domain will be an instance of at least one of the leaves of the top-level of universals. Figure 2.9 presents the class taxonomy of this ontology.

---

[20] Another important notion is *unity*. However, it has not been used to classify the properties of this top-level ontology of universals. Therefore, such a notion will not be presented until Chapter 3, where the OntoClean method is described.

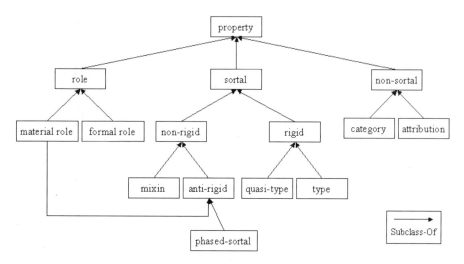

Figure 2.9: Class taxonomy of the top-level ontology of universals.

The *top-level ontology of particulars* (Gangemi et al., 2001) holds general concepts (for example, `object`) to which domain concepts can be linked with the relation *Subclass-Of*. Figure 2.10 shows part of the class taxonomy of this ontology. As we can see, the ontology contains three roots (`abstract`, `concrete` and `relation`). It is being developed following the principles established in the OntoClean method (Welty and Guarino, 2001) for cleaning ontologies, described in Section 3.8.3.

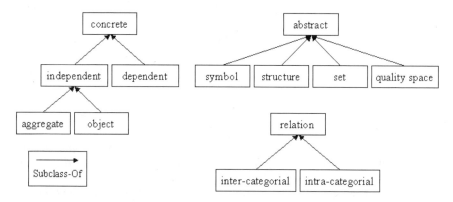

Figure 2.10: Partial view of the class taxonomy of top-level ontology of particulars.

Let us suppose that we want to link concepts of our travel domain to the top-level ontologies of universals and particulars. In this case, the domain concepts (i.e., `car`, `traveler`, etc.) will be subclasses of concepts of the top-level ontology of particulars, and they will also be instances of concepts of the top-level ontology of universals. Instances like `my car` or `John Smith` are instances of classes linked to the top-level of particulars.

Both the top-level ontology of universals and the top-level ontology of particulars are available in the ontology engineering workbench WebODE, which will be presented in Chapter 5. At the end of the year 2002, the former had 15 concepts while the latter had over 30 concepts.

2.2.2 Sowa's top-level ontology

Sowa's top-level ontology includes the basic categories and distinctions that have been derived from a variety of sources in logic, linguistics, philosophy, and artificial intelligence (Sowa, 1999). Sowa's top-level ontology has 27 concepts, all of them identified in Figure 2.11.

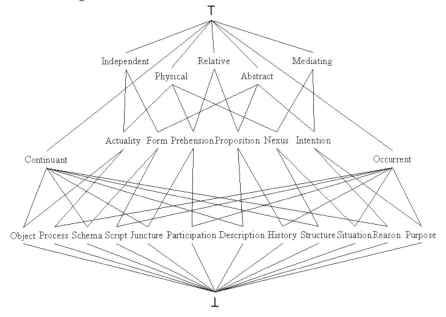

Figure 2.11: Sowa's top-level ontology.

This ontology has a lattice structure where the top concept is the *universal type* (represented as T in Figure 2.11), and the bottom concept is the *absurd type* (⊥). The *universal type* contains all the possible instances of the ontology. The *absurd type* does not have instances and is a subclass of every concept of the taxonomy. The direct subclasses of the *universal type* are the following: *independent*, *relative*, *mediating*, *continuant*, *physical*, *abstract*, and *occurrent*. By combining these primitive concepts more concepts of the lattice are obtained, for example,

```
history = proposition ∩ occurrent
```

The structure of this top-level ontology is a lattice (see a definition in Section 3.6.2) because every pair of concepts of the taxonomy has, at least, a common direct or indirect superclass, and each pair of concepts has, at least, a common direct or indirect subclass. Let us take as an example the pair {*proposition, occurrent*}, where the common superclass is of the *universal type*, and a common subclass is *history*. In this example, the class *history* could be represented as the intersection of *proposition* and *occurrent*. In this top-level ontology, concepts can be obtained by combining concepts from the upper levels.

2.2.3 Cyc's upper ontology

Cyc's Upper Ontology is contained in the Cyc Knowledge Base (Lenat and Guha, 1990), which holds a huge amount of common sense knowledge. The Cyc KB is being built upon a core of over 1,000,000 assertions hand-entered and designed to gather a large portion of what people normally consider consensus knowledge of the world. It is divided into hundreds of microtheories (bundles of assertions in the same domain) and is implemented in the CycL language.

Cyc's Upper Ontology[21] contains about 3,000 terms arranged in 43 topical groups (fundamentals, time and dates, spatial relations, etc.). The class *Thing* is the root of the ontology, and it is also the universal set. This means that when we link terms from a domain ontology to Cyc's Upper Ontology through the *genls* relation (which is the *Subclass-Of* relation in CycL), every concept of the domain ontology is a subclass of *Thing*, therefore, every instance of the domain ontology is an instance of *Thing*. Cyc's Upper Ontology has been built by performing the following steps: (1) dividing the universal set into tangible and intangible, into the static thing versus the dynamic process, into collection versus individual, etc.; and (2) refining the result when new knowledge is introduced (such as new concepts, new *Subclass-Of* relations, etc.). During the refining process, some of these categories might disappear.

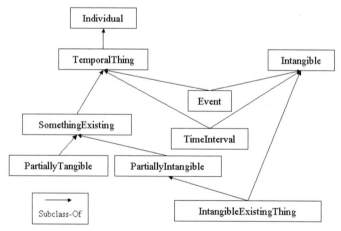

Figure 2.12: Fragment of the class taxonomy of Cyc's Upper Ontology.

---

[21] http://www.cyc.com/cyc-2-1/cover.html

Figure 2.12 shows a fragment of Cyc's Upper Ontology. As we can see, the concepts *TimeInterval* and *Event* are subclasses of the concepts *TemporalThing* and *Intangible*. A *TemporalThing* is an *Individual*. *SomethingExisting*, which is a subclass of the concept *TemporalThing*, is partitioned in the concepts *PartiallyTangible* and *PartiallyIntangible*. An *IntangibleExistingThing* is something *PartiallyIntangible* and *Intangible*.

Cycorp[22], the company supplier of Cyc's Upper Ontology, provides several tools to assist users in the handling of this ontology. Such tools include hypertext links that permit browsing directly some of the taxonomies and navigating among the references (a topical listing of the upper ontology divided into subject-areas to facilitate systematic study, etc.).

2.2.4 The Standard Upper Ontology (SUO)

The Standard Upper Ontology[23] is the result of a joint effort to create a large, general-purpose, formal ontology (Pease and Niles, 2002). It is promoted by the IEEE Standard Upper Ontology working group, and its development began in May 2000. The participants were representatives of government, academia, and industry from several countries. The effort was officially approved as an IEEE standard project in December 2000.

There are currently two "starter documents" agreed by the working group and that may be developed into a draft standard. One of the documents is known as the IFF (Information Flow Framework) Foundation Ontology, a meta-ontology based on Mathematics and viewed from the set-theoretic perspective. The other one is known as SUMO (Suggested Upper Merged Ontology). Part of its current structure is shown in Figure 2.13.

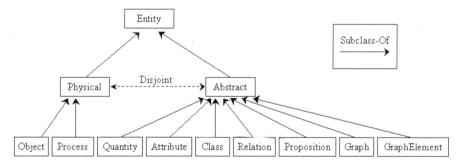

Figure 2.13: Structure of the first levels of SUMO (May 2002).

---

[22] http://www.cyc.org/
[23] http://suo.ieee.org/

The goal of SUMO is to create a comprehensive and consistent top-level ontology from some of the best public sources, such as:

- CNR's group mereotopology (Borgo et al., 1996; Borgo et al., 1997).
- Upper-level ontologies; e.g., Sowa's upper ontology and Russell and Norvig's upper-level ontology (1995).
- Time theories; e.g., James Allen's temporal axioms (Allen, 1984).
- Plan and process theories (Pease and Carrico, 1997); etc.

Therefore, SUMO considers some high level distinctions, and contains temporal concepts and processes. It is a modular ontology, that is, the ontology is divided into sub-ontologies. The dependencies between the various sub-ontologies can be outlined as Figure 2.14 shows.

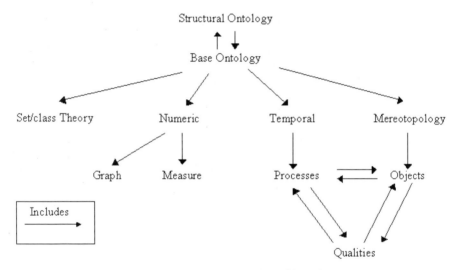

Figure 2.14: Modular structure of SUMO.

To decide which concepts should be removed, added or preserved during the evolution of this top-level ontology, a series of steps must be performed (Niles and Pease, 2001):

1) Take the current version of the top-level ontology as the base and add, one by one, lower-level ontologies to this base.
2) Eliminate from the top-level ontology the concepts not related to any concept of the domain ontologies, and add other top-level concepts suitable to model the lower level ontologies.

The people involved in the SUMO development are currently in the process of augmenting each of the records in the noun database of WordNet with pointers to SUMO concepts.

2.3 Linguistic Ontologies

This section collects information on linguistic ontologies. The purpose of this type of ontology is to describe semantic constructs rather than to model a specific domain. They offer quite a heterogeneous amount of resources, used mostly in natural language processing. The main characteristic of these ontologies is that they are bound to the semantics of grammatical units (words, nominal groups, adjectives, etc.).

Most linguistic ontologies use words as grammatical units. In fact, of the ontologies reviewed in this section, only the Generalized Upper Model (GUM) and SENSUS gather information on grammatical units that are bigger than words. Other ontologies focus on the word meaning (e.g., WordNet). Moreover, in some of the ontologies there is a one-to-one mapping between concepts and words in a natural language (e.g., wordnets of EuroWordNet), while in others many concepts may not map to any word in a language or may map to more than one in the same language (e.g., Mikrokosmos).

There are also differences with respect to their degree of language dependency; some linguistic ontologies depend totally on a single language (e.g., WordNet); others are multilingual – i.e., are valid for several languages – (e.g., GUM); some others contain a language-dependent part and a language-independent part (e.g., EuroWordNet); and others are language independent (e.g., Mikrokosmos).

The origin and motivations of these ontologies are varied and thus we have: on-line lexical databases (e.g., WordNet), ontologies for machine translation (e.g., Sensus), ontologies for natural language generation (e.g., GUM), etc.

In the next sections we present the following ontologies: WordNet, EuroWordNet, GUM, Mikrokosmos, and SENSUS. Some of these, as for example SENSUS and GUM, are also considered top-level ontologies since they chiefly contain very abstract concepts.

2.3.1 WordNet

WordNet (Miller et al., 1990; Miller, 1995) is a very large lexical database for English created at Princeton University and based on psycholinguistic theories. Psycholinguistics is an interdisciplinary field of research concerned about the cognitive bases of linguistic competence (Fellbaum and Miller, 1990). WordNet attempts to organize lexical information in terms of word meanings rather than word forms, though inflectional morphology is also considered. For example, if you search for *trees* in WordNet, you will have the same access as if you search for *tree*.

WordNet 1.7 contains 121,962 words and 99,642 concepts. It is organized into 70,000 sets of synonyms ("synsets"), each representing one underlying lexical concept. Synsets are interlinked via relationships such as synonymy and antonymy, hypernymy and hyponymy (*Subclass-Of* and *Superclass-Of*), meronymy and holonymy (*Part-Of* and *Has-a*). Approximately one half of the synsets include brief explanations of their intuitive sense in English. WordNet divides the lexicon into five categories: nouns, verbs, adjectives, adverbs, and function words. Nouns are organized as topical hierarchies. Figure 2.15 shows part of the noun hierarchy where terms concerning a person, his (her) components, his (her) substances, and his (her) family organization, appear related. The only relations that we can see in the figure are *meronymy*, *antonymy*, and *hyponymy*, since it is a very reduced view of the noun hierarchy.

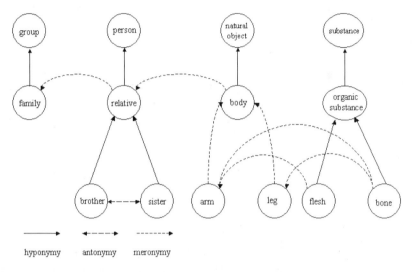

Figure 2.15: A partial view of the category of nouns of WordNet.

Verbs are organized according to a variety of entailment relations. For example, the verbs *succeed* and *try* are related through a backward implication, and *buy* and *pay* are related through a temporal inclusion. With adjectives and adverbs the relations of similarity and antonymy play an important role. For instance, *dry* is related to *sere, anhydrous, arid*, etc., through the relation of similarity. *Wet* is also related to *humid, watery,* or *damp* through the relation of similarity. Besides, *dry* and *wet* are related by means of the relation of antonymy.

2.3.2 EuroWordNet

EuroWordNet (Vossen, 1998; 1999)[24] is a multilingual database with wordnets for several European languages (Dutch, Italian, Spanish, German, French, Czech, Estonian). Some of the institutions involved in this project are: University of Amsterdam (The Netherlands), UNED (Spain), and University of Sheffield (United Kingdom).

The wordnets are structured in EuroWordNet in the same way as WordNet is for English, with interrelated synsets. The wordnets are linked to an Inter-Lingual-Index. Through this index the languages are interconnected so that it is possible to go from the words in one language to similar words in any other language, and to compare synsets and their relations across languages. The index also gives access to

---

[24] http://www.hum.uva.nl/~ewn/

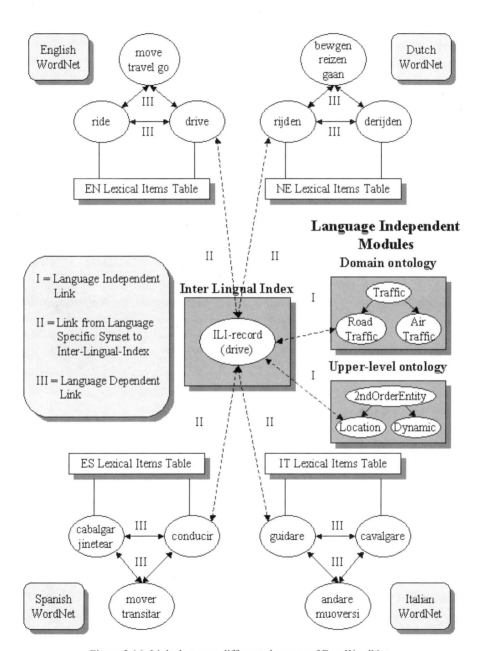

Figure 2.16: Links between different elements of EuroWordNet.

a shared upper-level ontology of 63 semantic distinctions. This upper-level ontology provides a common semantic framework for all the languages, while language specific properties are maintained in individual wordnets. This index can be used for monolingual and cross-lingual information retrieval.

Figure 2.16 shows a small section of EuroWordNet. We can see that the English words: *move*, *ride*, *drive*, etc., are related to words in other languages with similar meaning through the Inter-Lingual-Index. Therefore, we can find language dependent links inside words in the same language (represented by III), independent language links that connect the Inter-Lingual-Index with the domain ontologies and with the upper-level ontology (represented by I), and links that connect the Inter-Lingual-Index with the synsets of other different languages (represented by II).

The EuroWordNet project was completed in the summer of 1999, and the design of the EuroWordNet database, the defined relations, the upper ontology and the Inter-Lingual-Index are now frozen. Nevertheless, many other institutes and research groups are developing similar wordnets in other languages (European and non-European) using the EuroWordNet specification. If compatible, these wordnets can be added to the database and, through the index, connected to any other wordnet. Wordnets are currently developed, at least, for the following languages: Swedish, Norwegian, Danish, Greek, Portuguese, Basque, Catalan, Romanian, Lithuanian, Russian, Bulgarian and Slovene.

The cooperative framework of EuroWordNet is continued through the Global WordNet Association[25], a free and public association created to stimulate the building of new wordnets in EuroWordNet and WordNet.

2.3.3 The Generalized Upper Model

The Generalized Upper Model (GUM)[26] (Bateman et al., 1995) is the result of a continuous evolution that began with the Penman Upper Model, used in the Penman text generation system (Bateman et al., 1990). Three organizations were involved in the development of GUM: the Information Sciences Institute (ISI, USA), GMD/IPSI (Germany), and the Institute for the Technological and Scientific Research (CNR, Italy).

GUM is a linguistic ontology bound to the semantics of language grammar constituents. Unlike other linguistic ontologies, such as WordNet, it does not describe the semantics of words but the semantics that can be expressed in bigger grammatical units such as nominal groups, prepositional phrases, etc.

This ontology has two hierarchies, one of concepts and another of relations. Figure 2.17 shows the first levels of these hierarchies.

---

[25] http://www.hum.uva.nl/~ewn/gwa.htm
[26] http://www.darmstadt.gmd.de/publish/komet/gen-um/newUM.html

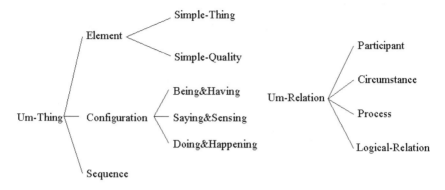

Figure 2.17: First levels of GUM hierarchies.

These taxonomies have their origin in Halliday's (1985) functional grammar, but can be applied to any theory. The concept hierarchy represents the basic semantic entities and includes *configurations* of the processes, and the different kinds of *objects* and *qualities*. A *configuration* is a set of objects that participate in some activity or that are in some state. An example of *configuration* is *being&having*, which indicates the existence of something or a relation of identity, possession, attribution, etc. The relation hierarchy represents the *participants* and the *circumstances* involved in the *processes*, and the *logical combinations* between them. The *actor*, the *message*, or the *attribute* are examples of *participants*. *Company, comparison, cause, mode, time, space*, etc., express *circumstances*.

2.3.4 The Mikrokosmos ontology

The Mikrokosmos Ontology[27] (Mahesh and Nirenburg, 1995; Mahesh, 1996) is a language-independent ontology that is part of the Mikrokosmos machine translation project on the domain of mergers and acquisitions of companies. The New Mexico State University, Carnegie Mellon University and some other organizations of the US government have participated in this project.

Mikrokosmos is not committed to any particular ontological theory, it is built on more practical considerations (Mahesh, 1996). Its main design principle is a careful distinction between language-specific knowledge represented in the lexicon, and language-neutral knowledge represented in the ontology. Lexicon entries represent word or phrase meanings by mapping these entries to concepts of the ontology.

Figure 2.18 shows the first levels of the ontology. Currently, this ontology has several thousands of concepts, most of which have been generated by retrieving objects, events, and their properties from different sources. Each concept is represented by a frame, which has a name in English, and the following attributes (Mahesh and Nirenburg, 1995): a definition that contains an English string used solely for human browsing purposes, a time-stamp for bookkeeping, taxonomy links

---

[27] http://crl.nmsu.edu/mikro (user and password are required)

(*Subclass-Of* and *Instance-Of*), etc. English terms are also used to refer to each concept in the ontology.

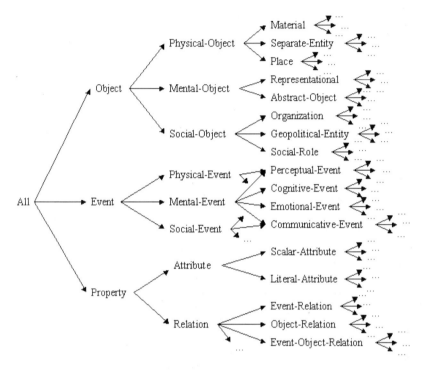

Figure 2.18: Mikrokosmos class taxonomy (from Mahesh and Nirenburg, 1995).

In parallel to the development of the Mikrokosmos ontology, a Spanish lexicon of several thousands words has been built. These words cover a wide variety of categories, though they put particular emphasis on the domain of mergers and acquisitions of companies.

2.3.5 SENSUS

SENSUS[28] (Swartout et al., 1997) is a natural language-based ontology developed by the Natural Language group at ISI to provide a broad conceptual structure for working in machine translation.

SENSUS contains more than 70,000 nodes representing commonly encountered objects, entities, qualities and relations. This ontology provides a hierarchically structured concept base (Knight and Luck, 1994). The upper (more abstract) region of the ontology is called the Ontology Base and consists of approximately 400 items that represent essential generalizations for the linguistic processing during translation. The middle region of the ontology provides a framework for a generic

---

[28] http://www.isi.edu/natural-language/projects/ONTOLOGIES.html

world model and contains items representing many word senses in English. The lower (more specific) regions of the ontology provide anchor points for different languages.

The current content of the SENSUS ontology was obtained by extracting and merging information from various electronic knowledge sources. This process, as shown in Figure 2.19, began by merging, manually, the PENMAN Upper Model, ONTOS (a very high-level linguistically-based ontology) and the semantic categories taken from a dictionary. As a result, the Ontology Base was produced. WordNet was then merged (again, by hand) with the Ontology Base, and a merging tool was used to merge WordNet with an English dictionary. Finally, and to support machine translation, the result of this merge was increased by Spanish and Japanese lexical entries from the Collins Spanish/English dictionary and the Kenkyusha Japanese/English dictionary.

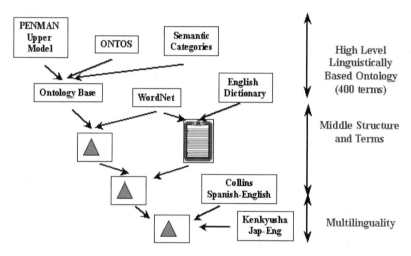

Figure 2.19: SENSUS ontology building process, by extracting and merging information from existing electronic resources (adapted from Swartout et al., 1997).

2.4 Domain Ontologies

As we explained in Chapter 1, domain ontologies (Mizoguchi et al., 1995; van Heijst et al., 1997) are reusable vocabularies of the concepts within a domain and their relationships, of the activities taking place in that domain, and of the theories and elementary principles governing that domain. In this section, we will deal with representative ontologies in the domains of e-commerce, medicine, engineering, enterprise, chemistry, and knowledge management.

2.4.1 E-commerce ontologies

The popularity of the Internet and the huge growth of new Internet technologies in recent years have brought about the creation of many e-commerce applications (Fensel, 2000; Berners-Lee, 1999). Technology is not the only key factor for the development of the current e-applications; the context of e-commerce, especially the context of B2B (Business to Business) applications, requires an effective communication between machines. As a consequence, several standards and initiatives started to ease the information exchange between customers and suppliers, and among different suppliers, by providing frameworks to identify products and services in global markets.

In this section, we present five different proposals to classify products in the e-commerce domain: UNSPSC[29], NAICS[30], SCTG[31], e-cl@ss[32] and RosettaNet[33]. These proposals have been agreed by a wide group of people and organizations, and are codified using different computation languages and formats. Therefore, they provide consensus and also top-level terms that can be used to classify products and services in vertical domains[34]. However, they cannot be considered heavyweight ontologies but simply lightweight ones, since they consist of concept taxonomies and some relations among them.

The United Nations Standard Products and Services Codes (UNSPSC) has been created by the United Nations Development Programme (UNDP) and Dun & Bradstreet. UNSPSC is a global commodity code standard that classifies general products and services and is designed to facilitate electronic commerce through the exchange of product descriptions.

Initially the UNDP managed the code of the Electronic Commerce Code Management Association (ECCMA)[35]. This partnership finished, and as a result there are now two different versions of the UNSPSC: the United Nations Standard Products and Services Codes owned by the UNDP, and the Universal Standard Products and Services Classification managed by the ECCMA. In October 2002, both organizations signed an agreement in which they proposed to have one single version of the classification, which has marked the beginning of the UNSPSC unification project.

The UNSPSC coding system is organized as a five-level taxonomy of products, each level containing a two-character numerical value and a textual description. These levels are defined as follows:

---

[29] http://www.unspsc.org/
[30] http://www.naics.com
[31] http://www.bts.gov/programs/cfs/sctg/welcome.htm
[32] http://www.eclass.de/
[33] http://www.rosettanet.org/
[34] Vertical portals usually serve a particular industry and provide deep domain expertise and content. They are normally related with traditional industry segments, such as Electronics, Automotive, Steel, etc. Horizontal portals are characterized by the large number of disperse suppliers and of distributors and resellers.
[35] http://www.eccma.org

- *Segment.* The logical aggregation of families for analytical purposes.
- *Family.* A commonly recognized group of inter-related commodity categories.
- *Class.* A group of commodities sharing a common use or function.
- *Commodity.* A group of products or services that can be substituted.
- *Business Function.* The function performed by an organization in support of the commodity. This level is seldom used.

UNSPSC version 6.0315 contains about 20,000 products organized in 55 segments. Segment 43, for instance, which deals with computer equipment, peripherals and components, contains about 300 kinds of products. Figure 2.20 shows part of this segment.

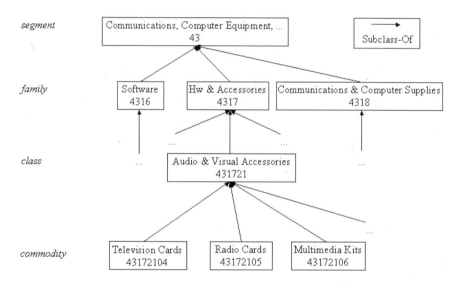

Figure 2.20: Part of the classification of UNSPSC for computer equipment.

NAICS (North American Industry Classification System) was created by the Census Office of USA in cooperation with the Economic National Classification Committee of USA, Statistics Canada, and Mexico's *Instituto Nacional de Estadística, Geografía e Informática* (INEGI). It classifies products and services in general, and is used in USA, Canada and Mexico. NAICS was developed after the Standard Industrial Classification (SIC) was revised. SIC was created in the 1930s to classify establishments according to the type of activity they were primarily engaged in and to promote the comparison of their data describing various facets of the US economy.

NAICS products are identified by means of a six-digit code, in contrast to the four-digit SIC code. The NAICS code includes a greater number of sectors and permits more flexibility to design subsectors. It also provides additional details not necessarily appropriate for all three NAICS countries. The international NAICS agreement fixes only the first five digits of the code. The sixth digit, when used, identifies subdivisions of NAICS industries that consider the user's needs in individual countries. Thus, six-digit US codes may differ from counterparts in Canada or Mexico, but up to the five-digit level they are standardized. The general structure is:

XX	Industry Sector (20 broad sectors up from 10 SIC)
XXX	Industry Subsector
XXXX	Industry Group
XXXXX	Industry
XXXXXX	US, Canadian, or Mexican National specific

Table 2.5 presents the correspondence between some NAICS Sectors and SIC Divisions. Many of the new sectors reflect parts of SIC divisions, such as the *Utilities* and *Transportation* sectors, that are split from the SIC division *Transportation, Communications, and Public Utilities*.

Table 2.5: Correspondence between some NAICS Sector and SIC Divisions.

Code	NAICS Sectors	SIC Divisions
11	Agriculture, Forestry, Fishing, and Hunting	Agriculture, Forestry and Fishing
21	Mining	Mining
23	Construction	Construction
31-33	Manufacturing	Manufacturing
22	Utilities	Transportation, Communications, and Public Utilities
48-49	Transportation and Warehousing	
42	Wholesale Trade	Wholesale Trade
44-45	Retail Trade	Retail Trade
72	Accommodation and Food Services	
52	Finance and Insurance	Finance, Insurance, and Real Estate
53	Real Estate, Rental and Leasing	

SCTG (Standard Classification of Transported Goods) was sponsored by the Bureau of Transportation Statistics (BTS). It is a product classification for collecting and reporting Commodity Flow Survey (CFS) data. SCTG was developed by the US Department of Transportation's (DOT), Volpe National Transportation Systems Center (Volpe Center), Standards and Transportation Divisions of Statistics Canada, US Bureau of the Census (BOC), and the US Bureau of Economic Analysis (BEA).

This classification has four levels, each of which follows two important principles. First, each level covers the universe of transportable goods, and second, each category in each level is mutually exclusive. The general structure is:

XX	Product Category
XXX	Commodities or Commodity Groups (different in US and Canada)
XXXX	Domestic Freight Transportation Analyses
XXXXX	Freight Movement Data

The first level of the SCTG (two digits) consists of 43 product categories. These categories were designed to emphasize the link between industries and their outputs.

The second level (three digits) is designed to provide data for making comparisons between the Canadian goods and the US goods. Categories specified at this level consist of commodities or commodity groups for which very significant product movement levels have been recorded in both the United States (US) and Canada. The third level (four digits) is designed to provide data for domestic freight transportation analyses. Four-digit categories may be of major data significance to either the US or Canada, but not necessarily to both. The fourth level (five digits) is designed to provide categories for collecting (and potentially reporting) freight movement data. Product codes at this level have been designed to create statistically significant categories for transportation analysis.

Figure 2.21 presents a partial view of this classification. We can see that in this particular classification levels two and three do not contribute with additional classes to the root of the hierarchy. This is so because every branch of the tree has four levels.

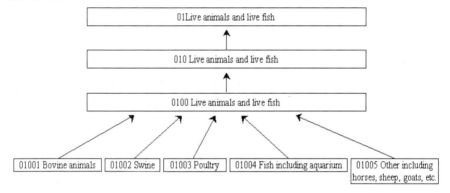

Figure 2.21: Partial view of the SCTG classification.

E-cl@ss is a German initiative to create a standard classification of material and services for information exchange between suppliers and their customers, and companies such as BASF, Bayer, Volkswagen-Audi, SAP, etc., make use of it.

The e-cl@ss classification consists of four levels of concepts (called *material classes*), with a numbering code similar to the one used in UNSPSC (each level adds two digits to its previous level). These four levels are: *Segment, Main Group, Group* and *Commodity Class*. Inside the same commodity class we can have several products (in this sense, several products can share the same code).

E-cl@ss contains about 12,000 products organized in 21 segments. Segment number 27[36], which deals with *Electrical Engineering*, contains about 2,000 products. The main group 27-23, which deals with *Process Control Systems* and with other computer devices, contains about 400 concepts. Figure 2.22 shows a partial view of this classification.

---

[36] Please note that the numbering of segments is not consecutive.

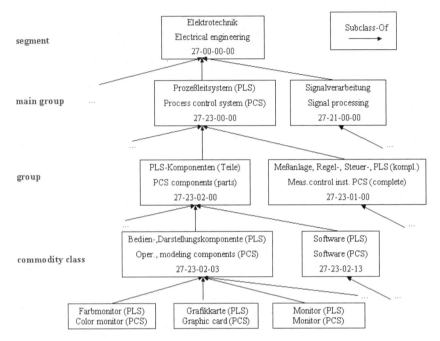

Figure 2.22: Part of the classification of e-cl@ss for electrical engineering products (German and English).

E-cl@ss provides a set of attributes for every product that is a leaf in the classification. The set of attributes is an addition of individual characteristics describing the related commodity. This set distinguishes e-cl@ss from UNSPSC and offers a solution to the shallowness of that. For example, *PC System* (with code 24-01-99-03) has attributes like *product type*, *product name*, etc., in e-cl@ss.

The e-cl@ss search tool, which is available on-line[37], allows finding terms with an interface in different languages (German, Spanish, English and Czech). In fact, the terms found are presented in any of these languages. The e-cl@ss classification can also be downloaded from the same URL.

The **RosettaNet** classification has been created by RosettaNet, which is a self-funded, non-profit consortium of about 400 companies of Electronic Components, Information Technology, Semiconductor Manufacturing and Solution Provider companies. Started in the IT industry, RosettaNet is currently being expanded to other vertical areas, notably the automotive, consumer electronics and telecommunications industries.

The RosettaNet classification does not use a numbering system, as UNSPSC does, but is based on the names of the products it defines. This classification is

---

[37] http://www.eclass.de/

related to the UNSPSC classification and provides the UNSPSC code for each product defined in RosettaNet. This classification has only two levels in its product taxonomy:

- *RN Category*. A group of products, such as *Video Products*.
- *RN Product*. A specific product, such as *Television Card*, *Radio Card*, etc.

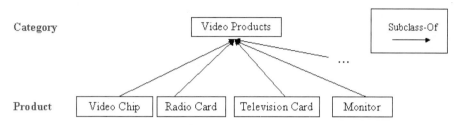

Figure 2.23: Partial view of the RosettaNet classification.

The RosettaNet classification consists of 14 categories and about 150 products. It should be added that RosettaNet is more specific than the UNSPSC classification. Figure 2.23 shows a small section of the RosettaNet classification related to video products for computer equipment, and table 2.6 presents the classification structured as in its original Microsoft Excel format. Unlike in the previous formats, the order of contents here is of great importance, since the relationship between products and the category they belong to are given by the order in which they appear. Hence *Monitor*, *RadioCard*, *TelevisionCard* and *VideoChip* are products from the category *Video Products* in the RosettaNet classification.

Table 2.6: Source format for the RosettaNet classification of video products.

RosettaNet Category Name	RosettaNet Product Name	UNSPSC Code	UNSPSC Code Name
Video Products			
	Monitor	43172401	Monitors
	Radio Card	43172105	Radio Cards
	Television Card	43172104	Television Cards
	Video Chip	321017	Hybrid Integrated Circuits

In this section, we have described five classifications of products and services (UNSPSC, NAICS, SCTG, e-cl@ss, and RosettaNet), which present a big overlap between them, so that a product or service could be classified in different places in each classification. The proliferation of initiatives reveals that B2B markets have not reached a consensus on coding systems, on level of detail, on granularity, etc., which is an obstacle for the interoperability of applications following different standards. For instance, an application that uses the UNSPSC code cannot interoperate with an application that follows the e-cl@ss coding system. To align such initiatives, some works have proposed to establish ontological mappings between existing standards (Bergamaschi et al., 2001; Corcho and Gómez-Pérez, 2001; Gordijn et al., 2001).

Figure 2.24 shows an example of *Equivalent-To* and *Subclass-Of* relations between concepts of the RosettaNet and the UNSPSC classifications. The concept *Video Chip* of the RosettaNet classification is a subclass of the concept *Hybrid Integrated Circuits* of the UNSPSC classification, the concept *Monitor* of RosettaNet is equivalent to the concept *Monitors* of UNSPSC, etc. As we can see, two sibling concepts in RosettaNet are classified in different UNSPSC classes: *Monitor* and *Radio Card* are subclasses of the same concept in RosettaNet (*Video Products*), while their equivalent concepts in UNSPSC (*Monitors* and *Radio Cards* respectively) are subclasses of different concepts in that classification (*Monitors & Displays* and *Radio Cards* respectively).

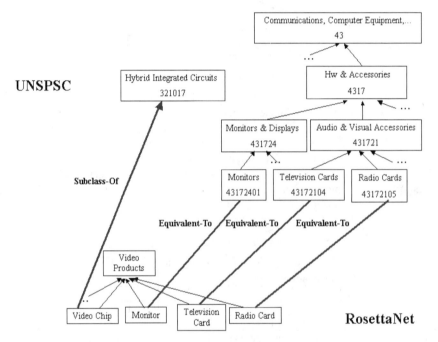

Figure 2.24: Equivalence relationships between the RosettaNet and UNSPSC classifications (Corcho and Gómez-Pérez, 2001).

2.4.2 Medical ontologies

Medical ontologies are developed to solve problems such as the demand for the reusing and sharing of patient data, the transmission of these data, or the need of semantic-based criteria for statistical purposes. The unambiguous communication of complex and detailed medical concepts is a crucial feature in current medical information systems. In these systems several agents must interact between them in order to share their results and, thus, they must use a medical terminology with a clear and non-confusing meaning.

GALEN[38] (Rector et al., 1995), developed by the non-profit organization OpenGALEN, is a clinical terminology represented in the formal and medical-oriented language GRAIL (Rector et al., 1997). This language was specially developed for specifying restrictions used in medical domains. GALEN was intended to be used with different natural languages and integrated with different coding schemata. It is based on a semantically sound model of clinical terminology known as the GALEN COding REference (CORE) model. Figure 2.25 shows the GALEN CORE top-level ontology.

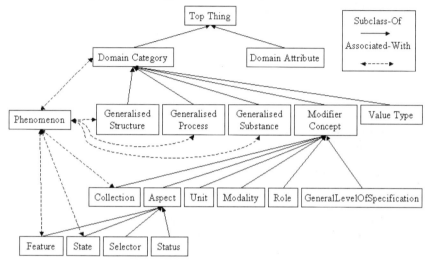

Figure 2.25: GALEN CORE top-level ontology.

The GALEN CORE top-level ontology establishes four general categories (which are subclasses of *DomainCategory*):

- Structures (*GeneralisedStructure*), which are abstract or physical things with parts that are time-independent (such as *microorganism*, *protocol* or *heart*).
- Substances (*GeneralisedSubstance*), which are continuous abstract or physical things that are time-independent, such as *bile*, *drugs* or *radiation*.
- Processes (*GeneralisedProcess*), which are changes that occur over time, such as *irradiation*, *clinical act* or *breathing*.
- Modifiers (*ModifierConcept*), which refine or modify the meaning of the other three categories, such as *severe diabetes*. In this ontology the following types of modifiers are considered: modifiers of *aspect* (classified in *feature*, *state*, *selector*, and *status*), *unit*, *modality*, *role*, *general level of specification*, and *collection*.

The category *ValueType* is also a subclass of *DomainCategory*. It defines value types such as *Integer*, *Ordinal*, etc. Besides, the category *Phenomenon* is included in this top-level ontology, as shown in figure 2.25. It gathers the medical intuitions of *Disease* and *Disorder* and it is associated with domain categories, more specifically

---

[38] http://www.opengalen.org/

with structures, processes, and substances, and with the modifiers of feature, state, and collection.

Finally, the GALEN CORE top-level ontology defines relationships between concepts that belong to general categories. These relationships are called attributes (*DomainAttribute*) and are divided into two types: *constructive attributes*, which link processes, structures and substances together; and *modifier attributes*, which link processes, structures and substances to modifiers.

UMLS[39] (Unified Medical Language System), developed by the United States National Library of Medicine, is a large database designed to integrate a great number of biomedical terms collected from various sources (over 60 sources in the 2002 edition) such as clinical vocabularies or classifications (MeSH, SNOMED, RCD, etc.).

UMLS is structured in three parts: *Metathesaurus, Semantic Network* and *Specialist Lexicon*.

- The *Metathesaurus* contains biomedical information about each of the terms included in UMLS. If a term appears in several sources, which is usual, a concept will be created in UMLS with a preferred term name associated to it. The original source information about the terms (such as, definition, source, etc.) is attached to the concept and some semantic properties are also specified, such as concept synonyms, siblings and parents, or the relationships between terms. In the UMLS edition of the year 2002, the *Metathesaurus* contained about 1,5 million terms.

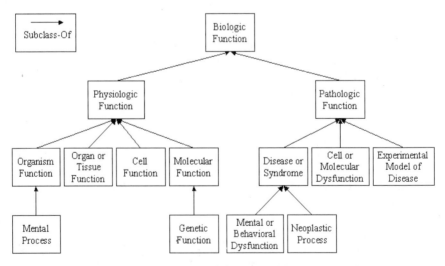

Figure 2.26: Part of the Semantic Network of the UMLS ontology.

---

[39] http://www.nih.gov/research/umls/

- The *Semantic Network* is a top-level ontology of biomedical concepts and relations among these concepts. Figure 2.26 shows a partial view of this top-level ontology. The *Semantic Network* was not derived from the biomedical sources integrated in UMLS but created as a part of UMLS with the aim of providing a consistent structure or categorization in which the *Metathesaurus* concepts are included. Each Metathesaurus concept is attached to a concept or concepts of the *Semantic Network*. Thus, the *Semantic Network* was introduced in order to solve the heterogeneity among the UMLS sources, and it could be considered the result of the integration of the UMLS sources. In the 2002 edition, the *Semantic Network* contained 134 top-level concepts and 54 relationships among them.
- The *Specialist Lexicon* contains syntactic information about biomedical terms to be used in natural language processing applications.

ON9[40] (Gangemi et al., 1998) is a medical set of ontologies that includes some terminology systems, like UMLS. Figure 2.27 shows an inclusion network of some ON9 ontologies. Here, ontologies are represented with boxes. Thick dashed boxes are sets of ontologies (some show the elements explicitly). Continuous arrows mean *included in*, and dashed arrows mean *integrated in*. The ontologies at the top of the hierarchy are the *Frame Ontology* and the set of *KIF ontologies* (Gangemi et al., 1998).

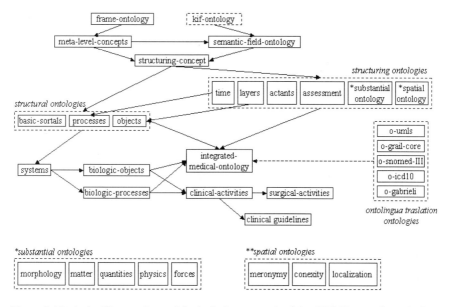

Figure 2.27: A significant subset of the inclusion network of the ON9 library of ontologies (from Gangemi et al., 1998).

---

[40] http://saussure.irmkant.rm.cnr.it/ON9/index.html

To link these ontologies with the generic ontology library several ontologies have been defined: *Structuring-Concepts*, *Meta-Level-Concepts* and the *Semantic-Field-Ontology*. The sets of *Structural ontologies* and of *Structuring ontologies* contain generic ontologies. Particularly, the *Integrated-Medical-Ontology* includes all the generic ontologies used to gather the terminological ontologies of the five terminological systems.

2.4.3 Engineering ontologies

Engineering ontologies contain mathematical models that engineers use to analyze the behavior of physical systems (Gruber and Olsen, 1994). These ontologies are created to enable the sharing and reuse of engineering models among engineering tools and their users. Among the various engineering ontologies, the EngMath ontologies and PhysSys deserve special mention.

EngMath (Gruber and Olsen, 1994) is a set of Ontolingua ontologies developed for mathematical modeling in engineering. These ontologies include conceptual foundations for scalar, vector, and tensor quantities as well as functions of quantities, and units of measure.

When the EngMath ontologies were designed, the developers had three kinds of uses in mind. First, these ontologies should provide a machine and human-readable notation for representing the models and domain theories found in the engineering literature. Second, they should provide a formal specification of a shared conceptualization and a vocabulary for a community of interoperating software agents in engineering domains. And third, they should put the base for other formalization efforts including more comprehensive ontologies for engineering and domain-specific languages.

In Figure 2.28, we can see some of the ontologies that make up EngMath:
- *Abstract-Algebra*. It defines the basic vocabulary for describing algebraic operators, domains, and structures such as *fields*, *rings*, and *groups*.
- *Physical-Quantities*. This ontology models the concept of physical quantity. A physical quantity is a measure of quantifiable aspect. The ontology *Physical-Quantities* has 11 classes, three relations, 12 functions (*addition*, *multiplication*, *division*, etc.), and two instances.
- *Standard-Dimensions*. It models the physical quantities most commonly used. It has 18 classes (*mass quantity*, *length quantity*, *temperature quantity*, etc.), and 27 instances.
- *Standard-Units*. This ontology defines a set of basic units of measure. It has one class (*Si-Unit*, that is, unit of the International System), and 60 instances (*kilogram*, *meter*, *Celsius-degree*, etc.).
- *Scalar-Quantities*. This ontology permits modeling quantities whose magnitude is a real number, for example, "6 kilograms". It has one class (*scalar quantity*), six functions (which specialize functions of the ontology *Physical-Quantities* for scalar quantities), and one instance.

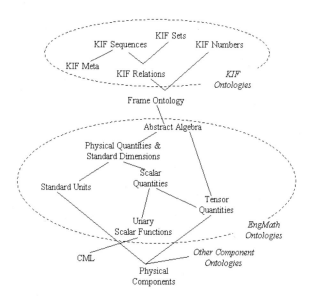

Figure 2.28: Structure of the EngMath ontologies (from Gruber and Olsen, 1994).

EngMath has been an important experimental base to establish the design criteria for building ontologies described in Section 1.6.

PhysSys (Borst, 1997) is an engineering ontology for modeling, simulating and designing physical systems. It forms the basis of the OLMECO library[41], a model component library for physical systems such as heating systems, automotive systems and machine tools. PhysSys formalizes the three viewpoints of physical devices: system layout, physical process behavior and descriptive mathematical relations.

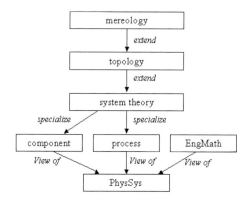

Figure 2.29: Structure of the PhysSys ontologies (from Borst, 1997).

---

[41] http://www.rt.el.utwente.nl/bnk/olmeco.htm

Figure 2.29 gives a general view of the structure of PhysSys ontology. As we can observe, this structure is a pyramid where the most specific ontologies (the nearest to the base) import the most general ones. Next, we describe briefly each of the PhysSys ontologies:

- *Mereology Ontology.* It defines the relation *Part-Of* and its properties. This relation permits stating that devices are formed by components, which in their turn, can be made up of smaller components. The *Mereology Ontology* is an Ontolingua implementation of the Classical Extensional Mereology described in Simons (1987).

- *Topology Ontology.* It defines the relation *is-connected-to* and its properties. This ontology is useful to describe the physical behavior of devices since it represents how the components interact inside the system.

- *System Theory Ontology.* It defines standard system-theoretic notions such as *system, sub-system, system boundary, environment,* etc.

- *Component Ontology.* It is focused on the structural aspects of devices and is useful for representing what kind of dynamic processes occur in the system. The *Component Ontology* is constructed with the *Mereology Ontology*, the *Topology Ontology*, and the *System Theory Ontology*.

- *Physical Process Ontology.* It specifies the behavioral view of physical systems.

- *Mathematical Ontology.* It defines the mathematics required to describe physical processes.

2.4.4 Enterprise ontologies

Enterprise ontologies are usually created to define and organize relevant knowledge about activities, processes, organizations, strategies, marketing, etc. All this knowledge is meant to be used by enterprises. Here, we will present the Enterprise Ontology and TOVE. Both have been essentially the experimental basis of some methodological approaches of ontology engineering presented in Chapter 3.

The **Enterprise Ontology**[42] (Uschold et al., 1998) was developed within the Enterprise Project by the Artificial Intelligence Applications Institute at the University of Edinburgh with its partners IBM, Lloyd's Register, Logica UK Limited, and Unilever. The project was supported by the UK's Department of Trade and Industry under the Intelligent Systems Integration Programme (project IED4/1/8032). This ontology contains terms and definitions relevant to businesses. It is implemented in Ontolingua and it has 92 classes, 68 relations, seven functions and 10 individuals. Figure 2.30 shows a partial view of the class taxonomy.

Conceptually, the Enterprise Ontology is divided into four main sections:
- Activities and processes. The central term here is *Activity*, which is intended to capture the notion of anything that involves doing, particularly when this indicates action. The concept of *Activity* is closely linked to the idea of the *Doer*, which may be a *Person, Organizational-Unit* or *Machine*.

---

[42] http://www.aiai.ed.ac.uk/~entprise/enterprise/ontology.html

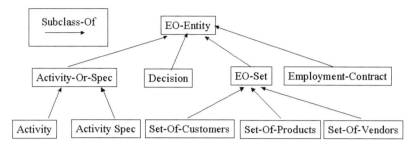

Figure 2.30: Partial view of the taxonomy of the Enterprise Ontology.

- Organization. The central concepts of the Organization section are: *Legal-Entity* and *Organizational-Unit*.
- Strategy. The central concept of this section is *Purpose*. *Purpose* captures the idea of something that a *Plan* can *help achieve* or the idea that an *Organization-Unit* can be responsible for. In fact, this section includes any kind of *purpose*, whether in a level of organization and time scale (normally called strategic), or in a detailed and short term.
- Marketing. The central concept of this section is *Sale*. A *Sale* is an agreement between two *Legal-Entities* for the exchange of a *Product* for a *Sale-Price*. Normally the *Products* are goods or services and the *Sale-Price* is monetary, although other possibilities are included. The *Legal-Entities* play the (usually distinct) roles of *Vendor* and *Customer*. A *Sale* may have been agreed on in the past, and a future *Potential-Sale* can be envisaged, whether the actual *Product* can or cannot be identified and whether it exists or not.

This ontology has been a relevant experimental foundation for the Uschold and King's (1995) approach to develop ontologies, which is described in Chapter 3.

The **TOVE**[43] (TOronto Virtual Enterprise) (Fox, 1992) project is being carried out by the Enterprise Integration Laboratory (EIL) at the University of Toronto. Its goal is to create a data model able (1) to provide a shared terminology for the enterprise that agents can both understand and use, (2) to define the meaning of each term in a precise and unambiguous manner, (3) to implement the semantics in a set of axioms that will enable TOVE to deduce automatically the answer to many "common sense" questions about the enterprise, and (4) to define a symbology for depicting a term, or the concept constructed thereof in a graphical context.

TOVE ontologies are implemented with two different languages: C++ for the static part, and Prolog for the axioms.

Figure 2.31 shows the structure of the TOVE ontologies. Up to now, the existing ontologies developed to model Enterprises are: Foundational Ontologies (Activity and Resource) and Business Ontologies (Organization, Quality, Products and Requirements). These ontologies cover activities, state, causality, time, resources, inventory, order requirements, and parts. They have also axiomatized the definitions for portions of the knowledge of activity, state, time, and resources.

---

[43] http://www.eil.utoronto.ca/tove/toveont.html

Axioms are implemented in Prolog and provide answers for common-sense questions via deductive query processing.

Enterprise Ontologies
- Enterprise Design Ontology
- Project Ontology
- Material Flow Ontology
- Business Process Ontology

Derivative Ontologies
- Transportation Ontology
- Inventory Ontology
- Quality Ontology
- Product Design Ontology
- Goals Ontology
- Scheduling Ontology
- Operating Strategies Ontology
- Product Requirements Ontology
- Information Resource Ontology
- Intended Action Ontology
- Electro Mechanical Product Ontology

Core Ontologies
- Product Ontology
- Service Ontology
- Activity Ontology
- Organization Ontology
- Resource Ontology

Figure 2.31: Structure of the TOVE ontologies.

According to TOVE developers, their future work will be confined to the development of ontologies and axioms for quality, activity-based costing, and organization structures.

This ontology has been an important experimental basis for the Grüninger and Fox's (1995) method to develop ontologies, described in Chapter 3.

2.4.5 Chemistry ontologies

Chemistry ontologies model the composition, structure, and properties of substances, processes and phenomena. They can be used for many purposes: for education (to teach students the periodic table of elements, the rules for molecule composition, etc.), for environmental science (to detect environmental pollutants), for scientific discovery (to analyze publications to learn about new molecules' composition or to synthesize chemicals), etc. We will describe the set of chemistry ontologies developed by the Ontology Group of the Artificial Intelligence Laboratory at UPM: *Chemicals* (composed of *Chemical Elements* and *Chemical*

Crystals), *Ions* (composed of *Monatomic Ions* and *Poliatomic Ions*) and *Environmental Pollutants*. All of them are available in WebODE, and both the *Chemical Elements* and the *Chemical Crystals* ontologies are also implemented in Ontolingua and available in the Ontolingua Server.

Figure 2.32 shows how all these ontologies are integrated in a hierarchical architecture. It should be interpreted that the ontologies on top of this hierarchy include the lower-level ontologies. Note that this hierarchical architecture facilitates future users the comprehension, design and maintenance of ontologies. As we can see, *Chemical Elements* is a key point in this ontology structure. It imports the *Standard-Units* ontology available in the Ontolingua Server, which, in its turn, imports other ontologies in the same ontology server, such as *Standard-Dimensions*, *Physical-Quantities*, *KIF-Numbers* and the *Frame-Ontology*.

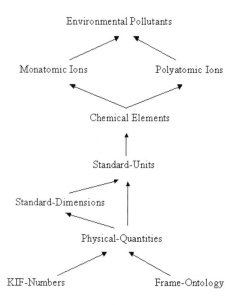

Figure 2.32: Relationship between the chemistry ontologies described in this section and other ontologies in the Ontolingua Server.

Chemicals is composed of two ontologies: *Chemical Elements* and *Chemical Crystals*. These ontologies were used to elaborate METHONTOLOGY (Fernández-López et al., 1999), an ontology development methodology that will be described in Chapter 3.

The *Chemical Elements* ontology models knowledge of the chemical elements of the periodic table, such as what elements these are (*Oxygen*, *Hydrogen*, *Iron*, *Gold*, etc.), what properties they have (*atomic number*, *atomic weight*, *electronegativity*, etc.), and what combination constraints of the attribute values they have. *Chemical Elements* contains 16 classes, 20 instance attributes, one function, 103 instances and 27 formal axioms.

Chemical Crystals was built to model the crystalline structure of the chemical elements. Therefore, *Chemical Elements* imports this ontology. The ontology contains 19 classes, eight relations, 66 instances and 26 axioms.

Ions is built on top of *Chemical Elements* and is also composed of two ontologies: *Monatomic Ions* (which model ions composed of one atom only) and *Polyatomic Ions* (which model ions composed of two or more atoms). Ions contains 62 concepts, 11 class attributes, three relations and six formal axioms.

Finally, the **environmental pollutants** ontology (Gómez-Pérez and Rojas, 1999) imports *Monatomic Ions* and *Polyatomic Ions* and is composed of three ontologies: *Environmental Parameters*, *Water* and *Soil*. The first ontology defines parameters that might cause environmental pollution or degradation in the physical environment (air, water, ground) and in humans, or more explicitly, in their health. The second and third ontologies define water and soil pollutants respectively. These ontologies define the methods for detecting pollutant components of various environments, and the maximum concentrations of these components permitted according to the legislation in force.

2.4.6 Knowledge management ontologies

The objectives of knowledge management (KM) in an organization are to promote knowledge growth, knowledge communication and knowledge preservation in the organization (Steels, 1993). To achieve these objectives corporate memories can be created. A corporate memory is an explicit, disembodied, persistent representation of knowledge and information in an organization (van Heijst et al., 1996). According to Dieng-Kuntz and colleagues (1998, 2001), a corporate memory can be built following different techniques that can be combined: document-based, knowledge-based, case-based, groupware-based, workflow-based and distributed. Ontologies are included among the knowledge-based techniques for building corporate memories.

Basically, Abecker and colleagues (1998) distinguish three types of KM ontologies:
- *Information ontologies*. They describe the different kinds of information sources, their structure, access permissions, and format properties.
- *Domain ontologies*. They model the content of the information sources.
- *Enterprise ontologies*. They model the context of an organization, business process, organization of the enterprise, etc., as described in Section 2.4.4.

Figure 2.33 shows an example of the existing relations between the aforementioned ontologies. The ontologies presented in the figure have been built for the corporate memory of the Artificial Intelligence Laboratory at UPM in Madrid. There are two domain ontologies: *Hardware&Software* (which models the hardware equipment of the laboratory and the software installed in it) and *Documentation* (which models all the documents generated in the laboratory: publications, theses, faxes, etc.). There are four enterprise ontologies: *Organization* and *Groups* (which model the structure of the laboratory and its organization in different research groups), *Projects* (which models the projects that are developed in the laboratory), and *Persons* (which models the members of the laboratory: research staff, administrative staff, students, etc.). Three of these ontologies are also information ontologies: *Documentation*, *Projects* and *Persons* since they describe the information sources of the corporate memory and store information.

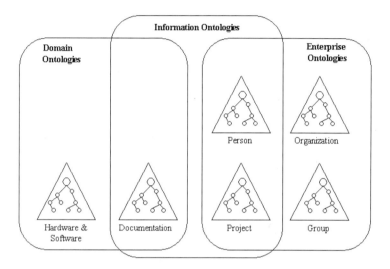

Figure 2.33: Information, domain and enterprise ontologies in a corporate memory for a research and development laboratory.

The **(KA)²** **ontologies** (Decker et al., 1999) are also good examples of KM ontologies. They were built inside the Knowledge Annotation Initiative of the Knowledge Acquisition community (Benjamins et al., 1999), also known as the (KA)² initiative. Its goal was to model the knowledge-acquisition community with the ontologies built by 15 groups of people at different locations. Each group focused on a particular topic of the (KA)² ontologies (problem solving methods, ontologies, etc.). The result was seven related ontologies: an *organization ontology*, a *project ontology*, a *person ontology*, a *publication ontology*, an *event ontology*, a *research-topic ontology* and a *research-product ontology*. They formed the basis to annotate WWW documents of the knowledge acquisition community, and thus to enable intelligent access to these Web documents.

The first release of the (KA)² ontologies was built in the FLogic language (Kifer et al., 1995), which is described in Chapter 4. These FLogic ontologies were translated into Ontolingua with ODE translators (Blázquez et al., 1998) to make them accessible to the entire community through the European mirror of the Ontolingua Server in Madrid[44]. The updated version of (KA)² is not in Ontolingua

---

[44] http://granvia.dia.fi.upm.es:5915/ Log in as "ontologias-ka2" with password "adieu007"

but in DAML+OIL and is maintained at the AIFB (Institute for Informatics and Formal Description Methods) of the University of Karlsruhe[45].

In the context of the European IST project Esperonto[46], five KM ontologies have been developed in WebODE to describe **R&D projects**: *Project, Documentation, Person, Organization,* and *Meeting*. These ontologies describe R&D projects and their structure, documents that are generated in a project, people and organizations participating in it, and meetings (administrative, technical, etc.) held during a project lifecycle. Figure 2.34 shows the relationships between all these ontologies (a project has associated meetings, a document belongs to a project, a document summarizes a meeting, people have a role in a project, etc.).

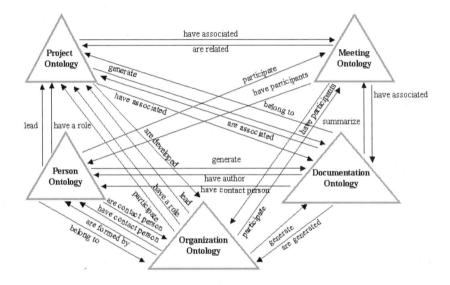

Figure 2.34: Main ad hoc relationships between KM ontologies for R&D projects.

Part of the concept taxonomy of the *Documentation* ontology is presented in Figure 2.35. As the figure shows, we have distinguished four types of documents in a project: management documents, technical documents, publications and additional documents. Some of the technical documents generated in a project are deliverables, manuals and presentations. Publications can be done as books or articles, and there are different types of articles, depending on where they are published: in workshops, as part of the proceedings of a conference, in books or in magazines and journals.

These ontologies can be accessed at the Esperonto Web site, powered by the knowledge portal ODESeW[47].

---

[45] http://ka2portal.aifb.uni-karlsruhe.de
[46] http://www.esperonto.net/
[47] http://webode.dia.fi.upm.es/sew/index.html

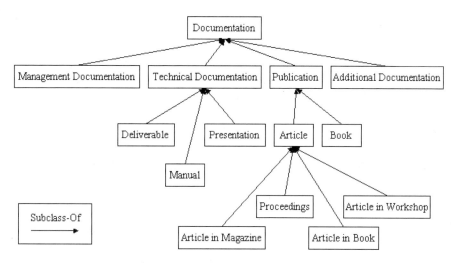

Figure 2.35: Fragment of the *documentation ontology* of R&D projects.

2.5 Bibliographical Notes and Further Reading

To those readers who want to have a thorough grounding in the contents of this chapter, we recommend the following readings, grouped by topics:

- *Ontologies in general.* The deliverable D.1.1 "Technical Roadmap" of the OntoWeb thematic network, funded by the European Commission, contains brief descriptions of and references to the most outstanding ontologies. The OntoRoadMap application, which has been created inside the project OntoWeb (*http://babage.dia.fi.upm.es/ontoweb/wp1/OntoRoadMap/index.html*),   lets researchers consult and update the information on existing ontologies.

- *Knowledge representation ontologies.* We recommend to download the KR ontologies that have been presented in Section 2.1: the Frame Ontology and the OKBC   Ontology   (available   at   the   Ontolingua   Server: *http://ontolingua.stanford.edu/*), the RDF and RDF Schema KR ontologies (available at *http://www.w3.org/RDF/*), the OIL KR ontology (available at *http://www.ontoknowledge.org/oil/*), the DAML+OIL KR ontology (available at *http://www.daml.org/language/*), and the OWL KR ontology (available at *http://www.w3.org/2001/sw/WebOnt/*).

- *Top-level ontologies.* More information about top-level ontologies can be found in   *http://www-sop.inria.fr/acacia/personnel/phmartin/RDF/phOntology.html*. We also advise to consult the SUO Web page at *http://suo.ieee.org/*.

- *Linguistic ontologies.* For linguistic ontologies, we recommend periodically access to the Web page of the OntoWeb SIG on Language Technology in Ontology Development and Use (*http://dfki.de/~paulb/ontoweb-lt.html*). Other linguistic ontologies different to the ones dealt with in this chapter are: Corelex, which is presented in *http://www.cs.brandeis.edu/~paulb/CoreLex/corelex.html*

and (Buitelaar, 2001); EDR, presented in *http://www.iijnet.or.jp/edr/* and (Miyoshi et al., 1996); and the Goi-Takei's ontology, presented in (Ikehara et al., 1997) and *http://www.kecl.ntt.co.jp/icl/mtg/topics/lexicon-index.html*.

- *E-commerce ontologies.* You can read about e-commerce ontologies in the deliverable D3.1 of OntoWeb (IST-2000-29243), which deals with e-commerce content standards. This deliverable is available in the following URL: *http://www.ontoweb.org/download/deliverables/D3.1.pdf.* We also recommend to read about the initiatives for aligning e-commerce classifications (Bergamaschi et al., 2001; Corcho and Gómez-Pérez, 2001; Gordijn et al., 2000).

- *Medical ontologies.* More information about the GALEN ontology can be found in *http://www.opengalen.org/resources.html.* We recommend to download the open source tool OpenKnoME (*http://www.topthing.com*) to compile and to browse the GALEN sources. Access to UMLS sources and resources (applications and documentation) is free, though it is necessary to sign the UMLS license agreement at *http://www.nlm.nih.gov/research/umls/license.html.* A general overview of medical ontologies is presented by Bodenreider (2001).

- *Chemistry ontologies.* One of the data sets included in the DAML data sources wishlist (*http://www.daml.org/data/*) is the periodic table of the chemical elements, which would be considered as a reference data set for chemical and related industries, probably combined with other chemistry ontologies including elements, compounds, etc. So we recommend to take a close look at this effort.

- *Content standards.* We recommend to have a look at the Special Interest Group on Content Standards of OntoWeb (IST-2000-29243), whose URL is: *http://www.ladseb.pd.cnr.it/infor/ontology/OntoWeb/SIGContentStandards.htm.* The goal of this SIG is to coordinate cooperation and participation with current initiatives related to ontology-based content standardization and content harmonization across different standards.

- *Legal ontologies.* We recommend to have a look at the Legal Ontologies Working Group within the OntoWeb Content Standards SIG, whose URL is: *http://ontology.ip.rm.cnr.it/legontoweb.html.* The objective of this working group is (1) to collect the (possibly formalized) ontologies proposed so far in the literature and still maintained or 'alive'; (2) to contact the reference persons; (3) to create a Web page in which a general outline of Legal Ontologies is presented; and (4) to provide a preliminary description of the steps to reach a "Common Core Legal Ontology Library". Several events have dealt with legal ontologies, such as *http://lri.jur.uva.nl/jurix2001/legont2001.htm*, h*ttp://www.cs.wustl.edu/icail2001/*, and *http://www.cfslr.ed.ac.uk/icail03/*. Other URLs related to legal ontologies are: *http://www.csc.liv.ac.uk/~lial/*, *http://www.lri.jur.uva.nl*, *http://www.idg.fi.cnr.it/researches/researches.htm*, and *http://www.austlii.edu.au/au/other/col/1999/35/*.

Chapter 3

Methodologies and Methods for Building Ontologies

The 1990s and the first years of this new century have witnessed the growing interest of many practitioners in approaches for building ontologies from scratch, for reusing other ontologies and for using semiautomatic methods that reduce the knowledge acquisition bottleneck of the ontology development process. Until the mid-1990s, this process was an art rather than an engineering activity. Each development team usually followed their own set of principles, design criteria and phases for manually building the ontology. The absence of common and structured guidelines slowed the development of ontologies within and between teams, the extension of any ontology, the possibility of ontologies of being reused in others, and the use of ontologies in final applications.

In 1996, the first workshop on Ontological Engineering was held in conjunction with the 12th European Conference on Artificial Intelligence. Its goal was to explore a suite of principles, design decisions, and rules of good practice from which other ontology designers could profit. A second workshop was held in 1997 with the same topic though this time it took place with the AAAI Spring Symposium Series in Stanford. One of the main aspects dealt with in this workshop was the use of methodologies to design and evaluate ontologies. Since then, methodological aspects related to different activities of the ontology development process and its lifecycle are included in most of the international conferences on the Ontological Engineering field (EKAW, FOIS, K-CAP, KAW, etc.) and workshops held in conjunction with AAAI, ECAI and IJCAI.

The goal of this chapter is to present the main methodologies and methods used to build ontologies from scratch, by reusing and re-engineering other ontologies, by a process of merging or by using an ontology learning approach.

In the literature, the terms *methodology, method, technique, process, activity,* etc., are used indiscriminately (de Hoog, 1998). To make clear the use of these terms on the Ontological Engineering field, we have adopted the IEEE definitions for such terms in this chapter. Thus, all the works presented in this chapter are presented uniformly, independently of how each author uses its own terminology.

The IEEE defines a **methodology** as "*a comprehensive, integrated series of techniques or methods creating a general systems theory of how a class of thought-intensive work ought be performed*" (IEEE, 1990). Methodologies are broadly used in Software Engineering (Downs et al., 1998; Pressmann, 2000) and Knowledge Engineering (Waterman, 1986; Wielinga et al., 1992; and Gómez-Pérez et al., 1997). As we can read in the previous definition of methodology, both methods and techniques are parts of methodologies. A **method** is a set of "*orderly process or procedure used in the engineering of a product or performing a service*" (IEEE, 1990). A **technique** is "*a technical and managerial procedure used to achieve a given objective*" (IEEE, 1990).

De Hoog (1998) explores the relationships between methodologies and methods for building Knowledge Based Systems (KBS). According to him, methodologies and methods are not the same because "*methodologies refer to knowledge about methods*". Methodologies state "what", "who" and "when" a given activity should be performed. Greenwood (Greenwood, 1973) also explores the differences between methods and techniques. A method is a general procedure while a technique is the specific application of a method and the way in which the method is executed. For example, the method to build a circumference consists in plotting a line whose points have the same distance with respect to the center. There are several techniques for applying this method: plotting the line with a compass, with a pencil tied to a string, with a circumference template, etc.

According to the IEEE methodology definition, methods and techniques are related. In fact, methods and techniques are used to carry out tasks inside the different processes of which a methodology consists. A process is a "*function that must be performed in the software life cycle. A process is composed of activities*" (IEEE, 1996). An activity is "*a constituent task of a process*" (IEEE, 1996). A task is the smallest unit of work subject to management accountability. "*A task is a well-defined work assignment for one or more project members. Related tasks are usually grouped to form activities*" (IEEE, 1996). For example, the system design in Software Engineering is a process that has to be performed in every project. To execute this process, the following activities have to be carried out: database design, architectural design, interface design, etc. The database design activity, in turn, requires performing different tasks like data conceptual modeling, physical structure design, etc. To carry out each task different methods can be used. For example, physical structure design can be performed through the functional dependency method, or through conceptual model transformation rules. In addition, each method has associated its own techniques.

The relationships between the aforementioned definitions are summarized in Figure 3.1, where we can see that a methodology is composed of methods and techniques. Methods are composed of processes and are detailed with techniques. Processes are composed of activities. Finally, the activities make groups of tasks.

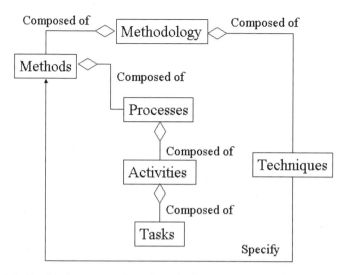

Figure 3.1: Graphical representation of terminological relationships in methodologies.

3.1 Ontology Development Process

In 1997, the ontology development process (Fernández-López et al., 1997) was identified on the framework of the METHONTOLOGY methodology for ontology construction. Such a proposal was based on the IEEE standard for software development (IEEE, 1996). The ontology development process refers to *which* activities are performed when building ontologies. It is crucial to identify these activities if agreement is to be reached on ontologies built by geographically distant cooperative teams. It is advisable to carry out the three categories of activities presented in Figure 3.2 and steer clear of anarchic constructions:

Ontology management activities include scheduling, control and quality assurance. The *scheduling* activity identifies the tasks to be performed, their arrangement, and the time and resources needed for their completion. This activity is essential for ontologies that use ontologies stored in ontology libraries or for ontologies that require a high level of abstraction and generality. The *control* activity guarantees that scheduled tasks are completed in the manner intended to be performed. Finally, the *quality assurance* activity assures that the quality of each and every product output (ontology, software and documentation) is satisfactory.

Ontology development oriented activities are grouped, as presented in Figure 3.2, into pre-development, development and post-development activities.
    During the pre-development, an *environment study* is carried out to know the platforms where the ontology will be used, the applications where the ontology will be integrated, etc. Also during the pre-development, the *feasibility study* answers

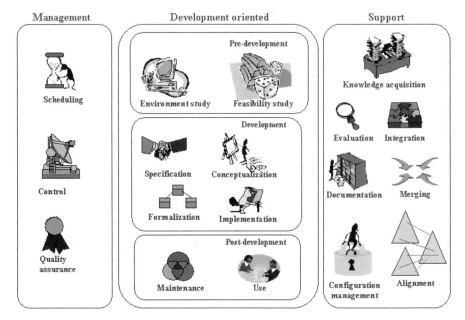

Figure 3.2: Ontology development process.

questions like: is it possible to build the ontology? is it suitable to build the ontology?, etc.

Once in the development, the *specification* activity[1] states why the ontology is being built, what its intended uses are and who the end-users are. The *conceptualization* activity structures the domain knowledge as meaningful models at the knowledge level (Newell, 1982). The *formalization* activity transforms the conceptual model into a formal or semi-computable model. The *implementation* activity builds computable models in an ontology language (in Chapter 4 we describe several languages used to implement ontologies).

During the post-development, the *maintenance* activity updates and corrects the ontology if needed. Also during the post-development, the ontology is *(re)used* by other ontologies or applications.

Finally, **ontology support activities** include a series of activities performed at the same time as the development-oriented activities, without which the ontology could not be built. They include knowledge acquisition, evaluation, integration, merging, alignment, documentation and configuration management. The goal of the *knowledge acquisition* activity is to acquire knowledge from experts of a given domain or through some kind of (semi)automatic process, which is called ontology learning (Kietz et al., 2000). The *evaluation* activity (Gómez-Pérez et al., 1995)

---

[1] In (Fernández-López et al., 1997) we considered *specification* as a pre-development activity. However, following more strictly the IEEE standard for software development, we have considered the specification activity as being part of the proper development process. In fact, the result of this activity is an ontology description (usually in natural language) that will be transformed into a conceptual model by the *conceptualization* activity.

makes a technical judgment of the ontologies, of their associated software environments, and of the documentation. This judgment is made with respect to a frame of reference during each stage and between stages of the ontology's life cycle. The *integration* activity is required when building a new ontology by reusing other ontologies already available. Another support activity is *merging* (Gangemi et al., 1999; Noy and Musen, 2001; Stumme and Maedche, 2001), which consists in obtaining a new ontology starting from several ontologies on the same domain. The resulting ontology is able to unify concepts, terminology, definitions, constraints, etc., from all the source ontologies (Pinto et al., 1999). The merge of two or more ontologies can be carried out either in run-time or design time. The *alignment* activity establishes different kinds of mappings (or links) between the involved ontologies. Hence this option preserves the original ontologies and does not merge them. The *documentation* activity details, clearly and exhaustively, each and every one of the completed stages and products generated. The *configuration management* activity records all the versions of the documentation and of the ontology code to control the changes.

From this analysis we can conclude that the ontology development process identifies which activities are to be performed. However, it does not identify the order in which the activities should be performed (Fernández-López et al., 1997) (see also IEEE, 1996). The ontology life cycle identifies *when* the activities should be carried out, that is, it identifies the *set of stages* through which the ontology moves during its life time, describes what activities are to be performed in each stage and how the stages are related (relation of precedence, return, etc.).

3.2 Ontology Methodology Evolution

Basically, a series **of methods and methodologies for developing ontologies** have been reported. In 1990, Lenat and Guha (1990) published some general steps and some interesting points about the Cyc development. Some years later, in 1995, on the basis of the experience gathered in developing the Enterprise Ontology (Uschold and King, 1995) and the TOVE (TOronto Virtual Enterprise) project ontology (Grüninger and Fox, 1995) both in the domain of enterprise modeling, the first guidelines were proposed and later refined in (Uschold and Grüninger, 1996; Uschold, 1996).

At the 12th European Conference for Artificial Intelligence (ECAI'96), Bernaras and colleagues (1996) presented a method to build an ontology in the domain of electrical networks as part of the Esprit KACTUS project (KACTUS, 1996). The METHONTOLOGY methodology (Gómez-Pérez et al., 1996) appeared simultaneously and was extended in further papers (Fernández-López et al., 1997; Gómez-Pérez, 1998; Fernández-López et al., 1999). In 1997, a new method was proposed for building ontologies based on the SENSUS ontology (Swartout et al., 1997).

Then some years later, the On-To-Knowledge methodology appeared within the project with the same name (Staab et al., 2001).

But methods and methodologies have not been created only for building ontologies from scratch. When (re)using an existing ontology it might happen that the ontology is implemented in a language with an underlying knowledge representation paradigm different to the knowledge representation conventions used by the ontology that reuses it, or that the ontology to be reused has different ontological commitments, etc. For solving some of these problems METHONTOLOGY includes a **re-engineering method** (Gómez-Pérez and Rojas, 1999).

Although one of the main purposes of ontologies is to reduce the knowledge acquisition bottleneck, to acquire knowledge for building ontologies still requires a lot of time and resources. As a consequence, **ontology learning methods** have been thought up to decrease the effort made during the knowledge acquisition process (Aussenac-Gilles et al., 2000a; Kietz et al., 2000). Such methods are used with several purposes: to create a new ontology from scratch, to enrich an existing one with new terms, and to acquire knowledge for some tasks. We present in this chapter ontology learning methods mainly based on natural language analysis from texts.

Ontologies aim to capture *consensual* knowledge of a given domain in a generic and formal way to be reused and shared across applications and by groups of people. From this definition we could *wrongly* infer that there is only one ontology for a domain. In fact, we can find in the literature several ontologies that model, though in different ways, the same kind of knowledge or domain. Noy and Musen (1999) distinguish two approaches for unifying the terminologies of the ontologies: ontology alignment and ontology merging. **Ontology alignment methods** establish different kinds of mappings (or links) between the ontologies, hence this option preserves the original ontologies. However, **ontology merging methods** propose to generate a unique ontology from the original ontologies. The merging process usually requires to establish mappings between the ontologies to merge. Given the current state of affairs and in the context of the Semantic Web, it is more suitable to establish ontological mappings between existing ontologies on the same topic than to pretend to build *the* unified knowledge model for such a topic from scratch. In this chapter, we present the ONIONS methodology (Gangemi et al., 1999), FCA-Merge method (Stumme and Maedche, 2001), Chimaera (McGuinness et al., 2000) and PROMPT (Noy and Musen, 2000) for merging ontologies. We also present the method used by AnchorPROMPT (Noy and Musen, 2001) for ontology alignment.

All the aforementioned approaches do not consider **collaborative and distributed construction of ontologies**. In fact, the first method that included a proposal for collaborative construction was Co4 (Euzenat, 1995; 1996). This method includes a protocol for agreeing new pieces of knowledge with the rest of the knowledge architecture, which has been previously agreed upon.

Ontologies cannot be reused by other ontologies or used by applications without **evaluating** first their content from a technical point of view. As for guidelines to evaluate ontologies, the first publications were (Gómez-Pérez et al., 1995; Gómez-Pérez, 1996); and she has continued working on the evaluation of taxonomic knowledge (Gómez-Pérez, 1999; 2001). Guarino and colleagues have developed OntoClean (Welty and Guarino, 2001), a method to analyze and clean the taxonomy of an existing ontology by means of a set of principles based in philosophy. Other interesting works on knowledge base evaluation with ontologies are those of Kalfoglou and Robertson (1999a; 1999b).

To conclude, the purpose of this chapter is not to evaluate which methodology is the best. As de Hoog says (1998, with his own emphasis), "*it is extremely difficult to judge the value of a methodology in an objective way. Experimentation is of course the proper way to do it, but it is hardly feasible because there are too many conditions that cannot be controlled*". On the one hand "*introducing an experimental toy problem will violate the basic assumption behind the need for a methodology: a complex development process.* On the other hand, if we extrapolate the argument that de Hoog provides for knowledge based systems to the ontology field, it is not very likely that someone will pay twice for building the same complex ontology with different approaches.

3.3 Ontology Development Methods and Methodologies

This section presents and compares the classical methodologies and methods used to build ontologies from scratch or by reusing other ontologies. In particular the approaches dealt with are the Cyc method, the Uschold and King's method, the Grüninger and Fox's methodology, the KACTUS approach, METHONTOLOGY, the SENSUS method, and the On-To-Knowledge methodology.

3.3.1 The Cyc method

In the middle of the 1980s, the Microelectronics and Computer Technology Corporation (MCC) started to create Cyc, a huge knowledge base (KB) with common sense knowledge. Cyc was built upon a core of over 1,000,000 hand-entered assertions designed to capture a large portion of what people normally consider consensus knowledge about the world.

To implement Cyc, the CycL language was used. This is a hybrid language that combines frames with predicate calculus. The CycL inference engine allows: multiple inheritance, automatic classification, maintenance of inverse links, firing of daemons, constraint checking, agenda-based best-first search, etc.; it also has a truth maintenance system, a contradiction detection and a resolution module.

The reason why Cyc can be considered as an ontology is because it can be used as a substrate for building different intelligent systems that can communicate and interact.

As Figure 3.3 illustrates, during the development of Cyc the following processes were carried out (Lenat and Guha, 1990):

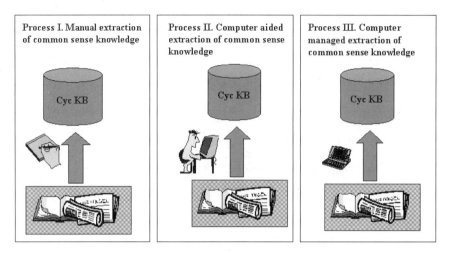

Figure 3.3: Processes proposed by the Cyc method.

Process I. Manual coding of articles and pieces of knowledge. This first process was carried out by hand because existing natural language systems and learning machines did not handle enough common sense knowledge to search for this kind of new knowledge. This knowledge was acquired in three ways:

- *Encoding the knowledge required to understand books and newspapers.* This does not mean encoding the contents of such works, but searching and representing the underlying common sense knowledge that the writers of those articles assumed their readers already possessed.
- *Examination of articles that are unbelievable,* for example, a paper that says that an airplane was flying for one year without filling up. The purpose of this examination is to study the rationale that makes some articles unbelievable.
- *Identification of questions that "anyone" should be able to answer by having just read the text.* The KB is augmented to be able to answer such questions.

Process II. Knowledge coding aided by tools using the knowledge already stored in the Cyc KB. This second process can be performed when tools for analyzing natural language and machine learning tools can use enough common sense knowledge to search for new common sense knowledge.

Process III. Knowledge codification mainly performed by tools using knowledge already stored in the Cyc KB. This third process delegates most of the work to the tools. To work with Cyc tools users only recommend the system the knowledge sources to be read and explain the most difficult parts of the text.

Two activities are performed in all of the three previous processes:

Activity 1. Development of a knowledge representation and top level ontology containing the most abstract concepts. As we saw in Chapter 2, terms like `attribute` or `attribute value` are examples of knowledge representation terms, and `thing`, `intangible` or `collection` are examples of abstract concepts.

Activity 2. Representation of the knowledge of different domains using such primitives.

Up to now, this method has been used only for building the Cyc KB; however, Cyc has different micro-theories to gather the knowledge of domains from different viewpoints. A micro-theory (Guha, 1991) is a theory of some topic, e.g., a theory of mechanics, chemical elements, etc. Different micro-theories might take different assumptions and simplifications about the world, be seen from different perspectives, and be used in different areas.

With regard to the applications in which Cyc ontologies are used, there are several modules integrated into the Cyc KB and the CycL inference engine. One of these is the Heterogeneous Database Integration System, which maps the Cyc vocabulary into database schemas, that is, the data stored on the databases are interpreted according to the Cyc vocabulary. Other module is the Knowledge-Enhanced Searching of Captioned Information, which permits making queries over images using their captions in natural language. Another module is the Guided Integration of Structured Terminology (GIST), which allows users to import and simultaneously manage and integrate multiple thesauri.

Cyc agents have also been built. All these agents have a common core with knowledge of the Cyc KB plus domain knowledge from the specific domain of the agent.

Finally, the WWW Information Retrieval module uses the natural language tools to access the Cyc KB and allows extending the Cyc KB with information available on the Web.

3.3.2 Uschold and King's method

Uschold and King (1995) proposed the first method for building ontologies, which was extended in (Uschold and Grüninger, 1996). They proposed some guidelines based on their experience of developing the Enterprise Ontology. As described in Section 2.4.4, this ontology was developed as a part of the Enterprise Project by the Artificial Intelligence Applications Institute at the University of Edinburgh with its partners IBM, Lloyd's Register, Logica UK Limited, and Unilever.

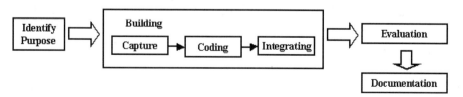

Figure 3.4: Main processes of the Uschold and King's method.

␣o build an ontology according to Uschold and King's approach, the following processes must be performed: (1) identify the purpose of the ontology, (2) build it, (3) evaluate it, and (4) document it. During the building process, the authors propose capturing knowledge, coding it and integrating other ontologies inside the current ontology. These processes, shown in Figure 3.4, are:

Process 1. To identify the purpose and the scope. The goal here is to clarify why the ontology is being built, what its intended uses are (to be reused, shared, used, used as a part of a KB, etc.) and what the relevant terms on the domain will be. Considering our traveling example, the purpose of building a travel ontology would be, for instance, to provide a consensual knowledge model of the traveling domain that will be used by travel agencies. Such ontology could be also used for other purposes, for instance, for developing a catalogue about lodgings or transport means. Concerning the scope, the list of relevant terms to be included are: `places` and `types of place`, `lodging` and `types of lodging` (`hotel`, `motel`, `camping`, etc.), `trains`, `buses`, `undergrounds`, etc.

Process 2. To build the ontology. It is broken down into three activities:

Activity 2.1. Ontology capture. The following tasks are proposed for capturing knowledge: to identify key concepts and relationships in the domain of interest; to produce precise and unambiguous textual definitions for such concepts and relationships; to identify the terms that refer to such concepts and relationships and thus to reach an agreement. The textual definitions are not created following the style of classical dictionaries but are built by referring to other terms and including notions such as class, relation, etc. Consequently, these natural language definitions determine the knowledge representation ontology to be used. Some concepts and relations identified for our travel agency ontology could be (with their associated terms and definitions) the following:

- `Transport means`: it is a class. Each transport means has a `starting point`.
- `Bus`: it is a class. It is a kind of `Transport means`.
- `Local bus`: it is a class. It is a `bus` whose `departure place`, `destination place` and `stops` are at the same `Location`.

To identify the concepts in the ontology, Uschold and Grüninger (1996) pointed out three strategies: bottom-up, top-down, and middle-out.

The *bottom-up strategy* proposes identifying first the most specific concepts and then, generalizing them into more abstract concepts. The authors affirm that a bottom-up approach results in a very high level of detail. This approach: (1) increases the overall effort, (2) makes it difficult to spot commonality between related concepts, and (3) increases the risk of inconsistencies which leads to (4) re-work and even to more effort. In our example, if we want to represent transport means following a bottom-up strategy, we identify first the following types of means, as we can see in Figure 3.5: `London underground`, `London local bus`, `London taxi`, `Madrid underground`,

Madrid local bus and Madrid taxi. Such transport means could be grouped not only into underground, local bus and taxi, but also into Madrid transport means and London transport means. These last concepts may not be interesting for our ontology. We omit the concept bus and other types of buses like a shuttle bus, which might be important.

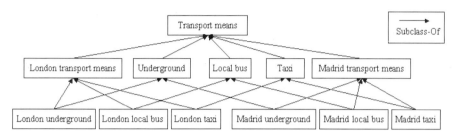

Figure 3.5: Example of a taxonomy built following the bottom-up approach.

With the *top-down strategy* the most abstract concepts are identified first, and then specialized into more specific concepts. The main result of using a top-down approach is a better control of the level of detail; however, starting at the top can result in choosing and imposing arbitrary and possibly not needed high level categories. Because these do not arise naturally, there is a risk of less stability in the model, what leads to reworking and to greater effort. The emphasis on dividing up rather than putting together also results, for a different reason, in missing the commonality inherent in the complex web of inter-connected concepts. In our example, as Figure 3.6 illustrates, we start building the taxonomy with the concept object and we distinguish between concrete object and abstract object. Then, we consider the different transport means as abstract objects that use concrete objects (taxi, bus, train). With this strategy we can generate too many concepts (object,

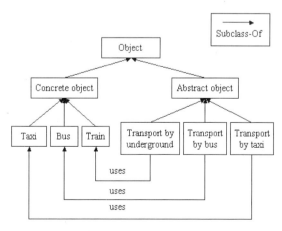

Figure 3.6: Example of a taxonomy built following the top-down approach.

concrete object, etc.), and we may make an unnecessary distinction between transport means and the objects they need.

Finally, the *middle-out strategy* recommends identifying first the core of basic terms, and then specifying and generalizing them as required. Uschold and Grüninger claim that a middle-out approach, by contrast, strikes a balance in terms of the level of detail. Detail only arises as necessary by specializing the basic concepts, so some efforts are avoided. If we start with the most important concepts first, and define higher level concepts in terms of them, these higher level categories arise naturally and thus are more likely to be stable. This, in turn, leads to less re-work and less overall effort. In the example on the transport domain, as can be seen in Figure 3.7, we have identified first the concepts: underground, bus and taxi, which are the most important for us. Then, we have generated the top and the bottom concepts for bus, which are local bus, shuttle bus and coach.

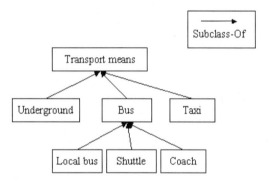

Figure 3.7: Example of a taxonomy built following the middle-out approach.

Activity 2.2. Coding. This activity involves two tasks: (a) committing to basic terms that will be used to specify the representation ontology (e.g., class, entity, relation), and (b) writing the code.

Activity 2.3. Integrating existing ontologies. This activity refers to how and whether to use ontologies that already exist. Integration can be done in parallel with the previous activities of this process. Examples of ontologies that could be reused are: the *Frame Ontology* for modeling the domain ontology using a frame-based approach, *KIF-Numbers* to represent numbers, or the *Standard-Units* that contains descriptions of units of measure. This last ontology is useful for representing different kind of distances (meter, kilometer, etc.).

Process 3. To evaluate. The authors take the definition from Gómez-Pérez and colleagues (1995) and affirm that: "*to make a technical judgment of the ontologies, their associated software environment, and documentation with respect to a frame of reference ... the frame of reference may be requirement specifications, competency questions, and/or the real world*".

Process 4. To document. On this process, the guidelines for documenting the ontology are established and are possibly different, according to the type and purpose of the ontology. A guideline example is to locate similar definitions together or to create naming conventions such as: using upper or lowercase letters to name the terms, or writing the terms of the representation ontology in uppercase.

According to Uschold and Grüninger (1996), the aforementioned processes are not sufficient to have a methodology. Every methodology should also include a set of techniques, methods, and principles for each of the above four stages, and it should indicate what relationships between the stages exist (e.g., recommended order, interleaving, inputs/outputs).

The main drawback of this method is the lack of a conceptualization process before implementing the ontology. The goal of a conceptualization process is to provide a domain model less formal than the implementation model but more than the definition of the model in natural language. Other problems provoked by this lack of a conceptualization process are (Fernández-López et al., 1999) that: (1) domain experts, human users, and ontologists have many difficulties in understanding ontologies implemented in ontology languages; and (2) domain experts are not able to build ontologies in their domain of expertise. So the bottleneck in knowledge acquisition still persists! To obtain the conceptual model from the ontology implementation, we can apply the process of re-engineering explained in Section 3.4.

3.3.3 Grüninger and Fox's methodology

Based on the experience of the TOVE project on the enterprise domain, which was developed at the University of Toronto, Grüninger and Fox (1995) published a formal approach to build and evaluate ontologies. This methodology has been used to build the TOVE ontologies, which are the pillars of the Enterprise Design Workbench[2], a design environment that permits the user to explore a variety of enterprise designs.

Grüninger and Fox's methodology is inspired by the development of knowledge based systems using first order logic. They propose identifying intuitively the main scenarios, that is, possible applications in which the ontology will be used. Then, a set of natural language questions, called competency questions, are used to determine the scope of the ontology. These questions and their answers are both used to extract the main concepts and their properties, relations and formal axioms of the ontology. On the other hand, knowledge is formally expressed in first-order logic. This is a very formal methodology that takes advantage of the robustness of classic logic and can be used as a guide to transform informal scenarios in computable models.

The processes identified in this methodology are shown in Figure 3.8:

---

[2] http://www.eil.toronto.ca/eil.html

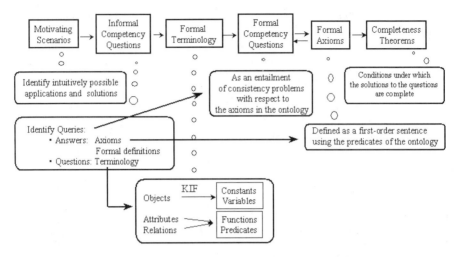

Figure 3.8: Processes in Grüninger and Fox's methodology.

Process 1. To identify motivating scenarios. The development of ontologies is motivated by scenarios related to the applications that will use the ontology. Such scenarios describe a set of the ontology's requirements that the ontology should satisfy after being formally implemented. A motivating scenario also provides a set of intuitively possible solutions to the scenario problems. These solutions give a first idea of the informal intended semantics of the objects and relations that will later be included in the ontology. In our example, the purpose of building a travel ontology is to provide a consensual knowledge model of the traveling domain that could be used by travel agencies.

Process 2: To elaborate informal competency questions. Given the set of informal scenarios, a set of informal competency questions are identified. Informal competency questions are those written in natural language to be answered by the ontology once the ontology is expressed in a formal language. The competency questions play the role of a type of requirement specification against which the ontology can be evaluated. Examples of informal competency questions are:

a) Given the preferences of a traveler (cultural travel, mountain travel, beach travel, etc.) and some constraints (economical or about the travel itself), which destinations are the most appropriate?

b) Given a young traveler with a budget for lodging, what kinds of lodgings are available?

This methodology proposes to stratify the set of competency questions. An ontology is not well-designed if all the competency questions are simple queries, that is, if the questions cannot be decomposed or composed into more specific or general questions, respectively. Competency questions can be split off into more specific (or atomic) competency questions, and the answer to a question can be used to answer more complex questions. For example, the competence question (a) could be decomposed to deal separately with cultural and economical constraints on the following:

a.1)   Given the preferences of a traveler (cultural
       travel, mountain travel, beach travel, etc.) and
       some economical constraints, which destinations
       are the most appropriate?

a.2)   Given the preferences of a traveler (cultural
       travel, mountain travel, beach travel, etc.) and
       some traveling constraints (i.e., the traveler
       hates traveling by plane), which destinations are
       the most appropriate?

Each competency question is useful as a base for obtaining assumptions, constraints, the necessary input data, etc., as Figure 3.9 illustrates.

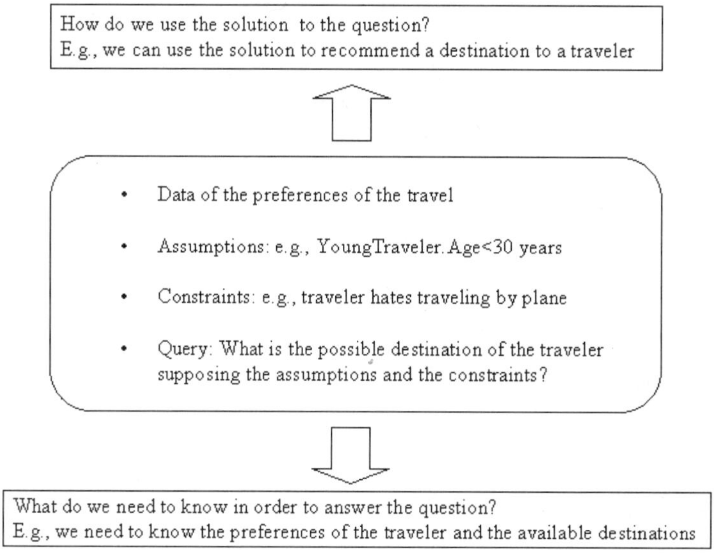

Figure 3.9: An example of a competency question.

Process 3: To specify the terminology using first order logic. The ontologist can use informal competency questions to extract the content of the ontology. Such content will be formally represented in the ontology. From the informal competency questions, the ontologist extracts the terminology that will be formally represented by means of concepts, attributes and relations in a first-order logic language. From the answers in natural language to the competency questions, the ontologist extracts the knowledge to be included in the formal definitions of concepts, relations, and formal axioms.

To build the ontology in first-order logic, the designers should carry out the tasks of a traditional formalization in first-order logic:

- *Identifying objects in the universe of discourse.* Examples of objects, which are instances, of the traveling domain are: Paris, Madrid, London, New York, Flight IB2140, Bus 125, Train C4, Hotel Palace in Madrid, Hotel Travel Lodge in Newcastle, etc.

- *Identifying predicates.* Unary predicates are used for representing concepts, binary predicates for attributes, and binary relations and n-ary predicates for n-ary relations. Examples of predicates that represent concepts are[3]:
  o transport-means ($transport)
  o bus ($bus)
  o train ($train)
  o traveler ($traveler)
  o young-traveler ($traveler)
  o adult-traveler ($traveler)
  o old-traveler ($traveler)
  o destination ($destination)
  o lodging ($lodging)
  o camping ($camping)
  o hotel ($hotel)
  o travel-information ($travelinfo)
  o location ($location), etc.

  Examples of predicates that represent attributes are:
  o traveler-name ($traveler,$string)
  o hotel-name ($hotel,$string)
  o bus-number ($bus,$integer), etc.
  Note that we cannot use the attribute name to refer to the name of a traveler, a hotel, and a bus, since predicates are only distinguished by their name and their arity. We have created the predicates traveler-name, hotel-name, and bus-number.

  Examples of predicates that represent binary relations are:
  o has-destination ($travelinfo,$location)
  o has-departure ($travelinfo,$location), etc.
  Where has-destination represents that the travel $travelinfo arrives at the location $location. And has-departure means that the travel $travelinfo departs from the location $location.

  As we will see later, the *Subclass-Of* relation can be represented with the implication if we make some assumptions.

---

[3] Variables are preceded by the symbol "$".

Process 4: To write competency questions in a formal way using formal terminology. Informal competency questions are written as an entailment of consistency problems with respect to the axioms in the ontology. Such axioms will be defined in process 5. For instance, the previous informal competency question "Given a set of traveler's preferences (cultural travel, mountain travel, beach travel, etc.) and some economical constraints, which destinations are the most appropriate?" would be formally represented in first-order logic as follows:

```
∃$x $y (destination ($x) ∧ travel-information ($y) ∧
        wants-to-travel (c,$y) ∧
        age(c,a) ∧ preferences(c,e) ∧ max-expense(c,b) ∧
        has-destination ($y, $x))      ?
```

where the meaning of the constants is: c is a traveler, b is the maximum quantity that the traveler can spend, a is the age of the traveler, and e are its preferences.

Process 5: To specify axioms using first-order logic. This methodology proposes using axioms to specify the definitions of terms in the ontology and constraints in their interpretation; axioms are defined as a first-order sentences using predicates of the ontology. The following axiom expresses that a traveler is a young traveler if and only if his age is equal or lower than 29.

```
∀$x (traveler ($x) ∧
     (∃$y integer($y) ∧ age($x,$y) ∧ ($y<30)) ↔
         young-traveler($x))
```

To represent the *Subclass-Of* relation the logical implication[4] can be used:

```
∀$x (local-bus($x) → bus($x))
```

If the proposed axioms are insufficient to represent the formal competency questions and to characterize the solutions to the questions, other axioms or objects are added.

Process 6. To specify completeness theorems. Once the competency questions have been formally stated, we must define the conditions under which the solutions to the questions are complete. This is the basis of completeness theorems for the ontology. In our example, a formal formulation for completeness is not needed since we only have to state that the system shows the traveler all the options.

As the main conclusion to this methodology, we can say that it is well-founded for building and evaluating ontologies, even though some management and support activities are missing.

---

[4] Note that ∀x (P(x) → Q(x)) in classic first order logic does not have exactly the same meaning as Subclass-Of(P,Q) in the paradigm of frames. For example, non-monotonic reasoning is usually considered when reasoning with frames, and disregarded in classic first order logic. To learn more about the relationships between frames and first order logic, consult Brewka (1987).

3.3.4 The KACTUS approach

This approach was proposed by Amaya Bernaras and her colleagues (1996), inside the Esprit KACTUS project (KACTUS, 1996). An objective of this project was to investigate the feasibility of knowledge reuse in complex technical systems and the role of ontologies to support it (Schreiber et al., 1995).

This approach for developing ontologies is conditioned by application development. Thus, every time an application is built, the ontology that represents the knowledge required for the application is refined. The ontology can be developed by reusing others and can be integrated into ontologies of later applications. Therefore, every time an application is developed, the following processes occur (Bernaras et al., 1996):

Process 1. Specification of the application, which provides context to an application and a view of the components that the application tries to model. In this process a list of terms and tasks have to be provided. For example, in our ontology for a travel agency, we will have terms such as: `place, the name of the place, a cultural place`, etc., and tasks such as: `obtain the most suitable place for a client`, etc.

Process 2. Preliminary design based on relevant top-level ontological categories, where the list of terms and tasks developed during the previous process are used as input for obtaining several views of the global model in accordance with top-level ontological categories, for example, concept, relation, attribute, etc. This design process involves searching ontologies already developed (perhaps for other applications). These ontologies are then refined and extended to be used in the new application, as Figure 3.10 shows. Let us imagine that before developing the travel agency application, another application in the geography domain had been developed for educational purposes. The designers of the travel agency application should try to adapt the knowledge on locations of the former application to the travel domain.

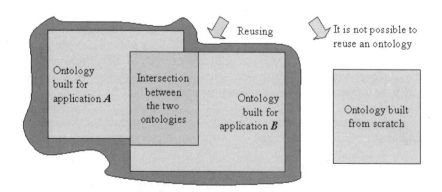

Figure 3.10: Design in KACTUS method.

Process 3. Ontology refinement and structuring to achieve a definitive design following the modularization and hierarchical organization principles. For the application the designers should follow the traditional Software and Knowledge Engineering recommendations and methodologies. Given that the travel agency ontology has concepts such as `client, transport means`, etc., we should create a separate ontology for clients, another for transport means, etc.

The KACTUS project illustrates this approach. The authors present the development of three ontologies as the result of the development of the same number of applications. The purpose of the first application is to diagnose faults in an electrical network. The second concerns scheduling service resumption after a fault in that network. By the time the development of the ontology of this application started, the fault ontology had also been built. Then, the developers refined and augmented the domain concepts by looking at the top-level ontological categories, and modified the relevant domain concepts already identified in the diagnosis ontology in order to meet the needs of restoration. Afterwards, they refined the structure of the ontology and obtained its definitive design. The third application controls the electrical network. This application is based on the other two. The ontology of this application can be considered as the junction between the domain ontology for diagnosis and service recovery planning. The union of the ontologies yields a set of sub-ontologies that belong to the intersection and other sets used for one application or the other but not for both at the same time. The sub-ontologies of the intersection are more likely to be reused, since the relevant adaptations in these ontologies should be carried out in, at least, two different applications.

3.3.5 METHONTOLOGY

This methodology was developed within the Ontology group at Universidad Politécnica de Madrid. METHONTOLOGY (Fernández-López et al., 1997; Gómez-Pérez, 1998; Fernández-López et al., 1999) enables the construction of ontologies at the knowledge level. METHONTOLOGY has its roots in the main activities identified by the software development process (IEEE, 1996) and in knowledge engineering methodologies (Gómez-Pérez et al., 1997; Waterman, 1986). This methodology includes: the identification of the ontology development process (already presented in Section 3.1), a life cycle based on evolving prototypes, and techniques to carry out each activity in the management, development-oriented, and support activities.

ODE (Blázquez et al., 1998) and WebODE (Arpírez et al., 2003) were built to give technological support to METHONTOLOGY. Other ontology tools and tool suites can also be used to build ontologies following this methodology, for example, Protégé-2000 (Noy et al., 2000), OntoEdit (Sure et al., 2002a), etc. METHONTOLOGY has been proposed[5] for ontology construction by the

---

[5] http://www.fipa.org/specs/fipa00086/ (last access, March 30, 2003)

Foundation for Intelligent Physical Agents (FIPA), which promotes inter-operability across agent-based applications.

3.3.5.1 Ontology crossed life cycles

The ontology development process of Section 3.1 was proposed on the framework of this methodology and refers to those activities performed during ontology building. This process does not identify the order in which such activities should be performed. This is the role of the ontology life cycle. METHONTOLOGY proposes an ontology building life cycle based on *evolving prototypes* because it allows adding, changing, and removing terms in each new version (prototype).

For each prototype, METHONTOLOGY proposes to begin with the schedule activity that identifies the tasks to be performed, their arrangement, and the time and resources needed for their completion. After that, the ontology specification activity starts and at the same time several activities begin inside the management (control and quality assurance) and support processes (knowledge acquisition, integration, evaluation, documentation, and configuration management). All these management and support activities are performed in parallel with the development activities (specification, conceptualization, formalization, implementation and maintenance) during the whole life cycle of the ontology.

Once the first prototype has been specified, the conceptual model is built within the ontology conceptualization activity. This is like assembling a jigsaw puzzle with the pieces supplied by the knowledge acquisition activity, which is completed during the conceptualization. Then the formalization and implementation activities are carried out. If some lack is detected after any of these activities, we can return to any of the previous activities to make modifications or refinements. When tools like the WebODE ontology editor are used, the conceptualization model can be automatically implemented into several ontology languages using translators. Consequently, formalization is not a mandatory activity in METHONTOLOGY.

Figure 3.11 shows the ontology life cycle proposed in METHONTOLOGY, and summarizes the previous description. Note that the activities inside the management and support processes are carried out simultaneously with the activities inside the development process.

Related to the support activities, the figure also shows that the knowledge acquisition, integration and evaluation is greater during the ontology conceptualization, and that it decreases during formalization and implementation. The reasons for this greater effort are:

- Most of the knowledge is acquired at the beginning of the ontology construction.
- The integration of other ontologies into the one we are building is not postponed to the implementation activity. Before the integration at the implementation level, the integration at the knowledge level should be carried out.
- The ontology conceptualization must be evaluated accurately to avoid propagating errors in further stages of the ontology life cycle.

The relationships between the activities carried out during ontology development are called *intra-dependencies*, or what is the same, they define the ontology life cycle.

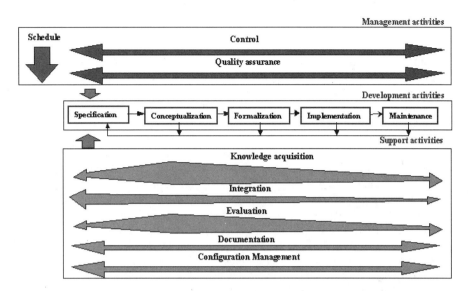

Figure 3.11: Development process and life cycle of METHONTOLOGY.

METHONTOLOGY also considers that the activities performed during the development of an ontology may involve performing other activities in other ontologies already built or under construction (Fernández-López et al., 2000). Therefore, METHONTOLOGY considers not only intra-dependencies, but also inter-dependencies. *Inter-dependencies* are defined as the relationships between activities carried out when building different ontologies. Instead of talking about the life cycle of an ontology, we should talk about crossed life cycles of ontologies. The reason is that, most of the times and before integrating an ontology in a new one, the ontology to be reused is modified or merged with other ontologies of the same domain.

Let us illustrate now the activities commented before with an ontology we made in the past. Suppose that you want to build an ontology about monatomic ions to be used in environmental-pollutants-related studies. You should know that some knowledge about chemical elements and their properties, as well as units of measure of some properties, is required to represent knowledge about ionic concentration.

Before developing the monatomic ions ontology we should look for existing ontologies that could be reused. So we looked for ontologies in the domain of chemical elements of the periodic table and for ontologies describing units of measure. It is important to mention here that the inter-dependencies between the monatomic ions ontology and other ontologies started when the requirements of the monatomic ions ontology were identified. Let us see now in more detail that process. The initial activities performed were:

a) *To find candidate ontologies to be reused.* We located the *Standard Units* ontology (Gruber, 1993b) at the Ontolingua Server; this ontology defines basic units of measure. We also located the *Chemical Elements* ontology (Fernández-

López et al., 1999), which defines the chemical elements of the periodic table. The *Chemical Elements* ontology was built with ODE (Blázquez et al., 1998) and its Ontolingua code is available at the Ontolingua Server. Finally, we found some measure units and chemical entities (*atom*, *ion*, *molecule*, and *radical*) in the Cyc upper-level ontology at the Cyc server.

b) *To inspect the content and granularity of the candidate ontologies.* The *Standard Units* ontology includes for each unit: natural language definition, physical quantity and some factors of conversion to other units of the same quantity. The Cyc ontology includes only a natural language definition.

c) *To select the ontologies to be reused.* We selected the *Chemical Elements* and the *Standard Units* ontologies because they were more suitable for our purposes, and we used Cyc ontologies for reference purposes.

d) *To evaluate the selected ontologies from a knowledge representation point of view.* The ontologists did a preliminary evaluation of the *Standard Units* and *Chemical Elements* ontologies from a KR point of view. As described in (Gómez-Pérez and Rojas, 1999), several problems were met at the *Standard Units* and *Chemical Elements* ontologies. The most important was that *Standard Units* lacked taxonomic organization since all the instances were of the root class. The result of the review process in *Chemical Elements* showed that different versions of the ontology needed to be merged to output a new unified and corrected ontology.

Simultaneously with the previous evaluation, the domain experts also did a preliminary evaluation of the *Chemical Elements* ontology as they understood its conceptual model. However, we postponed the *Standard Units* domain expert evaluation because the domain experts were unable to understand the Ontolingua code.

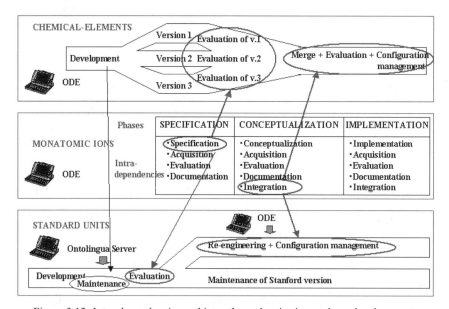

Figure 3.12: Inter-dependencies and intra-dependencies in ontology development.

As Figure 3.12 illustrates, the specification of monatomic ions provoked the evaluation of different versions of *Chemical Elements* and the evaluation of *Standard Units*. During the conceptualization activity of the *Monatomic Ions* ontology we built its conceptual model and, simultaneously, we started the integration activity with the goal of reusing definitions from the *Standard Units* and *Chemical Elements*. It was at this integration activity of the *Monatomic ions* where most of the inter-dependencies with the other ontologies appeared.

With respect to *Chemical Elements*, we evaluated each of the versions before merging them manually. Once they were merged, we evaluated the resulting ontology. During the whole process, we also performed the configuration management of *Chemical Elements*.

With respect to *Standard Units*, we re-engineered the old version and carried out the configuration management of the new one. Some of the most important motivations that we had for re-engineering the *Standard Units* ontology were:

- No conceptual model of the ontology existed, just its implementation code in the Ontolingua language.

- There was no taxonomic organization; there was a single class to which all the instances were subordinated.

- Some definitions had a poor, informal language description, which did not give any information.

Let us analyze the *Standard Units* life cycle presented in Figure 3.12. The *Standard Units* ontology was built at the beginning of the 1990s and, probably, several applications now use its definitions. Since the *Standard Units* ontology was built to the present day, only a few changes have been carried out in its version at the Ontolingua Server and several ontologies and applications reuse the ontology. So, we can say that the *Standard Units* ontology life cycle was "latent" or "hibernating". When we developed *Chemical Elements* in 1996, we identified some units of measure that did not appear at *Standard Units,* and which we added to the ontology at the Ontolingua Server. We updated the ontology with the new units but we did not carry out big changes in its structure nor in its content. Consequently, these updates could be seen as maintenance activities. And now we can say that the *Standard Units* life cycle "wakes up" when *Standard Units* is reused by the *Monatomic Ions* ontology and the re-engineering process over the *Standard Units* ontology starts. At this point, the *Standard Units* life cycle is alive since we have modified its structure and content.

It is interesting to observe in Figure 3.12 how the *Standard Units* ontology life cycle branches out in two. Thus, two *Standard Units* ontologies – the *Standard Units* at the Ontolingua Server and the re-engineered *Standard Units* – were available after running a re-engineering process on the original one. The opposite occurs with *Chemical Elements* where several ontologies coexist, each one with its own life cycle, and converge with the new life cycle of the merged *Chemical Elements* ontology after the merging process.

These confluences and forkings of life cycles call for a global management of ontologies. The configuration management of each ontology must not be carried out separately from the ones in which they are integrated, though it must be global and should affect simultaneously all the ontologies handled.

3.3.5.2 Conceptual modeling in METHONTOLOGY

In this section we present the METHONTOLOGYs proposal for ontology conceptualization. This activity deserves a special attention because it determines the rest of the ontology construction. Its objective is to organize and structure the knowledge acquired during the knowledge acquisition activity, using external representations that are independent of the knowledge representation paradigms and implementation languages in which the ontology will be formalized and implemented. Consequently, the conceptualization activity has a strong relationship with the knowledge acquisition activity.

Once the conceptual model is built, the methodology proposes to transform the conceptual model into a formalized model, which will be implemented in an ontology implementation language. That is, along this process the ontologist is moving gradually from the knowledge level to the implementation level, increasing slowly the degree of formality of the knowledge model so that it can be understood by a machine.

In that sense, in Figure 3.13 we adapt Blum's essential process model (Blum, 1996) of software engineering to the ontological engineering field. The transformation T_1, which refers to the conceptual modeling process, can be seen as a transformation of an idea of a domain into a conceptual model that describes such an idea. The transformation T_2 converts the conceptual model into a formalized model. The transformation T_3 transforms the formalized model into a model which can be executed in a computer. The figure presents T_1 and T_3 in a continuous line, and T_2 in a discontinuous one. They are represented differently because some domain knowledge may lost when transforming the conceptual model into the formalized model. This happens when the components used to create conceptual models are more expressive than those used to create formal models.

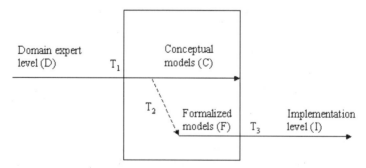

Figure 3.13: Essential process model in ontology development, adapted from Blum (1996) and Gómez-Pérez and colleagues (1997).

The conceptualization activity in METHONTOLOGY organizes and converts an informally perceived view of a domain into a semi-formal specification using a set of intermediate representations (IRs) based on tabular and graph notations that can be understood by domain experts and ontology developers. METHONTOLOGY proposes to conceptualize the ontology using a set of tabular and graphical IRs that extend those used in the conceptualization phase of the IDEAL methodology for knowledge-based systems development (Gómez-Pérez et al., 1997). These IRs bridge the gap between the people's perception of a domain and the languages used to implement ontologies. The expressiveness of the METHONTOLOGY IRs eases the transformation process. In fact, we have proven that our IRs allow conceptualizing the main components (concepts, attributes, relations, formal axioms, rules, etc.) of the traditional ontology languages described in Chapter 4: Ontolingua (Farquhar et al., 1997), LOOM (MacGregor, 1991), OKBC (Chaudhri et al., 1998) OCML (Motta, 1999), and FLogic (Kifer et al., 1995). ODE and WebODE translators transform the conceptual model of the ontology into several ontology languages, as presented in Chapter 5.

When dealing with ontologies, ontologists should not be anarchic in the use of modeling components in the ontology conceptualization. They should not define, for instance, a formal axiom if the terms used to define the axiom are not precisely defined on the ontology. METHONTOLOGY includes in the conceptualization activity the set of tasks for structuring knowledge, as shown in Figure 3.14.

The figure emphasizes the ontology components (concepts, attributes, relations, constants, formal axioms, rules, and instances) attached to each task, and illustrates the order proposed to create such components during the conceptualization activity. This modeling process is not sequential as in a waterfall life cycle model, though some order must be followed to ensure the consistency and completeness of the knowledge represented. If new vocabulary is introduced, the ontologist can return to any previous task.

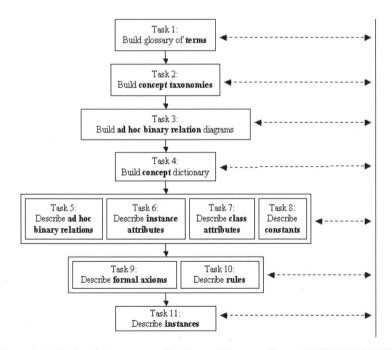

Figure 3.14: Tasks of the conceptualization activity according to METHONTOLOGY.

Our experience of building ontologies has revealed that ontologists should carry out the following tasks:

Task 1: To build the glossary of terms that identifies the set of terms to be included on the ontology, their natural language definition, and their synonyms and acronyms.

Task 2: To build concept taxonomies to classify concepts. The output of this task could be one or more taxonomies where concepts are classified.

Task 3: To build ad hoc binary relation diagrams to identify ad hoc relationships between concepts of the ontology and with concepts of other ontologies.

Task 4: To build the concept dictionary, which mainly includes the concept instances[6] for each concept, their instance and class attributes, and their ad hoc relations.

Once the concept dictionary is built, the ontologist should define in detail each of the ad hoc binary relations, instance attributes and class attributes identified on the concept dictionary, as well as the main constants of that domain.

Task 5: To describe in detail each ad hoc binary relation that appears on the ad hoc binary relation diagram and on the concept dictionary. The result of this task is the ad hoc binary relation table.

Task 6: To describe in detail each instance attribute that appears on the concept dictionary. The result of this task is the table where instance attributes are described.

Task 7: To describe in detail each class attribute that appears on the concept dictionary. The result of this task is the table where class attributes are described.

Task 8: To describe in detail each constant and to produce a constant table. Constants specify information related to the domain of knowledge, they always take the same value, and are normally used in formulas.

Once that concepts, taxonomies, attributes and relations have been defined, the ontologist should describe formal axioms (task 9) and rules (task 10) that are used for constraint checking and for inferring values for attributes. And only optionally should the ontologists introduce information about instances (task 11).

We will show now how to apply this knowledge structuring activity with an example in the traveling domain.

Task 1: To build the glossary of terms. First, the ontologist builds a glossary of terms that includes all the relevant terms of the domain (concepts, instances, attributes that represent concept properties, relations between concepts, etc.), their natural language descriptions, and their synonyms and acronyms. Table 3.1 illustrates a section of the glossary of terms of the travel ontology. It is important to mention that on the initial stages of the ontology conceptualization the glossary of terms might contain several terms that refer to the same concept. Then the ontologist should detect that they appear as synonyms.

---

[6] Although instances can be created when the ontology is used (after its construction) the ontologist can decide whether to model relevant instances or not. This field is optional.

Table 3.1: An excerpt of the Glossary of Terms of our travel ontology.

Name	Synonyms	Acronyms	Description	Type
American Airlines Flight	--	AA Flight	Flight operated by American Airlines.	Concept
Bed and Breakfast	--	--	An establishment (as an inn) offering lodging and breakfast	Concept
British Airways Flight	--	BA Flight	Flight operated by British Airways.	Concept
Business Trip	--	--	A special package for businessmen, consisting of a flight and a good quality hotel.	Concept
Camping	--	--	Temporal lodging in a camp.	Concept
Economy Trip	--	--	An economic package, usually costing less than 1000$.	Concept
European Location	--	--	A location in Europe.	Concept
Five-star Hotel	--	--	High quality hotel.	Concept
Flight	--	--	A journey by plane identified by a flight number.	Concept
Hotel	--	--	An establishment that provides lodging and usually meals, entertainment, and various personal services for the public	Concept
Iberia Flight	--	IB Flight	Flight operated by Iberia.	Concept
Japan Location	--	--	A location in Japan.	Concept
Location	Place	--	A position or site occupied or available for occupancy or marked by some distinguishing feature.	Concept
Lodging	Accommodation	--	A temporary place to stay during a trip, sleeping accommodations.	Concept
Luxury Trip	--	--	A luxury and expensive trip.	Concept
Spain Location	--	--	A location in Spain.	Concept
Train Travel	Rail Travel	--	A journey by train.	Concept
Travel	--	--	A journey from place to place.	Concept
Travel Package	--	--	A travel package that a person can ask for. It consists of one or several means of transport and one or several accommodations.	Concept
USA Location	--	--	A location in the United States.	
maximum Number of Travelers in a Plane	-	--	The maximum number of travelers in a plane at the same time.	Constant
arrival Date	--	--	Date of arrival of the trip.	Instance Attribute
departure Date	--	--	Date of departure of the trip.	Instance Attribute
final Price	--	--	The final price of the package for a traveler.	Instance Attribute
name	--	--	The location name.	Instance Attribute
single Fare	--	--	Fare of a single ticket.	Instance Attribute
departure Place (Travel, Location)	--	--	The location where the travel departs from.	Relation
placed in (Lodging, Location)	--	--	The place where a lodging is located.	Relation

Task 2: To build concept taxonomies. When the glossary of terms contains a sizable number of terms, the ontologist builds concept taxonomies to define the concept hierarchy. As explained in Section 3.3.2, any of the three approaches proposed by Uschold and Grüninger (1996) can be used: top-down, bottom-up, and middle-out.

To build concept taxonomies, the ontologist selects terms that are concepts from the glossary of terms. For this, it is really important to identify in the concept taxonomy sets of disjoint concepts, that is, concepts that cannot have common instances. METHONTOLOGY proposes to use the four taxonomic relations defined in the Frame Ontology and the OKBC Ontology: *Subclass-Of*, *Disjoint-Decomposition*, *Exhaustive-Decomposition*, and *Partition*.

A concept C_1 is a *Subclass-Of* another concept C_2 if and only if every instance of C_1 is also an instance of C_2. For example, as Figure 3.15 illustrates, Iberia Flight is a subclass of Flight, since every flight operated by Iberia is a flight. A concept can be a subclass of more than one concept in the taxonomy. For instance, the concept AA0488 is a subclass of the concepts American Airlines Flight and Iberia Flight, since it is a code-shared flight.

A *Disjoint-Decomposition* of a concept C is a set of subclasses of C that do not have common instances and do not cover C, that is, there can be instances of the concept C that are not instances of any of the concepts in the decomposition. For example, the concepts BA0068, BA0066 and BA0069 make up a disjoint decomposition of the concept British Airways Flight because no flight can be simultaneously a BA0068 flight, a BA0066 flight, and a BA0069 flight. Besides, there may be instances of the concept British Airways Flight that are not instances of any of the three classes. This disjoint decomposition is also shown in Figure 3.15.

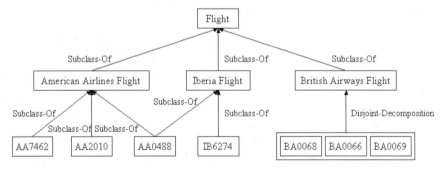

Figure 3.15: An excerpt of the Concept Taxonomy of flights in our travel ontology.

An *Exhaustive-Decomposition* of a concept C is a set of subclasses of C that cover C and may have common instances and subclasses, that is, there cannot be instances of the concept C that are not instances of at least one of the concepts in the decomposition. For example, the concepts Economy Trip, Business Trip and Luxury Trip make up an exhaustive decomposition of the concept Travel Package because there are no travel packages that are not instances of at least one of those concepts, and those concepts can have common instances. For example, a business trip can be economic or very expensive. This exhaustive decomposition is shown in Figure 3.16.

Figure 3.16. An exhaustive decomposition in our travel ontology.

A *Partition* of a concept C is a set of subclasses of C that does not share common instances but that covers C, that is, there are not instances of C that are not instances of one of the concepts in the partition. For example, Figure 3.17 shows that the concepts International Flight and Domestic Flight make up a partition of the concept Flight because every flight is either international or domestic.

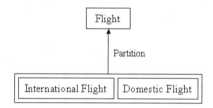

Figure 3.17: A partition in our travel ontology.

Once the ontologist has structured the concepts in the concept taxonomy, and before going ahead with the specification of new knowledge, s(he) should examine that the taxonomies contain no errors. In Section 3.8.2 we describe several types of taxonomic errors that can be evaluated: loops in the hierarchy, common instances in a partition, etc.

Task 3: To build ad hoc binary relation diagrams. Once the taxonomy has been built and evaluated, the conceptualization activity proposes to build ad hoc binary relation diagrams. The goal of this diagram is to establish ad hoc relationships between concepts of the same (or different) concept taxonomy. Figure 3.18 presents a fragment of the ad hoc binary relation diagram of our travel ontology, with the relations arrival Place and departure Place, and their inverses is Arrival Place of and is Departure Place of. Such relations connect the root concepts (Travel and Location) of the concept taxonomies of travels and locations. From an ontology integration perspective, such ad hoc relations express that the flight ontology will include the location ontology and vice versa.

Before going ahead with the specification of new knowledge, the ontologist should check that the ad hoc binary diagrams have no errors. The ontologist should figure out whether the domains and ranges of each argument of each relation delimit exactly and precisely the classes that are appropriate for the relation. Errors appear when the domains and ranges are imprecise or over-specified.

Figure 3.18: An excerpt of the Diagram of ad hoc Binary Relations of our travel ontology.

Task 4: To build the concept dictionary. Once the concept taxonomies and ad hoc binary relation diagrams have been generated, the ontologist must specify which are the properties and relations that describe each concept of the taxonomy in a concept dictionary, and, optionally, their instances.

A concept dictionary contains all the domain concepts, their relations, their instances, and their class and instance attributes. The relations specified for each concept are those whose domain is the concept. For example, the concept `Travel` has two relations: `departure Place` and `arrival Place`. Relations, instance attributes and class attributes are local to concepts, which means that their names can be repeated in different concepts. For example, the attribute `name` is repeated in the concepts `Location` and `Travel Package`. The relation `arrival Place` is also repeated in the concepts `Travel` and `Travel Package`. Table 3.2 shows a small section of the concept dictionary of our travel ontology.

Table 3.2: An excerpt of the Concept Dictionary of our travel ontology.

Concept name	Class attributes	Instance attributes	Relations
AA7462	--	--	same Flight as
American Airlines Flight	company Name	--	--
British Airways Flight	company Name	--	--
Five-star Hotel	number of Stars	--	--
Flight	--	--	same Flight as
Location	--	name size	is Arrival Place of is Departure Place of
Lodging	--	price of Standard Room	placed in
Travel	--	arrival Date company Name departure Date return Fare single Fare	arrival Place departure Place
Travel Package	--	budget final Price name number of Days travel Restrictions	arrival Place departure Place accommodated in travels in
USA Location	--	--	--

As we said before, once the concept dictionary has been built, the ontologist must describe in detail each of the ad hoc binary relations, class attributes, and instance attributes appearing in it. In addition, the ontologist must describe accurately each of the constants that appear in the glossary of terms. Though METHONTOLOGY does all these tasks, it does not propose a specific order to perform them.

Task 5: To define ad hoc binary relations in detail. The goal of this task is to describe in detail all the ad hoc binary relations included in the concept dictionary, and to produce the ad hoc binary relation table. For each ad hoc binary relation, the ontologist must specify its name, the names of the source and target concepts, its cardinality, its inverse relation and its mathematical properties. Table 3.3 shows a section of the ad hoc binary relation table of our travel ontology, which contains the definition of the relations `same Flight as`, `placed in`, and `accommodated in`, and two definitions of the relations `arrival Place` and `departure Place`.

Table 3.3: An excerpt of the ad hoc Binary Relation Table of our travel ontology.

Relation name	Source concept	Source card. (Max)	Target concept	Mathematical properties	Inverse relation
same Flight as	Flight	N	Flight	Symmetrical Transitive	--
placed in	Lodging	1	Location	--	--
accommodated in	Travel Package	N	Lodging	--	--
arrival Place	Travel	1	Location	--	is Arrival Place of
departure Place	Travel	1	Location	--	is Arrival Place of
arrival Place	Travel Package	1	Location	--	is Departure Place of
departure Place	Travel Package	1	Location	--	is Departure Place of

Task 6: To define instance attributes in detail. The aim of this task is to describe in detail all the instance attributes already included in the concept dictionary by means of an instance attribute table. Each row of the instance attribute table contains the detailed description of an instance attribute. Instance attributes are those attributes whose value(s) may be different for each instance of the concept. For each instance attribute, the ontologist must specify the following fields: its name; the concept it belongs to (attributes are local to concepts); its value type; its measurement unit, precision and range of values (in the case of numerical values); default values if they exist; minimum and maximum cardinality; instance attributes, class attributes and constants used to infer values of the attribute; attributes that can be inferred using values of this attribute; formulae or rules that allow inferring values of the attribute; and references used to define the attribute.

Table 3.4 shows a fragment of the instance attribute table of our travel ontology. Some of the previous fields are not shown for the sake of space. This table contains the attributes `price of Standard Room` of a lodging, `departure Date` and `arrival Date` of a travel, etc. The use of measurement units in numerical attributes causes the integration of the *Standard Units* ontology. This is an example of how METHONTOLOGY proposes to integrate ontologies during the conceptualization activity, and not to postpone the integration to the ontology implementation activity.

Table 3.4: An excerpt of the Instance Attribute Table of our travel ontology.

Instance attribute name	Concept name	Value type	Measurement unit	Preci-sion	Range of values	Cardi-nality
budget	Business Trip	Float	Currency Quantity	0.01	1000....3000	(0,1)
budget	Economy Trip	Float	Currency Quantity	0.01	0....1000	(0,1)
name	Location	String	--	--	--	(1,N)
size	Location	Integer	Square Meters	1	--	(1,1)
price of Standard Room	Lodging	Float	--	--	--	(0,1)
budget	Luxury Trip	Float	Currency Quantity	0.01	--	(0,1)
arrival Date	Travel	Date	--	--	--	(0,1)
company Name	Travel	String	--	--	--	(0,N)
departure Date	Travel	Date	--	--	--	(0,1)
return Fare	Travel	Float	Currency Quantity	0.01	--	(0,1)
single Fare	Travel	Float	Currency Quantity	0.01	--	(0,1)
budget	Travel Package	Float	Currency Quantity	0.01	--	(0,1)
final Price	Travel Package	Float	Currency Quantity	0.01	--	(0,1)
number of Days	Travel Package	Integer	days	1	--	(0,1)
travel Restrictions	Travel Package	String	--	--	--	(0,1)

Task 7: To define class attributes in detail. The aim of this task is to describe in detail all the class attributes already included in the concept dictionary by means of a class attribute table. Each row of the class attribute table contains a detailed description of the class attribute. Unlike instance attributes, which describe concept instances and take their values in instances, class attributes describe concepts and take their values in the class where they are defined. Class attributes are neither inherited by the subclasses nor by the instances. For each class attribute, the ontologist should fill the following information: name; the name of the concept where the attribute is defined; value type; value; measurement unit and value precision (in the case of numerical values); cardinality; the instance attributes whose values can be inferred with the value of this class attribute; etc.

Table 3.5 shows the class attributes company Name and number of Stars defined in our travel ontology. For example, the class attribute number of Stars takes value 5 in the class Five-stars Hotel. Note that, given that these attributes are not inherited, they are defined in different concepts.

Table 3.5: An excerpt of the Class Attribute Table of our travel ontology.

Attribute name	Defined at concept	Value type	Measurement unit	Precision	Cardinality	Values
company Name	American Airlines Flight	String	--	--	(1,1)	AA
company Name	British Airways Flight	String	--	--	(1,1)	BA
company Name	Iberia Flight	String	--	--	(1,1)	IB
number of Stars	Five-star Hotel	Integer	star	1	(1,1)	5
number of Stars	Four-star Hotel	Integer	star	1	(1,1)	4
number of Stars	Three-star Hotel	Integer	star	1	(1,1)	3
number of Stars	Two-star Hotel	Integer	star	1	(1,1)	2
number of Stars	One-star Hotel	Integer	star	1	(1,1)	1

Task 8: To define constants in detail. The aim of this task is to describe in detail each of the constants defined in the glossary of terms. Each row of the constant table contains a detailed description of a constant. For each constant, the ontologist must specify the following: name, value type (a number, a mass, etc.), value, the measurement unit for numerical constants, and the attributes that can be inferred using the constant. Table 3.6 shows a fragment of the constant table of our travel ontology, where the constant `maximum Number of Travelers in a Plane` is defined. The attributes that can be inferred with the constant are omitted.

Table 3.6: An excerpt of the Constant Table of our travel ontology.

Name	Value Type	Value	Measurement unit
maximum Number of Travelers in a Plane	Integer	200	person

Formal axioms and rules are important ontology modeling components in heavyweight ontologies, as we commented in Chapter 1. Formal axioms are logical expressions that are always true and are normally used to specify constraints in the ontology. Rules are generally used to infer knowledge in the ontology, such as attribute values, relation instances, etc. METHONTOLOGY proposes to describe formal axioms and rules in parallel once concepts and their taxonomies, ad hoc relations, attributes, and constants have been defined.

Task 9: To define formal axioms. To perform this task, the ontologist must identify the formal axioms needed in the ontology and describe them precisely. For each formal axiom definition, METHONTOLOGY proposes to specify the following information: name, NL description, the logical expression that formally describes the axiom using first order logic, the concepts, attributes and ad hoc relations to which the axiom refers, and the variables used.

Table 3.7: An excerpt of the Formal Axiom Table of our travel ontology.

Axiom name	Train inside Europe
Description	Every train that departs from a European location must arrive at another European location
Expression	forall(?X,?Y,?Z) ([Train Travel](?X) and [departure Place](?X,?Y) and [arrival Place](?X,?Z) and [European Location](?Y) -> [European Location](?Z))
Concepts	Train Travel European Location
Referred attributes	--
Ad hoc binary relations	departure Place arrival Place
Variables	?X ?Y ?Z

As we have already commented, METHONTOLOGY proposes to express formal axioms in first order logic. Table 3.7 shows a formal axiom in our travel ontology that states that "every train that departs from a European location must arrive at another European location"[7]. The row that corresponds to the referred attributes is empty because the axiom only mentions concepts and relations. The variables used are ?X for `Train Travel`, ?Y for the `departure Place` and ?Z for the `arrival Place`.

Task 10: To define rules. Similarly to the previous task, the ontologist must identify first which rules are needed in the ontology, and then describe them in the rule table. For each rule definition, METHONTOLOGY proposes to include the following information: name, NL description, the expression that formally describes the rule, the concepts, attributes and relations to which the rule refers, and the variables used in the expression.

METHONTOLOGY proposes to specify rule expressions using the template *if* *<conditions> then <consequent>*. The left-hand side of the rule consists of conjunctions of atoms, while the right-hand side of the rule is a single atom.

Table 3.8 shows a rule that states and establishes that "every ship that departs from Europe is arranged by the company Costa Cruises". This rule would let us infer the company name of a ship given the fact that it departs from Europe. As shown in the figure, the rule refers to the concepts `Ship` and `European Location`, to the attribute `company Name`, and to the relation `departure Place`. The variables used are ?X for the `Ship`, and ?Y for the `European Location`.

Table 3.8: An excerpt of the Rule Table of our travel ontology.

Rule name	Costa Cruises rule
Description	Every ship that departs from Europe is arranged by the company Costa Cruises
Expression	if [European Location](?Y) and Ship(?X) and [departure Place](?X,?Y) then [company Name](?X, "Costa Cruises")
Concepts	Ship European Location
Referred attributes	company Name
Ad hoc binary relations	departure Place
Variables	?X ?Y

Task 11: To define instances. Once the conceptual model of the ontology has been created the ontologist might define relevant instances that appear in the concept dictionary inside an instance table. For each instance, the ontologist should define: its name, the name of the concept it belongs to, and its attribute values, if known. Table 3.9 presents some instances of the instance table of our travel domain:

---

[7] We suppose that travel agencies work only with travel, accommodation, etc., in Europe and America.

`AA7462_Feb08_2002` and `AA7462_Feb16_2002`). Both of them are instances of the concept `American Airlines Flight`, as defined in the concept dictionary, and they have some attribute and relation values specified: `company Name`, `departure Date`, `arrival Date`, and `single Fare`. These instances could have more than one value for the attributes whose maximum cardinality is higher than one.

Table 3.9: An excerpt of the Instance Table of our travel ontology.

Instance Name	Concept Name	· Attribute	Values
AA7462_Feb08_2002	AA7462	company Name	American Airlines
		departure Date	02/08/2002
		arrival Date	02/08/2002
		single Fare	300
AA7462_Feb16_2002	AA7462	company Name	American Airlines
		departure Date	02/16/2002
		arrival Date	02/16/2002
		single Fare	300

Embedded in the conceptualization activity itself, there are a series of controls for verifying that each IR is used correctly and that the knowledge represented is valid, that is, the semantics of the conceptualized knowledge is what it should be. For example, in the formal axiom expression that appears in Table 3.7, we use the attribute `arrival Place`, applied to an instance of the concept `Train Travel`. One of the verifications proposed by the conceptualization activity is to check that this attribute can be applied to that instance, which is true, since `Train Travel` is a subclass of the concept `Travel`, in which this attribute is defined.

It is important to mention here that different domain ontologies may have different knowledge representation needs. METHONTOLOGY suggests reducing or extending the set of intermediate representations according to the KR needs in a domain as well as modifying the fields of the intermediate representations by adding, removing or changing some of the fields previously presented. For instance, if an ontologist is building a lightweight ontology with only concepts, attributes and relations between concepts, (s)he does not need to use the intermediate representations that model rules and formal axioms.
METHONTOLOGY has been used at UPM to build the following ontologies:

- *Chemicals* (Fernández-López, 1996; Gómez-Pérez et al., 1996; Fernández-López et al., 1999), which contains knowledge within the domain of chemical elements and crystalline structures, as presented in Chapter 2. OntoGeneration (Aguado et al., 1998) is a system that uses the Chemicals ontology and the linguistic ontology GUM (Bateman et al., 1995) to generate Spanish text descriptions in response to queries of the Chemistry domain.
- *Monatomic Ions* (Rojas, 1998), which gathers information about monatomic ions, as explained in Chapter 2.
- *Environmental Pollutant* ontologies (Mohedano, 2000). They represent methods to detect pollutant components in various media: water, air, soil, etc., and the maximum concentrations of these components permitted taking into account the legislation in force. This ontology was also commented on Chapter 2.

- *Silicate* (Pinilla-Ponz, 1999). It models properties in the domain of minerals, paying special attention to silicates.
- The *Reference Ontology* (Arpírez et al., 1998) and the *OntoRoadMap* ontology, which extends the former. They are ontologies in the domain of ontologies that play the role of ontology yellow pages. They provide features for describing ontologies, ontology development methodologies, tools and languages for implementing ontologies, ontology-based applications, ontology events (conferences, workshops, etc.), etc. Two applications use these ontologies: (Onto)^{2}Agent (Arpírez et al., 2000) and the OntoRoadMap application[8]. (Onto)^{2}Agent is an ontology-based WWW broker about ontologies that uses the Reference-Ontology as a knowledge source and retrieves descriptions of ontologies that satisfy a given set of constraints. The OntoRoadMap application (developed as an evolution of (Onto)^{2}Agent) uses the *OntoRoadMap* ontology. It permits users to introduce, access and modify information about ontologies, ontology tools, ontology methodologies and ontology-based applications. It was developed in the framework of the OntoWeb thematic network[9].
- The restructured version of the *(KA)^2* ontology (Blázquez et al., 1998), which contains knowledge about the scientific community in the field of Knowledge Acquisition, particularly scientists, research topics, projects, universities, etc. Also described in Chapter 2.
- *Knowledge management* ontologies (KM-LIA), which provide vocabulary in the domains of people, publications, lessons learned, hardware and software, etc., of the Laboratory of Artificial Intelligence.
- Ontologies developed at the MKBEEM project[10] (Léger et al., 2000) on the domains of traveling, cloth catalogues, and lodging, which have been used in a multilingual platform for e-commerce.
- Ontologies for describing R&D projects and their structure, documents generated in R&D projects, persons and organizations participating in them, and meetings (administrative, technical, etc.) held during a project. The Esperonto project[11] uses these ontologies on the Esperonto knowledge portal.

3.3.6 SENSUS-based method

In this section, we present a method for building the skeleton of the domain ontology starting from a huge ontology, the SENSUS ontology, described in Section 2.3.5. The method proposes to link domain specific terms to the huge ontology and to prune, in the huge ontology, those terms that are irrelevant for the new ontology we wish to build.

The result of this process is the skeleton of the new ontology, which is generated automatically using the process described below and the OntoSaurus tool described in Chapter 5.

---

[8] http://babage.dia.fi.upm.es/ontoweb/WP1/OntoRoadMap/index.html
[9] http://www.ontoweb.org/
[10] http://www.mkbeem.com/
[11] http://www.esperonto.net/

According to this method, to build an ontology in a specific domain the following processes should be taken:

Process 1: To identify seed terms (key domain terms). For example, if we wish to build an ontology on flights we could take the terms presented in Figure 3.19 as seed: `Europe-Africa flight`, `Europe-America flight`, `London-Liverpool flight` and `Madrid-Barcelona flight`.

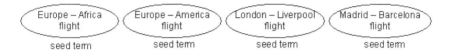

Figure 3.19: Process 1. Identify seed terms.

Process 2: To link manually the seed terms to SENSUS. As Figure 3.20 illustrates, the first two types of flight of the example are linked to SENSUS as hyponyms (subclasses) of `international flight`, and the other terms are linked as hyponyms of `domestic flight`. To perform this example we have used OntoSaurus.

Process 3: To add paths to the root. All the concepts in the path, from the seed terms to the root of SENSUS, are included. OntoSaurus provided the set of concepts presented in Figure 3.21.

Process 4: To add new domain terms. In this process, terms that could be relevant within the domain and that have not yet appeared are manually added. Then processes 2 and 3 are repeated to include concepts in the path going from the new terms to the root of SENSUS. In our example, we can add the terms `origin` and `destination`, as shown in Figure 3.22. We should also add the ascendants of the new identified terms.

Process 5. To add complete subtrees. In this process, the ontologist has to pay special attention to those nodes that have a large number of paths through them in the tree now generated. Then, for the subtree under each of these nodes, the ontologist should decide whether to add a node or not. The criterion taken into account in this process is that if many of the nodes in a subtree have been found to be relevant, then the other nodes in the subtree are likely to be relevant, too. As Figure 3.23 shows, we could add the entire subtree of `flight trip` and then the concepts `redeye` (night flight) and `nonstop flight` (a flight without intermediate landings between source and destination).

This process is done manually, since it seems that the ontologist requires some understanding of the domain to take the decision of adding new nodes. Obviously, very high level nodes in the ontology will always have many paths through them, but it is not appropriate to include the entire subtrees under these nodes.

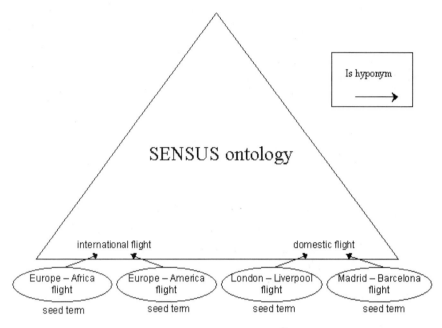

Figure 3.20: Process 2. To link the seed terms to SENSUS.

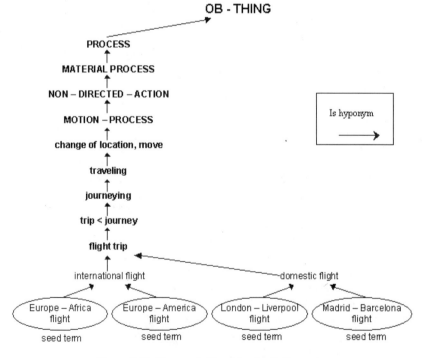

Figure 3.21: Process 3. To add paths to the root.

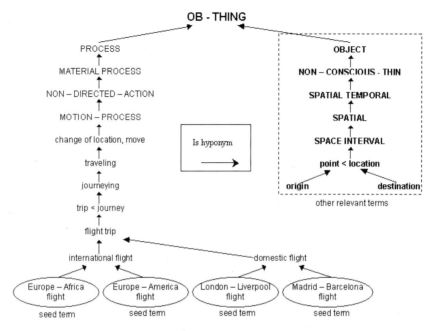

Figure 3.22: Process 4. To add new domain terms.

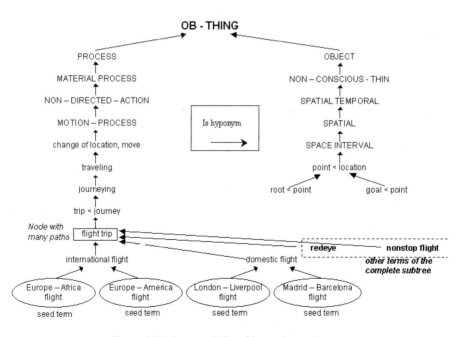

Figure 3.23: Process 5. To add complete subtrees.

The approach adopted in SENSUS promotes knowledge shareability as the same base ontology is used to develop ontologies in specific domains. A major advantage of this approach is that if two ontologies are developed independently, the broad coverage of the ontology (SENSUS) acts as a "hinge" that couples the terminology and organization of one ontology with the other (Swartout et al., 1997).

SENSUS has also been applied for building an ontology for military air campaign planning. It contains an overview of the basic elements that characterize air campaign plans such as campaign, scenario, participants, commanders, etc. (Valente et al., 1999). It also includes ontologies of weapons, systems in general, fuel, etc.

3.3.7 On-To-Knowledge

The aim of the On-To-Knowledge project (Staab et al., 2001) is to apply ontologies to electronically available information for improving the quality of knowledge management in large and distributed organizations. Some of the partners of this project are the Institute AIFB of the University of Karlsruhe, the Vrije Universiteit of Amsterdam, and British Telecom. In this project, they developed a methodology and tools for intelligent access to large volumes of semi-structured and textual information sources in intra-, extra-, and internet-based environments. The methodology includes a methodology for building ontologies to be used by the knowledge management application. Therefore, the On-To-Knowledge methodology for building ontologies proposes to build the ontology taking into account how the ontology will be used in further applications. Consequently, ontologies developed with this methodology are highly dependent of the application. Another important characteristic is that On-To-Knowledge proposes ontology learning for reducing the efforts made to develop the ontology.

The methodology also includes the identification of goals to be achieved by knowledge management tools, and is based on an analysis of usage scenarios (Staab et al., 2001).

We consider On-To-Knowledge as a methodology because it has a set of techniques, methods, principles for each of its processes, and because it indicates the relationships between such processes (e.g., recommended order, interleaving, input/outputs). The processes proposed by this methodology are shown in Figure 3.24.

Process 1: Feasibility study. On-To-Knowledge adopts the kind of feasibility study described in the CommonKADS methodology (Schreiber et al., 1999). According to On-To-Knowledge, the feasibility study is applied to the complete application and, therefore, should be carried out before developing the ontologies. In fact, the feasibility study serves as a basis for the kickoff process.

Process 2: Kickoff. The result of this process is the ontology requirements specification document that describes the following: the domain and goal of the ontology; the design guidelines (for instance, naming conventions); available

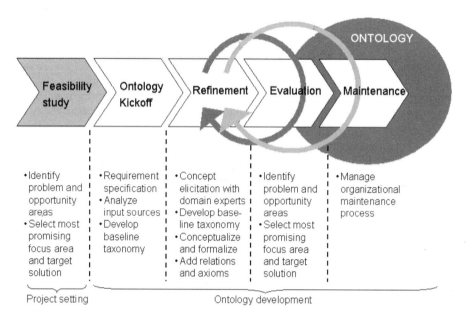

Figure 3.24: On-To-Knowledge processes (Staab et al., 2001) (© 2001 IEEE).

knowledge sources (books, magazines, interviews, etc.); potential users and use cases as well as applications supported by the ontology.

Competency questions, discussed in Section 3.3.3, can be useful to elaborate the requirements specification document. The requirement specification should lead the ontology engineer to decide about the inclusion or exclusion of concepts in the ontology, and about their hierarchical structure. In fact, this specification is useful to elaborate a draft version containing few but seminal elements. This first draft is called "baseline ontology". The most important concepts and relations are identified on an informal level.

In the kickoff process the developers should look for potentially reusable ontologies already developed.

Process 3: Refinement. The goal here is to produce a mature and application-oriented "target ontology" according to the specification given in the kickoff process. This refinement process is divided into two activities:

Activity 1: Knowledge elicitation process with domain experts. The baseline ontology, that is, the first draft of the ontology obtained in process 2, is refined by means of interaction with experts in the domain. When this activity is performed, axioms are identified and modeled. During the elicitation, the concepts are gathered on one side and the terms to label the concepts on the other. Then, terms and concepts are mapped. The On-To-Knowledge methodology proposes the use of intermediate representations to model the knowledge. In this aspect, it follows METHONTOLOGY's basic ideas. If several experts participate in the building of the ontology, it is necessary to reach an agreement.

A complementary way to enrich the ontology is to use it as seed in an ontology learning process, as explained in Section 3.5.

Activity 2: Formalization. The ontology is implemented using an ontology language. Such language is selected according to the specific requirements of the envisaged application. To carry out the formalization, On-To-Knowledge recommends the OntoEdit ontology editor, which generates automatically the ontology code in several languages. Other ontology editors that perform similar functions can be also used, as described in Chapter 5.

Process 4: Evaluation. The evaluation process serves as a proof of the usefulness of the developed ontologies and their associated software environment. The product obtained is called ontology based application. During this process two activities are carried out:

Activity 1: Checking the requirements and competency questions. The developers check whether the ontology satisfies the requirements and "can answer" the competency questions.

Activity 2: Testing the ontology in the target application environment. Further refinement of the ontology can arise in this activity.

This evaluation process is closely linked to the refinement process. In fact, several cycles are needed until the target ontology reaches the envisaged level.

Process 5: Maintenance. It is important to clarify who is responsible for the maintenance and how this should be carried out. On-To-Knowledge proposes to carry out ontology maintenance as part of the system software.

On-To-Knowledge has been adopted to build virtual enterprises, to organize corporate memories, and to help desk functionality in call centers. This last application provides customers with appropriate information on products and services and decides about the ability of a company to establish successful and stable relationships with their clients.

3.3.8 Comparing ontology development methods and methodologies

Which method or methodology is the most useful to build your ontology? To help you answer this question we have elaborated a framework to compare the following methods and methodologies: the Cyc method, Uschold and King's method, Grüninger and Fox's methodology, the KACTUS method, METHONTOLOGY, the SENSUS method, and the On-To-Knowledge methodology.

3.3.8.1 Comparison framework
The comparison framework takes into account the ontology construction strategy of methodologies and methods, their software support, the ontology development processes that they propose, and how they have been used to develop ontologies or in applications, projects, etc. This framework is based on the one presented by Fernández-López and Gómez-Pérez (2002a).

To compare the *construction strategy* of methods and methodologies we propose the following set of criteria, summarized in Table 3.10:

- Life cycle proposal. The life cycle identifies the set of stages through which the ontology moves during its life time. It also describes which activities have to be performed at each stage and how the stages are related, such as relations of precedence, simultaneity, etc. Examples of life cycles are:
  - Incremental life cycle (McCracken and Jackson, 1982). According to this approach, the ontology would grow by layers, allowing the inclusion of new definitions only when a new version is planned. This model prevents the inclusion of new definitions if they are not planned, but it does permit an incremental development.
  - Evolving prototypes (Kendall and Kendall, 1995). According to this approach, the ontology grows according to the needs. This model permits modifying, adding, and removing definitions in the ontology at any time.
- Strategy according to the application. This criterion is related to the degree of dependency of the ontology with the application using it. Considering this criterion, the methodologies and methods can be classified into the following types:
  - Application dependent. Ontologies are built on the basis of the applications that use them.
  - Application semi-dependent. The possible scenarios of ontology use are identified in the specification stage.
  - Application-independent. The process is totally independent of the uses of the ontology in applications.
- Use of core ontologies. In this criterion we analyze whether it is possible or not to use a core ontology as a starting point in the development of the domain ontology.
- Strategy to identify concepts. There are three possible strategies for identifying concepts: from the most concrete to the most abstract (bottom-up), from the most abstract to the most concrete (top-down), or from the most relevant to the most abstract and most concrete (middle-out). A more precise explanation of this criterion can be found in Section 3.3.2, where we described Uschold and King's method.

Concerning the *technological support*, it is important to know which tools give full or partial support to the methodologies and methods. Table 3.11 enumerates these tools and tool suites.

Table 3.12 summarizes the *ontology development processes* in all the methods and methodologies. Each cell of the table can be filled with three types of values. The value 'described' means that the method or methodology describes how to perform each task in the proposed activity, when to do it, who has to do it, etc. The value 'proposed' means that the methodology just identifies the process. The value 'NP' means that public documentation does not mention the non-considered activity.

Table 3.10: Summary of the construction strategies.

Feature	Cyc	Uschold & King	Grüninger & Fox	KACTUS	METHONTOLOGY	SENSUS	On-To-Knowledge
Life cycle proposal	Evolving prototypes	Non-proposed	Evolving prototypes or incremental	Evolving prototypes	Evolving prototypes	Non-proposed	Incremental and cyclic with evolving prototypes
Strategy with respect to the application	Application independent	Application independent	Application semi-dependent	Application dependent	Application independent	Application semi-dependent	Application dependent
Strategy to identify concepts	Not specified	Middle-out	Middle-out	Top-down	Middle-out	Not specified	Top-down Bottom-up Middle-out
Use of a core ontology	Yes	No	No	No	Depends on the available resources	Yes	Depends on the available resources

Table 3.11: Technological support of the approaches.

Feature	Cyc	Uschold & King	Grüninger & Fox	KACTUS	METHONTOLOGY	SENSUS	On-To-Knowledge
Tools that give support	Cyc tools	No specific tool	No specific tool	No specific tool	ODE WebODE OntoEdit Protégé-2000	No specific tool (usually OntoSaurus)	OntoEdit with its plug-ins.

Table 3.12: Summary of the ontology development process.

Feature		Cyc	Uschold & King	Grüninger & Fox	KACTUS	METHONTOLOGY	SENSUS	On-To-Knowledge[12]
Ontology management activities	Scheduling	NP	NP	NP	NP	Proposed	NP	Described[12]
	Control	NP	NP	NP	NP	Proposed	NP	Described
	Quality assurance	NP	NP	NP	NP	Proposed	NP	Described
Ontology development-oriented activities	Pre-development processes — Environment study	NP	NP	NP	NP	NP	NP	Proposed
	Feasibility study	NP	NP	NP	NP	NP	NP	Described
	Development processes — Specification	NP	Proposed	Described in detail	Proposed	Described in detail	Proposed	Described in detail
	Conceptualization	NP	NP	Described in detail	Proposed	Described in detail	NP	Proposed
	Formalization	NP	NP	Described in detail	Described	Described	NP	Described
	Implementation	Proposed	Proposed	Described	Proposed	Described in detail	Described	Described
	Post-development processes — Maintenance	NP	NP	NP	NP	Proposed	NP	Proposed
	Use	NP	NP	NP	NP	NP	NP	Proposed
Ontology support activities	Knowledge acquisition	Proposed	Proposed	Proposed	NP	Described in detail	NP	Described
	Evaluation	NP	Proposed	Described in detail	NP	Described in detail	NP	Proposed
	Integration	Proposed[13]	Proposed	Proposed	Proposed	Proposed	NP	Proposed
	Configuration management	NP	NP	NP	NP	Described	NP	Proposed
	Documentation	Proposed	Proposed	Proposed	NP	Described in detail	NP	Described
	Merging and Alignment	NP	NP	NP	NP	NP	NP	NP

[12] Each On-To-Knowledge description consists of (a) an explanation of the general ideas of how to carry out the activity; (b) references to authors that have written about such an activity; and (c) the activity software support.

[13] Cyc proposes the integration of different micro-theories.

Table 3.13: Summary of the use of methods and methodologies.

Feature	Cyc	Uschold & King	Grüninger & Fox	KACTUS	METHONTOLOGY	SENSUS	On-To-Knowledge
Projects where they have been used	High Performance Knowledge Bases (HPKB)	Enterprise Project	TOVE	KACTUS	MKBEEM, OntoWeb, Esperonto, ContentWeb, Environmental Ontologies.	Military air campaign planning (DARPA project)	On-To-Knowledge, OntoWeb, SemiPort, AIFB Website, COST action
Acceptance by external organizations	Unknown	Unknown	Unknown	Unknown	Recommended by FIPA for ontology development http://www.fipa.org/specs/fipa00086/ (last access, March 30, 2003)	Unknown	VU Amsterdam, CognIT, Aidministrator, SwissLife, EnerSearch BT, Ontoprise GmbH, DFKI Kaiserslautern, Fraunhofer Institute for Integrated Publication and Information Systems, FIZ
Ontologies created	Cyc	Enterprise Ontology	TOVE	Electrical network ontologies	- Chemicals, Monatomic Ions, Silicate and Environmental Pollutants - Reference and OntoRoadMap - $(KA)^2$ ontologies - KM ontologies - MKBEEM ontologies - Esperonto ontologies	Military air campaign planning ontologies	- Skills Management - Virtual Organization - OntoShare - OntoWeb Portal - AIFB Portal
Ontology domains	Cyc's different micro-theories	Enterprise	Enterprise	Electrical network	- Chemical and Environment Ontologies - Knowledge management - Computer Science - Travel - etc.	Military air campaign	See above
Applications that use such ontologies	- Heterogeneous DB integration - Searching of Captioned Information - Thesauri Integration	Enterprise Toolset	Enterprise Design Workbench Supply Chain Management Project	Diagnosis and service resumption in electrical networks	- OntoGeneration - OntoRoadMap - $(Onto)^2$ Agent - ODEClean - MKBEEM prototype - Esperonto Web Site - ODESeW	Unknown	See above

Finally, and in relation with the *use of ontologies* built according to a method or methodology, we have analyzed the use of the ontologies in projects; the acceptation of the methodology or method by other groups different to the one that has elaborated it; the ontologies developed following the methodology or method; the domains of such ontologies; and the systems where they have been used. Table 3.13 summarizes all these features.

3.3.8.2 Conclusions

The conclusions reached from the analysis of the tables are:

- The prevailing life cycle model is evolving prototypes, although there are approaches that do not propose any life cycle model.
- There is a wide diversity of ontology development strategies. Some approaches consider the application-dependent strategy, others the application-semidependent, and others the application-independent.
- There is also a wide diversity of strategies to identify concepts in the taxonomy, although the middle-out approach is the most commonly used.
- None of the approaches covers all the processes involved in ontology building. However, the following scale can be established between the methodologies and methods presented, from the most to the least complete.
  - METHONTOLOGY is the approach that provides the most accurate descriptions of each activity.
  - The On-To-Knowledge methodology describes more activities than the other approaches.
  - The strength of Grüninger and Fox's methodology is its high degree of formality. However, the ontology life cycle is not completely specified. Several ontologies have been developed with this methodology and some applications use these ontologies, but the methodology has only been tested on the business domain.
  - Uschold and King's method has the same omissions as Grüninger and Fox's and it is less detailed.
  - The SENSUS-based method does not mention the ontology life cycle and it has some of the shortcomings of the above approaches. However, it easily allows generating skeleton ontologies from huge ontologies.
  - Bernaras and colleagues' method has been used to build only a few ontologies and applications and it has also the aforementioned omissions.
- Most of the approaches are focused on development activities, specially on the ontology implementation, and they do not pay too much attention to other important aspects related to the management, evolution and evaluation of ontologies. This is due to the fact that the ontological engineering field is relatively new. However, a low compliance with the criteria formerly established does not mean a low quality of the methodology or method. As de Hoog (1998) states, a not very specified method can be very useful for an experienced group.
- Most of the approaches present some drawbacks in their use. Some of them have not been used by external groups and, in some cases, they have been used in a single domain.

- Most of the approaches do not have a specific tool that gives them technology support. Besides, none of the available tools covers all the activities necessary in ontology building.

3.4 Method for Re-engineering Ontologies

Ontologists can come across an ontology that might be reused in the ones that they are developing. It might happen, however, that this ontology has not been developed according to the modeling criteria and the ontological commitments that the ontologists are following. It might also be possible that the domain experts do not completely agree with the contents of the ontology to be reused. Or it might happen that the conceptual model of the ontology, or even its design, is missing and the only thing available is the ontology implementation in a formal language. In all these cases, a re-engineering process is needed.

Ontological re-engineering (Gómez-Pérez and Rojas, 1999) is defined as the process of retrieving a conceptual model of an implemented ontology and transforming this conceptual model to a more suitable one, which is then re-implemented in the same language or in another ontology language. Figure 3.25 presents the proposal of a method for re-engineering ontologies, which adapts Chikofsky and Cross II's (1990) software re-engineering schema to the ontology domain. This adaptation is an extension of METHONTOLOGY for ontology re-engineering.

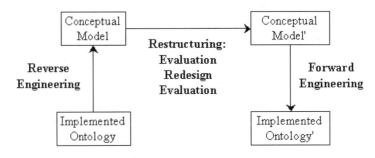

Figure 3.25: Ontological re-engineering process.

Three main activities are identified in the ontology re-engineering process:

Activity 1. Reverse Engineering. Its objective is to derive the ontology conceptual model from its implementation code. To build this conceptual model, the set of intermediate representations proposed by METHONTOLOGY might be used, as well as any ontology editor able to import ontologies in that specific language or format too.

For example, suppose that during the construction of our travel agency ontology we want to reuse an ontology of places written in Ontolingua, as shown in Figure 3.26. If we do not have the ontology conceptualization, we must obtain it from its Ontolingua code.

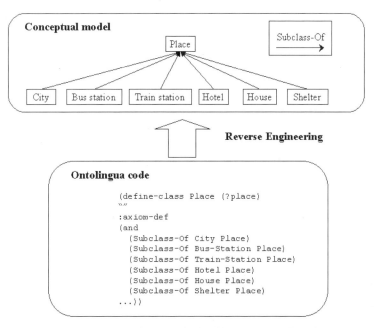

Figure 3.26: Taxonomy of places obtained by reverse engineering.

Activity 2. Restructuring. The goal here is to reorganize the initial conceptual model into a new one. The restructuring activity is carried out in two phases, analysis and synthesis. The analysis phase includes evaluation, whose general purpose is to evaluate the ontology from a technical point of view (Gómez-Pérez et al., 1995). The synthesis phase seeks to correct the ontology after the analysis phase and to document all the changes made. Hence, activities related to configuration management have appeared in this context. The aim of configuration management is to keep a record of the ontology evolution as well as a strict change control. Figure 3.27 shows an example of a control report of a change made in our travel ontology.

> **Description of the Change**: Modify the taxonomy shown in Figure 3.26 as all the classes are subclasses of the root class.
> **Need for the Change**: It is advisable to create an intermediate layer with concepts that distinguish stations and accommodations.
> **Effects of the Change**: The taxonomy has been modified and two new classes are included.
> **Alternatives**: The only alternative is the one shown in Figure 3.28.
> **Date of change**: 03/03/2002.
> **Changes made**: Changes are shown in Figure 3.28.

Figure 3.27: Change control report of the restructuring of the travel ontology.

In our example, a problem in the ontology structure has been detected during the analysis phase: there is no taxonomic organization identifying intermediate concepts between the concept `Place` and the next level of the concept taxonomy. That is, all the stations and all the accommodations are at the same level. In the synthesis phase, we can modify the conceptual model of the ontology of locations through a specialization of concepts. The objective here is to create general concepts that are superclasses of existing concepts in the old taxonomy. For example, the concepts `Bus station` and `Train station` can be defined as subclasses of the concept `Station`, and the concepts `Hotel`, `House` and `Shelter` can be defined as subclasses of the concept `Accommodation`, as shown in Figure 3.28.

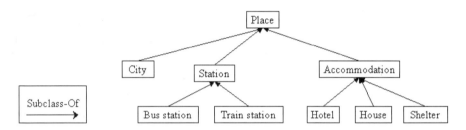

Figure 3.28: Taxonomy of places restructured.

Activity 3. Forward Engineering. The aim of this activity is to output a new ontology implementation on the basis of the new conceptual model. For example, if we need the ontology in OWL, we can implement the new conceptual model automatically with many of the ontology tools described in Chapter 5.

We tested this re-engineering method when we developed the environmental ontologies described in Section 2.4.5, because we had to re-engineer the *Standard-Units* ontology of the Ontolingua Server, as presented by Gómez-Pérez and Rojas (1999).

We also applied this method to re-engineer ontologies in the context of the IST project MKBEEM (Léger et al., 2000). The MKBEEM ontologies were developed by different groups and with two different ontology tools: CONE (Kankaanpää, 1999), a frame-based ontology editor, and WebODE (Arpírez et al., 2003), based on a combination of frames and first order logic as will be described in Chapter 5. These ontologies had to be transformed into the description logic language CARIN (Levy and Rousset, 1998) because we were interested in using the inference services provided by PICSEL (Goasdoué et al., 2000), which worked with that language. To exchange ontologies between both tools we decided to use an XMLization of CARIN, called X-CARIN. Figure 3.29 shows how ontologies developed with CONE were transformed into X-CARIN and then imported through a reverse engineering process into WebODE. There, the ontologies were re-engineered, integrated with the other ontologies, and transformed back into X-CARIN using WebODEs X-CARIN translator.

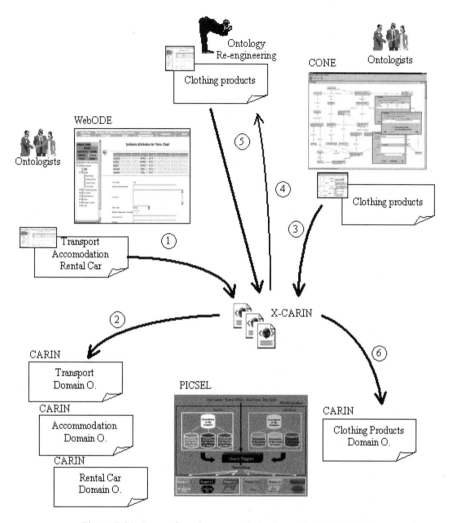

Figure 3.29: Re-engineering example in the project MKBEEM.

3.5 Ontology Learning Methods

Although one of the main purposes of ontologies is to reduce the effort during the knowledge acquisition process, acquiring knowledge for building an ontology from scratch, or for refining an existing ontology requires much time and many resources. There are, however, several approaches for the partial automatization of the knowledge acquisition process. This automatization can be carried out by means of natural language analysis and machine learning techniques. Alexander Maedche and Steffen Staab (2000a) distinguish the following ontology learning approaches:

1) *Ontology learning from texts.* Ontology learning from texts is based on the use of text corpora. A *corpus of texts* is a set of texts that should be representative of the domain (complete), prepared to be processed by a computer, and accepted by the domain experts (Enery and Wilson, 2001). To understand the different methods and techniques identified by Maedche and colleagues for ontology learning from texts, it is important to distinguish between the linguistic level and the conceptual level. The main characteristic of the linguistic level is that knowledge is described through linguistic terms, while in the conceptual level knowledge is described through concepts and relations between concepts (Brachman, 1979; Guarino, 1994). According to this distinction, the learnt concepts and relations are at the conceptual level, and the texts used during the learning are, obviously, at the linguistic level. Therefore, the different techniques of ontology learning from texts are based on how linguistic level structures are 'projected' on the conceptual level. These kind of techniques are classified into:

1.1) *Pattern-based extraction* (Hearst, 1992). Relations at the conceptual level are recognized from sequences of words in the text that follow a given pattern.

For example, in English a pattern can establish that if a sequence of n names is detected, then the n-1 first names are hyponyms of the nth. According to this pattern, the term `Spain location` could be used to obtain the hyponymy relationship between the term `Spain location` and the term `location`. This relation at the linguistic level is projected on the conceptual level as the *Subclass-Of* relation between the concept associated to the term `Spain location` and the concept associated to the term `location`.

This kind of technique is applied in the ontology field by Maedche and colleagues (Kietz et al., 2000), as well as by Aussenac-Gilles and colleagues (2000a; 2000b).

1.2) *Association rules.* Association rules were initially defined on the database field as follows (Agrawall et al., 1993): "*Given a set of transactions, where each transaction is a set of literals (called items), an association rule is an expression of the form X implies Y, where X and Y are sets of items. The intuitive meaning of such a rule is that transactions of the database which contain X tend to contain Y*". Association rules are used on the data mining process to discover information stored in databases provided that we have a rough idea of what we are looking for (Adriaans and Zantinge, 1996).

In the ontology field (Maedche and Staab, 2000b) association rules have been used to discover non-taxonomic relations between concepts, using a concept hierarchy as background knowledge, and statistics of co-occurrences of terms in texts. Thus, for example, if the word `train` frequently co-occurs with the word `travel` in the texts to be analyzed, then we could add to the ontology a relation between the concept associated to `train` and the concept associated to `travel`.

1.3) *Conceptual clustering* (Michalsky, 1980; Faure et al., 2000). A set of concepts are taken as input and then are grouped according to the semantic distance between them. A way to group concepts is to consider that two concepts belong to the same group if their semantic distance is lower than a predefined threshold. A way to calculate the distance between concepts is based on the use of the syntactical functions that the terms associated to such concepts play in the text.

For example, if `train` and `car` appear with the same syntactical function (e.g., the subject) in sentences with the same verb (e.g., `Peter travels by train`, `John travels by car`, etc.), then the concepts associated to `train` and `car` are considered semantically as close concepts and should be grouped.

Conceptual clustering is explicitly proposed in the two ontology learning methods that we will present in this section.

1.4) *Ontology pruning* (Kietz et al., 2000). The objective of ontology pruning is to elicit a domain-ontology using a core ontology and a corpus, or even several corpora of texts. A method that uses ontology pruning is presented in Section 3.5.1.

1.5) *Concept learning* (Hahn and Schulz, 2000). A given taxonomy is incrementally updated as new concepts are acquired from real-world texts. To update the taxonomy, techniques already considered in other approaches (*pattern based extraction, ontology clustering*, etc.) could be applied. A method that uses concept learning is also presented in Section 3.5.1.

2)   *Ontology learning from instances* (Morik and Kietz, 1989). Particular instances, for example, those taken from files, are used to generate the ontology.

3)   *Ontology learning from schemata.* Relational database schemas, Entity/Relationship models, and XML schemas can be used to generate ontologies by a re-engineering process.

4)   *Ontology learning for interoperability.* Semantic mappings between similar elements from two ontologies are learnt. The learned mappings can be used for ontology merging, and also when a system needs to operate with the two ontologies.

Up to now, the most well-known ontology learning methods use techniques that belong to the category of ontology learning from texts. Two of these methods will be presented in this section: Maedche and colleagues' and Aussenac-Gilles and colleagues'.

3.5.1 Maedche and colleagues' method

Maedche and colleagues' method (Kietz et al., 2000) assumes that documents from a domain describe most of the domain concepts and relations to be included in an ontology as well as the domain terminology. This method proposes to learn the ontology using as a base a core ontology (SENSUS, WordNet, etc.), which is enriched with the learned concepts.

New concepts are identified using natural language analysis techniques over the resources previously identified by the user. The resulting ontology is pruned and then focused on a specific domain by means of several approaches based on statistics. Finally, relations between concepts are established applying learning methods. Such relations are added to the resulting ontology.

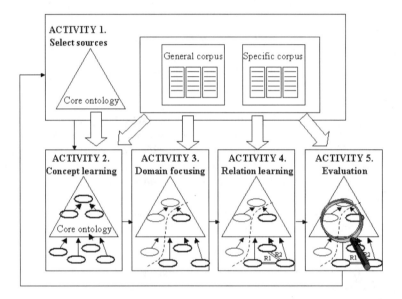

Figure 3.30: Activities followed in Maedche and colleagues' method for ontology learning.

Figure 3.30 shows the five activities proposed in this method:

Activity 1. Select sources. In this method, sources are either ontologies or documents. The process starts with the selection of a core ontology, which is used as a base in the learning process. This ontology should contain generic and domain specific concepts. In this first activity the ontologist should specify which documents should be used in the steps to follow to refine and extend the previous ontology. By its own nature, documents are heterogeneous in their formats and contents. They can be free text, semi-structured text, domain text, and generic text documents. Documents will make up two corpora: one with domain specific terms, and another with general terms.

Activity 2. Concept learning. Its goal is to acquire new generic and domain specific concepts. Both types of concepts are extracted from texts by means of mainly natural language processing (NLP) tools that use pattern-based extraction and conceptual clustering. The selection of the tools depends on the languages to be processed (Spanish, English, German, etc.).
The method suggests linking the learned concepts to the core ontology using, above all, the *Subclass-Of* relation.

Activity 3. Domain focusing. Its purpose is to prune the enriched core ontology and remove general concepts. The results of the analysis of the term frequency in the generic and the specific corpora are used to prune the ontology. The terms appearing more frequently in the domain-specific corpus than in the generic corpus should be proposed to the ontologist for deciding whether they should be kept in the whole enriched ontology.

Activity 4. Relation learning. ad hoc relations between concepts of the domain are learnt by means of pattern-based extraction and association rules.

Activity 5. Evaluation. Its goal is to evaluate the resulting ontology (the core ontology enriched and pruned in the previous activities) and to decide whether it is necessary to repeat the process again.

This method is supported by the tool Text–To–Onto (Maedche and Volz, 2001), and has been applied inside the project On-To-Knowledge, whose methodology was described in Section 3.3.7.

3.5.2 Aussenac-Gilles and colleagues' method

This is a method for ontology learning based on knowledge elicitation from technical documents, as described by Aussenac-Gilles and colleagues (2000a, 2000b). The method allows creating a domain model by analyzing a corpus with NLP tools. The method combines knowledge acquisition tools based on linguistics with modeling techniques to keep links between models and texts. During the learning process, it is assumed that (Aussenac-Gilles et al., 2002):
1) The ontology builder should have a comprehensive knowledge about the domain, so that (s)he will be able to decide which terms (nouns, phrases, verbs or adjectives) are domain terms and which concepts and relations are labeled with these domain terms.
2) Concerning the output, a similar implicit assumption is that the ontology builder knows well how the ontology will be used.

After selecting a corpus, the method proposes to obtain linguistic knowledge (terms, lexical relations, and groups of synonyms) at the linguistic level. This linguistic knowledge is then transformed into a semantic network in the normalization activity. The semantic network includes concepts, relationships between concepts and attributes for the concepts, and is implemented in the formalization activity. Figure 3.31 illustrates the activities proposed by the method:

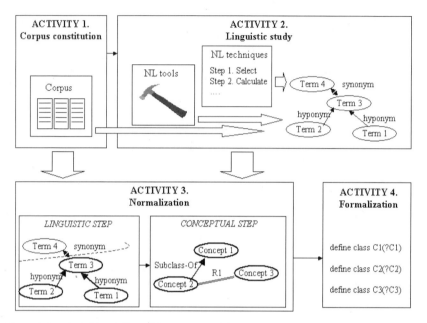

Figure 3.31: Activities followed in Aussenac-Gilles and colleagues' method for ontology learning.

Activity 1. Corpus constitution. Texts are selected from among the technical documentation available taking into account the ontology requirement specification document. The authors recommend that the selection of texts be made by an expert in texts of the domain, and that the corpus should be complete, that is, it should cover the entire domain specified by the application. To perform this activity it is very useful to have a glossary of the domain terms. Thus, the expert selects texts containing the terms of the glossary. If we compare this activity with the first activity proposed by Maedche and his colleagues, we can observe that they differ in: (1) the kind of sources used (this method does not require a core ontology to build the new ontology), and (2) the kind of texts to be analyzed, because the method shown in Section 3.5.1 is not necessarily focused on technical texts.

Activity 2. Linguistic study. This activity consists in selecting adequate linguistic tools and techniques (for example, pattern-based extraction and conceptual clustering), and applying them to the texts being analyzed to obtain domain terms, lexical relations, and groups of synonyms.

Activity 3. Normalization. The result of this activity is a conceptual model expressed by means of a semantic network. This conceptual model is rather informal and can be easily understood by the ontology builder. Normalization includes two steps: a linguistic step and a conceptual modeling one.

- During the *linguistic step*, the ontologist has to choose the relevant terms and the lexical relations (hyperonym, hyponym, etc.). According to the authors this choice is mainly subjective. Terms and lexical relations are kept when they seem important both for the domain and for the application where the ontology will be used. Also in this linguistic step, the ontologist adds a natural language definition to these terms according to the senses they have in the source texts. If there are terms with several meanings, the most relevant senses are taken.
- During the *conceptual step*, terms and lexical relations are transformed into concepts and semantic relations, which are defined in a normalized form using the terms associated to concepts and relations.

The result of the normalization activity has to be checked in accordance with differentiation rules that require that for any given concept the following information should be made explicit in the model:
- The concept must have, at least, one common attribute or relation with its father concept (generally an inherited attribute or relation).
- The concept must have, at least, one specific attribute or relation that makes it different from its father concept.
- The concept must have, at least, one property that makes it different from its sibling concepts.

Activity 4. Formalization. Concepts and relations of the semantic network are implemented in a formal language.

Several tools give support to different activities of this method. Lexter (Bourigault et al., 1996) is used in the linguistic study activity to obtain domain terms. Géditerm (Aussenac-Gilles, 1999) and Terminae (Biébow and Szulman, 1999) are used in the normalization activity to choose terms, and Terminae is also used in the formalization activity. This method was applied, as an experiment, to organize the concepts of the Knowledge Engineering domain in French (Aussenac-Gilles et al., 2000a).

3.6 Ontology Merging Methods and Methodologies

Ontologies aim to capture consensual knowledge of a given domain in a generic and formal way, to be reused and shared across applications and by groups of people. From this definition we could wrongly infer that there is only one ontology for modeling a domain. However, we can find on the literature several ontologies that model the same knowledge in different ways. For instance, as we saw in Section 2.2, there are several top-level ontologies that differ in the criteria followed to classify the most general concepts of the taxonomy, and in the e-commerce field there are several standards and joint initiatives for the classification of products and services (UNSPSC, e-cl@ss, RosettaNet, NAICS, SCTG, etc.). This heterogeneity of ontologies also happens in many domains (medicine, law, art, sciences, etc.).

Noy and Musen (1999) defined ontology alignment and merging as follows: (1) *ontology alignment* consists in establishing different kinds of mappings (or links) between two ontologies, hence preserving the original ontologies; and (2) *ontology merging* proposes to generate a unique ontology from the original ontologies. This section will be focused on ontology merging, though some ideas presented in this section can be used for aligning ontologies. In fact, before merging two ontologies there has to be a correspondence between terms of the ontologies to merge. This section presents the following methods: ONIONS (Steve et al., 1998; Gangemi et al., 1999), FCA-Merge (Stumme and Maedche, 2001) and PROMPT (Noy and Musen, 2000).

3.6.1 ONIONS

One of the most elaborated proposals for ontology merging is ONIONS, developed by the Conceptual Modeling Group of the CNR in Rome, Italy. With this method we can create a library of ontologies originated from different sources. In the first stages of the integration, the sources are unified without considering the generic theories that will be used in the modeling (part-whole or connectedness theories, for example). Later, these theories are incorporated as a base of the library and they are integrated as faces of the same polyhedron. In this way, the ontologies of the library are connected through the terms of the shared generic theories.

The specific activities proposed by ONIONS are shown in Figure 3.32:
Activity 1. The creation of a corpus of validated sources. The selection of sources (electronic dictionaries, informal is-a hierarchies, etc.) is made taking into account their diffusion and validation inside the domain community, for example, traveling.

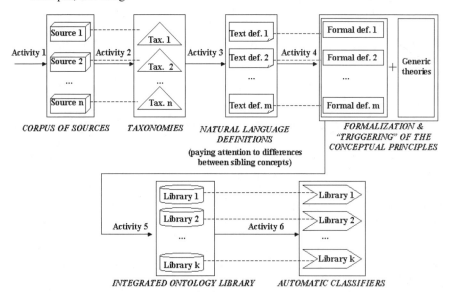

Figure 3.32: Activities followed in the ONIONS method for ontology merging.

Activity 2. Taxonomic analysis. The taxonomy contained in each single source is inferred.

Activity 3. Local definition analysis. A unified definition in natural language is given for each concept of the corpus. When the unified definition is created, it is important to establish the differences between sibling concepts. For example, if we have the sibling concepts domestic flight and international flight, we have to distinguish them by introducing in the definitions expressions such as "the departure and the arrival places belong to the same country" or "the departure and the arrival places belong to different countries". It is also important to detect and remove ambiguities and modal expressions ("it is usually characterized by..."). This activity is called "local" because the definitions are not yet connected through generic theories.

Activity 4. Multi-local definition analysis: triggering paradigms. In this activity, each term is formalized without including formal axioms. The definition can contain terms like *Subclass-Of*, *Part-Of*, *Transmitted-By*, etc., which have to be searched in theories containing them. This activity is called "multi-local" because the links between the ontology definitions and the generic theories have to be made explicit. For instance, in a definition that contains the term *Part-Of*, we have to specify that such a term should be defined in a mereology theory.

Activity 5. The building of an integrated ontology library. The definitions are enriched with formal axioms, and domain and generic ontologies are integrated in the same library. Sometimes, the generic ontologies may have to be extended and integrated in the library since they are not intended to be used in all the different domain ontologies.

Activity 6. The classification of the library. The ontology libraries are implemented in a language with automatic classification capabilities, such as LOOM.

In this process, we should make a clear distinction between the linguistic level and the conceptual level. So, polysemy, homonymy and synonymy appear:
- *Polysemy.* Different concepts have to be defined for any set of polysemic senses of a term. Polysemy occurs when two concepts with overlapping or disjoint meanings have the same name. For example, flight can be: an instance of traveling by plane; a scheduled trip by plane between designated airports; etc., as we explained in Section 1.5. Therefore, a different concept for each meaning of flight has to be created.
- *Homonymy.* It occurs when two disjoint concepts have the same name. For example, flight in the sense of instance of traveling by plane, and flight meaning a set of steps between one floor or landing. The homonymy has to be solved using a different name for each concept, or preventing the homonyms to be included in the same module namespace.
- *Synonymy.* It is the converse of homonymy, and occurs when two concepts with different names has the same meaning. Synonyms can be preserved linked to the concept.

When the library is built, the activities to incorporate new ontologies are (Gangemi et al., 1999):

Activity 7. Ontology representation. Each ontology is implemented in the language of the library. For example, the authors of this method use the LOOM language.

Activity 8. Text analysis and formalization. If texts on the domain of the ontologies are available, they are analyzed and formalized.

Activity 9. Integration of intermediate products. The intermediate products obtained in the previous activities are integrated in the library. To carry out this activity the difference between each of the sibling concepts is obtained, and this difference is formalized by axioms that reuse (if available) concepts and relations of the library. The new concepts are linked to the library through the *Subclass-Of* and *Superclass-Of* relations. Moreover, the aforementioned synonym, homonym and polysemy terms have to be dealt with. A term of a new source can have some of these relations with another term of a new source, or with a term of the library.

Activity 10. Ontology mapping. The source ontologies are explicitly mapped in the integrated ontologies to allow interoperability (maybe partial). The only explicit mappings are *equivalent* and *coarser equivalent*. The equivalent mapping is $C_1 = C_2$, whereas the coarser equivalent mapping is $C_1 = C_2 \cup C_3$, where C_2 and C_3 are disjoint.

The library ON.9.2 has been created with ONIONS and it unifies medical ontologies like GALEN or UMLS. These medical ontologies have been presented in Chapter 2. Nowadays, ONIONS is evolving from the versions presented in the mid-1990s. The last version is more tightly integrated with foundational ontologies and linguistic processing. We do not present it here because it has not been published yet. However, it is being applied to several industrial projects (banking regulations, service-level agreements, fishery terminologies, etc.).

3.6.2 FCA-Merge

FCA-Merge (Stumme and Maedche, 2001) was developed at the Institute AIFB of the University of Karlsruhe, Germany. This approach is very different from the other approaches presented in this section. FCA-Merge takes as input the two ontologies to be merged and a set of documents on the domains of the ontologies, as shown in Figure 3.33. The merging is performed by extracting, from the documents, instances that belong to concepts of both ontologies. Thus, if the concept C_1 of the ontology O_1 has instances in the same documents as the concept C_2 of the ontology O_2, then C_1 and C_2 are candidates to be considered the same concept. To establish this relation between concepts and documents, we have created a table for each ontology. Each table relates each concept C of the associated ontology with the documents where instances of C appear. A lattice structure is generated from the tables and, finally, the merged taxonomy is obtained from the structure. At present, this method works only for lightweight ontologies.

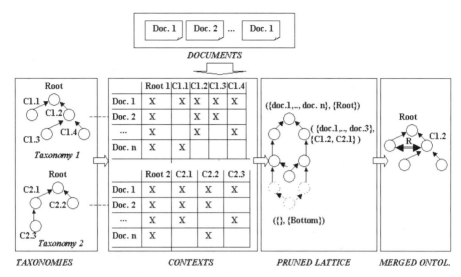

Figure 3.33: General view of FCA-Merge.

An algebra $(L; \wedge, \vee)$ is called a lattice[14] if L is a nonempty set, $\wedge$ and $\vee$ are binary operations on L, both $\wedge$ and $\vee$ are idempotent, commutative, and associative, and they satisfy the absorption law. The lattices used by Stumme and Maedche (2001) can be expressed:

- Each element of L is a pair of sets $(\{d_1, d_2, ..., d_n\}, \{c_1, c_2, ..., c_m\})$, where each d_i is a document, and each c_i is a concept. $\{c_1, c_2, ..., c_m\}$ represents the concept $c_1 \cap c_2 \cap ... \cap c_m$.
- $(A,B) \wedge (A',B') = (A \cap A', B'')$, where B'' contains every concept of B and every concept of B'.
- $(A,B) \vee (A',B') = (A \cup A', B'')$, where the concept represented by B'' is the union of the concept represented by B and the concept represented by B'.
- Two elements (A,B) and (A',B') of L are graphically linked if and only if $A \subseteq A'$.

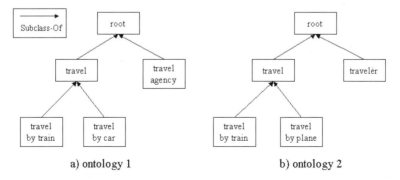

a) ontology 1   b) ontology 2

Figure 3.34: Sample ontologies to be merged through FCA-Merge.

---

[14] http://mathworld.wolfram.com/Lattice.html

Suppose that we want to merge the two ontologies of Figure 3.34 with FCA-merge. To do this with the FCA-Merge method the following activities must be carried out:

Activity 1. To extract instances. We get a table for each ontology to merge, by using NL analysis tools. Each table relates each document with the ontology concepts that have instances in the document. For example, Tables 3.14 and 3.15 show the concepts of the ontology O_1 and O_2 respectively, related to the documents where they have instances. Thus, the concept `travel` of O_1 has instances in the documents 1, 2, 3 and 4, and the concept `travel` of O_2 has instances in the same documents. For the sake of clarity, we will add a suffix to every term to distinguish the source ontologies where they are defined. Thus, for instance, the terms `travel_1` and `travel_2` are used to refer to the terms `travel` of O_1 and `travel` of O_2 respectively.

Table 3.14: Appearance of instances of the O_1 concepts in the documents considered.

	root	travel	travel agency	travel by train	travel by car
doc1	X	X		X	X
doc2	X	X	X	X	X
doc3	X	X	X		X
doc4	X	X	X	X	
doc5	X				

Table 3.15: Appearance of instances of the O_2 concepts in the documents considered.

	root	travel	traveler	travel by train	travel by plane
doc1	X	X		X	
doc2	X	X	X	X	X
doc3	X	X	X		X
doc4	X	X		X	X
doc5	X		X		

Activity 2. To generate the pruned concept lattice structure. From the tables generated in the former activity, a lattice structure is automatically generated and pruned. To do this, the following tasks are carried out:

Task 2.1. Lattice structure generation. Stumme and Maedche (2001) define each lattice node as a combination of columns of the tables. A node is represented by a pair composed by a set of documents and the set of concepts from the two ontologies that have instances in such documents. It is represented as:

```
({document_1, document_2, ... , document_n},
    {concept_1, concept_2, ... , concept_m})
```

For example, in Figure 3.35 the node (`{doc2, doc3, doc4}`, `{travel_agency_1, travel_by_plane_2}`) represents those concepts that have instances in the documents 2, 3 and 4. A node N_1 is a child of other node N_2 if and only if the set of documents of N_1 is included in the set of documents of N_2.

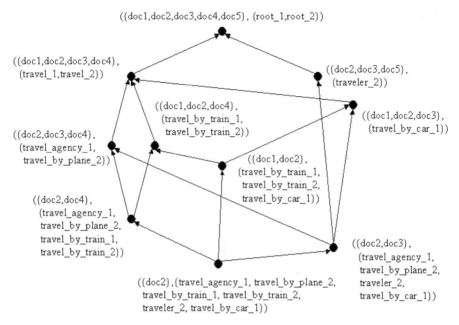

Figure 3.35: Lattice structure generated by FCA-Merge for the ontologies of Figure 3.34 and the documents of Tables 3.14 and 3.15.

The node ({doc2, doc3, doc4}, {travel_agency_1, travel_by_plane_2}) is a child of the node ({doc1, doc2, doc3, doc4}, {travel_1, travel_2}) because {doc2, doc3, doc4} is included in {doc1, doc2, doc3, doc4}.

Task 2.2. Lattice structure pruning. Once the lattice structure has been generated, it is pruned. A node remains in the lattice structure if and only if it represents a concept of some of the two source ontologies, or has some child that represents a concept of some of the two source ontologies. Otherwise, it is pruned.

For example, as we can see in Figure 3.36, ({doc2, doc3, doc4}, {travel_agency_1, travel_by_plane_2}) remains in the pruned lattice, since it represents both the concept travel_agency_1 and travel_by_plane_2. However, the node ({doc2, doc3}, {travel_agency_1, travel_by_plane_2, traveler_2, travel_by_car_1}) should be removed from the lattice structure, since such a node represents the intersection travel_agency_1 ∩ traveler_2 ∩ travel_by_car_1 or the intersection

`travel_by_plane_2 ∩ traveler_2 ∩ travel_by_car_1`,
but it does not represent a single concept of any ontology, and no concept of any ontology is represented by some child node.

The result of pruning the lattice of Figure 3.35 appears in Figure 3.36, where dashed lines mean that the edge and its origin node have been pruned, and where continuous lines are used for edges kept in the lattice.

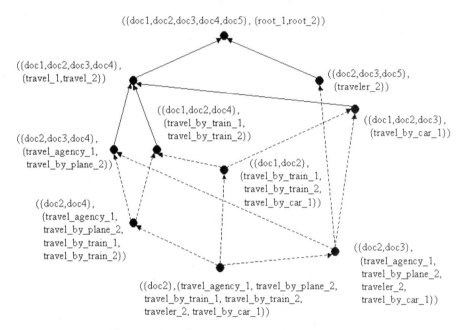

Figure 3.36: Lattice structure pruned by FCA-Merge.

Activity 3. To derive the merged ontology. Starting from the pruned lattice structure, the engineer obtains the target ontology. This activity can be software aided, although the role of the ontologist is fundamental. Some of the decisions to be made for each node are:

- If the node really represents a single concept. For example, the node (`{doc2, doc3, doc4}`, `{travel_agency_1, travel_by_plane_2}`) should be revised, since the ontologist may suspect that the terms `travel_agency` and `travel_by_plane` do not represent the same concept. This may happen because only a few documents have been used for merging the two ontologies. The Figure 3.37 shows that we have decided to generate two concepts from this node: `travel agency` and `travel by plane`.

- If the node could represent a relation. Relations can be obtained from the intersection of concepts. For example, the same node (`{doc2, doc3, doc4}`, `{travel_agency_1, travel_by_plane_2}`) could derive the following ad hoc relation: a travel agency `recommends` a travel by plane. This relation is shown in Figure 3.37.

As in any process that uses texts to extract knowledge, a crucial decision in FCA-Merge is which documents should be selected.

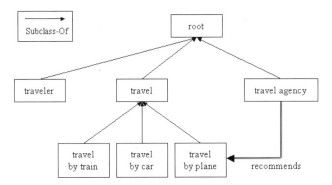

Figure 3.37: Resulting ontology from merging the ontologies of Figure 3.34.

3.6.3 PROMPT

The PROMPT method (Noy and Musen, 2000) has been elaborated by the Stanford Medical Informatics group at Stanford University. The main assumption of PROMPT is that the ontologies to be merged are formalized with a common knowledge model based on frames. A plug-in of Protégé-2000 merges ontologies according to the PROMPT method. In fact, this section is intertwined with Section 5.3.1, where we describe how to use the PROMPT plug-in.

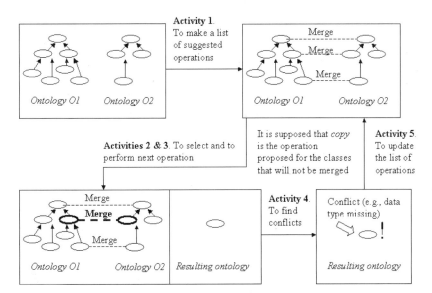

Figure 3.38: Activities followed in the PROMPT method for ontology merging.

As we can observe in Figure 3.38, this method proposes first to elaborate a list with the operations to be performed to merge the two ontologies (e.g., merge two classes, merge two slots, etc.). This activity is carried out automatically by the PROMPT plug-in. Afterwards, a cyclic process starts. In each cycle the ontologist selects an operation of the list and executes it. Then a list of conflicts resulting from the execution of the operation must be generated, and the list of possible operations for the following iterations is updated. Some of the new operations are included in the list because they are useful to solve the conflicts.

Let us suppose that we want to merge the ontologies of Figure 3.39 using the PROMPT method.

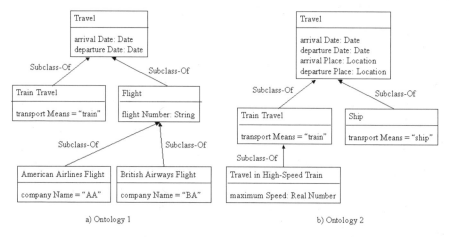

a) Ontology 1   b) Ontology 2

Figure 3.39: Sample ontologies to be merged through PROMPT.

The set of activities to be performed are:

Activity 1. To make the initial list of suggested operations. The set of ontology-merging operations here identified includes both the operations normally performed during traditional ontology editing and the operations specific to merging and alignment and these are[15]:

- Creating a new class in the new ontology by merging classes of the original ontologies.
- Creating a new slot in the new ontology by merging slots of the original ontology.
- Creating a new binding between a slot and a class in the new ontology by merging bindings between a slot and a class of the original ontologies.
- Creating a new class in the new ontology by performing a deep copy of a class from one of the original ontologies. A deep copy consists in copying all the parents of a class up to the root of the hierarchy, and all the classes and slots it refers to.

---

[15] This catalogue of possible operations might grow as PROMPT authors gain more experience.

- Creating a new class in the new ontology by performing a shallow copy of a class from one of the original ontologies. A shallow copy consists in copying only the class and not its parents or the classes and slots it refers to.

The initial list of possible operations for the two ontologies of Figure 3.39 would be the one that appears in Table 3.16. We propose to merge those classes that have similar names in both ontologies (e.g., Travel of *Ontology 1*, and Travel of *Ontology 2*). We also propose to make a deep or shallow copy of the classes that are not common to both ontologies, depending on whether they have subclasses (e.g., Flight of *Ontology 1*) or not (e.g., Ship of *Ontology 2*) respectively.

Table 3.16: Initial list of possible operations.

Operation	Travel Ontology 1	Travel Ontology 2
Merge	Travel	Travel
Merge	Train Travel	Train Travel
Deep copy	Flight	--
Shallow copy	--	Ship
Shallow copy	--	Travel in High-Speed Train
Shallow copy	American Airlines Flight	--
Shallow copy	British Airlines Flight	--

The following process is repeated until the two ontologies are merged:

Activity 2. To select next operation. The ontologist chooses an operation of the list. This decision might be based on different aspects: what (s)he wants to focus on, what (s)he considers important, etc. For example, the ontologist may decide that (s)he is only interested in merging parts of the ontology and just ignore other parts. Let us suppose that, in our travel domain, the ontologist chooses to merge the class Travel of both ontologies.

Activity 3. To perform the selected operation. The PROMPT plug-in executes the operation selected by the ontologist in the previous activity. After this point, the ontologist might order the PROMPT plug-in to carry out additional changes associated to the proposed operation. For instance, when the merging of the class travel of both ontologies is carried out, all the original slots of travel in *Ontology 1*, and of *Ontology 2* can be included in the resulting class.

Activity 4. To find conflicts. This activity is performed by analyzing the resulting ontology. The following conflicts might appear in the resulting ontology after the execution of these operations[16]:

- naming conflicts (more than one frame with the same name);
- dangling references (a frame refers to another frame that does not exist);
- redundancy in the class hierarchy (more than one path from a class to a parent other than root); and
- slot-value restrictions that violate class inheritance.

Following with our example, when we create the class `Travel` in the resulting ontology, the attributes `arrival Place`, `departure Place`, `arrival Date` and `departure Date` must be included though the classes defining their datatypes (`Location` and `Date`) are not.

Activity 5. To update the list of operations. For updating the list the PROMPT plug-in does not only consider the linguistic-similarity but also the structure of the ontology. This activity could be carried out with the algorithm AnchorPROMPT (Noy and Musen, 2001), though this is not the only option. AnchorPROMPT finds mappings between classes of two ontologies by means of the structure of such ontologies.

Besides, the PROMPT plug-in analyzes the relationships and definitions of the concepts that were involved in the latest operation executed.

Table 3.17 shows the updated list of possible operations after merging the class `Travel` of both ontologies. As we can see, the proposal of copying the data types `Date` and `Location` is found from the conflict list.

Table 3.17: Updated list of possible operations after the first cycle.

Operation	Travel Ontology 1 term	Travel Ontology 2 term
Copy	Data type `Date`	Data type `Date`
Copy	Data type `Location`	Data type `Location`
Merge	`Train Travel`	`Train Travel`
Deep copy	`Flight`	--
Shallow copy	--	`Ship`
Shallow copy	--	`Travel by High-Speed Train`
Shallow copy	`American Airlines Flight`	--
Shallow copy	`British Airlines Flight`	--

After performing several iterations, the resulting ontology of our example might be the one appearing in Figure 3.40.

---

[16] As with the merge operations, this catalogue of possible conflicts might grow as PROMPT authors gain more experience.

To perform the merge of our two travel ontologies, we have used the PROMPT plug-in, which gives support to this method.

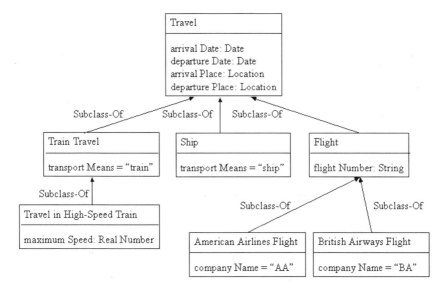

Figure 3.40: Ontology resulting from merging the ontologies of Figure 3.39.

3.7 Co4: a Protocol for Cooperative Construction of Ontologies

One of the essential characteristics of ontologies is that they provide consensual knowledge in a given domain. However, most of the methods previously presented do not propose guidelines for reaching consensus when ontologies are built cooperatively. We will describe a protocol for reaching consensus between different knowledge bases.

Co4 (Rechenmann, 1993; Euzenat, 1995; 1996) is a protocol developed at INRIA for the collaborative construction of knowledge bases (KBs). Its goal is to allow discussing and committing to the knowledge in the KBs of a system.

The protocol takes as an input a set of KBs organized in a tree. The leaves of this tree are called user KBs, and the intermediate nodes, group KBs. The user KBs do not need to have consensual knowledge, while group KBs represent the consensual knowledge among its sons (called subscriber KBs). A KB can be subscribed to only one group KB. Besides, the knowledge in a KB can be transferred to another KB.

Let us think about two groups developing ontologies in Europe (group 1.1 and group 1.2) and two groups in America (group 2.1 and group 2.2) who are building collaboratively our travel agency ontology. Figure 3.41 represents a possible KB tree. The European groups must reach consensus in KB.1, and the American groups must reach consensus in KB.2. Moreover, all of them must reach consensus in the KB.0.

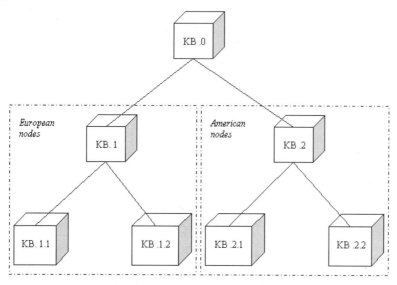

Figure 3.41: KB tree structure of the travel agency ontology construction according to the Co4 protocol.

To reach consensus for different KBs, every KB modification proposal must be submitted to the upper node in the tree, so that it can be analyzed by the rest of the sibling groups. The modification proposal is accepted only when all the sibling groups accept it.

Let us suppose that group 1.1 proposes a modification to be accepted by all the groups. Figure 3.42 shows the process followed until consensus is reached:
(1) The KB 1.1 sends a message to the KB 1.
(2) The KB 1 sends a call for comments to all its subscriber KBs (in our case, the KB 1.2).
(3) The KB 1.2 replies.
(4) The KB 1 sends the decision to all its subscribers.

If the modification proposal is accepted, the European groups have reached consensus, and the process follows on:
(5) The KB 1 sends the proposal to the KB 0.
(6) The KB 0 transmits a call for comments to the KB 2.
(7) The KB 2 sends the call for comments to its subscriber KBs (KB 2.1 and KB 2.2).
(8) The KB 2.1 and the KB 2.2 send their replies to the KB 2.
(9) The KB 2 replies to the KB 0.

If the proposal is accepted, that is, if there is a general agreement, the KB 0 propagates the acceptance decision to all its subscriber KBs. This decision is sent recursively until the leaves of the KB tree are reached, as shown at the bottom of Figure 3.42.

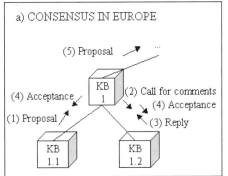
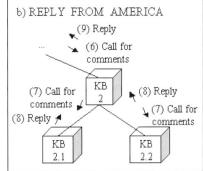

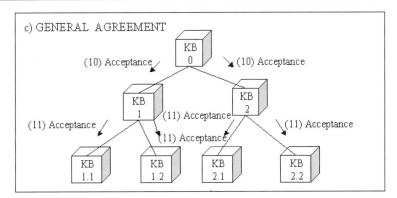

Figure 3.42: Example of agreement following the Co4 model.

In the process described above, we have supposed that all the reply messages from subscriber KBs to their corresponding group KB accept the modification proposal. However, any of them could have rejected it, what means lack of agreement.

One of the characteristics of this protocol is that the absence of agreement about a modification proposal does not prevent other users from accepting the modification. For example, if the KB 1.1 modification proposal is only accepted by the KB 1.2 and the KB 2.1, then the modification will be carried out in all the European KBs and in the American KB 2.1, but not in the KB 0 nor in the KB 2.2.

Co4 also considers the possibility of subscribing a new KB when the construction of the rest of KBs has already started. In this case, all the knowledge that has been already agreed by the KB group to which the KB subscribes is included in this KB.

Moreover, independent KBs can take part as "observers", so they can see any modifications in the tree but cannot submit them.

Co4 originated from two experiences with knowledge bases in the domain of molecular genetics. The first, ColiGene (Perrière and Gautier, 1993), describes the regulation mechanism of gene expression in the *E. coli* bacterial genome. The second allows the description and manipulation of mammal genomic maps at the cytogenetic, genetic, and physical levels. The Co4 protocol is supported by the Co4 system (Alemany, 1998).

3.8 Methods for Evaluating Ontologies

As any other resource used in software applications, the content of ontologies should be evaluated before (re)using it in other ontologies or applications. In that sense, we could say that it is unwise to publish an ontology or to implement a software application that relies on ontologies written by others (even yourself) without evaluating first its content, that is, its concepts definitions, taxonomy and axioms. A well-evaluated ontology will not guarantee the absence of problems, but it will make its use safer.

The first works on ontology content evaluation started in 1994 (Gómez-Pérez, 1994a; 1994b). In the last two years the interest of the Ontological Engineering community in this issue has grown. The main efforts to evaluate ontology content were made by Gómez-Pérez (1996; 2001) in the framework of METHONTOLOGY, and by Guarino and colleagues (Welty and Guarino, 2001) with the OntoClean method.

This section summarizes both approaches and presents a few definitions of the most common terms used in this area. However, we will not evaluate specific ontologies implemented in a given language, nor how well-known ontology development tools perform content evaluation. We will present two approaches for evaluating taxonomies.

3.8.1 Ontology evaluation terminology

A study of the knowledge based systems (KBS) evaluation ideas served as a precedent for evaluating ontologies and also for learning from KBS successes and mistakes (Gómez-Pérez, 1994b). The main ideas taken from this study were committed to prepare a framework for ontology evaluation, which includes: (1) the division of evaluation into two kinds: technical (carried out by developers) and users' evaluation; (2) the provision of a set of terms for ontology evaluation process and the standard definitions of such terms; (3) the definition of a set of criteria to carry out the user's and the technical evaluation processes; (4) the inclusion of evaluation activities in methodologies for building ontologies; (5) the construction of tools for evaluating existing ontologies; and (6) the inclusion of evaluation modules in tools used to build ontologies.

With regard to terminology and its definitions, the main terms (borrowed from the KBS evaluation field) are (Gómez-Pérez et al., 1995): "evaluation", "verification", "validation" and "assessment".

Ontology evaluation (Gómez-Pérez, 1996) is a technical judgment of the content of the ontology with respect to a frame of reference[17] during every phase and between phases of their lifecycle. Ontology evaluation includes ontology verification and ontology validation. Ontology evaluation should be carried out on the following components at the ontology:

- Every individual definition and axiom.
- Collections of definitions and axioms stated explicitly in the ontology.
- Definitions imported from other ontologies.
- Definitions that can be inferred from other definitions and axioms.

Ontology Verification refers to building the ontology correctly, that is, ensuring that its definitions[18] implement correctly the ontology requirements and competency questions, or function correctly in the real world.

Ontology Validation refers to whether the ontology definitions really model the real world for which the ontology was created. The goal is to prove that the world model (if it exists and is known) is compliant with the world modeled formally.

Finally, **Ontology Assessment** is focused on judging the ontology content from the user's point of view. Different types of users and applications require different means of assessing an ontology.

In summary, the goal of the evaluation process is to determine what the ontology defines correctly, what it does not, and what it does incorrectly. To evaluate the content of a given ontology, the following criteria were identified (Gómez-Pérez, 1996): consistency, completeness and conciseness.

Consistency refers to whether it is possible to obtain contradictory conclusions from valid input definitions. A given definition is consistent if and only if the individual definition is consistent and no contradictory knowledge can be inferred from other definitions and axioms.

Completeness. Incompleteness is a fundamental problem in ontologies, even more when ontologies are available in such an open environment as the Semantic Web. In fact, we cannot prove the completeness of an ontology nor the completeness of its definitions, but we can prove the incompleteness of an individual definition, and therefore we can deduce the incompleteness of an ontology if at least one definition is missing in the established reference framework. So, an ontology is complete if and only if:

- All that is supposed to be in the ontology is explicitly stated in it, or can be inferred.

---

[17] A frame of reference can be: requirements specifications, competency questions (Grüninger and Fox, 1995) the real-world, etc.
[18] A definition is written in natural language (informal definition) and in a formal language (formal definition).

- Each definition is complete. This is determined by figuring out: (a) what knowledge the definition specifies and if it defines explicitly the world; and (b) for all the knowledge that is required but not explicit, it should be checked whether it can be inferred from other definitions and axioms. If it can, the definition is complete; otherwise, it is incomplete.

Conciseness. An ontology is concise if: (a) it does not store any unnecessary or useless definitions, (b) explicit redundancies between definitions of terms do not exist, and (c) redundancies cannot be inferred from other definitions and axioms.

3.8.2 Taxonomy evaluation

In addition to providing the terminology for ontology evaluation described in Section 3.8.1, Gómez-Pérez has identified and classified different kinds of errors in taxonomies. Such an identification can be used as a check list for taxonomy evaluation. The following list presents a set of possible errors that can be made by ontologists when modeling taxonomic knowledge in an ontology under a frame-based approach. They are classified in: inconsistency, incompleteness, and redundancy errors, as shown in Figure 3.43. The ontologist should not postpone the evaluation until the taxonomy is finished; the control mechanisms should be performed during the construction of the taxonomy.

It is important to mention that we have slightly modified the terminology presented by Gómez-Pérez (2001) in order to be consistent with the vocabulary used in other sections of this book.

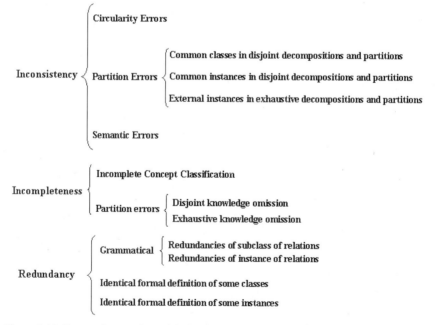

Figure 3.43: Types of errors that might be made when developing taxonomies with frames.

Inconsistency Errors can be classified in circularity errors, semantic inconsistency errors, and partition errors.

- **Circularity errors**. They occur when a class is defined as a specialization or generalization of itself. Depending on the number of relations involved, circularity errors can be classified as circularity errors at distance zero (a class with itself), circularity errors at distance 1, and circularity errors at distance *n*. Figure 3.44 illustrates these errors. For example, if we say that `Traveler` is a subclass of `Person`, and that `Person` is a subclass of `Traveler`, then the ontology has a circularity error of distance 1.

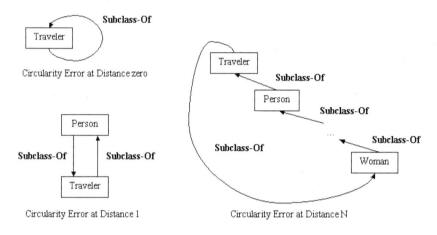

Figure 3.44: Circularity errors.

- **Semantic inconsistency errors**. They usually occur because the ontologist makes an incorrect semantic classification, that is, (s)he classifies a concept as a subclass of a concept to which it does not really belong; for example, (s)he classifies the concept `Airbus` as a subclass of the concept `Train`. The same might happen when classifying instances.

- **Partition errors**. Concept classifications can be defined in a disjoint (disjoint decompositions), a complete (exhaustive decompositions), and a disjoint and complete manner (partitions). The following types of partition errors are identified:
  - *Common classes in disjoint decompositions and partitions.* These occur when there is a disjoint decomposition or a partition *class_p₁,...,class_pₙ* defined in a class *class_A*, and one or more classes *class_B₁,...,class_Bₖ* are subclasses of more than one *class_pᵢ*.

    Figure 3.45a shows an error of this type in a disjoint decomposition. The classes `Air Transport`, `Sea Transport` and `Ground Transport` form a disjoint decomposition of the class `Transport`. This error appears if we define the class `Seaplane` as a subclass of the classes `Air Transport` and `Sea Transport`.

Figure 3.45b shows an error of this type in a partition. The classes `International Flight` and `Domestic Flight` form a partition of the class `Flight`. This error occurs if the class `Non Stop Flight` is defined as a subclass of the classes `International Flight` and `Domestic Flight` simultaneously.

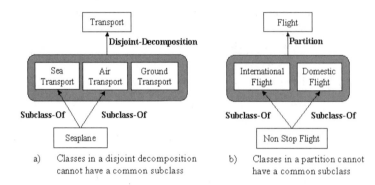

Figure 3.45: Common classes in disjoint decompositions and partitions.

- *Common instances in disjoint decompositions and partitions.* These errors happen when one or several instances belong to more than one class of a disjoint decomposition or partition.

    Figure 3.46a shows an error of this type in a disjoint decomposition. The classes `Air Transport`, `Sea Transport` and `Ground Transport` form a disjoint decomposition of the class `Transport`. This error happens if we define `Seaplane HA-14` as an instance of the classes `Air Transport` and `Sea Transport`.

    Figure 3.46b shows an error of this type in a partition. The classes `International Flight` and `Domestic Flight` form a partition of the class `Flight`. This error occurs if a specific flight is defined as an instance of both classes.

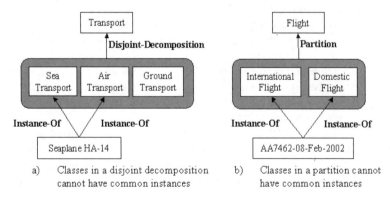

Figure 3.46: Common instances in disjoint decompositions and partitions.

- *External instances in exhaustive decompositions and partitions.* These errors occur when we have defined an exhaustive decomposition or a partition of the base class (*Class_A*) into the set of classes *class_p₁,...,class_pₙ*, and there are one or more instances of the *class_A* that do not belong to any class *class_pᵢ* of the exhaustive decomposition or partition.

  Figure 3.47a shows an error of this type in an exhaustive decomposition. The classes `Economy Trip`, `Business Trip`, and `Luxury Trip` form an exhaustive decomposition of the class `Travel Package`. This error happens if we define an instance `John's Package` as an instance of the class `Travel Package`.

  Figure 3.47b shows an error of this type in a partition. The classes `International Flight` and `Domestic Flight` form a partition of the class `Flight`. This error occurs if we define the flight `AA7462` that departs on February 8, 2002 as an instance of the class `Flight` instead of as an instance of the class `International Flight`

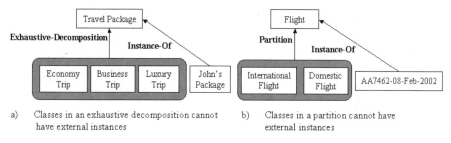

a)   Classes in an exhaustive decomposition cannot   b)   Classes in a partition cannot have
     have external instances   external instances

Figure 3.47: External instances in exhaustive decompositions and partitions.

Detecting incompleteness on taxonomies. Errors appear when the superclasses of a given class are imprecise or over-specified, and when information about subclasses that belong to disjoint decompositions, exhaustive decompositions, and partitions is missing. Very often, when a concept taxonomy is built, the ontologist only uses the *Subclass-Of* relation to build the taxonomy and omits disjoint knowledge between classes. We present here common omissions when building taxonomies.

- **Incomplete Concept Classification**. Generally, an error of this type is made whenever concepts are classified without accounting for them all, that is, concepts existing in the domain are overlooked. On the traveling domain, an error of this type occurs if we classify locations only taking into account beach locations and mountain locations, and we do not consider cultural locations, skiing locations, etc.

- **Partition Errors.** They could happen when the definition of disjoint and exhaustive knowledge between classes is omitted. We have identified two types of errors:

  - *Disjoint knowledge omission.* The ontologist identifies the set of subclasses of a given class, but omits to model, in the taxonomy, that the subclasses are disjoint. An example would be to define the classes South American Location and North American Location as subclasses of American Location, without specifying that they form a disjoint decomposition of the class American Location.

- *Exhaustive knowledge omission.* The ontologist defines a decomposition of a class, omitting the completeness constraint between the subclasses and the base class. An example would be to define South American Location and North American Location as a disjoint decomposition of an American Location without specifying that they form an exhaustive decomposition.

Redundancy detection. It occurs in taxonomies when there is more than one explicit definition of any of the hierarchical relations, or when we have two classes or instances with the same formal definition.

- **Redundancies of *Subclass-Of* relations** occur between classes that have more than one *Subclass-Of* relation. We can distinguish direct and indirect repetition. A *Direct repetition* exists when two or more *Subclass-Of* relations between the same source and target classes are defined. An *Indirect repetition* exists when two or more *Subclass-Of* relations between a class and its indirect superclasses are defined. For example, Figure 3.48 shows an indirect repetition, because the class AA2010 is defined as a subclass of AmericanAirlinesFlight and Flight, and AmericanAirlinesFlight is defined as a subclass of Flight.

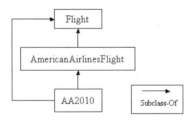

Figure 3.48: Indirect repetition.

- **Redundancies of *Instance-Of* relations**. As in the above case, we can distinguish between direct and indirect repetition.

- **Identical formal definition of classes**. Different classes have the same formal definition, although they have different names.

- **Identical formal definition of instances**. Different instances have the same definition, although they have different names.

3.8.3 OntoClean

OntoClean is a method elaborated by the Ontology Group of the CNR in Padova (Italy). Its goal is to remove wrong *Subclass-Of* relations in taxonomies according to some philosophical notions such as *rigidity*, *identity* and *unity*. These notions are applicable to properties, but can be extended to concepts, as we did in Chapter 2. The notions of *rigidity* and *identity* were explained in Section 2.2.1. Let us remember them:

- *Rigidity*. A property is rigid (+R) if and only if it is necessarily essential to all its instances. For example, the concept person is rigid, since every person is necessarily a person in every possible situation. On the other hand, a property is anti-rigid (~R) if and only if it is not essential for all its instances (for example, student). Finally, a property is non-rigid (-R) if and only if it is not essential for some of its instances. For example, the concept red is non-rigid, since there are instances of red which are essentially red (Drop of Blood), and instances that are not essentially red (My Pullover).

- *Identity*. A property (for example being a person) *carries* an identity criterion (IC), which is denoted by the symbol (+I), if and only if all its instances can be (re)identified by means of a suitable "sameness" relation (for example, DNA). The IC must be applicable to every instance in every moment. A property *supplies* an identity criterion (+O) if and only if such a criterion is not inherited by any subsuming property belonging to the ontology.

It might occur that a given property could inherit an identity criterion from any of its parents, and the property might have its own identity criterion at the same time. In such a case, the property carries two identity criteria and supplies its own identity criterion, but not the inherited criterion from its parents.

Sometimes it is hard to find and make explicit a suitable IC even though we know that the IC exists. Suppose that a non-expert in art makes a taxonomy about pictures, and (s)he wants to identify an identity criterion for Picasso's painting. In that case, it is quite hard for the non-expert to identify which is the identity criterion of the property Picasso's painting. However, we know that experts in art could identify easily Picasso's paintings. So, the identity criterion exists, and we could tag the property Picasso's painting with (+I).

We will now provide simplified and approximated definitions related to the notion of unity, considering that for understanding the idea of unity, it is necessary to know the idea of *whole* previously. To have more precise definitions, you can consult (Gangemi et al., 2001).

- *Whole*. We can say that an individual *w* is a *whole* if and only if it is made up of a set of parts unified by a relation *R* that links every pair of parts of *w*, and no part of *w* is linked by *R* to something that is not part of *w*, as we can see in Figure 3.49.

    Let us suppose that we want to represent the concept Piece of Metal and that a piece of metal is composed of different sections. As we can see in Figure 3.50, every pair of sections of a piece of metal is intimately `connected` with the other pieces, which means that the metal of the different sections is linked at the molecular level. However, we can say that two or more pieces of metal in mere contact are not `intimately connected` in the sense we have mentioned before. Since each section could be considered as a part, every piece of metal is a (topological) whole because every part is related through the relation intimately connected to any of the others, and there is no part of the piece of metal intimately connected to something that is outside such a piece.

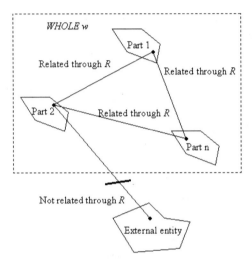

Figure 3.49: The notion of *whole*.

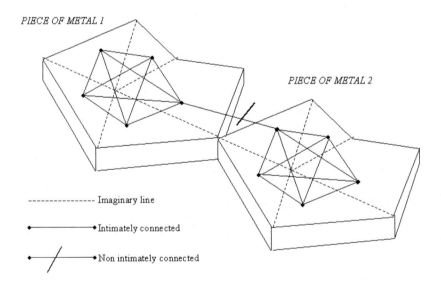

Figure 3.50: An example of the notion of *whole*: relations between parts of a piece of metal.

- *Unity*. A property *P* is said to *carry unity* (+U) if there is a *common* unifying relation *R* such that *all* the instances of *P* are wholes[19] under *R*. According to the previous example, we can say that the concept Piece of Metal carries unity (+U) because every piece of metal is a whole under the relation intimately connected. This relation is named unity criterion (UC). As it happens with the identity criterion, the unity criterion can be inherited from any of its parents.

If a property does not carry unity, it can be tagged with (-U). There are two cases of properties that do not carry unity (-U):

Properties carrying anti-unity. A property carries *anti-unity* (~U) if and only if *all* its instances can possibly be non-wholes. That is, there is not any instance that can be unified by a relation *R* in any situation (permanently). To explain anti-unity, we will think of the concept Metal. We may find a relation *R* that unifies a particular instance of metal in a particular moment, for example, we can find the relation metal belonging to the same car; however, this relation is not permanent, since a car can be dismantled, and the metal of such a car does not belong to the same car any more. Therefore, metal carries anti-unity (~U).

Properties that do not apply a common *unity criterion to all its instances*. This case differs from the other in that it is possible that some, or even every instance *i* has a permanent relation R_i that unifies it. However, this relation is not the same for all the instances. Thus, some (or even all) instances can be wholes, but with different unity criteria. An example is Legal Agent (Welty and Guarino, 2001), which could include people, companies, etc.

Bearing in mind these meta-properties, wrong *Subclass-Of* relations in a taxonomy can be cleaned. According to CNRs proposal, the OntoClean method proposes five activities for cleaning taxonomies (Welty and Guarino, 2001). Let us take the taxonomy of Figure 3.51 as an example.

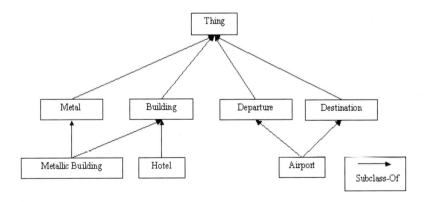

Figure 3.51: Example of taxonomy to be evaluated.

---

[19] In the actual definition, the OntoClean authors use *essential wholes* instead of *wholes*.

Activity 1. Assigning meta-properties to every property. This activity proposes to assign values to the meta-properties for each concept in the taxonomy. Thus, the ontologist tags all the concepts with the following symbols: *is rigid (+R)*; *is anti-rigid (~R)*, *is non-rigid (-R)*, *carries identity criterion (+I)*, *supplies identity criterion (+O)*, *carries unity (+U)*, and *carries anti-unity (~U)*. With regard to (-U), although it could be used for any concept that does not carry unity, it will be reserved for those concepts that carry neither unity nor anti-unity, as explained previously with the concept `Legal Agent`.

The *top-level ontologies of universals* and *particulars* presented in Section 2.2.1 can be used to set up these meta-properties. However, how to carry out this is out of the scope of this book. Figure 3.52 shows the result of assigning meta-properties to the taxonomy of Figure 3.51. For each concept in the taxonomy, we have followed this order: rigidity, identify and unity. This assignment has been made without taking into account the top-level ontologies.

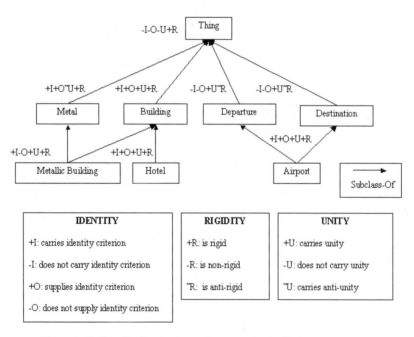

Figure 3.52: Result of assigning meta-properties to the taxonomy.

Rigidity. We can say that the concepts `Thing`, `Metal`, `Metallic Building`, `Building`, `Hotel` and `Airport` are rigid (+R) because any instance of any of these concepts has to be an instance of this concept in any situation. For example, `Building` is rigid since every building is necessarily a building in every possible situation. The concepts `Departure` and `Destination` are anti-rigid (~R), since a departure (or a destination) can stop being a departure, for instance, due to political or economical reasons.

Identity. Let us start with the concept on top of the taxonomy. There is not a unique identity criterion valid for everything. We can say that `Thing` neither carries (-I) nor supplies identity criterion (-O). Let us think now of the case of `Building`. Which features allow us to identify a building? We know that we can identify a building by its shape, materials, the little details of its front, etc. Therefore, `Building` carries an identity criterion (+I), though it may be very complex to define it as we said before when explaining the identity notion. As the parent of `Building` (`Thing`) does not carry identity criterion, the identity criterion of building is not inherited, therefore, we can say that `Building` supplies identity criterion (+O).

Let us suppose that when we built our taxonomy we wanted to model `hotel` from a legal point of view. Now, when we are assigning meta-properties, the identity criterion that better reflects what we had in mind is the `hotel legal code`. Hence, the `hotel legal code` is one of its identity criterion, and `Hotel` carries identity criterion (+I). Since the `hotel legal code` criterion is not inherited from `Building`, we can say that `Hotel` supplies identity criterion (+O).

As in the case of `Building`, we know that `Metal` can be identified by an identity criterion and that it carries identity (+I). As the parent of `Metal` (`Thing`) does not carry identity criterion, the identity criterion of metal is not inherited, therefore, we can say that `Metal` supplies identity criterion (+O).

`Metallic Building` inherits its identity criterion from `Building` and from `Metal`, hence, it just carries two identity criteria (+I), but it does not supply them (-O).

Let us think now of `Departure` and `Destination`, and let us suppose that airports, bus stops, train stations, etc., played the role of departures and destinations when we built the taxonomy. In this case, there is not a common identity criterion, neither for `Departure` nor for `Destination` because if the identity criterion existed, it could be applied to all of them (airports, bus stops, etc.). Therefore, `Departure` and `Destination` do not carry identity criterion (-I). And since they do not carry identity criterion (they do not own nor inherit it from `thing`), they do not supply it (-O).

With regard to `Airport`, the `airport legal code` can be considered as one of its identity criteria. So, `Airport` carries identity criterion (+I). As the identity criterion is not inherited from `Departure` and `Destination`, we can say that `Airport` supplies identity criterion (+O).

To sum up, `Metal`, `Building`, `Hotel` and `Airport` carry (+I) and supply (+O) identity criterion, `Metallic Building` carries identity criterion (+I) but it does not supply (-O) it, and `Thing`, `Departure` and `Destination` neither carry (-I) nor supply (-O) identity criterion.

Unity. Sometimes it is not easy to find the unity relation. However, it is possible to know that a property has a unity criterion, although we do not know exactly which.

Concerning Thing, there are things unified by a functional unity criterion, other things unified by a topological unity criterion, etc. Therefore, there is not a unique unity criterion valid for everything. As a consequence, Thing neither carries unity nor anti-unity, for which it is tagged with (-U).

With regard to the case of Building, a building is constructed according to its function (to lodge people, to store goods, etc.). Different parts of the building are designed according to such a function. So, the unity criterion depends on the function of the building. On the other hand, the different parts of the building are topologically connected. Consequently, a building is a whole under a unity criterion that is a combination of a functional and topological unity. Therefore we can say that Building carries a unity criterion (+U) that is not only functional but also topological.

Let us consider now the case of Hotel. For a hotel to carry out its function, workers, utilities, services, etc. must work properly. Therefore, the different parts of the hotel are unified to carry out the function of lodging people. As a consequence, we know that Hotel has to carry a functional unity criterion (+U).

As we said when dealing with the unity notion, Metal carries anti-unity (~U). Metallic Building does not inherit the unity criterion from metal but from Building. So Metallic Building carries unity (+U).

In the case of Departure and Destination, let us suppose that when we built the ontology we only had in mind departures and destinations as places from where passengers depart from and arrive at. So, departures and destinations are unified to carry out a function. Therefore, Departure and Destination carry a functional unity criterion (+U).

As for the case of Airport, applying a similar argument as the one used for Hotel, we can say that it carries a functional unity criterion (+U).

In summary, Hotel, Building, Metallic Building, Airport, Destination, and Departure carry unity (+U); Metal carries anti-unity (~U), and Thing carries neither unity nor anti-unity (-U).

Activity 2. Focusing only on the rigid properties. The goal of this activity is to identify which are the essential parts of the taxonomy. A taxonomy with only rigid properties is called *backbone taxonomy*, which is the base of the rest of the taxonomy. In our example, in this activity, we have focused on Thing, Metal, Metallic Building, Building, Hotel and Airport, and we have disregarded Departure and Destination at this moment, as Figure 3.53 illustrates.

Activity 3. Evaluating the taxonomy according to principles based on the meta-properties. To perform this evaluation, we will present three rules (Welty and Guarino, 2001) that are related with the identification of conflicts between identity criteria, unity criteria and between anti-unity and unity.

Rule 1: Checking identity
The rule for detecting conflicts between identity criteria, inspired in Lowe (1989), states that properties carrying (+I) incompatible identity criteria are necessarily disjoint. Following this rule, two properties carrying incompatible identity criteria cannot have common individuals. If two concepts with incompatible identity criteria had common individuals, the individuals would inherit two identity criteria which are incompatible. So the candidate concepts that could breach the rule are:

• Concepts that are not disjoint.
• Concepts that carry identity (+I).

Besides, if there is incompatibility between the identity criteria carried by both concepts, we can state that the two concepts do not satisfy the rule.

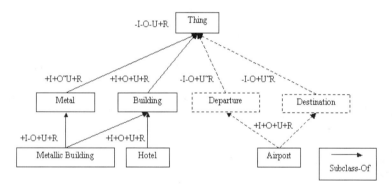

Figure 3.53: Backbone taxonomy.

We can see in Figure 3.53 that Hotel is a subclass of Building. So, they are not disjoint. Besides, both Hotel and Building carry identity (+I); therefore, they are "suspects" of breaching the rule. Now, we have to search for possible incompatible ICs between them. According to what we said when we tagged the taxonomy, Hotel has its own identity criterion and inherits the IC of Building because Building supplies identity criterion (+O). This means that every hotel could be identified by the features of its building. However, given that Hotel is considered here from the legal point of view, a hotel can legally exist even when it does not have a building. Consequently, the features of its building cannot be used to identify the hotel. Hence, there exists a conflict between the identity criteria when we say that Hotel is a subclass of Building. So, the inherited identity criterion from building is incompatible with its own identity criterion; therefore, we remove the *Subclass-Of* relation between `Hotel` and `Building`. The solution proposed in this example is to link directly `Hotel` with `Thing` using the *Subclass-Of* relation, but this solution does not represent that a hotel has a building. Thus, we propose to create the relation `has Building` between `Hotel` and `Building`. By doing this, we model that a hotel has a building, but it is not a building. With this solution we can represent hotels that do not have a building.

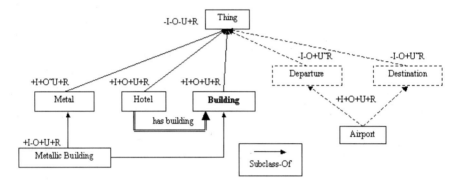

Figure 3.54: Result of restructuring the backbone taxonomy after applying the identity rule.

Rule 2: Checking unity

The rule for detecting conflicts between unity criteria states that properties carrying incompatible unity criteria (UCs) are necessarily disjoint. According to this rule, two properties carrying incompatible unity criteria cannot have common individuals. If two concepts with incompatible unity criteria had common individuals, the individuals would inherit two unity criteria which are incompatible. So the candidate concepts that could breach the rule are:

- Concepts that are not disjoint.
- Concepts that carry unity (+U).

If there is incompatibility between the unity criteria carried by both concepts; then we can state that the two concepts do not satisfy the rule.

If we analyze Figure 3.54, we can say that rule 2 has not been breached. To show how to work with this rule, we will take the taxonomy as it appeared in Figure 3.53. The unity notion can be used to reinforce that `hotel` cannot be a subclass of `Building`. Looking at Figure 3.53, we can notice that hotel and building are not disjoint and both carry unity (+U). So, they are "suspects" of breaching the rule. Now, we have to search for possible incompatible UCs between them. As we have said before, `Building` carries a functional and topological unity criterion. However, `Hotel` carries only a functional unity criterion and not a topological one. That is, a topological unity criterion is not applicable to `Hotel`. Therefore, there is a breach of rule 2.

This violation is problematic because if the hotel has several buildings, we should have several instances for the same hotel. The solution shown in Figure 3.54 also solves this incompatibility.

Rule 3: Checking unity and anti-unity
The rule for detecting conflicts between properties with anti-unity (~U) and properties carrying unity (+U) states that a property carrying anti-unity (~U) has to be disjoint with a property carrying unity (+U). If a property P_1 carries anti-unity (~U) and a property P_2 carries unity (+U), why cannot P_1 have common individuals with P_2? That is, why must they be disjoint?. If we know that P_1 carries anti-unity (~U), no common individual would be a whole under a common unifying relation. If we know that P_2 carries unity (+U), all common individuals would be a whole under a common unifying relation (which is the unity criterion). In other words, any common individual would be a whole and would not be a whole, which is a contradiction. So the concepts that could violate the rule are:
- Concepts that are not disjoint, and
- One of the concepts that carries anti-unity (~U) and another that carries unity (+U).

For instance, we can see in Figure 3.54 that `Metallic Building` and `Metal` are not disjoint, since `Metallic Building` is a subclass of `Metal`. Besides, `Metallic Building` is tagged with +U, whereas `Metal` is tagged with ~U. Therefore, there is a violation of the rule. A solution against the violation of rule 3 is to say that a metallic building is constituted by metal, as we can see in Figure 3.55.

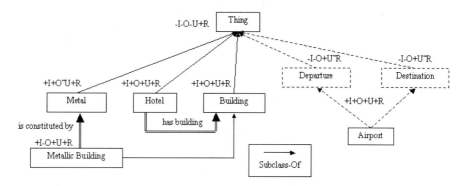

Figure 3.55: Result of restructuring the backbone taxonomy after applying the unity and anti-unity rule.

Activity 4. Considering non-rigid properties. When the backbone taxonomy has been examined, the ontology developer has to evaluate non-rigid (-R) and anti-rigid (~R) properties. A useful rule to perform such an evaluation is the following:

Rule 4. Checking rigidity (+R) and anti-rigidity (~R)

The rule for detecting conflicts between rigid and anti-rigid properties states that an anti-rigid property cannot subsume a rigid property, which means that a rigid concept cannot be a subclass of an anti-rigid one. So the concepts that could violate the rule are:

- The parent concept is tagged with ~R.
- The child concept is tagged with +R.

We can see in Figure 3.55 that `Airport` is a subclass of `Departure` and `Destination`. Besides, `Airport` is rigid (+R) and `Departure` and `Destination` are anti-rigid (~R). Therefore, there are two violations of rule 4: `Airport` can be neither a subclass of `Departure` nor of `Destination`.

   This violation causes problems because any instance of airport is a departure and a destination according to the taxonomy presented in Figure 3.56. However, it might happen that for any reason the airport stopped being a departure or a destination for our travel agency. To solve this problem, we have two options. The first consists in considering `Departure` and `Destination` as subclasses of `Airport` but not the opposite. And the second consists in introducing the concept `Travel` and converting the concepts `Departure` and `Destination` in relations, as Figure 3.56 illustrates.

   This last option forces us to extend the scope of the ontology and to carry out more knowledge acquisition, modeling, evaluation, etc.

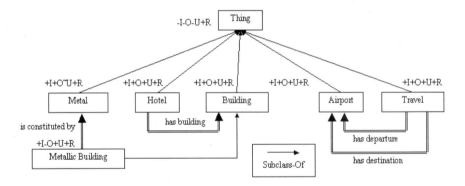

Figure 3.56: Result of considering non-rigid properties and looking for missing concepts.

Activity 5. Completing the taxonomy with other concepts and relations. We have several reasons to introduce new concepts. One is the transformation of concepts into relations, for example, when we have added the concept `Travel`. Given that we have introduced new concepts, we must repeat the process starting from the activity 1.

As we can see, OntoClean evaluation is not only useful to clean the concept taxonomy, but also to make explicit the ontological commitments assumed in the definitions of the ontology terms. Thus, for example, the assignment of meta-properties to `Departure` and `Destination` has forced us to reflect on the exact sense of such terms in our ontology.

OntoClean is being used in the Eureka European project, where WordNet is being restructured; it is also used in the construction of a domain ontology in the financial field; and in the TICCA Italian project, where an ontology of social interaction is being created; etc.

At the time of writing this book WebODE is the unique ontology platform that includes a module for evaluating ontologies according to OntoClean method (Fernández-López and Gómez-Pérez, 2002b).

3.9 Conclusions

Throughout this chapter, we have presented in detail the ontology development process and the methods and methodologies that support the building of ontologies from scratch. Also, we have discussed particular methods that allow carrying out specific activities already identified in the ontology development process. Special attention must be given to the re-engineering method; to the ontology learning methods that help reduce the effort during the knowledge acquisition process; to the merging of ontologies that generates a unique ontology from several ontologies; to the ontology alignment that establishes different types of mapping between ontologies (hence preserving the original ones); and to the ontology evaluation methods used for evaluating the ontology content. For each methodology and method, we have given an example on the traveling domain.

The main conclusion (taken from the analysis of Tables 3.10 to 3.14) is that none of the approaches presented in Section 3.3 cover all the processes identified on the ontology development process. Most of the methods and methodologies for building ontologies are focused on the development activities, specially on the ontology conceptualisation and ontology implementation, and they do not pay too much attention to other important aspects related to management, learning, merge, integration, evolution and evaluation of ontologies. In fact, such types of methods should be added to the methodologies for ontology construction of Section 3.3. An attempt to include some methods into a methodology occurs in METHONTOLOGY, where re-engineering methods and the two evaluation methods presented in Section 3.8 are being integrated.

In this chapter, we have seen that although all the methods and methodologies presented in Section 3.3 propose to reuse existing ontologies, the SENSUS method automates the construction of domain ontologies from the reuse of the knowledge contained on huge ontologies (the SENSUS ontology). Specific methods for merging and alignment ontologies presented in Section 3.6 also favor the reuse of existing knowledge resources.

Now, we conclude with the specific methods presented in this chapter:

- *Ontology re-engineering methods (Section 4).* The method presented is just a sound initial approach to carry out the aforementioned process although it must be improved in further studies with more complex ontologies. In order to increase the reusability of the ontology to be re-engineered, we need new guidelines and criteria to achieve a higher degree of reusability in the restructuring process.

- *Ontology learning methods (Section 5).* Ontology learning is a novel research area, and most of its approaches are based on extracting knowledge from text using a corpus that guides the natural language analysis. We propose to integrate ontology learning methods into the knowledge acquisition activity of ontology building methodologies.

- *Ontology merging methods and methodologies (Section 6).* The strategies presented for merging ontologies are quite diverse and are able to merge concept taxonomies, attributes and relations. However, they should include new methods for merging other ontology components, such as axioms.

- *Cooperative construction of ontologies (Section 7).* Co4 is a protocol for collaborative construction of consensual knowledge bases. Specific methods are needed for reaching consensus on ontology building.

- *Ontology evaluation methods (Section 8).* The field of ontology evaluation is just emerging. From the methodological perspective, evaluation activities should be introduced in more detail into some activities (e.g., conceptualisation and implementation) of the ontology development process.

Finally, we would like to point out that Ontologies are dynamic entities that evolve over time. The management of ontology evolution and the relationships between different versions of the same ontology are crucial problems to be solved. In this section we have not summarized the work carried out in this area, but we have identified the need to create and integrate robust methods inside the current methodologies to distinguish and recognize versions, with procedures for updates and changes in ontologies.

3.10 Bibliographical Notes and Further Reading

To those readers who want to read more about the contents of this chapter, we recommend the deliverable D.1.4 "A survey on methodologies for developing, maintaining, integrating, evaluating and re-engineering ontologies" of the OntoWeb thematic network. This deliverable contains detailed descriptions and references of these and other methods and methodologies for ontology construction. The descriptions can also be consulted and updated in the OntoRoadMap application (*http://babage.dia.fi.upm.es/ontoweb/wp1/OntoRoadMap/index.html*).

In addition, the following readings, grouped by topics, are recommended:
- *Ontology development methods and methodologies.* Extended information on the methods and methodologies presented in Section 3.3 can be found for: the Cyc method (*http://www.cyc.com/publications.html*), the Uschold and King's

method (*http://www.aiai.ed.ac.uk/project/enterprise/enterprise/ontology.html*), the Grüninger and Fox's methodology (*http://www.eil.utoronto.ca/enterprise-modelling/papers/*), and the METHONTOLOGY framework (*http://delicias.dia.fi.upm.es/papers/methontology.html*).

- *Method for re-engineering ontologies.* Papers on this issue are also available in the METHONTOLOGY's URL.

- *Ontology learning methods.* We recommend reading the book "Ontology Learning for the Semantic Web", from Alexander Maedche (2002), which contains descriptions of ontology learning algorithms and implementations such as the Text-To-Onto system. We also recommend the deliverable D1.5 "A survey on ontology learning methods and techniques" of the OntoWeb thematic network.

- *Ontology merging methods and methodologies.* ONIONS publications can be found at *http://saussure.irmkant.rm.cnr.it/onto/publ.html.* Maedche and colleagues' ontology merging method publications can be found in *http://wwwneu.fzi.de/wim/eng/publications.php.* Concerning the PROMPT method, all the related publications can be found in Natasha Noy publications' Web page (*http://smi.stanford.edu/people/noy/publications.html*).

- *Co4: a protocol for cooperative construction of ontologies.* The papers of Co4 can be found in *http://www.inrialpes.fr/sherpa/publi.html.*

- *Ontology evaluation methods.* Publications related to ontology evaluation can be found at *http://delicias.dia.fi.upm.es/papers/evaluation.html.* Papers about OntoClean and its theoretical foundations are available at *http://ontology.ip.rm.cnr.it/Publications.html.* Finally, there are also interesting papers related to ontology evaluation in Yannis Kalfoglou's home page *http://www.ecs.soton.ac.uk/~yk1/publications.html.*

Chapter 4

Languages for Building Ontologies

One of the key decisions to take in the ontology development process is to select the language (or set of languages) in which the ontology will be implemented. In the last decades, many ontology implementation languages have been created and other general Knowledge Representation (KR) languages and systems have been used for implementing ontologies though these were not specifically created with this purpose.

Usually, the selection of an ontology language is not based on the KR and inference mechanisms needed by the application that uses the ontology, but on the developer's individual preferences. Our experience tells us that a wrong selection of the language used to implement an ontology may cause problems once the ontology is being used in an application.

In this chapter, we will try to clarify the following questions:

- Which language(s) should I use to implement my ontology?
- What expressiveness does an ontology language have?
- What are the inference mechanisms attached to an ontology language?
- Does any ontology development tool support the language?
- Is the language appropriate for exchanging ontologies between applications?
- Does the language ease the integration of the ontology in an application?
- Is the language integrated in other languages used to represent knowledge and information on the Web, such as HTML and XML?
- Are there translators that transform the ontology implemented in a source language into a target language?
- How do such translators minimize the loss of knowledge in the translation process?

4.1 Ontology Language Evolution

At the beginning of the 1990s, a set of AI-based ontology languages was created. Basically, the KR paradigms underlying such ontology languages were based on first order logic (e.g., KIF), on frames combined with first order logic (e.g., CycL, Ontolingua, OCML and FLogic), and on description logics (e.g., LOOM). OKBC was also created as a protocol to access ontologies implemented in different languages with a frame-based KR paradigm. The overall layout of these languages is shown in Figure 4.1.

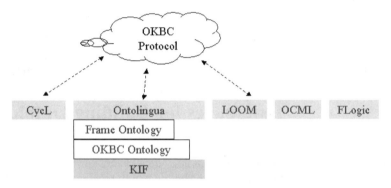

Figure 4.1: Traditional ontology languages.

Of the previous set of languages, **CycL** (Lenat and Guha, 1990) was the first to be created. CycL is based on frames and first order logic and was used for building the Cyc Ontology.

KIF (Genesereth and Fikes, 1992; NCITS, 1998) was created later, in 1992, and was designed as a knowledge interchange format; KIF is based on first order logic. Since ontologies were difficult to create directly in KIF, **Ontolingua** (Farquhar et al., 1997) was created on top of it. Hence, Ontolingua builds on KIF, and is the ontology language supported by the Ontolingua Server. This language has a Lisp[1]-like syntax and its underlying KR paradigm are frames and first order logic. Ontolingua was considered a standard *de facto* by the ontology community in the 1990s.

At the same time, **LOOM** (MacGregor, 1991) was built, though it was not intended to implement ontologies but for general knowledge bases. LOOM is based on description logics (DL) and production rules and provides automatic concept classification features. **OCML** (Motta, 1999) was developed later, in 1993, as a kind of "operational Ontolingua". In fact, most of the definitions that can be expressed in OCML are similar to the corresponding definitions in Ontolingua. OCML was built for developing executable ontologies and models in problem solving methods (PSMs). Finally, in 1995 **FLogic** (Kifer et al., 1995) was developed as a language that combined frames and first order logic though it did not have Lisp-like syntax.

---

[1] For those unaware of this term, Lisp is a family of languages whose development started, in the late 1950s, for list processing in Artificial Intelligence.

In the spring of 1997, the High Performance Knowledge Base program (HPKB) was started. This research program was sponsored by DARPA and its objective was to solve many of the problems that usually appear when dealing with large knowledge bases (concerning efficiency, content creation, integration of the content available in different systems, etc.). One of the results of this program was the development of the **OKBC** (Open Knowledge Base Connectivity) protocol (Chaudhri et al., 1998). This protocol allows accessing knowledge bases stored in different Knowledge Representation Systems, which may be based on different KR paradigms. Of the languages aforementioned Ontolingua, LOOM and CycL are OKBC compliant.

The boom of the Internet led to the creation of ontology languages for exploiting the characteristics of the Web. Such languages are usually called *web-based ontology languages* or *ontology markup languages*. Their syntax is based on existing markup languages such as HTML (Raggett et al., 1999) and XML (Bray et al., 2000), whose purpose is not ontology development but data presentation and data exchange respectively. The relationships between these languages are shown in Figure 4.2.

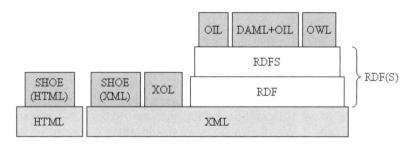

Figure 4.2: Ontology markup languages.

The first ontology markup language to appear was **SHOE** (Luke and Heflin, 2000). SHOE is a language that combines frames and rules. It was built as an extension of HTML, in 1996. It used tags different from those of the HTML specification, thus allowing the insertion of ontologies in HTML documents. Later its syntax was adapted to XML.

The rest of ontology markup languages presented here are based on XML. **XOL** (Karp et al., 1999) was developed as a XMLization of a small subset of primitives from the OKBC protocol, called OKBC-Lite. **RDF** (Lassila and Swick, 1999) was developed by the W3C (the World Wide Web Consortium) as a semantic-network based language to describe Web resources. Its development started in 1997, and RDF was proposed as a W3C Recommendation in 1999. The **RDF Schema** (Brickley and Guha, 2003) language was also built by the W3C as an extension to RDF with frame-based primitives. This language was proposed as a W3C Candidate Recommendation in 2000 and then it suffered a major revision in November 2002, so that its reference document was published as a W3C Working Draft. Later, it was revised in January 2003. The combination of both RDF and RDF Schema is normally known as **RDF(S)**.

These languages have established the foundations of the Semantic Web (Berners-Lee, 1999). In this context three more languages have been developed as extensions to RDF(S): OIL, DAML+OIL, and OWL. **OIL** (Horrocks et al., 2000) was developed at the beginning of the year 2000 in the framework of the European IST project On-To-Knowledge[2]. It adds frame-based KR primitives to RDF(S) and its formal semantics is based on description logics. **DAML+OIL** (Horrocks and van Harmelen, 2001) was created later (between the years 2000 and 2001) by a joint committee from the US and the EU in the context of the DARPA project DAML[3]. It was based on the previous DAML-ONT specification, which was built at the end of 2000, and on OIL. DAML+OIL adds DL-based KR primitives to RDF(S). In 2001 the W3C formed a working group called Web-Ontology (WebOnt) Working Group[4]. The aim of this group was to make a new ontology markup language for the Semantic Web. The result of their work is the **OWL** language (Dean and Schreiber, 2003), which is a W3C Working Draft (March 2003). OWL covers most of the features of DAML+OIL and has renamed most of the primitives that appeared in that language.

4.2 The Selection of an Ontology Language

Not all of the existing languages have the same expressiveness nor do they reason the same way. KR paradigms underlying ontology implementation languages are diverse: frames, description logic, first (and second) order logic, semantic networks, etc. This fact makes even more important the correct selection of the language in which the ontology is to be implemented. In fact, a KR paradigm may prove to be very appropriate for a specific task but not for others carried out in an application.

Therefore, before coding the ontology we should detect first what we need, in terms of expressiveness and reasoning, and then which languages satisfy such requirements. For this task we strongly recommend the use of the evaluation framework described in Corcho and Gómez-Pérez (2000). This framework allows analyzing and comparing the expressiveness and reasoning capabilities of ontology languages. Sections 4.2.1 and 4.2.2 are based on this framework.

In this chapter, we present how to implement our travel ontology with 11 languages (KIF, Ontolingua, LOOM, OCML, FLogic, SHOE, XOL, RDF(S), OIL, DAML+OIL, and OWL) and with the OKBC protocol. Other languages could have been included here, but we have selected only those we consider the most representative.

All language descriptions will be divided into two main dimensions, which are strongly related to each other: knowledge representation and reasoning mechanisms. We will comment on the main features that each dimension presents.

---

[2] http://www.ontoknowledge.org/
[3] http://www.daml.org/
[4] http://www.w3.org/2001/sw/WebOnt/

4.2.1 Knowledge representation

We first discuss how terms from other ontologies can be imported into an ontology. This is of great relevance since we will be able to create and maintain modular ontologies more easily if we can import terms from other ontologies. We also focus on the ontology header and the information included there, which is usually documentation about the ontology, authors, maturity of the ontology, etc.

Then, we show how to implement different ontology components in the language taking into account the KR paradigm underlying the language.

We start describing how **concepts** are built. Concepts are the central modeling component in most of the languages, regardless of the underlying KR formalism. We will include how to define concept **attributes**. Two kinds of attributes are usually distinguished: *instance attributes* (which describe concept instances and can take their values in those instances) and *class attributes* (which describe the concept and take their values in it). Besides, instance attributes are inherited by the subclasses of the class where they are defined and by the instances of this class and of its subclasses, while class attributes are not. We will then show how attributes can be constrained according to their *type of value*, *cardinalities* (how many values the attribute can take), *default values* and other constraints.

Once we have learned how to define concepts in the language, we present how to create concept **taxonomies**. Concept taxonomies are implemented in frame-based and DL-based languages differently. In frame-based languages, the *subclass-of* relationships between concepts must be always represented explicitly at design time. In DL-based languages, the inference engine (usually called classifier) can infer them at run time even if they are not represented explicitly. The representation of *disjoint* and *exhaustive* knowledge in concept taxonomies will also be explained.

Relations are very important components in ontology modeling as they describe the relationships that can be established between concepts, and consequently, between the instances of those concepts. Depending on the KR paradigms underlying the language, relations will be given different names. They are usually called *relations* or *slots* in frame-based languages and are known as *roles* or *properties* in DL-based languages. At this point we discuss how binary and non-binary relations can be represented in the language. We will see that, while all languages allow defining binary relations, not all of them allow defining n-ary relations. In this case, we can represent n-ary relations by means of reification. Finally we focus on the constraints that can be used to restrict relation arguments, such as *type* and *cardinalities*.

Then we describe **functions**, in case they can be defined in the language. We can observe that in many languages functions are usually defined as special cases of relations.

Once we have learned how to implement concepts, concept taxonomies, relations and functions, we present how to define formal **axioms**. They usually represent those pieces of knowledge that cannot be implemented in the ontology with the rest of modeling components. Formal axioms can appear *embedded* in other ontology definitions or as *independent* definitions in the ontology.

Sometimes ontologies include **instances**. We comment how instances can be created, how their attribute values can be filled and how a relation that holds between instances can be represented in the language.

Finally we present the **other components** that can be expressed in the language, such as rules, procedures, ontology mappings, etc.

4.2.2 Reasoning mechanisms

After having described how all the components in the ontology can be modeled, we are going to deal with the reasoning mechanisms attached to the language. A central issue for KR formalisms is the tradeoff between expressive power and reasoning mechanisms (Levesque and Brachman, 1985), that is to say, the more expressive a language is the more complex results to create an inference engine with the corresponding deductive mechanisms.

Hence we first present the main features of **inference engines** attached to the language if there are any. In the case of DL-based languages, we will observe whether there is an **automatic classifier** available for the language that computes the concept taxonomy automatically from the ontology concept definitions.

Another reasoning mechanism to which we will pay attention is the management of **simple** and/or **multiple inheritance** of concept attributes and relations through concept taxonomies.

Once inheritance mechanisms are described, we present how inference engines manage **exceptions** in concept taxonomies (this is also called non-monotonic reasoning). A common example of an exception in a concept taxonomy is the following: suppose that we have created the concept Bird with the attribute flies, whose value is True; suppose now that we have created the concept Ostrich with the attribute flies, whose value is False; if the inference engine is able to deal with exceptions and we have an instance of the concept Ostrich, the value of attribute flies of that instance will be False.

Finally we present if the inference engine provides **constraint checking** functionalities for detecting inconsistencies in the ontology and describe how inferences in the language are made (whether the inference engine uses backward or forward chaining for rules, which algorithms it uses, etc.).

4.3 Traditional Ontology Languages

In this section we present how to implement ontologies with the following ontology languages: Ontolingua and KIF, LOOM, OKBC, OCML and FLogic. As we have commented above, OKBC is not an ontology language but a protocol that allows the access to KR systems using primitives based on frames.

4.3.1 Ontolingua and KIF

Ontolingua (Gruber, 1992; Farquhar et al., 1997) was released in 1992 by the Knowledge Systems Laboratory of Stanford University. It is an ontology language based on KIF (Genesereth and Fikes, 1992; NCITS, 1998) and on the Frame Ontology (Gruber, 1993a). Ontolingua is the ontology-building language used by the Ontolingua Server[5] (Farquhar et al., 1997), which will be described in Chapter 5.

KIF (*Knowledge Interchange Format*) was developed in the context of the ARPA Knowledge Sharing Effort (Neches et al., 1991). The purpose for KIFs development was to solve the problem of language heterogeneity in knowledge representation, and to allow the interchange of knowledge between diverse information systems. KIF is a prefix notation of first order predicate calculus with some extensions. It permits the definition of objects, functions and relations with functional terms and equality. KIF has declarative semantics (it is possible to understand the meaning of expressions without an interpreter to manipulate them) and permits the representation of meta-knowledge, reifying functions and relations, and non-monotonic reasoning rules.

As KIF is an interchange format, to implement ontologies with it is a very tedious task. But with the *Frame Ontology* (Gruber, 1993a), built on top of KIF, this task becomes easier. As we mentioned in Chapter 2, the *Frame Ontology* is a KR ontology for modeling ontologies under a frame-based approach and provides primitives such as *Class*, *Binary-Relation*, *Named-Axiom*, etc. Since it was built on the basis of KIF and a series of extensions of this language, this ontology can be completely translated into KIF with the Ontolingua Server's translators. In 1997, the *Frame Ontology* was modified because another representation ontology, the *OKBC Ontology*, was included between KIF and the *Frame Ontology*, as shown in Figure 4.1. As a result, several definitions from the *Frame Ontology* were moved to the *OKBC Ontology*. Definitions from both ontologies are shown in Figures 1.11 and 1.12.

Both the *Frame Ontology* and the *OKBC Ontology* are less expressive than KIF. This means that not all the knowledge that can be expressed in KIF can be expressed only with the primitives provided by these KR ontologies. Thus Ontolingua allows adding KIF expressions to the definitions implemented with the *Frame Ontology* and the *OKBC Ontology*. With the Ontolingua language we can build ontologies according to any of the four following approaches: (1) using the *Frame Ontology* vocabulary; (2) using the *OKBC Ontology* vocabulary; (3) using KIF expressions; and (4) combining the *Frame Ontology* vocabulary, the *OKBC Ontology* vocabulary and KIF expressions simultaneously.

Recently a theorem prover (JTP[6]) has been developed for KIF expressions. Since all the expressions implemented in Ontolingua can be translated into KIF, JTP can be used to reason with Ontolingua ontologies.

Ontolingua ontologies are kept at the Ontolingua Server, which besides storing Ontolingua ontologies it allows users to build ontologies using its ontology editor, to import ontologies implemented in Ontolingua, and to translate ontologies from Ontolingua into KIF (Genesereth and Fikes, 1992), OKBC (Chaudhri et al., 1998),

---

[5] http://ontolingua.stanford.edu/
[6] Java Theorem Prover (http://www.ksl.stanford.edu/software/JTP/)

LOOM (MacGregor, 1991), Prolog, CORBAs IDL (Mowbray and Zahavi, 1995), Epikit (Genesereth, 1990) and CML (Stanley, 1986).

4.3.1.1 Knowledge representation

In this section we present how ontologies are implemented in Ontolingua (either by combining the *Frame Ontology* vocabulary and KIF, or by using KIF exclusively). Now we present examples with the *OKBC Ontology* vocabulary since this protocol is described in Section 4.3.3. Several examples that have been extracted from our travel ontology are shown, and the main features of this language are pointed out. Some of the Ontolingua definitions that we present in this section were presented in Chapter 1.

The header of an Ontolingua ontology defines the ontology name, natural language (NL) documentation, level of maturity, and generality. The last two measures, maturity and generality, are assigned arbitrarily by the ontology developer, and their value ranges from *very low* to *very high*. Besides, the header refers to the ontologies imported. In our travel ontology, we import the following: the `Frame-Ontology`, `kif-numbers`, `standard-units` and `time`.

```
(define-ontology Travel-Ontology
  (Frame-Ontology kif-numbers standard-units time)
  "Sample ontology for travel agencies"
  :maturity :medium
  :generality :high)
```

The definition above is valid only for Ontolingua. KIF does not provide special means for defining the header of an ontology nor for importing terms from other ontologies. So if we want to import these terms, we must repeat their formal definitions in the new ontology.

Let us now describe in detail the components that can be implemented in Ontolingua. We start with the definition of **concepts**, which are called classes in Ontolingua. Classes are defined by their name, by an optional documentation and by one or several sentences defining constraints on the attributes of the class or on the class itself:

- The keywords *:def*, *:sufficient* and *:iff-def* establish necessary, sufficient, and necessary and sufficient conditions that any instance of the class must satisfy respectively.
- The keyword *:equivalent* establishes conditions for the equivalence of classes.
- The keywords *:constraints* and *:default-constraints* establish necessary conditions on attributes of the class and on the default values of the attributes of the class respectively. These constraints are inherited by its subclasses.
- The keywords *:axiom-def*, *:axiom-constraints* and *:axiom-defaults* allow defining second-order axioms about the class itself.
- The keywords *:class-slots* and *:instance-slots* can be used for defining class and instance attributes respectively. We can also define them inside the keyword *:def* and *:iff-def*, as presented below in the definition of the class `Travel`.

- The keyword *:default-slot-values* defines default values for attributes of the class.
- The keyword *:issues* is used for adding extra documentation to the class.

Below, we show the Ontolingua code that defines the concept `Travel`. This code was presented in Chapter 1. In this definition, the documentation of the class has been included and some necessary constraints (*:def*) of the types of values of the instance attributes `companyName` and `singleFare` have been defined. Necessary and sufficient constraints (*:iff-def*) of the types of values of the instance attributes `arrivalDate` and `departureDate` have also been defined. Finally, with *:axiom-def* we have defined those expressions related to the class and not to its instances, such as the taxonomic relationships (*Subclass-Of* and *Superclass-Of*) and the exact cardinalities and maximum cardinalities of some of the attributes of the concept (with *Template-Facet-Value*). Note that the *Superclass-Of* primitive is not commonly used in Ontolingua class definitions, since it would be redundant to define that the class X is a superclass of the class Y, and that the class Y is a subclass of the class X. Hence, the primitive *Subclass-Of* is more frequently used.

```
(define-class Travel (?X)
   "A journey from place to place"
:iff-def
  (and (arrivalDate ?X Date)(departureDate ?X Date))
:def
  (and (companyName ?X String)
       (singleFare ?X CurrencyQuantity))
:axiom-def
  (and (Superclass-Of Travel Flight)
       (Subclass-Of Travel Thing)
       (Template-Facet-Value Cardinality
             arrivalDate Travel 1)
       (Template-Facet-Value Cardinality
             departureDate Travel 1)
       (Template-Facet-Value Maximum-Cardinality
             singleFare Travel 1)))
```

Class attributes are defined with the keyword *:class-slots*. In the next example, `transportMeans` is defined as a class attribute of the class `Flight`, whose value is "plane". As described in Section 4.2.1, this attribute is not inherited to the subclasses nor to the instances of the class `Flight`. To be able to express that an attribute of a concept has some values that are inherited to its subclasses and instances, we would need default values, which cannot be represented in Ontolingua.

Besides, `Flight` is a subclass of `Travel` that has exactly one `flightNumber`. Note that in the previous definition the concept `Travel` was defined as a superclass of the concept `Flight`.

```
(define-class Flight (?X)
   "A journey by plane"
:axiom-def
 (and (Subclass-Of Flight Travel)
      (Template-Facet-Value Cardinality
             flightNumber Flight 1))
:class-slots ((transportMeans "plane")))
```

We have noted in the previous examples that we can restrict the type, cardinality, and maximum cardinality of attributes. We can also restrict their minimum cardinality and state their default values. Moreover, we can define arbitrary constraints on attributes, which are expressed by KIF sentences.

The concepts aforementioned (Travel and Flight) have been defined with primitives from the *Frame Ontology*. These concepts are transformed into unary relations in KIF. The definitions that follow next present the concepts Travel and Flight expressed in KIF, as provided by the Ontolingua Server[7]. Note that some of the KIF definitions shown in this section have redundant information. For instance, classes are defined both as classes and as relations with arity 1.

```
(defrelation Travel (?X)
:= (and (arrivalDate ?X Date)(departureDate ?X Date)))
(Subclass-Of Travel Thing)
(Superclass-Of Travel Flight)
(Class Travel)
(Arity Travel 1)
(Documentation Travel "A journey from place to place")
(=>(Travel ?X)
   (and (companyName ?X String)
        (singleFare ?X CurrencyQuantity)))
(Template-Facet-Value Cardinality
                      departureDate Travel 1)
(Template-Facet-Value Cardinality arrivalDate Travel 1)
(Template-Facet-Value Maximum-Cardinality
                      singleFare Travel 1)

(defrelation Flight)
(Class Flight)
(Arity Flight 1)
(Documentation Flight "A journey by plane")
(Subclass-Of Flight Travel)
(Template-Facet-Value Cardinality
                      flightNumber Flight 1)
(transportMeans Flight "plane")
```

---

[7] All the KIF definitions presented in this section are presented here as they are automatically translated by the Ontolingua Server.

Both concepts are represented as instances of the class *Class* that are also unary relations: (Arity Flight 1) (Arity Travel 1). Their documentation is defined using the *Documentation* relation. In the first definition, the necessary and sufficient conditions for the concept Travel are expressed with KIF sentences after the symbol :=. Necessary conditions are expressed as logical implication (=>). In the second one Flight is defined as a subclass of Travel, and it expresses the restriction on the cardinality of the attribute flightNumber. The value for the class attribute transportMeans is stated in the last sentence.

The Ontolingua definition of the concept Flight shows how to represent concept **taxonomies** using the *Subclass-Of* relation. We want to emphasize that in Ontolingua, a class must be always a subclass of, at least, another class, except for the generic class Thing. This class is the root class of the *HPKB-upper-level* ontology, which is a top level ontology converted from the *Cyc* upper-level ontology. If a class is not explicitly defined by the ontologist as a subclass of Thing, this knowledge is set by default by the Ontolingua Server.

Knowledge about disjoint and exhaustive concept decompositions and about partitions can also be represented in Ontolingua, with the primitives *Disjoint-Decomposition*, *Exhaustive-Decomposition*, and *Partition* respectively. These three primitives are defined in the Frame Ontology and can be found in the Ontolingua Server. Figure 4.3 illustrates their KIF definitions. The axioms included in both definitions deserve special attention as they define the meaning of these relations. The definition of *Exhaustive-Decomposition* imposes only a necessary condition (represented by :=> instead of :=), that is, it does not define all the constraints of the relation, but only some of them.

If we reuse these definitions, we can build disjoint and exhaustive decompositions, and partitions. We show below two definitions that present the disjoint decomposition of the concept AmericanAirlinesFlight into AA7462, AA2010 and AA0488 (see also Figure 4.4a), and the partition of Location into the concepts EuropeanLocation, AsianLocation, AfricanLocation, AustralianLocation, AntarcticLocation, NorthAmericanLocation, and SouthAmericanLocation:

```
(define-class AmericanAirlinesFlight (?X)
:def (Flight ?X)
:axiom-def
  (Disjoint-Decomposition AmericanAirlinesFlight
            (Setof AA7462 AA2010 AA0488)))

(define-class Location (?X)
:axiom-def
  (Partition Location
          (Setof EuropeanLocation NorthAmericanLocation
                SouthAmericanLocation AsianLocation
                AfricanLocation AustralianLocation
                AntarcticLocation)))
```

```
(defrelation Disjoint-Decomposition (?c ?decomposition)
:= (and  (Class ?c)
         (Class-Partition ?decomposition)
         (=> (Member ?subclass ?decomposition)
             (Subclass-Of ?subclass ?c))))
(Relation Disjoint-Decomposition)
(Arity Disjoint-Decomposition 2)
(Binary-Relation Disjoint-Decomposition)
(Domain Disjoint-Decomposition Class)
(Range Disjoint-Decomposition Class-Partition)
(Documentation Disjoint-Decomposition
 "A disjoint-decomposition of a class C is a set of subclasses of C that
   are mutually disjoint")
```

a) Disjoint-Decomposition

```
(defrelation Exhaustive-Decomposition (?c ?decomposition)
:=> (=> (Member ?subclass ?decomposition)
        (Subclass-Of ?subclass ?c)))
(Domain Exhaustive-Decomposition Class)
(Relation Exhaustive-Decomposition)
(Arity Exhaustive-Decomposition 2)
(Binary-Relation Exhaustive-Decomposition)
(Documentation Exhaustive-Decomposition
 "An exhaustive decomposition of a class C is a set of subclasses of C such
   that there cannot be another subclass of the class that is not in the set
   (or is a subclass of a class in the set).
  Note: this does not necessarily mean that the elements of the set are
   disjoint (see partition - a partition is a disjoint exhaustive
   decomposition) .")
```

b) Exhaustive-Decomposition

```
(defrelation Partition (?c ?class-partition)
:= (and  (Disjoint-Decomposition ?c ?class-partition)
         (=> (Instance-Of ?instance ?c)
             (exists (?subclass)
                (and (Member ?subclass ?class-partition)
                     (Member ?instance ?subclass))))))
(Relation Partition)
(Arity Partition 2)
(Binary-Relation Partition)
(Subrelation-Of Partition Exhaustive-Decomposition)
(Subrelation-Of Partition Disjoint-Decomposition)
(Documentation Partition
 "A subrelation-partition of a class C is a set of mutually-disjoint classes
   which covers C. Every instance of C is is an instance of exactly one of
   the subclasses in the partition")
```

c) Partition

Figure 4.3: KIF definition of *Disjoint-Decomposition*, *Exhaustive-Decomposition* and *Partition*.

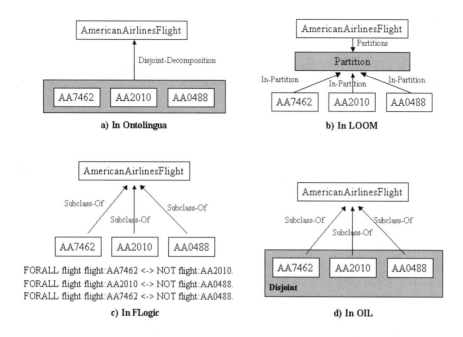

Figure 4.4: Disjoint decompositions in Ontolingua, LOOM, FLogic, and OIL.

The previous definitions are translated completely into KIF as follows:

```
(defrelation AmericanAirlinesFlight)
(Class AmericanAirlinesFlight)
(Arity AmericanAirlinesFlight 1)
(Subclass-Of AmericanAirlinesFlight Flight)
(Disjoint-Decomposition AmericanAirlinesFlight
                        (setof AA7462 AA2010 AA0488))

(defrelation Location)
(Class Location)
(Arity Location 1)
(Partition Location
    (setof EuropeanLocation NorthAmericanLocation
           SouthAmericanLocation AsianLocation
           AfricanLocation AustralianLocation
           AntarcticLocation))
```

As we can see in the KIF definition of the concept AmericanAirlinesFlight, this concept is defined as a subclass of the concept Flight. If we observe its definition in Ontolingua, we notice that we have used the expression :def (Flight ?X) instead of the expression :axiom-def (Subclass-Of AmericanAirlinesFlight Flight), used in the definition of the concept Travel. The KIF translation shows that both expressions mean the same, hence they can be used indistinctly. In the first one, we say that all the instances of the concept `AmericanAirlinesFlight` are necessarily instances of `Flight`, while in the second we say that the concept `AmericanAirlinesFlight` is a subclass of the concept `Flight`.

Binary **relations** are used to describe both the attributes of a concept and the relationships between two concepts. The following example, which combines the *Frame Ontology* vocabulary (*define-relation* and *:def*) and KIF expressions (the one attached to the *:def* primitive), shows the definition of the instance attribute `singleFare` and the binary relation `arrivalPlace`. The domains (concepts to which they are applied) and ranges (destination concepts or types of values) of both terms are explicitly described in these definitions.

```
(define-relation singleFare (?travel ?fare)
   "The single fare of a journey is a currency quantity"
:def (and (Travel ?travel) (CurrencyQuantity ?fare)))

(define-relation arrivalPlace (?travel ?arrPlace)
   "A journey ends at a location"
:def (and (Travel ?travel) (Location ?arrPlace)))
```

The equivalent KIF definitions for these relations are presented below. In KIF, we explicitly declare twice that the relations are binary (by stating that they are binary relations and that their arity is 2). We also explicitly define the domain and range of both relations and their documentation.

```
(defrelation singleFare
   (Relation singleFare)
   (Binary-Relation singleFare)
   (Arity singleFare 2)
   (Domain singleFare Travel)
   (Range singleFare CurrencyQuantity)
   (Documentation singleFare
 "The single fare of a journey is a currency quantity"))

(defrelation arrivalPlace
   (Relation arrivalPlace)
   (Binary-Relation arrivalPlace)
   (Arity arrivalPlace 2)
   (Domain arrivalPlace Travel)
   (Range arrivalPlace Location)
   (Documentation arrivalPlace
       "A journey ends at a location"))
```

Ontolingua presupposes the unique name assumption for the names of all the terms of an ontology. For instance, in the case of relations this means that relation names must be unique in an ontology. We may want that two different concepts share the name of a relation, then the domain of the relation must be defined as being the union of both concepts (or (Ship ?X) (Flight ?X)), and the range of the relation must be restricted depending on the concept to which the relation is applied (specifying the value type with Template-Facet-Value value-type). Below there is an example where the relation departurePlace is different for the concepts Flight and Ship. The departure place of a flight must be an airport, while the departure place of a ship must be a port. In our travel ontology, both Airport and Port are defined as subclasses of Location.

```
(define-relation departurePlace (?X ?Y)
:def (or (Ship ?X) (Flight ?X))
:axiom-def
  ((Template-Facet-Value
          value-type departurePlace Ship Port)
  (Template-Facet-Value
          value-type departurePlace Flight Airport)))
```

This definition is presented below in KIF. It is explicitly stated that it is a binary relation, that its domain is Ship or Flight (expressed with :=>), and that its value type is Port or Airport, depending on whether its domain is Ship or Airport respectively (expressed with *Template-Facet-Value*).

```
(defrelation departurePlace (?X ?Y)
:=> (or (Ship ?X) (Flight ?X)))
(Relation departurePlace)
(Arity departurePlace 2)
(Binary-Relation departurePlace)
(Template-Facet-Value
     Value-Type departurePlace Ship Port)
(Template-Facet-Value
     Value-Type departurePlace Flight Airport)
```

As was stated in Chapter 1, higher arity relations are used to represent relationships between more than two concepts. Also in Chapter 1 we presented an Ontolingua definition for the ternary relation connects, which states that a road connects two cities provided they are different. This definition combines the *Frame Ontology* vocabulary and KIF expressions.

```
(define-relation connects (?city1 ?city2 ?road)
   "A road connects two different cities"
:def
 (and
  (Location ?city1)(Location ?city2)(Road-Section ?road)
  (not (part-of ?city1 ?city2))
  (not (part-of ?city2 ?city1))
  (or (and (start ?road ?city1)(end ?road ?city2))
      (and (start ?road ?city2)(end ?road ?city1)))))
```

In KIF we have a relation whose arity is 3. The types of arguments are defined using the *Nth-Domain* primitive, which states the position of the relation argument and its type. Finally, all the logical sentences of the relation definition in Ontolingua are the same as those in KIF. Let us see the KIF definition of the relation connects:

```
(defrelation connects (?city1 ?city2 ?road)
   (Documentation connects
        "A road connects two different cities")
   (Relation connects)
   (Arity connects 3)
   (Nth-Domain connects 1 Location)
   (Nth-Domain connects 2 Location)
   (Nth-Domain connects 3 RoadSection)
   (not (part-of ?city1 ?city2))
   (not (part-of ?city2 ?city1))
   (or (and (start ?road ?city1) (end ?road ?city2))
       (and (start ?road ?city2) (end ?road ?city1))))
```

Functions in Ontolingua are special kinds of relations, where the last argument (the output argument of the function) can be obtained from the set of input arguments. This relationship between input arguments and the output argument is expressed within *:lambda-body*. In Chapter 1, the next definition of the function Pays was presented. This function is used to obtain a room price after applying a discount.

```
(define-function Pays (?room ?discount) :-> ?finalPrice
   "Price of the room after applying the discount"
:def (and (Room ?room)
          (Number ?discount)
          (Number ?finalPrice)
          (Price ?room ?price))
:lambda-body
          (- ?price (/ (* ?price ?discount) 100)))
```

The equivalent KIF definition appears below. It is similar to the previous aforementioned of the relation connects, although it uses the primitive *deffunction*. In fact, in KIF functions are also a type of relations where the value of the output is always the same for a fixed set of the n-1 input arguments.

```
(deffunction Pays (?room ?discount ?finalPrice)
   (Documentation Pays
       "Price of the room after applying the discount")
   (Function Pays)
   (Arity Pays 3)
   (Nth-Domain Pays 1 Room)
   (Nth-Domain Pays 2 Number)
   (Nth-Domain Pays 3 Number)
```

```
(=    (Pays ?room ?discount)
      (- ?price (/ (* ?price ?discount) 100)))
(=>  (Pays ?room ?discount ?finalPrice)
      (Price ?room ?price)))
```

With regard to formal **axioms**, we can add that they can be defined in Ontolingua either as independent elements in the ontology or as embedded in other terms (inside concept definitions, relations, etc.). These axioms are represented directly in KIF but cannot be expressed with the *Frame Ontology* vocabulary. The following first order axiom declares that trains cannot go from the USA to Europe.

```
(define-Axiom NoTrainfromUSAtoEurope
 "It is not possible to travel from the USA to Europe by
train"
:= (forall (?travel)
    (forall (?city1)
      (forall (?city2)
        (=> (and (Travel ?travel)
                 (arrivalPlace ?travel ?city1)
                 (departurePlace ?travel ?city2)
                 (EuropeanLocation ?city1)
                 (USALocation ?city2))
            (not (TrainTravel ?travel)))))))
```

Finally, an **instance** (which is also called an individual) is defined with the instance name, the class it belongs to and the values of the instance attributes. These instance attributes must be defined within the class to which the instance belongs or in any of the superclasses. The following example shows the definition of an instance of AA7462 flight in Ontolingua. Our instance has a single fare of 300 US Dollars, departs on February 8, 2002, and arrives in Seattle. 300USDollars, Feb8-2002 and Seattle are instances of CurrencyQuantity, Date and Location respectively.

```
(define-instance AA7462-Feb-08-2002 (AA7462)
:def ((singleFare AA7462-Feb-08-2002 300USDollars)
      (departureDate AA7462-Feb-08-2002 Feb8-2002)
      (arrivalPlace AA7462-Feb-08-2002 Seattle)))
```

In KIF, instances are called objects and are defined in the same way as instances in Ontolingua. Here, the class to which the instance belongs and the values of the instance attributes must be defined explicitly.

```
(defobject AA7462-Feb-08-2002
           (AA7462 AA7462-Feb-08-2002)
           (singleFare AA7462-Feb-08-2002 300USDollars)
           (departureDate AA7462-Feb-08-2002 Feb8-2002)
           (arrivalPlace AA7462-Feb-08-2002 Seattle))
```

Other components, such as procedures, can be expressed in Ontolingua though their examples are not shown since they are not included in the common definition of heavyweight ontologies, as was explained in Chapter 1.

4.3.1.2 Reasoning mechanisms

JTP[8] is the theorem prover implemented for Ontolingua ontologies (actually, it is implemented for KIF and Ontolingua ontologies can be translated completely into KIF). JTP can be used for deducing information from axioms or for checking constraints in ontologies. It converts arbitrary first order logic sentences into clausal form, as presented in Russell and Norvig (1995), and it uses an iterative deepening search to find proofs extending the resolution techniques employed by Prolog, and avoiding getting lost in endless paths, as Prolog. In addition, JTP deals with inheritance.

The Ontolingua Server does not include JTP though it includes the following reasoning mechanisms: single and multiple **inheritance** and **constraint checking**. With regard to multiple inheritance, conflicts are not resolved in the Ontolingua Server. Furthermore, in the Ontolingua Server, inheritance is basically monotonic (that is, the Ontolingua Server does not deal with exceptions in concept taxonomies). The only non-monotonic capabilities of the Ontolingua Server are related to default values for slots and facets. The Ontolingua Server also checks the types and cardinalities of concept attributes and relation arguments.

4.3.2 LOOM

LOOM (MacGregor, 1991; LOOM tutorial, 1995) was being developed from 1986 until 1995 by the Information Science Institute (ISI) of Southern California University. LOOM was not exactly built as a language for implementing ontologies but as an environment for the construction of general-purpose expert systems and other intelligent applications.

LOOM is a descendant of the KL-ONE (Brachman and Schmolze, 1985) family of languages. Consequently, it is based on the description logics (DL) paradigm and is composed of two different sublanguages: the "description" and the "assertional" languages. The former is used for describing domain models through objects and relations (TBox), the latter allows asserting facts about individuals (ABox). LOOM also supports rules and predicate calculus, and procedural programming supported through pattern-directed methods.

4.3.2.1 Knowledge representation

Let us explain now how to import terms from other LOOM ontologies. As in Ontolingua, the ontology where the terms are defined should also be imported. Below we can see the header for our travel ontology, which imports LOOMs built-in theory (containing LOOM primitives) and other general ontologies on units and time.

---

[8] http://www.ksl.stanford.edu/software/JTP/

```
(defcontext TRAVEL-ONTOLOGY
:theory (LOOM::BUILT-IN-THEORY)
        (LOOM::TIME-ONTOL)
        (LOOM::UNITS-ONTOL))
```

DL languages usually provide two basic components for ontology modeling: concepts and roles. These components are created by combining different constructs that describe the DL language thoroughly. Now we are going to describe the pattern used for creating concept expressions in LOOM and then how to model concepts; later, we will describe the pattern used for creating role expressions in LOOM and how to model roles.

Let us start with **concept** modeling. The pattern for creating concept expressions in LOOM is presented below. It shows that LOOM definitions combine the following constructs, most of which were explained in Chapter 1:

- Conjunction (*:and*), disjunction (*:or*) and negation (*:not*) of concepts.
- Value restriction (*:all*) and existential restriction (*:some*).
- Number restriction (*:at-least, :at-most, :exactly*). The constructor *:the* is short for expressing value restriction (*:all*) and number restriction set to 1 (*:exactly 1*).
- Collection of individuals (*:one-of*).
- Equivalence (*:same-as*). For instance, we can represent that the concepts Person and HumanBeing are equivalent.
- Set inclusion (*:subset*). To express relations between value sets or individuals.
- Role fillers (*:filled-by, :not-filled-by*). To represent the values of a role for a specific concept.
- Comparison (<|>|<=|>=|=|/=) and relation between values (*:relates*). To establish relationships between the values of slots.
- First-order logic expressions (*:satisfies*) that every instance of the concept satisfies. This expression will be used for query answering.

```
concept-name |
({:and|:or} concept-expr+) |
(:not concept-expr) |
({:all|:some|:the} relation-expr concept-name) |
({:at-least|:at-most|:exactly} integer relation-expr) |
({:one-of {instance|constant}+) |
({:same-as|:subset} relation-expr relation-expr) |
({:filled-by|:not-filled-by} relation-expr
          {instance|constant}+) |
({<|>|<=|>=|=|/=} relation-expr {relation-expr|number}) |
(:relates relation-expr relation-expr
          {relation-expr |constant}) |
(:satisfies (?variable) query-expr)
```

LOOM distinguishes between primitive and defined concepts. The definition of a primitive concept just states necessary conditions for any instance belonging to it. These primitive concepts are defined in LOOM with the *:is-primitive* keyword. On the other hand, defined concepts state necessary and sufficient conditions for any instance belonging to it. These are defined in LOOM with the *:is* keyword.

Taking into account the previous explanation of what primitive and defined concepts are, we can say that the concept Travel of our travel ontology is a primitive concept, and that the concept Flight is a defined concept. The former means that instances of the concept Travel have necessarily the attributes arrivalDate, departureDate, companyName and singleFare, with their corresponding cardinality restrictions. The latter means that instances of the concept Flight will also be instances of the concept Travel, will have one flightNumber and the value for their attribute transportMeans will be "plane". Besides, it means that if we have an instance with these characteristics we can infer that it is an instance of the concept Flight.

Both concept definitions take the construct *:all* to express the type of the instance attributes, and the constructs *:exactly* and *:at-most* to express cardinality constraints on those attributes. Finally, we use the keyword *:filled-by* to define the value "plane" for the class attribute transportMeans.

```
(defconcept Travel
    "A journey from place to place"
 :is-primitive
    (:and
      (:all arrivalDate Date) (:exactly 1 arrivalDate)
      (:all departureDate Date) (:exactly 1 departureDate)
      (:all companyName String)
      (:all singleFare CurrencyQuantity)
      (:at-most singleFare 1)))

(defconcept Flight
    "A journey by plane"
 :is
    (:and
      Travel
      (:all flightNumber Number) (:exactly 1 flightNumber)
      (:filled-by transportMeans "plane")))
```

If we compare the definition of the concept Travel kept in Ontolingua and in LOOM, we can observe that in Ontolingua we expressed necessary conditions (*:def*) and necessary and sufficient conditions (*:iff-def*) for the same concept definition, whereas in LOOM we cannot define both kinds of conditions for the same concept. In LOOM, the concept Travel is defined as a primitive concept (we only establish necessary conditions for an instance that belongs to the concept).

Regarding the definition of the concept Flight, we have used the *:filled-by* constructor to define the necessary and sufficient condition stating that all the instances of this concept take the value "plane" for their attribute transportMeans. Consequently, this definition differs from the one shown with Ontolingua, since in that case the attribute value was applied to the concept

`Flight`, and not to its subclasses and instances. In LOOM it is not possible to specify class attributes, as was the case with Ontolingua.

With regard to concept **taxonomies** in LOOM, we have already defined the concept `Flight` as a subclass of the concept `Travel`. Non-exhaustive and exhaustive decompositions can also be represented in taxonomies using the *:partitions* and *:exhaustive-partitions* keywords inside concept definitions respectively. Figure 4.4b shows how to represent a non-exhaustive decomposition in LOOM: the decomposition is defined in the superclass (`AmericanAirlinesFlight`), and the concepts that belong to the decomposition (`AA7462`, `AA2010` and `AA0488`) are explicitly linked to it. We can see below the concepts `AmericanAirlinesFlight` and `Location`, and their corresponding non-exhaustive and exhaustive decompositions.

```
(defconcept AmericanAirlinesFlight
  :partitions $AAPartition$)
(defconcept AA7462 :in-partition $AAPartition$)
(defconcept AA2010 :in-partition $AAPartition$)
(defconcept AA0488 :in-partition $AAPartition$)

(defconcept Location
  :exhaustive-partitions $continent$)
(defconcept EuropeanLocation
     :in-partition $continent$)
(defconcept NorthAmericanLocation
     :in-partition $continent$)
(defconcept SouthAmericanLocation
     :in-partition $continent$)
(defconcept AsianLocation
     :in-partition $continent$)
(defconcept AfricanLocation
     :in-partition $continent$)
(defconcept AustralianLocation
     :in-partition $continent$)
(defconcept AntarcticLocation
     :in-partition $continent$)
```

Neither the non-exhaustive decomposition of the concept `AmericanAirlinesFlight` nor the exhaustive decomposition of the concept `Location` specify disjointness constraints between the concepts in the decompositions. Therefore, the previous defintions are not equivalent to the ones presented in the Ontolingua section. Disjointness between concepts cannot be defined explicitly in LOOM but they are inferred by the LOOM classifier, taking into account the concept definitions.

In LOOM **relations** between concepts are called roles. Binary relations can be used for representing both attributes of concepts and ad hoc relations between two concepts. As in the case of concepts, there are a set of constructs that can be used to create relation expressions in LOOM. The pattern for building these expressions in LOOM is:

```
relation-name |
(:and relation-expr+) |
({:domain|:range} concept-expr) |
(:domains concept-expr concept-expr+) |
(:inverse relation-expr) |
(:compose relation-expr+) |
(:satisfies (?variable ?variable+) query-expr) |
(:predicate (?variable ?variable+) lisp-expr+)
```

Relation expressions are built by means of conjunction (*:and*), inverse relations (*:inverse*) and relation composition (*:compose*). In the case of binary relations, the domain and range of the relation are expressed with the *:domain* and *:range* primitives. In the case of higher arity relations, the domains (first *n-1* arguments) and range (last argument) of the relation are expressed with the *:domains* and *:range* primitives.

The *:satisfies* primitive permits including an expression that every instance of the relation satisfies. As in the case of concept expressions, the logical sentence after the *:satisfies* primitive is used in query answering. The *:predicate* primitive permits including a Lisp formula. This formula returns a non-nil value when applied to an instance of the relation.

Let us see now how to represent the definition of the instance attribute singleFare, the binary relation arrivalPlace and the ternary relation connects. All these expressions use the *defrelation* primitive.

```
(defrelation singleFare
    "The single fare of a journey is a currency quantity"
:domain Travel
:range CurrencyQuantity)

(defrelation arrivalPlace
    "A journey ends at a location"
:domain Travel
:range Location)

(defrelation connects
    "A road connects two different cities"
:arity 3
:domains (Location Location)
:range RoadSection
:predicate
    ((?city1 ?city2 ?road)
    (:not (part-of ?city1 ?city2))
    (:not (part-of ?city2 ?city1))
```

```
(:or (:and (start ?road ?city1)(end ?road ?city2))
     (:and (start ?road ?city2)(end ?road ?city1)))))
```

In Ontolingua, we were able to define a relation with two different domains and different ranges for each domain (the departure place of a flight is an airport, while the departure place of a ship is a port). However, LOOM does not allow representing this kind of knowledge.

In LOOM, **functions** are represented as special kinds of relations that use the *:function* primitive inside the relation definition. With this primitive we state how to obtain the output value of the function from the input arguments. The definition of the function Pays uses the *:function* primitive as described below, the *:domains* primitive for stating the types of the input arguments (Room and Discount) and the *:range* primitive for the type of the output argument.

```
(defrelation Pays
:is
 (:function (?Room ?Discount)
   (- (Price ?Room) (/ (* (Price ?Room) ?Discount) 100)))
:domains (Room Number)
:range Number)
```

Formal **axioms** in LOOM are embedded in concept and relation definitions with the *:predicate* or the *:satisfies* primitives. Below is the axiom of the non-availability of trains from Europe to the USA inside the definition of the concept Train-Travel.

```
(defconcept Train-Travel
:is    (:and  Travel
              (:satisfies ?x (:for-all ?y (:for-all ?z
                 (:not (:and (arrivalPlace ?x ?y)
                             (EuropeanLocation ?y)
                             (departurePlace ?x ?z)
                             (USALocation ?z))))))))
```

All the definitions presented above use the LOOM "description" language (i.e., they are included in the TBox). **Instances** of concepts and relations are defined through LOOM's "assertion" language (i.e., they are included in the ABox). What follows is the code corresponding to the inclusion of an instance and the values for some of the instance attributes.

```
(tellm     (AA7462 AA7462-08-Feb-2002)
           (singleFare AA7462-08-Feb-2002 300USDollars)
           (departureDate AA7462-08-Feb-2002 Feb8-2002)
           (arrivalPlace AA7462-08-Feb-2002 Seattle))
```

Finally, with LOOM we can also define production **rules** as ontology components. These rules can be used either to derive new information or to derive concept taxonomies automatically with the LOOM classifier.

4.3.2.2 Reasoning mechanisms

The LOOM inference engine is called the LOOM classifier. This classifier makes use of two different reasoning mechanisms: classification and deductive reasoning.

The classification mechanism integrates concept definitions and production rules, and relies on subsumption tests. **Automatic classifications** can be used to delegate the task of concept classification and to detect inconsistencies in the definition of terms in the ontology.

LOOM allows both single and multiple **inheritance** and performs monotonic reasoning on the attribute values for concepts and instances (that is, it does not handle exceptions in concept taxonomies). It also checks type **constraints** for the role values.

In addition, LOOM provides deductive reasoning mechanisms for performing inferences through backward chaining. These mechanisms are used for query answering and make use of the expressions defined with the *:satisfies* keyword in concept and role definitions.

LOOMs main drawback is that it is too expressive to permit complete reasoning (i.e., it is undecidable).

LOOM and OntoSaurus (Swartout et al., 1997), which is the tool with which LOOM ontologies can be browsed, are distributed for non-commercial use by ISI (Information Science Institute) at the University of Southern California. LOOM sources are provided in Lisp and contain the LOOM classifier. Hence it requires a Lisp interpreter to run it. LOOM ontologies can be accessed easily through the API of the Lisp interpreter and also through this API the LOOM classifier can be used .

4.3.3 OKBC

OKBC (Chaudhri et al., 1998) is the acronym for *Open Knowledge Base Connectivity*, previously known as the *Generic Frame Protocol* (GFP) (Karp et al., 1995). OKBC is the result of the joint efforts of the Artificial Intelligence Center of SRI International and the Knowledge Systems Laboratory of Stanford University. The objective of OKBC was to create a frame-based protocol to access knowledge bases stored in different knowledge representation systems (KRSs), as Figure 4.1 shows. Some of the languages and systems that were adapted to become OKBC compliant are: Ontolingua (Farquhar et al., 1997), LOOM (MacGregor, 1991), CycL (Lenat and Guha, 1990), Protégé-2000 (Noy et al., 2000), Theo (Mitchell et al., 1991), SIPE-2 (Wilkins, 1999), Ocelot (Karp and Paley, 1995), JTP, CLOS (*Common Lisp Object System*) (Steele, 1990), Tuple-KB (Rice and Farquhar, 1998), and WebODE (Arpírez et al., 2003).

The GFP Knowledge Model, the implicit KR formalism underlying OKBC, contains a set of KR primitives commonly found in frame-based representation systems. These primitives were presented in Chapter 2, when describing the OKBC Ontology. OKBC also defines procedures (using a Lisp-like syntax) to describe complex operations that cannot be performed by simply using the protocol primitives.

Different implementations of the OKBC protocol have been provided for different KRSs. However, there are small differences among all the implementations. In fact, OKBC allows some flexibility on the KR primitives implemented for each KRS since these differences are sometimes difficult to unify for all KRSs. For instance, some KRSs distinguish between primitive and defined concepts while other KRSs do not consider this distinction in their knowledge models; the same applies to the behavior of default values in each KRS, which may be different in other implementations of OKBC.

4.3.3.1 Knowledge representation

In an OKBC ontology we can import terms from other ontologies accessible through the protocol independently of the KRS where the terms are available. The ontologies that hold the terms wanted must be imported as "parent knowledge bases". The OKBC code that follows has been used to create our travel ontology for Ontolingua and to import the next ontologies: `kif-numbers`, `standard-units` and `time`. We have used in all our examples the Lisp syntax described in Section 3.7 of the OKBC reference document (Chaudhri et al., 1998).

```
(create-kb TravelOntology
:kb-type Ontolingua
:initargs (list :parent-kbs
                (list kif-numbers standard-units time)))
```

Concepts in OKBC can be either primitive or defined. This distinction is only useful if we access KRSs that support both types of concepts (for instance, LOOM). In OKBC attributes are known as slots. This protocol distinguishes two types of slots: *template* and *own*. Basically, *template* slots are used to represent instance attributes, while *own* slots are used to represent class attributes[9]. OKBC allows representing for a slot some of its values, which are inherited to its subclasses and to its instances, and default values, which are also inherited to its subclasses and to its instances. The properties of slots are called facets according to the frames KR formalism terminology.

We will use the following code to create the primitive concept `Travel` and the defined concept `Flight`.

```
(create-class Travel
:own-slots
  ((:documentation "A journey from place to place"))
:template-slots
  ((arrivalDate) (departureDate) (companyName)
   (singleFare))
```

---

[9] This equivalence is not strict: the term "own slot" also refers to the attributes of an instance (aka individual). Therefore, we can say that own slots are those that take values in a frame, no matter whether it is a class frame or an instance frame.

```
:template-facets
  ((arrivalDate (:cardinality 1) (:value-type Date))
   (departureDate (:cardinality 1) (:value-type Date))
   (companyName (:value-type :string))
   (singleFare (:maximum-cardinality 1)
               (:value-type CurrencyQuantity))))

(create-class Flight
:primitive-p false
:direct-superclasses (Travel)
:own-slots
  ((transportMeans "plane")
   (:documentation "A journey by plane"))
:template-slots ((flightNumber))
:template-facets ((flightNumber (:cardinality 1))))
```

In addition to the types, cardinalities, and maximum cardinalities of attributes, in OKBC we can specify minimum cardinality, default values, enumerated values, and maximum and minimum values in case of numeric attributes. If more facets are needed, they can be created with the *create-facet* primitive.

The scope of attributes in OKBC depends on the behavior of the target KRS connected. Let us suppose that the target KRS does not permit specifying slots with unconstrained domain. If we want to create a slot without determining its domain, we will be notified that an error has occurred. A similar behavior will be observed if we try to create two slots with the same name in a KRS that does not permit defining different slots with the same name.

The following definition of the slot departurePlace states that this slot has two different ranges depending on which concept it is attached to. Depending on the target KRS, this definition will be permitted or not.

```
(put-facet-value Ship departurePlace value-type Port)
(put-facet-value Flight departurePlace
                          value-type Airport)
```

Concept **taxonomies** are defined with the *direct-superclasses* primitive. In OKBC, a concept may have several direct superclasses but unlike Ontolingua or LOOM, OKBC does not support the definition of disjoint nor exhaustive knowledge in concept taxonomies. Thus, neither disjoint nor exhaustive knowledge will be available if we use the OKBC protocol to access an ontology.

Binary **relations** in OKBC are represented as template slots. The following examples present the OKBC slot definitions singleFare and arrivalPlace, which correspond to an instance attribute and a binary relation respectively.

```
(create-slot singleFare
:frame-or-nil Travel
:slot-type :template
:doc "The single fare of a journey is a currency
     quantity"
:own-slots (:value-type CurrencyQuantity))

(create-slot arrivalPlace
:frame-or-nil Travel
:slot-type :template
:doc "A journey ends at a location"
:own-slots (:value-type Location))
```

Higher arity relations, such as the relation connects, cannot be built directly with the OKBC protocol primitives no matter what the target KRS is and whether n-ary relations can be defined or not in the target KRS. Higher arity relations must be built by reification as concepts with an attribute for each of their arguments. Let us explain now how to define the relation connects. For the sake of clarity, we have also created the class TernaryRelation, which represents the class of all the relations with three arguments. The relation connects would be an instance of the class TernaryRelation. In this definition, we cannot express some of the information held in the Ontolingua and LOOM definitions such as the fact that a city is not included in another city or that the road starts in one city and ends in the another city.

```
(create-class TernaryRelation
:own-slots
   ((firstArgument)
    (secondArgument)
    (thirdArgument)))

(create-class connects
   "A road connects two different cities"
:direct-types (TernaryRelation)
:template-slots
   ((firstArgument (:value-type Location))
    (secondArgument (:value-type Location))
    (thirdArgument (:value-type RoadSection))))
```

Functions cannot be represented in OKBC nor can formal **axioms**; OKBC does not guarantee what the deductive treatment of these components could be in each implementation.

As regard to **instances**, they are called individuals in OKBC. OKBC does not restrict the number of classes to which the individual belongs. We show below the definition of our instance of the flight AA7462:

```
(create-individual AA7462-Feb-08-2002
:direct-types (AA7462)
:own-slots   (singleFare 300USDollars)
             (departureDate Feb8-2002)
             (arrivalPlace Seattle))
```

Finally, **procedures** can also be defined in OKBC. Their syntax is described in Chaudhri and colleagues (1998, Chapter 5). Procedures define sequences of operations that can be executed using the *tell&ask* interface (that is, they are sequences of operations for creating concepts, removing concepts, creating roles, etc.). The *tell&ask* interface is supplied with all the implementations of the OKBC protocol. It consists of the method *tell*, which allows asserting information in the ontology, and the method *ask*, which allows examining the contents of an ontology through the OKBC protocol.

4.3.3.2 Reasoning mechanisms

OKBC does not provide any inference engine since it was built as an access protocol to existing KRSs. However, it permits configuring the *behavior* of the reasoning engines attached to its underlying KRSs.

A group of behaviors are related to **constraint checking**. They determine how constraint checking is performed by the underlying KRS and are: *constraint-checking-time* (states when the constraint checking is performed: immediate, deferred, background, or never), *constraint-report-time* (states when the constraint violations are reported: immediate or deferred) and *constraints-checked* (states which of the constraints are checked: cardinalities, value types, domains, etc.).

Another behavior deals with **default values**. It specifies whether slot default values are overridden by local values or whether local values are added to the default value (provided they are consistent).

Finally, another behavior determines if it is possible to define the two kinds of **slots** described: *own* and *template*.

All the features that have been described here are included in the implementations of bindings from OKBC to the different languages for which OKBC is available. There are also other inference engines that build on OKBC to perform their inferences. For example, the PAL inference engine (integrated in Protégé-2000) and the WebODE inference engine (integrated in the WebODE ontology editor) use OKBC primitives to perform inferences. Both will be described with their corresponding tools in Chapter 5.

4.3.4 OCML

OCML (Motta, 1999) stands for *Operational Conceptual Modeling Language*. It was developed at the Knowledge Media Institute (UK) in the context of the VITAL project (Shadbolt et al., 1993) to provide operational modeling capabilities for the VITAL workbench (Domingue et al., 1993).

Several pragmatic considerations were taken into account in its development. One was its compatibility with Ontolingua. In fact, OCML can be considered as a kind of "operational Ontolingua" that provides theorem proving and function evaluation facilities for its constructs.

As OCML is mainly based on Ontolingua, it is a frame-based language with a Lisp-like syntax. Thus, OCML provides primitives to define classes, relations, functions, axioms and instances. It also provides primitives to define rules (with backward and forward chaining) and procedural attachments. Besides, a general *tell&ask* interface is implemented for OCML as a mechanism to assert facts and/or examine the contents of an OCML model.

OCML has a basic ontology library holding 12 ontologies. The first group of ontologies (*lists*, *numbers*, *sets* and *strings*) gives basic definitions for handling basic data types. The second (*frames*, *relations* and *functions*) deals with definitions for knowledge representation in OCML. The third (*task-method*, *mapping* and *inferences*) is used for building problem solving methods. Finally, the last group (*meta* and *environment*) describes the OCML language.

We must add that for editing and browsing OCML ontologies the WebOnto ontology editor (Domingue, 1998) can be used. WebOnto is described in Chapter 5.

4.3.4.1 Knowledge representation
We start by describing the header of OCML ontologies. The header of any OCML ontology is defined with the *def-ontology* primitive followed by the ontology name, natural language documentation, imported ontologies (*:includes*) and the ontology type (*:type*), which in our case is a domain ontology (*:domain*). In addition to domain ontologies, other types of ontologies can be built in OCML: *:method*, *:task* and *:application*. Finally, the type *:basic* is used for the set of basic ontologies in the ontology library presented above.

```
(def-ontology travel-ontology
  "Sample ontology for travel agencies"
  :includes (time units)
  :type :domain)
```

Concepts in OCML are known as classes. A class is modeled with the *def-class* primitive followed by a list of its superclasses (which may be empty), its documentation (which is optional), and the formal definition of the attributes of the class. Here we present the definition of the concept Travel, which only contains instance attributes. In this definition, constraints on the types of attributes and their cardinalities are also stated.

```
(def-class Travel ()
  "A journey from place to place"
  ((arrivalDate :type Date :cardinality 1)
   (departureDate :type Date :cardinality 1)
   (companyName :type String)
   (singleFare :type CurrencyQuantity
               :max-cardinality 1)))
```

A class attribute can be created with the primitive *:own-slots*, as shown in the following definition of the attribute `transportMeans` of the concept `Flight`. The use of this primitive is equivalent to the one described for OKBC, that is, it is not inherited by the subclasses of the concept nor by its instances.

```
(def-class Flight (Travel)
  "A journey by plane"
  ((flightNumber :type Number :cardinality 1))
:own-slots ((transportMeans "plane")))
```

To represent an instance attribute whose values are inherited to all the subclasses and instances of the concept where the attribute is defined, we can use the primitive *:value*, as shown in the definition that follows. Default values can be represented similarly, with the primitive *:default-value*.

```
(def-class Flight (Travel)
  "A journey by plane"
  ((flightNumber :type Number :cardinality 1)
   (transportMeans :type String :value "plane"
                   :cardinality 1)))
```

In addition to the type, values, cardinality and maximum cardinality of attributes, we can specify their minimum cardinality, default values, documentation and the way attribute values can be inherited.

Concept **taxonomies** are built inside concept definitions. In the case of subclass-of relations, the concept superclasses are included in the more specialized concept, just after the concept name, as shown in the aforementioned definition of the concept `Flight`. Disjoint decompositions and partitions are represented with the primitives *Subclass-Partition* and *Exhaustive-Subclass-Partition* respectively, as shown below. There are no primitives to represent exhaustive decompositions of a concept, although this can be represented with formal axioms:

```
(def-class AmericanAirlinesFlight (Flight)
()
:axiom-def
  (Subclass-Partition AmericanAirlinesFlight
     (set-of AA7462 AA2010 AA0488)))

(def-class Location ()
()
:axiom-def
  (Exhaustive-Subclass-Partition Location
     (set-of EuropeanLocation NorthAmericanLocation
             SouthAmericanLocation AsianLocation
             AfricanLocation AustralianLocation
             AntarcticLocation)))
```

Relations are used to describe the relationships between two or several concepts. The following examples show how to define the binary relation arrivalPlace and the ternary relation connects. In these definitions we have taken the keyword *:argument-types* to define the types of the relation arguments. The keyword *:constraint* is used to specify relation constraints. In the definition of the relation connects, this same keyword is chosen to specify that cities connected by a road must be different. Note that this restriction is like the one provided in Ontolingua.

```
(def-relation arrivalPlace (?travel ?arrPlace)
   "A journey ends at a location"
:argument-types (Travel Location))

(def-relation connects (?city1 ?city2 ?road)
   "A road connects two different cities"
:argument-types (Location Location RoadSection)
:constraint
(and (not (part-of ?city1 ?city2))
     (not (part-of ?city2 ?city1))
     (or (and (start ?road ?city1)(end ?road ?city2))
         (and (start ?road ?city2)(end ?road ?city1)))))
```

There are many other options that can be used in the definition of OCML relations. In fact, there are two overlapping groups of primitives: one for specifying relations (*:iff-def, :sufficient, :constraint, :def* and *:axiom-def*) and another for defining their operational constraints (*:iff-def, :sufficient, :constraint, :def, :prove-by* and *:lisp-fun*). The primitives belonging to both groups specify relations and define their operational constraints at the same time. We will detail the meaning of all these primitives:

- *:iff-def* defines necessary and sufficient relation conditions.
- *:sufficient* defines sufficient relation conditions.
- *:constraint* and *:def* are equivalent. They define necessary relation conditions.
- *:axiom-def* defines sufficient relation conditions where the relation name appears.
- *:prove-by* and *:lisp-fun* define a logical expression and a Lisp expression respectively. Both types of expressions are used to check whether a tuple satisfies the relation or not.

In OCML, **functions** are used to compute values. They are built with a syntax similar to Ontolingua's. However, it differs from Ontolingua in that OCML functions can be executed. Constraints on the function arguments can be expressed with the keywords *:def* or *:constraint*. Besides, the body of the function can be defined either with a functional term (with the keyword *:body*) or with a procedural attachment in Lisp (with the keyword *:lisp-fun)*. Let us see the definition of the function Pays:

```
(def-function Pays (?room ?discount) -> ?finalPrice
  "Price of the room after applying the discount"
:def (and (Room ?room)(Number ?discount))
:body
  (- (Price ?room) (/ (* (Price ?room) ?discount) 100)))
```

OCML permits defining first-order and second-order formal **axioms**. These are defined either as independent elements in the ontology, with the *def-axiom* primitive, or embedded in other terms (inside concept definitions, relations, etc.). However, OCML does not give operational support to axioms, that is, axioms are simply added to the ontology not used in the reasoning process. Their syntax is like the one used in Ontolingua. The following axiom declares that trains cannot go from the USA to Europe.

```
(def-axiom NoTrainfromUSAtoEurope
  "It is not possible to travel from the USA to Europe by
train"
:def (forall (?travel)
       (forall (?city1)
         (forall (?city2)
           (=> (and (Travel ?travel)
                    (arrivalPlace ?travel ?city1)
                    (departurePlace ?travel ?city2)
                    (EuropeanLocation ?city1)
                    (USALocation ?city2))
             (not (TrainTravel ?travel)))))))
```

Finally, **instances** in OCML can just belong to one concept. The following example shows the definition of our instance of the AA7462 flight:

```
(def-instance AA7462-Feb-08-2002 AA7462
       ((singleFare 300USDollars)
        (departureDate Feb8-2002)
        (arrivalPlace Seattle)))
```

Other components such as procedures (by means of the *:body* and *:lisp-fun* keywords), and backward and forward rules (rules in which we can express their chaining mechanism) can also be expressed in OCML. Furthermore, we can define concept and relation mappings (which are useful for using OCML in PSMs). For a detailed description of such components we recommend (Motta, 1999).

4.3.4.2 Reasoning mechanisms

One of the main purposes of OCML was to model prototypes and to generate rapidly executable knowledge models. The OCML inference engine provides a function interpreter, a control interpreter and a proof system. We will focus on the proof system, which combines the frame-based definitions of OCML components with OCML backward and forward rules.

The OCML proof system performs **constraint checking** with the expressions defined by means of the keywords *:iff-def, :constraint* and *:def*. In the previous section, we presented other keywords that were used for defining operational constraints such as *:prove-by, :lisp-fun* and *:sufficient*. These keywords (the keyword *:iff-def* also included) are used by the proof system to **infer values**.

The OCML proof system deals with attribute **inheritance** through the concept taxonomy. However, it does not use a complete proof mechanism with respect to first-order logic statements (for instance, disjunctions are proved by testing each clause separately, and negations are proved by default). We can define the behavior of the inheritance mechanism when dealing with the default values of an attribute. The user can decide whether to override default values or to merge them with more specific values.

When the user requires more control over the operational use of a definition (for instance, in cases where the given specification is highly inefficient) procedural attachments (Weyhrauch, 1980) can be associated with term definitions. Procedural attachments can be defined in OCML or Lisp. For instance, in our example we may need a procedural attachment to verify the availability of seats for a travel package.

The OCML system is freely available for downloading[10]. It is distributed as source Lisp code, so it must be run in a Lisp interpreter. To integrate the OCML system in other applications so that we can handle OCML ontologies for any purpose, we can use the Java APIs, C++ APIs, etc., provided by many Lisp interpreters. The tell&ask interface has also proven to be very useful for this purpose. Applications that use OCML ontologies are: Planet-Onto (Domingue and Motta, 2000), ScholOnto (Buckingham-Shum et al., 2000), etc. All of them are built on top of a customized Web server called LispWeb (Riva and Ramoni, 1996), as described in Chapter 5.

4.3.5 FLogic

FLogic (Kifer et al., 1995) is the acronym of *Frame Logic*. It was created in 1995 at the Department of Computer Science of the State University of New York. FLogic was initially developed as an object oriented approach to first order logic. It was specially used for deductive and object-oriented databases, and was later adapted and used for implementing ontologies.

FLogic integrates features from object-oriented programming, frame-based KR languages and first order logic. Some of its most significant features are: object identity, complex objects, inheritance, polymorphic types, query methods and encapsulation. In FLogic, the term *object* is used instead of *frame*, and *attribute* instead of *slot* (which is the term commonly used in frame-based languages, as we have seen when describing other frame-based languages).

FLogic has a model-theoretic semantics and a sound, complete resolution-based proof theory. FLogic can be combined with other specialized logics, like HiLog

---

[10] http://kmi.open.ac.uk/projects/ocml/download.html

(Chen et al., 1993) and Transaction Logic (Bonner and Kifer, 1995), to improve ontology reasoning.

FLogic ontologies can be built with different ontology development tools such as OntoEdit, Protégé-2000 and WebODE. Applications of this language range from object-oriented and deductive databases to ontologies. For instance, FLogic was used in the ontology-related project $(KA)^2$ (Benjamins et al., 1999), for information integration applications (Ludäscher et al., 1998), etc.

4.3.5.1 Knowledge representation
FLogic does not provide any reusable KR ontology with KR high-level primitives. Its modeling primitives are included directly as part of the language syntax.

In this language, we can export and import FLogic terms using "modules". Classes and their attributes can be exported and imported independently, as they are in object-oriented programming. This means that not all the attributes of a class can be imported (or visible) into other modules. The following example shows how to export the concept Travel. The instance attributes arrivalDate and departureDate are public. The instance attribute companyName is private and the instance attribute singleFare is exported to an ontology called accountOntology[11].

```
module travelOntology
   Travel[
      public:   arrivalDate => Date; departureDate => Date;
      private:  companyName =>> STRING;
      export-to(accountOntology):
               singleFare => CurrencyQuantity].
```

Concepts are essential components in FLogic because this language is based on the frame paradigm. We will confine our presentation now to the definition of the concept Travel in FLogic. The instance attributes of this concept are represented inside the concept definition using double arrows (both => and =>>). The number of edges of the arrow represents the maximum cardinality of the attribute: a single edge (=>) restricts the maximum cardinality of the attribute to one, while a double edge does not constrain the maximum cardinality. The type of attributes is defined on the right side of its definition and definitions are separated by semicolons.

```
Travel[
      arrivalDate => Date;
      departureDate => Date;
      companyName =>> STRING;
      singleFare => CurrencyQuantity].
```

In FLogic, there are two types of attributes: *instance* and *class* attributes. We have already presented how instance attributes are defined. Class attributes are identified with a single arrow (-> and ->>). The number of edges has the same meaning as

---

[11] Note that all FLogic definitions end with a period.

instance attributes have. The definition of the concept `Flight`, which contains a class attribute called `transportMeans`, whose value is "plane", and an instance attribute called `flightNumber` whose type is `String`, can be modeled as:

```
Flight[
       flightNumber => NUMBER;
       transportMeans -> "plane"].
```

In the previous definition, the attribute `transportMeans` is not inherited by the subclasses nor the instances of the class `Flight`. It represents a property of the class. If our aim is to assign values to an attribute so that they are inherited by the subclasses and instances of the class, we must use the symbols `o->` and `o->>`. Default values cannot be represented in FLogic.

The minimum cardinality of attributes cannot be defined in FLogic and it is not possible to restrict the maximum cardinality of an attribute to other values different from 1 or N. Furthermore, FLogic does not have constructs for documenting ontology components as other languages do. Thus, to document concepts we can use a class attribute, called `documentation`, in each class, and we can add the following attribute definition to the concept `Travel`:

```
documentation -> "A journey from place to place"
```

Concept **taxonomies** are defined using the symbol `::`, as can be seen in the example that follows (a `Flight` is a subclass of `Travel`). However, it is not possible to represent disjoint and exhaustive knowledge easily in FLogic. This should be defined by means of formal axioms, which will be discussed later in this section.

```
Flight :: Travel.
```

Binary **relations** do not exist in this language. Thus we must define them as attributes inside concepts, as we did with the concept `Travel`. Higher arity relations must be modeled by reifying the relation and converting it into a frame with one attribute for each argument of the relation, as the following example (relation `Connects`) illustrates. The constraints on the relation arguments will be expressed by axioms.

```
TernaryRelation[
    firstArgument => Object;
    secondArgument => Object;
    thirdArgument => Object].
Connects::TernaryRelation.
Connects[
    firstArgument=>Location;
    secondArgument=>Location;
    thirdArgument=>RoadSection].
```

Functions in FLogic are methods defined inside a concept. The output value of a function is calculated with a deductive rule that is defined separately in the ontology. The following example shows the function `pays` that has as input arguments instances of the concept `Buyer`, of the concept `Room`, and of the concept `Number`, and it outputs an instance of the concept `Number`. In the rule that comes next we express the constraints on the input arguments and the relationship between the output value of the function and the input arguments.

```
Buyer[pays@Room,Number => Number].
B[pays@Prod,D -> F] ←
     B:Buyer AND Prod:Room AND D:Number AND F:Number
     AND Prod[price->P] AND F = P - (P * D / 100).
```

In FLogic, formal **axioms** are independent components that are defined with first-order logic. The following example is an axiom that states that trains cannot travel from the USA to Europe.

```
FORALL x:Train
   x[arrivalPlace -> arr;departurePlace -> dep]
      AND arr:EuropeanLocation
 → NOT (dep:USALocation).
```

As we pointed out when defining the relation `Connects`, formal axioms can be used to express the constraints on the relation arguments. The example shows two axioms that state that two cities connected by a road are not part of each other, and that the road actually has its starting and end points in these cities.

```
FORALL c:Connects
   c[firstArgument -> c1; secondArgument -> c2]
   → NOT (c1[partOf -> c2]) AND NOT (c2[partOf -> c1]).
FORALL c:Connects
   c[firstArgument -> c1;
     secondArgument -> c2;
     thirdArgument -> r]
   → ((r[start -> c1]) AND (r[end -> c2])) OR
     ((r[start -> c2]) AND (r[end -> c1])).
```

Formal axioms can be used to represent disjoint and exhaustive knowledge in FLogic. We now present the axioms that state that the concepts `AA7462`, `AA2010`, and `AA0488` are disjoint (they appear in Figure 4.4c), and that `EuropeanLocation`, `AsianLocation`, `AustralianLocation`, `AfricanLocation`, `AntarcticLocation`, `NorthAmericanLocation`, and `SouthAmericanLocation` form a partition of the concept `Location`.

```
AA7462 :: AmericanAirlinesFlight.
AA2010 :: AmericanAirlinesFlight.
AA0488 :: AmericanAirlinesFlight.
```

```
FORALL flight flight:AA7462 <-> NOT flight:AA2010.
FORALL flight flight:AA7462 <-> NOT flight:AA0488.
FORALL flight flight:AA0488 <-> NOT flight:AA2010.


EuropeanLocation :: Location.
NorthAmericanLocation :: Location.
SouthAmericanLocation :: Location.
AsianLocation :: Location.
AfricanLocation :: Location.
AustralianLocation :: Location.
AntarcticLocation :: Location.
FORALL location location:Location <->
     (location:EuropeanLocation OR
      location:NorthAmericanLocation OR
      location:SouthAmericanLocation OR
      location:AsianLocation OR
      location:AfricanLocation OR
      location:AustralianLocation OR
      location:AntarcticLocation).
```

Finally, an **instance** in FLogic is defined with the name of the instance, the concept it belongs to and the values of the instance attributes.

```
AA7462Feb082002:AA7462[
        singleFare -> 300USDollars;
        departureDate -> Feb082002;
        arrivalPlace -> Seattle].
```

4.3.5.2 Reasoning mechanisms

Several inference engines can be used to reason with FLogic ontologies: Ontobroker (Fensel et al., 1999; Decker et al., 1999), FLORA (Ludäscher et al., 2000), and FLORID (FLOgic Reasoning In Databases) (Frohn et al., 2000).

OntoBroker uses a sound, complete algorithm for the monotonic part of the language. Its proof algorithm is independent of the sequence of the rules written in FLogic, and of the sequence of the statements inside these rules. This is different from languages such as Prolog, where the sequence of statements establishes the order in which they will be executed. This means that the ontology terms may appear in any place in a FLogic ontology.

When dealing with **exceptions** in concept taxonomies, OntoBroker is not complete but only sound, what means that it does not ensure that all the solutions to a problem are reached though all the solutions proposed are correct.

OntoBroker can be used not only to infer new knowledge from the ontologies defined in FLogic but to **check constraints** in these ontologies.

OntoBroker has been used in many ontology-based applications such as the (KA)[2] initiative (Benjamins et al., 1999), and also as an inference engine for SILRI (Decker et al. 1998), and inside the ontology editor OntoEdit (Sure et al., 2002a).

FLORA is a translator from FLogic to XSB. XSB (Sagonas et al., 1994) is an open source, logic programming system that can be used as a deductive database engine, and whose syntax is similar to that of Prolog. This inference engine is sound, though not complete. It supports multiple inheritance, exception handling, and negation, but it does not support type constraint checking.

FLORID is mainly oriented to managing deductive object-oriented databases. It uses a bottom-up evaluation algorithm, what means that it computes the closure of a given set of facts and rules; that is, all the information that can be inferred from it. However, it is not complete. FLORID supports multiple inheritance, exception handling, and negation. Like FLORA it does not support type constraint checking.

4.4 Ontology Markup Languages

In this section, the following ontology markup languages are presented: SHOE, XOL, RDF(S), OIL, DAML+OIL, and OWL. As discussed in the introduction to this chapter, these languages have laid the foundations of the Semantic Web and some of them are still in a development phase. Therefore, the syntax and some constructs to be presented in the next sections may suffer changes in the future.

The syntax of these languages is based on existing Web markup languages like HTML – HyperText Markup Language – (Ragett et al., 1999) and XML – eXtensible Markup Language – (Bray et al., 2000). While we assume that most of our readers will be familiar with HTML, we think that XML may not be so well-known as it is less used. Therefore, we will present first a brief overview of XML, whose syntax is used in most of these ontology markup languages.

XML[12] (Bray et al., 2000) is a subset of the ISO standard SGML[13] (Standard Generalized Markup Language). SGML (ISO, 1986) was created to specify document markup languages or tag sets for describing electronic texts. These tag sets may be used to describe the text structural divisions (title page, chapter, scene, stanza), typographical elements (changing typefaces), and other features (grammatical structure, etc.). XML development was started in 1996 by the W3C XML Working Group, with the active participation of an XML Special Interest Group, and became a W3C Recommendation in February 1998.

XML was designed to overcome some of the drawbacks of HTML. For instance, HTML was meant to be consumed only by human readers since it dealt only with content presentation of Web resources, not with the structure of that content.

Currently, XML is being used not only to structure texts but to exchange a wide variety of data on the Web, allowing better interoperability between information systems.

Several design goals were taken into consideration to create XML: XML should be compatible with SGML; it should be usable straightforwardly over the Internet; it should support a wide variety of applications; XML documents should be easy to

---

[12] http://www.w3.org/XML/
[13] http://www.iso.org/iso/en/CatalogueDetailPage.CatalogueDetail?CSNUMBER=16387

create and process, human-legible, and reasonably clear; finally, its design should be formal and concise.

An XML document consists of the following components:

- Elements, which are the most basic information units. These are pieces of text or other nested XML elements enclosed in tags (one start tag and one end tag, both of them with the same name, and the latter starting with the symbol "/"). For instance, the following text is an XML element:

```
<Flight>AA7462</Flight>
```

This element might be used to express that AA7462 is a type of Flight. If there is not text nor XML elements enclosed inside the start and end tags we can use empty-element tags optionally. For instance, the following text is an XML element with an empty-element tag: <Flight/>.

- Attributes, which describe elements. They associate name-value pairs to elements and appear only in start tags or empty-element tags. For instance, the attribute price applied to the element with the tag Flight may specify the price of the flight being described. The element with this attribute would be as follows:

```
<Flight price="300 US dollars">AA7462</Flight>
```

- Entity references, which refer to the content of a named entity. A named entity is a character sequence associated with a name and whose function is similar to that of a macro definition in programming languages. An entity reference is formed with an ampersand (&), the entity name, and a semicolon (;), and is substituted in the text by the content of the corresponding entity. For instance, the *lower-than* symbol (<) can be written as <, as occurred in HTML. Entities are also used to refer to URLs that appear very often in an XML document, so as to avoid writing the complete URL every time we need to refer to it. For instance, if we want to refer to the URL of American Airlines, we can create the entity aa whose content is http://www.americanairlines.com/, and use &aa; every time that we refer to it. This entity must be created in the DTD of the XML document, as follows:

```
<!ENTITY aa "http://www.americanairlines.com/">
```

- Comments, which are pieces of text ignored by XML parsers. They are used to comment on parts of an XML document and are delimited by the symbols <!-- and -->. For instance, we can add the following comment to an XML document:

```
<!-- Flight AA7462: information -->
```

- Processing Instructions, which are commands that are meant to be passed and interpreted by specific applications that read the XML document. They are character sequences delimited by the symbols *<?* and *?>*. For instance, the following processing instruction is used to define the Cascade StyleSheet to be applied to an XML document:

```
<?xml:stylesheet type="text/css" href="style.css" ?>
```

- Prolog, which precedes the XML data. It includes the XML declaration (*<?XML version="1.0"?>*), and an optional reference to a document type definition, such as the following:

```
<!DOCTYPE travel SYSTEM "travel.dtd">
```

A Document Type Definition (DTD) is a document that specifies constraints on the valid tags and tag sequences that can appear in a SGML document (XML documents included). In other words, it defines the structure of a SGML document. It also defines entities, which were described above. We present below part of the WebODE ontology engineering platform's DTD[14] that defines the structure of the XML export and import format for WebODE ontologies. As we can see in this fragment, an ontology is described by its name, an optional description, an optional author, its creation date, zero or several related bibliographic references, an optional conceptualization, an optional set of instances, and an optional set of views. The ontology conceptualization, if contained in the XML document, contains lists (possibly empty) of imported terms, bibliographic references, concept descriptions, concept groups, ad hoc relations, formulae, constants, and relation properties. Each concept is described by its name, optional description, and lists (possibly empty) of class attributes, instance attributes, synonyms, abbreviations, and related bibliographic references. Finally, instance attributes contain their name, an optional NL description, their type (Integer, Float, String, etc.), minimum and maximum cardinalities, unit of measure, precision, a list of values and, as in the previous case, lists of related bibliographic references, synonyms, and abbreviations.

```
<!ELEMENT Ontology (Name, Description?, Author?,
   Creation-Date, Related-Reference*, Conceptualization?,
   Instances?, Views?)>

<!-- Conceptualization -->
<!ELEMENT Conceptualization (Imported-Term*, Reference*,
   Concept*, Group*, Term-Relation*, Formula*, Constant*,
   Property*)>

<!-- Term -->
<!ELEMENT Concept (Name, Description?, Class-Attribute*,
   Instance-Attribute*, Synonym*, Abbreviation*,
   Related-Reference*)>
```

---

[14] http://webode.dia.fi.upm.es/webode/DTD/webode_1_0.dtd

```
<!-- Instance attribute -->
<!ELEMENT Instance-Attribute (Name, Description?, Type,
  Minimum-Cardinality, Maximum-Cardinality,
  Measurement-Unit?, Precision?, Value*,
  Related-Reference*, Synonym*, Abbreviation*)>
```

XML schemas (Thompson et al., 2001; Biron and Malhotra, 2001) extend the capabilities of DTDs to specify the structure and constraints of XML documents (including datatypes, cardinalities, minimum and maximum values, etc.). Therefore, XML schemas can be used for specifying the structure of XML documents. For instance, a fragment of the previous DTD can be described as follows:

```
<xsd:schema
    xmlns:xsd="http://www.w3.org/2001/XMLSchema"
    xmlns="http://webode.dia.fi.upm.es/webode/XSD/
                    webode_schema.xsd">
  <xsd:element name="Ontology" type="OntologyType"/>
  <xsd:complexType name="OntologyType">
    <xsd:sequence>
     <xsd:element name="Name" type="xsd:string"/>
     <xsd:element name="Description" type="xsd:string"
                    minOccurs="0"/>
     <xsd:element name="Author" type="xsd:string"
                    minOccurs="0"/>
     <xsd:element name="Creation-Date" type="xsd:date"/>
     <xsd:element name="Related-Reference"
                    type="xsd:string"
                    minOccurs="0" maxOccurs="unbounded"/>
     <xsd:element name="Conceptualization"
                    type="ConceptualizationType"
                    minOccurs="0"/>
     <xsd:element name="Instances" type="InstancesType"
                    minOccurs="0"/>
     <xsd:element name="Views" type="ViewsType"
                    minOccurs="0"/>
    </xsd:sequence>
  </xsd:complexType>
...
</xsd:schema>
```

Depending on the absence or presence of a DTD or XML schema for an XML document, we can distinguish two types of XML documents: *well-formed* and *valid* documents respectively. In a well-formed XML document only one root element exists, all its elements are correctly nested (the start and end tags are balanced), and attribute values are delimited by quotes ("). However, its structure is not defined by a DTD or an XML schema. A valid XML document is a well-formed document whose structure is defined by a DTD or XML Schema and is compliant with it (that is, it follows the structure described in it).

We now present a fragment of the XML document describing the travel ontology in WebODE according to the DTD[15] presented above. It contains general information about the ontology and the concept `Flight` with its instance attribute `company Name`.

```xml
<?xml version="1.0" encoding="iso-8859-1"?>
<!DOCTYPE Ontology SYSTEM
'http://webode.dia.fi.upm.es/webode/DTD/webode_1_0.dtd'>

<Ontology>
  <!-- Ontology Description -->
  <Name>Travel Ontology</Name>
  <Author>ocorcho</Author>
  <Creation-Date>2002-06-21</Creation-Date>
  <Conceptualization>
    <Concept>
      <Name>American Airlines Flight</Name>
      <Instance-Attribute>
        <Name>company Name</Name>
        <Type>String</Type>
        <Minimum-Cardinality>1</Minimum-Cardinality>
        <Maximum-Cardinality>1</Maximum-Cardinality>
      </Instance-Attribute>
    </Concept>
...
  </Conceptualization>
</Ontology>
```

The last comment on XML is related to XML namespaces. They are a kind of mechanism to resolve naming conflicts between elements when each element comes from a different vocabulary. Each namespace identifies an XML vocabulary defined within a URL. We have used namespaces in the XML schema fragment presented previously where the term *xsd* was used to refer to the URL *http://www.w3.org/2001/XMLSchema*. Namespaces are used as prefixes of XML tags, specifying the URL where an element definition can be found. For instance, in a WebODE ontology we can define the namespace `odeKR` to refer to the URL `http://webode.dia.fi.upm.es/WebODEKR.xml#`, using the following code in the `Ontology` element:

```xml
<Ontology
 xmlns:odeKR="http://webode.dia.fi.upm.es/WebODEKR.xml#"
/>
```

If we want to refer to the Concept element defined in that URL, we will use:

---

[15] This XML document is also valid with respect to the corresponding XML schema, though the !DOCTYPE definition would not appear in it.

```
<odeKR:Concept>
```

which is an abbreviated expression for

```
http://webode.dia.fi.upm.es/ontology/time.xml#Concept
```

We show several examples of the use of XML namespaces when describing RDF(S), OIL, DAML+OIL, and OWL.

4.4.1 SHOE

SHOE (Luke and Heflin, 2000) stands for *Simple HTML Ontology Extension*. It was developed at the University of Maryland in 1996. SHOE was created as an extension of HTML with the aim of incorporating machine-readable semantic knowledge in Web documents. It provides specific tags for representing ontologies. As these tags are not defined in HTML, the information inside them is not shown in standard Web browsers. There is also a slight variant of the SHOE syntax for XML compatibility[16]. In our examples, we have used HTML syntax.

The main objective of the SHOE language was to make it possible to collect meaningful information about Web pages and documents with the aim of improving search mechanisms on the Web. Consequently, its intended use can be summarized in the following three steps: (1) to define an ontology that describes concepts and relationships between them; (2) to annotate HTML pages with concept instances that describe such pages or other pages, and (3) to let agents search SHOE annotated Web pages to keep information updated and to allow retrieving semantic information.

To help use SHOE, there are several tools available such as the SHOE Knowledge Annotator, Running SHOE, Exposé, Parka, XSB, SHOE Search, and SHOE Semantic Search. More information about these tools is provided in the section about reasoning mechanisms. Although SHOE is no longer maintained, these tools can still be downloaded and used.

SHOE developers have also contributed to the creation of other languages like DAML+OIL and OWL.

4.4.1.1 Knowledge representation
SHOE ontologies can import terms from other SHOE ontologies with the *USE-ONTOLOGY* tag. Inside this tag we must explicit the name and version of the ontology to be imported, the prefix used to refer to concepts of the imported ontology, and the URL where the ontology is available. As an example, our travel ontology imports two ontologies: the SHOE base ontology, which contains datatypes like STRING, NUMBER and Date, and top-level concepts like Entity and SHOEEntity, and a domain ontology about units. The SHOE base ontology should not be mistaken for a KR ontology because it does not provide a formal definition of SHOE KR primitives.

---

[16] Its DTD is available at *http://www.cs.umd.edu/projects/plus/SHOE/shoe_xml.dtd*

```
<!-- Ontology's name and version -->
<ONTOLOGY ID="Travel-Ontology" VERSION="1.0">

<!-- Importations from other ontologies -->
<USE-ONTOLOGY ID="base-ontology"
  VERSION="1.0" PREFIX="base"
  URL="http://www.cs.umd.edu/projects/plus/SHOE/
  base.html">
<USE-ONTOLOGY ID="units"
  VERSION="1.0" PREFIX="units"
  URL="http://delicias.dia.fi.upm.es/SHOE/units.html">
```

To use imported terms in an ontology these must be prefixed according to the ontology they belong to. Prefixes are defined in the *USE-ONTOLOGY* tag, as we have already mentioned. Hence, the concept USDollar from the units ontology must be referred to as units.USDollar. To improve the readability of the ontology, we can reduce the number of prefixes by renaming the imported terms using the *DEF-RENAME* tag. In a SHOE ontology, the following code lets us use USDollar when referring to the term units.USDollar.

```
<DEF-RENAME FROM="units.USDollar" TO="USDollar">
```

Concepts are known as categories in SHOE. They are created with the *DEF-CATEGORY* tag. Concepts include their name and, optionally, their NL documentation. In the following example, we can see the definition of the concepts Travel and Flight. In the definition of the concept Flight, we have also stated clearly its superclass.

```
<DEF-CATEGORY NAME="Travel"
  DESCRIPTION="A journey from place to place">

<DEF-CATEGORY NAME="Flight"
  DESCRIPTION="A journey by plane" ISA="Travel">
```

Attribute definitions are not included inside the concept definition. As in many other languages, attributes are defined as binary relations using the *DEF-RELATION* tag. We show below the definition of the instance attributes arrivalDate, departureDate, companyName and singleFare of the concept Travel. In these definitions, we have used FROM for the attribute domain and TO for the attribute value type. Note that in SHOE we cannot express cardinality restrictions on attributes nor default values nor other constraints.

```
<DEF-RELATION NAME="arrivalDate">
  <DEF-ARG POS="FROM" TYPE="Travel">
  <DEF-ARG POS="TO" TYPE="time.Date">
</DEF-RELATION>
```

```
<DEF-RELATION NAME="departureDate">
  <DEF-ARG POS="FROM" TYPE="Travel">
  <DEF-ARG POS="TO" TYPE="time.Date">
</DEF-RELATION>
<DEF-RELATION NAME="companyName">
  <DEF-ARG POS="FROM" TYPE="Travel">
  <DEF-ARG POS="TO" TYPE=".STRING">
</DEF-RELATION>
<DEF-RELATION NAME="singleFare">
  <DEF-ARG POS="FROM" TYPE="Travel">
  <DEF-ARG POS="TO" TYPE="units.CurrencyQuantity">
</DEF-RELATION>
```

In SHOE we cannot define class attributes nor instance attributes whose value is inherited for the concept subclasses and instances. Therefore, the attribute transportMeans of the concept Flight can only be defined as if it were an instance attribute although its value cannot be represented. The value type .STRING is not prefixed because it belongs to the base ontology.

```
<DEF-RELATION NAME="transportMeans">
  <DEF-ARG POS="FROM" TYPE="Flight">
  <DEF-ARG POS="TO" TYPE=".STRING">
</DEF-RELATION>
```

Concept **taxonomies** in SHOE are represented with the *ISA* keyword inside concept definitions, as shown in the definition of the concept Flight. A concept may be a subclass of several concepts, and is defined inside the *ISA* keyword by a whitespace-delimited list of the superclasses of the concept that is defined. Disjoint and exhaustive knowledge cannot be represented in this language.

Relations in SHOE can have any arity and they are represented with the *DEF-RELATION* tag. Arguments of a relation are defined with the *DEF-ARG* tag. Inside this tag, the position of that argument is specified with the keyword *POS*. The allowed values for this keyword are integers. In the case of binary relations, the terms *FROM* and *TO* can be used to represent the domain and range of the relation respectively, instead of using the keyword *POS* and the integers *1* and *2*.

We show next the definitions for the binary relation arrivalPlace and the ternary relation connects. With SHOE we cannot represent the constraint of: *cities are not part of each other.*

```
<DEF-RELATION NAME="arrivalPlace">
  <DEF-ARG POS="FROM" TYPE="Travel">
  <DEF-ARG POS="TO" TYPE="Location">
</DEF-RELATION>
```

```
<DEF-RELATION NAME="connects"
    DESCRIPTION="A road connects two different cities">
  <DEF-ARG POS="1" TYPE="Location">
  <DEF-ARG POS="2" TYPE="Location">
  <DEF-ARG POS="3" TYPE="RoadSection">
</DEF-RELATION>
```

Functions do not exist in SHOE nor can they be defined as relations. This is due to the fact that with SHOE we cannot represent any set of input arguments that output only one value.

But we can represent a very restricted type of formal **axioms**: inference rules. Inference rules are used to derive new knowledge from existing knowledge in the ontology. They are similar to Horn rules and are divided in two parts: the body (expressed inside the *INF-IF* tag), where we define one or several clauses, and the head (expressed inside the *INF-THEN* tag), where we define the consequence or consequences that can be inferred when the clauses in the body are true. If the USAGE attribute contains VAR in the body of the inference rule, it means that we are defining a variable with the name expressed in the VALUE attribute, which can take any value. The following inference rule states that we could infer that a person that takes a flight will arrive at the arrival place of that flight:

```
<DEF-INFERENCE>
 <INF-IF>
   <RELATION NAME="travelsIn">
       <ARG POS="1" VALUE="person" USAGE="VAR">
       <ARG POS="2" VALUE="journey" USAGE="VAR">
   </RELATION>
   <CATEGORY NAME="Traveler" FOR="person" USAGE="VAR">
   <CATEGORY NAME="Flight" FOR="journey" USAGE="VAR">
   <RELATION NAME="arrivalPlace">
       <ARG POS="FROM" VALUE="journey" USAGE="VAR">
       <ARG POS="TO" VALUE="place" USAGE="VAR">
   </RELATION>
 </INF-IF>
 <INF-THEN>
   <RELATION NAME="arrivesAt">
       <ARG POS="FROM" VALUE="person" USAGE="VAR">
       <ARG POS="TO" VALUE="place" USAGE="VAR">
   </RELATION>
 </INF-THEN>
</DEF-INFERENCE>
```

Constraints cannot be represented in SHOE. Hence, we will not be able to represent the axiom that does not allow trains to go from Europe to the USA.

Instances deserve a special treatment in SHOE since the main aim of this language is the annotation of instances in distributed Web documents. As a consequence, instances are not usually defined in the same document as the rest of the ontology definitions but inserted in disperse HTML documents. We show below the definition of our instance of flight AA7462, which may appear or be generated inside any of the Web pages of the American Airlines Web site. The value me is used to refer to the instance name.

```
<INSTANCE KEY="AA7462-Feb08-2002">
  <USE-ONTOLOGY ID="Travel-Ontology"
    URL="http://delicias.dia.fi.upm.es/SHOE/travel.html"
    VERSION="1.0" PREFIX="travel">
  <CATEGORY NAME="travel.AA7462">
  <RELATION NAME="travel.singleFare">
    <ARG POS=1 VALUE="me">
    <ARG POS=2 VALUE="300USDollars">
  </RELATION>
  <RELATION NAME="travel.departureDate">
    <ARG POS=1 VALUE="me">
    <ARG POS=2 VALUE="Feb8-2002">
  </RELATION>
  <RELATION NAME="travel.arrivalPlace">
    <ARG POS=1 VALUE="me">
    <ARG POS=2 VALUE="Seattle">
  </RELATION>
</INSTANCE>
```

As SHOE instances are distributed on the Web, SHOE considers the existence of claims, that is, information that has been asserted by an instance. In fact, different instances may provide contradictory information about something. These claims are correctly handled by the tools associated with the SHOE language and no other language provides this functionality.

4.4.1.2 Reasoning mechanisms
SHOE has been specially designed to allow inferences when querying an ontology. These inferences are performed with the inference rules defined in the corresponding ontologies.

As commented in the introduction to this language, there are several tools that handle SHOE ontologies, whose source code is available for downloading[17]. From the point of view of reasoning, the most interesting is Exposé (Heflin and Hendler, 2000), a Web crawler that searches Web pages with SHOE annotations, gathers the associated knowledge, and loads it into a knowledge representation system.

Currently, the KR systems available in Exposé are Parka, XSB, and any OKBC-compliant KR system. As we have presented OKBC in this chapter, we will only describe Parka and XSB.

Parka (Evett et al., 1994) is a frame-based system developed at the University of Maryland. Its main feature is the ability to handle very large knowledge bases. This

---

[17] http://www.cs.umd.edu/projects/plus/SHOE/downloads.html

system supports **exception handling** and multiple **inheritance**, and is able to handle **claims**. However, it lacks a general inference rule mechanism and does not allow making inferences with the **inference rules** defined in a SHOE ontology. It also provides the PIQ interface (Parka Interface for Queries) to allow querying a Parka knowledge base.

XSB was described in the FLogic's section. It is an open source, logic programming system that can be used as a deductive database engine. Its syntax is similar to that of Prolog. This system supports **exception handling**, multiple **inheritance**, inferences with the **inference rules,** and **claims**.

Other SHOE-related tools available at the above URL are the following:
- SHOE Knowledge Annotator (Heflin and Hendler, 2001); it can be used to annotate instances manually in HTML pages. It will be described in Section 5.4.4.
- Running SHOE (Heflin, 2001); it can be used to create wrappers for HTML and XML pages that generate annotations automatically.
- SHOE Semantic Search (Heflin and Hendler, 2000); it allows querying SHOE information that has been loaded in any of the previous knowledge bases.

Obviously, these tools are not related to reasoning with SHOE ontologies. However, we have considered them interesting enough to be included in this section.

4.4.2 XOL

XOL (Karp et al., 1999) stands for *XML-based Ontology exchange Language*. It was designed, in 1999, by Pangea Systems Inc. and the Artificial Intelligence Center of SRI International. The purpose of this language was to provide a format for exchanging ontology definitions among a heterogeneous set of software systems. Therefore, XOL was not intended for developing ontologies, it was created as an intermediate language for transferring ontologies among different database systems, ontology-development tools, and application programs.

In 1999, members from the bioinformatics community of several US universities and US firms evaluated different languages with the aim of studying the KR needs of experts in bioinformatics (McEntire et al., 1999), and selected several ontology languages such as Ontolingua (Farquhar et al., 1997), CycL (Lenat and Guha, 1990), OML (Kent, 1998) and RDF (Lassila and Swick, 1999). They also selected the ontology access protocol OKBC (Chaudhri et al., 1998) and other languages that had not been specifically created for implementing ontologies such as OPM (Chen and Markowitz, 1996), UML (Rumbaugh et al., 1998), ASN.1 (Dubuisson, 2000) and ODL[18]. Note that OIL, DAML+OIL, and OWL were not available at that time.

As a result of the evaluation carried out by these experts, the candidate languages for exchanging bioinformatics ontologies were Ontolingua and OML. However, both languages had important drawbacks: Ontolingua's Lisp syntax and OMLs lack of expressiveness. Therefore, they decided to create the language XOL by merging the high expressiveness of Ontolingua with the simple and readable

---

[18] http://www.odmg.org/standard/standardoverview.htm

syntax of OML (which uses XML). Finally, instead of Ontolingua they decided to use a subset of the OKBC knowledge model (Chaudhri et al., 1998), called OKBC-Lite, which had enough expressiveness to represent bioinformatics ontologies.

XOL ontologies are written in XML. XOL does not provide a KR ontology although it is based on the OKBC-Lite knowledge model. This reduced knowledge model allows representing classes, class taxonomies, slots, facets and individuals.

Generic text editors or XML editors should be used to author XOL files, as there are no specialized tools that permit developing ontologies with XOL. Neither are inference engines available for this language, because it is intended for exchanging ontologies among systems.

4.4.2.1 Knowledge representation

Unlike most of the languages already studied, XOL does not permit importing definitions from other ontologies. The header of XOL ontologies includes only information about the ontology's name and version, about ontology documentation and about the KR system in which the ontology will be available, as shown in the next definition:

```
<module>
  <name>Travel Ontology</name>
  <version>1.0</version>
  <documentation>Sample ontology for travel
      agencies</documentation>
  <kb-type>Ontolingua</kb-type>
  <package>user</package>
  ...
</module>
```

In XOL **concepts** are called classes. They are represented using the *class* tag, as shown in the following definition of the concept Travel. Concepts may also include, optionally, the NL documentation of the class:

```
<class>
  <name>Travel</name>
  <documentation>A journey from place to
      place</documentation>
</class>
```

Attributes in XOL are defined as slots. XOL distinguishes between *own* and *template* slots. The difference between both types of attributes was explained in Section 4.3.3. Attributes are defined with the *slot* tag followed by the type of attribute being defined (*own* or *template*). In the case of own slots it is not necessary to specify explicitly its type, since *own* is the default type. Let us see now the definition of the template slots arrivalDate, departureDate, companyName and singleFare of the concept Travel.

```
<slot type="template">
  <name>arrivalDate</name>
  <domain>Travel</domain>
  <slot-value-type>Date</slot-value-type>
  <slot-cardinality>1</slot-cardinality>
</slot>
<slot type="template">
  <name>departureDate</name>
  <domain>Travel</domain>
  <slot-value-type>Date</slot-value-type>
  <slot-cardinality>1</slot-cardinality>
</slot>
<slot type="template">
  <name>companyName</name>
  <domain>Travel</domain>
  <slot-value-type>String</slot-value-type>
</slot>
<slot type="template">
  <name>singleFare</name>
  <domain>Travel</domain>
  <slot-value-type>Currency Quantity</slot-value-type>
  <slot-maximum cardinality>1</slot-maximum cardinality>
</slot>
```

We may also define the name of the inverse slot, the minimum cardinality of the slot, and the minimum and maximum values for numeric slots. Furthermore, it is also possible to specify the values of own slots inside the definition of classes. Let us see the definition of the concept Flight, its own slot transportMeans, and its template slot flightNumber:

```
<class>
  <name>Flight</name>
  <documentation>A journey by plane</documentation>
  <subclass-of>Travel</subclass-of>
  <slot-values>
    <name>transportMeans</name>
    <value>plane</value>
  </slot-values>
</class>

<slot>
  <name>transportMeans</name>
  <domain>Flight</domain>
  <slot-value-type>String</slot-value-type>
  <slot-cardinality>1</slot-cardinality>
</slot>
```

```
<slot type="template">
  <name>flightNumber</name>
  <domain>Flight</domain>
  <slot-value-type>Number</slot-value-type>
  <slot-cardinality>1</slot-cardinality>
</slot>
```

Concept **taxonomies** are expressed in XOL with the *subclass-of* primitive, as we have already shown for concept Flight. A class can be a subclass of several classes. Disjoint and exhaustive knowledge cannot be expressed in this language.

Binary **relations** between concepts must be expressed in XOL as slots. We can define the documentation of the relation, its domain and range (*slot-value-type*). It is also possible to constrain the cardinality of the relations. As an example, we present the definition of the relation arrivalPlace between the concepts Travel and Location:

```
<slot type="template">
  <name>arrivalPlace</name>
  <documentation>A journey ends at a
      location</documentation>
  <domain>Travel</domain>
  <slot-value-type>Location</slot-value-type>
  <slot-cardinality>1</slot-cardinality>
</slot>
```

In XOL, ternary or higher arity relations cannot be expressed as such. They must be defined as classes by means of a reification process. Since XOL is less expressive than other languages, complex constraints for these relations cannot be expressed. For example, it is impossible to define that the ternary relation connects must be established between different cities.

```
<class>
  <name>connects</name>
  <documentation>A road connects two different
      cities</documentation>
</class>
<slot>
  <name>firstArgument</name>
  <domain>connects</domain>
  <slot-value-type>Location</slot-value-type>
  <slot-cardinality>1</slot-cardinality>
</slot>
<slot>
  <name>secondArgument</name>
  <domain>connects</domain>
  <slot-value-type>Location</slot-value-type>
```

```
  <slot-cardinality>1</slot-cardinality>
</slot>
<slot>
  <name>thirdArgument</name>
  <domain>connects</domain>
  <slot-value-type>RoadSection</slot-value-type>
  <slot-cardinality>1</slot-cardinality>
</slot>
```

Neither **functions** nor formal **axioms** can be expressed in XOL and this means a strong limitation of the expressiveness of this language.

Finally, in XOL **instances** are called individuals, and they must belong to only one class. The values of the slots attached to the instance must be defined inside the definition of an instance, as shown in the following example:

```
<individual>
  <name>AA7462 Feb08 2002</name>
  <instance-of>AA7462</instance-of>
  <slot-values>
      <name>singleFare</name>
      <value>300USDollars</value>
  </slot-values>
  <slot-values>
      <name>departureDate</name>
      <value>Feb08-2002</value>
  </slot-values>
  <slot-values>
      <name>arrivalPlace</name>
      <value>Seattle</value>
  </slot-values>
</individual>
```

4.4.2.2 Reasoning mechanisms
As it was stated in the introduction, no inference engines are available for XOL since this language is intended only for exchanging ontologies between different systems.

4.4.3 RDF(S): RDF and RDF Schema

RDF (Lassila and Swick, 1999) stands for *Resource Description Framework*. It is being developed by the W3C to create metadata for describing Web resources, and it has been already proposed as a W3C recommendation. As was commented in Chapter 2, the RDF data model is equivalent to the semantic networks formalism and consists of three object types: resources, properties and statements. The RDF KR ontology was also described in Section 2.1.2.

The RDF data model does not have mechanisms for defining the relationships between properties and resources. This is the role of the RDF Vocabulary Description language (Brickley and Guha, 2003), also known as RDF Schema or RDFS, which is a working draft of the W3C[19]. In Chapter 2, we also presented RDF Schema as a frame-based extension of RDF and described the RDFS KR ontology.

RDF(S) is the term commonly used to refer to the combination of RDF and RDFS. Thus, RDF(S) combines semantic networks with frames but it does not provide all the primitives that are usually found in frame-based knowledge representation systems. In fact, neither RDF, nor RDFS, and nor their combination in RDF(S) should be considered as ontology languages *per se*, but rather as general languages for describing metadata in the Web. From now on, we will always refer to RDF(S) in our examples and explanations.

RDF(S) is widely used as a representation format in many tools and projects, and there exists a huge amount of resources for RDF(S) handling, such as browsing, editing, validating, querying, storing, etc. In the section about further readings, we provide several URLs where updated information about RDF(S) resources can be found.

4.4.3.1 Knowledge representation

RDF(S) provides the most basic primitives for ontology modeling, achieving a balance between expressiveness and reasoning. It has been developed as a stable core of primitives that can be easily extended. In fact, as we will discuss later, languages such as OIL, DAML+OIL, and OWL reuse and extend RDF(S) primitives. In the following pages, we will review which types of ontology components may be represented in RDF(S).

In our examples we will use the XML syntax of RDF(S) (Beckett, 2003), and will also present the corresponding graphs for some of them. There is a syntax for RDF(S) based on triples (also called N-Triples notation[20]) but it will not be presented here.

Before analyzing which ontology components can be expressed in RDF(S), let us see how to define a RDF(S) ontology. An ontology in RDF(S) must start with the root node RDF. In this root node the namespaces for the RDF and RDFS KR ontologies must be included. These namespaces are usually identified with the prefixes *rdf* and *rdfs*, and they point to the standard URLs of both RDF and RDFS respectively. This definition is shown below:

```
<rdf:RDF
 xmlns:rdf="http://www.w3.org/1999/02/22-rdf-syntax-ns#"
 xmlns:rdfs="http://www.w3.org/2000/01/rdf-schema#">
```

The use of these namespaces allow us to use the prefixes *rdf* and *rdfs* for those KR primitives that belong to RDF and RDFS respectively.

---

[19] In this section, we describe the status of RDF(S) as of January 23, 2003. Some features of RDF or RDF Schema may change in the future, since they are still in a development phase.
[20] http://www.w3.org/TR/rdf-testcases/#ntriples

The file containing our ontology will be located in a specific URL (for instance, *http://www.ontologies.org/travel*). However, the definitions inside it could refer to a different URL (for instance, *http://delicias.dia.fi.upm.es/RDFS/travel*). In that situation, we must add an *xml:base* definition to the root node, pointing to the second URL, as follows:

```
<rdf:RDF
 xmlns:rdf="http://www.w3.org/1999/02/22-rdf-syntax-ns#"
 xmlns:rdfs="http://www.w3.org/2000/01/rdf-schema#"
 xml:base="http://delicias.dia.fi.upm.es/RDFS/travel">
```

Besides, if we want to import terms from other ontologies into our ontology, we should refer to them in any place of our ontology using the URL of those terms. For instance, if we want to import the concept CurrencyQuantity from a RDFS ontology of units that is placed at *http://delicias.dia.fi.upm.es/RDFS/units*, we should use the following identifier for the term when referring to it:

```
   http://delicias.dia.fi.upm.es/RDFS/units#CurrencyQuantity
```

As it is very tedious to write the previous expression every time we refer to this concept, we can create a XML entity units in the document type declaration that precedes the ontology definitions, as presented below, and use &units;CurrencyQuantity to refer to the concept CurrencyQuantity from that ontology, as we explained in the beginning of Section 4.4. In our examples, we will suppose that the following entities have been created:

```
<!ENTITY units
    'http://delicias.dia.fi.upm.es/RDFS/units#'>
<!ENTITY rdf
    'http://www.w3.org/1999/02/22-rdf-syntax-ns#'>
<!ENTITY rdfs 'http://www.w3.org/2000/01/rdf-schema#'>
<!ENTITY xsd
    'http://www.w3.org/2001/XMLSchema#'>
```

The entity xsd is normally used to refer to XML Schema datatypes (Biron and Malhotra, 2001), which are used as the range of many ontology properties. In the definitions we present in this section, the ontology terms will be referred to with three attributes: *rdf:ID*, *rdf:about* and *rdf:resource*. There are slight differences in the use of these attributes. The first (*rdf:ID*) is used only once for each ontology term to create an anchor-id for the term in the document where the ontology is defined. The second (*rdf:about*) is used to extend the definition of the resource to which it refers. The third (*rdf:resource*) is used to refer to an ontology term, without adding more knowledge. In the second and third cases, if the ontology term is defined in the same document as the reference is, we must precede its name by #.

Other attributes can be used to refer to terms in a RDF(S) file (*rdf:nodeID* and *rdf:bagID*) but they are out of the scope of this description. We refer to Beckett (2003) for a description of these attributes.

Concepts are known as classes in RDF(S). Though there exist several patterns to specify a class in RDF(S) with XML syntax, here we will use the most compact syntax. Classes are referenced either by their name or by a URL to a Web resource. They can also include their documentation and their superclasses. This is shown in the following code for the concept `Travel`.

```
<rdfs:Class rdf:ID="Travel">
   <rdfs:comment>A journey from place to
      place</rdfs:comment>
</rdfs:Class>
```

Figure 4.5 presents the graphical notation for the concept `Travel` and its attributes. This figure contains classes and properties that belong to the RDF KR ontology (*rdf:Property* and *rdf:type*), to the RDFS KR ontology (*rdfs:Literal*, *rdfs:Class*, *rdfs:domain* and *rdfs:range*), to a domain ontology about units (`units:currencyQuantity`), to XML Schema datatypes (`xsd:date`), and to our travel ontology (`Travel`, `companyName`, `singleFare`, `departureDate` and `arrivalDate`). The primitive *rdf:type* determines if a resource (represented by an ellipse) is a class or a property. For the properties of our ontology we should define their domain and range.

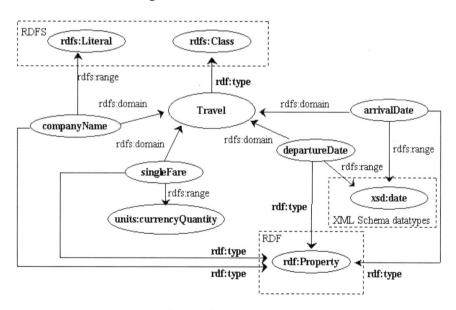

Figure 4.5: Definition of the class `Travel` in RDF(S).

Instance attributes of classes are defined as *properties* in RDFS. The *domain* of these properties is the class to which the attribute belongs, and the *range* for those properties is the type of the attribute values. No cardinality constraints nor default values can be defined for attributes.

In the definitions for properties of the example that follows, we use XML entities for referring to XML Schema datatypes (`&xsd;date` and `&xsd;integer`) and terms in other ontologies (`&units;CurrencyQuantity` and `&rdfs;Literal`).

```
<rdf:Property rdf:ID="arrivalDate">
  <rdfs:domain rdf:resource="#Travel"/>
  <rdfs:range rdf:resource="&xsd;date"/>
</rdf:Property>
<rdf:Property rdf:ID="departureDate">
  <rdfs:domain rdf:resource="#Travel"/>
  <rdfs:range rdf:resource="&xsd;date"/>
</rdf:Property>
<rdf:Property rdf:ID="companyName">
  <rdfs:domain rdf:resource="#Travel"/>
  <rdfs:range rdf:resource="&rdfs;Literal"/>
</rdf:Property>
<rdf:Property rdf:ID="singleFare">
  <rdfs:domain rdf:resource="#Travel"/>
  <rdfs:range rdf:resource="&units;CurrencyQuantity"/>
</rdf:Property>
```

Class attributes can be represented in RDF(S) similarly, although by defining the domain of the property as *rdfs:Class*, and including the property value in the class definition. For example, the following definitions represent the class attribute `transportMeans` and the concept `Flight`:

```
<rdf:Property rdf:ID="transportMeans">
  <rdfs:domain rdf:resource="&rdfs;Class"/>
  <rdfs:range rdf:resource="&rdfs;Literal"/>
</rdf:Property>

<rdfs:Class rdf:ID="Flight">
  <rdfs:comment>A journey by plane</rdfs:comment>
  <rdfs:subClassOf rdf:resource="#Travel"/>
  <transportMeans rdf:datatype="&rdfs;Literal">
    plane
  </transportMeans>
</rdfs:Class>
```

Concept **taxonomies** are built in RDF(S) by defining a class as a subclass of one or more classes. However, neither disjoint nor exhaustive knowledge in concept taxonomies can be expressed in this language.

Binary **relations** between classes are defined in RDF(S) as properties (in fact, all of the previous examples could be considered binary relations, as they relate two concepts). Therefore, as in the case of attributes, we may constrain their domain and range.

However, relations of higher arity cannot be represented directly in RDF(S). They must be defined with the same technique used for other languages, that is, by creating a class that represents the relation and whose attributes correspond to each of the arguments of this relation.

```
<rdfs:Class rdf:ID="connects">
  <rdfs:comment>A road connects two different
      cities</rdfs:comment>
</rdfs:Class>
<rdf:Property rdf:ID="firstArgument">
  <rdfs:domain rdf:resource="#connects"/>
  <rdfs:range rdf:resource="#Location"/>
</rdf:Property>
<rdf:Property rdf:ID="secondArgument">
  <rdfs:domain rdf:resource="#connects"/>
  <rdfs:range rdf:resource="#Location"/>
</rdf:Property>
<rdf:Property rdf:ID="thirdArgument">
  <rdfs:domain rdf:resource="#connects"/>
  <rdfs:range rdf:resource="#RoadSection"/>
</rdf:Property>
```

It is also important to mention here that in Section 7.3 of the RDF specification document (Lassila and Swick, 1999), the authors describe how to model non-binary relations between instances in RDF. Their description only shows how to represent that a non-binary relation holds among several instances (or values). However, if we follow those guidelines, we will not be able to represent that non-binary relations can hold between classes, as we did in the above definition. Our definition could be instantiated as follows ("the road 101 connects San Francisco and Los Angeles):

```
<connects rdf:ID="connects-SF-LA">
  <firstArgument rdf:resource="#SanFrancisco/>
  <secondArgument rdf:resource="#LosAngeles/>
  <thirdArgument rdf:resource="#101/>
</connects>
```

An important feature of RDF(S) is that it is possible to create hierarchies of relations using the *subPropertyOf* primitive. For example, we can express that the relation travelsByPlane (whose range is Flight) specializes the relation travels (whose range is Travel). This means that if the relation travelsByPlane holds between two instances, then the relation travels holds between the same two instances.

```
<rdf:Property rdf:ID="travelsByPlane">
  <rdfs:subPropertyOf rdf:resource="#travels"/>
  <rdfs:range rdf:resource="#Flight"/>
</rdf:Property>
```

Functions are not components of the RDF(S) knowledge model. And nor are formal **axioms**, though Maedche and colleagues (2000) have carried out some studies in order to include axioms in RDF(S) ontologies. These studies propose to embed sentences in FLogic into RDF(S) axioms, so that a FLogic inference engine can read the information of RDF(S) documents and reason with the knowledge described in the ontology. This approach could be followed with other languages as well.

Finally, and regarding **instances**, there are several patterns to define instances in an ontology. To do so we only need primitives from RDF (not RDFS). The definition of an instance includes the class to which the instance belongs and the corresponding set of property-value pairs. Depending on the range of each property, we have different representations of their value: a literal for `singleFare`, a typed literal for `departureDate` (its type is expressed with the *rdf:datatype* attribute), and a reference to a resource for `arrivalPlace`. The corresponding graphical notation of this instance is shown in Figure 4.6. The value representations of each property are also different depending on their range: a rectangle with the value `300 US Dollars` for `singleFare`, a rectangle with the value `2002-02-08^^xsd:date` for `departureDate`, which expresses that its type is `xsd:date` and its value `2002-02-08`, and an ellipse with the instance `Seattle` for `arrivalPlace`.

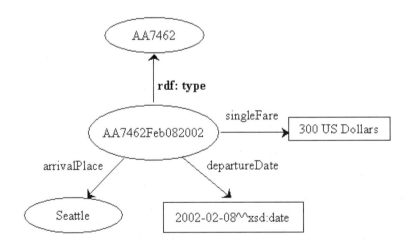

Figure 4.6: Definition of the instance AA7462Feb082002 in RDF(S).

```
<AA7462 rdf:ID="AA7462Feb082002">
  <singleFare>300 US Dollars</singleFare>
  <departureDate rdf:datatype="&xsd;date">
     2002-02-08
  </departureDate>
  <arrivalPlace rdf:resource="#Seattle"/>
</AA7462>
```

Assertions made by instances (aka claims) can be represented in RDF(S) using reification. Reification in RDF consists in transforming the value of a property into a statement[21]. In the following example, our instance `travelAgency1` claims that the `flightNumber` of the instance `AA7462Feb082002` is `7462`. This is represented in RDF(S) as a statement whose subject, predicate, and object are `AA7462Feb082002`, `flightNumber` and `7462` respectively, and whose property *claim:attributedTo* has the value `travelAgency1`. Observe that the property *claim:attributedTo* neither belongs to the RDF nor to the RDFS KR ontologies; it has been created as an example.

This definition is also shown in Figure 4.7, where the statement representing the claim is represented as an empty ellipse since we have not provided any identifier for it.

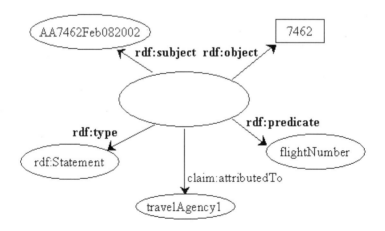

Figure 4.7: Definition of a claim in RDF

```
<rdf:Description>
  <rdf:subject rdf:resource="#AA7462Feb082002"/>
  <rdf:predicate rdf:resource="#flightNumber"/>
  <rdf:object>7462</rdf:object>
  <rdf:type rdf:resource="&rdf;Statement"/>
  <claim:attributedTo rdf:resource="#travelAgency1"/>
</rdf:Description>
```

Finally, some comments have to be made on RDF(S) **semantics**. At present, some studies are being carried out by the W3C on the definition of the RDF(S) model theory (Hayes, 2002). Previous to this work, the logical interpretation of this language (based on semantic networks) was explored by Conen and Klapsing (2000; 2001). The lack of formal semantics to create RDF(S) has caused several problems to define the semantics of other languages that extend RDF(S) like OIL, DAML+OIL, and OWL , which will be dealt with in the next sections.

4.4.3.2 Reasoning mechanisms
Currently, most of the inference systems for RDF(S) are mainly devoted to querying information about RDF ontologies as if they were a deductive database. In this context, some languages for querying RDF databases have appeared such as RQL (Karvounarakis and Christophides, 2002), RDFQL[22], and RDQL[23]. Standardization efforts will be needed to create a common query language for RDF(S).

In the following list we enumerate several RDF(S) inference systems (although it is by no means an exhaustive list): SilRI (Simple Logic RDF Inference) (Decker et al., 1998), included in Ontobroker; RIL[24] (RDF Inference Language), and TRIPLE (Sintek and Decker, 2001). Each of them has their own features though they are not dealt with here. There are also many other RDF(S) tools and APIs available for downloading, such as Amaya[25], the Jena toolkit[26], the ICS-FORTH RDFSuite[27], etc. These tools can be used to store RDF(S) ontologies, parse RDF(S), query RDF(S) ontologies, etc. Some of them are available in Java, others in C++, Lisp, Python, etc.

4.4.4 OIL

OIL (Horrocks et al., 2000; Fensel et al., 2001) stands for *Ontology Interchange Language* and *Ontology Inference Layer*. It was developed in the context of the European IST project On-To-Knowledge. Like the other languages previously presented, for example, SHOE and RDF(S), OIL was built to express the semantics of Web resources. OIL was superseded by DAML+OIL; however, software is still available to manage and reason with OIL ontologies.

OIL is a Web-based KR language that combines: (a) XML syntax; (b) modeling primitives from the frame-based KR paradigm, and (c) the formal semantics and

---

[22] http://www.intellidimension.com/RDFGateway/Docs/rdfqlmanual.asp
[23] http://www.hpl.hp.com/semweb/rdql.html
[24] http://rdfinference.org/index.html
[25] http://www.w3.org/Amaya/Amaya.html
[26] http://www.hpl.hp.com/semweb/jena-top.html
[27] http://www.ics.forth.gr/proj/isst/RDF/

reasoning support of description logics approaches (hence ensuring decidability and the existence of an efficient inference mechanism for the language). This is shown in Figure 4.8. Thus OIL can be defined as a frame-based language that uses DL to give clear semantics and also to permit efficient implementations of reasoners for the language. According to the DL terminology, OIL is a SHIQ language.

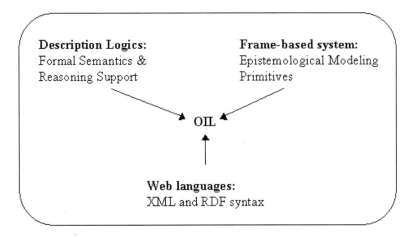

Figure 4.8: The three roots of OIL.

Figure 4.2 illustrates that OIL has been built on top of RDF(S), extending RDF(S) with new KR primitives.

OIL ontologies can be built with the following ontology tools: old versions of OILEd (which now supports DAML+OIL), Protégé-2000, OntoEdit and WebODE. OIL ontologies are not only implemented in XML, they can also be written as plain text files (known as OILs presentation syntax). We will use the XML syntax of OIL when explaining how to define the header of an OIL ontology and how to import terms from other ontologies, though we will use the OILs presentation syntax in the rest of the examples as it is much more readable.

4.4.4.1 Knowledge representation
In Section 2.1.3 we described the OIL KR ontology and the layered approach for OILs development, and we distinguished four layers: *Core OIL*, *Standard OIL*, *Instance OIL* and *Heavy OIL*. This layered structure of OIL is presented in Figure 2.3. In this section, we are focused on *Instance OIL*.

In OIL, the knowledge contained in an ontology is organized in three levels: the ontology container (holds information about the ontology, such as its author, URL, etc.), the ontology definition (holds the ontology terms definitions), and the object level (where the instances are stored – used only in *Instance OIL* and *Heavy OIL*).

We start with the *ontology container* level, which describes, as mentioned above, ontology meta data such as author, URL, name, subject, etc. This description makes use of the Dublin Core Meta data Element Set[28]. An OIL ontology in XML

---

[28] http://purl.oclc.org/dc/

syntax starts with the root node RDF. In this root node, the namespaces for the RDF, RDFS and OIL KR ontologies must be included. These namespaces are usually identified with the prefixes *rdf* and *rdfs* and *oil*, and they point to the standard URLs of the RDF, RDFS and OIL KR ontologies respectively.

```
<rdf:RDF
 xmlns:rdf="http://www.w3.org/1999/02/22-rdf-syntax-ns#"
 xmlns:rdfs="http://www.w3.org/2000/01/rdf-schema#"
 xmlns:oil="http://www.ontoknowledge.org/oil/rdf-
          schema/2000/11/10-oil-standard#">
```

Terms from other OIL or RDF(S) ontologies can be easily imported into OIL ontologies provided that we use OILs XML syntax. This import is done using namespaces and entities. For example, if we want to import the concept CurrencyQuantity from a units ontology, we must use the following code:

```
http://delicias.dia.fi.upm.es/OIL/units#CurrencyQuantity
```

As in RDF(S), if we define the entity units for the URL of the currency units ontology, we can use &units;CurrencyQuantity to refer to the concept CurrencyQuantity.

We will now deal with the *ontology definition* level. **Concepts** are known as classes in OIL and are defined by means of role restrictions that must be satisfied by instances belonging to the concepts. As in other DL languages, there are two types of concepts in OIL: *primitive* and *defined*. Let us see the definitions of the primitive concept Travel and the defined concept Flight:

```
class-def Travel
   documentation "A journey from place to place"
   slot-constraint arrivalDate cardinality 1 Date
   slot-constraint departureDate cardinality 1 Date
   slot-constraint companyName value-type string
   slot-constraint singleFare max-cardinality 1 integer

class-def defined Flight
   documentation "A journey by plane"
   subclass-of Travel
   slot-constraint flightNumber cardinality 1 integer
   slot-constraint transportMeans cardinality 1 string
```

In the previous definitions of the concepts Travel and Flight, we expressed the restrictions applied to their attributes (aka slots). Now we declare these slots. The slot *domain* and slot *range* is the set of classes to which the slot belongs and the type of slot values respectively. Slot default values cannot be defined in OIL.

Class attributes cannot be defined in OIL. Neither can instance attributes take a value in a class that is inherited by its subclasses and instances. Therefore, we are not able to express the value of the attribute `transportMeans` for the class `Flight` in the previous example.

```
slot-def arrivalDate
  domain Travel
  range Date
slot-def departureDate
  domain Travel
  range Date
slot-def companyName
  domain Travel
  range string
slot-def singleFare
  domain Travel
  range integer

slot-def flightNumber
  domain Flight
  range integer
slot-def transportMeans
  domain Flight
  range string
```

Concept **taxonomies** in OIL are expressed with the *subclass-of* primitive. We have used this primitive to define the concept `Flight`.

Besides, OIL allows expressing disjointness between concepts, exhaustive concept decompositions, and partitions by means of the *disjoint*, *covered*, and *disjoint-covered* primitives respectively. Figure 4.4d shows how to represent the disjoint decomposition of the concept `AmericanAirlinesFlight` into the concepts `AA7462`, `AA2010` and `AA0488`. We need to use the *disjoint* primitive to represent that these concepts are disjoint (as shown in the example below) and to declare explicitly that each concept in that disjoint set is a subclass of the class `AmericanAirlinesFlight`. The partition is easier to represent, as shown below for the concept `Location`. Exhaustive decompositions are defined similarly to partitions.

```
disjoint AA7462 AA2010 AA0488
class-def AA7462 subclass-of AmericanAirlinesFlight
class-def AA2010 subclass-of AmericanAirlinesFlight
class-def AA0488 subclass-of AmericanAirlinesFlight

disjoint-covered Location by EuropeanLocation
  NorthAmericanLocation SouthAmericanLocation
  AsianLocation AfricanLocation AustralianLocation
  AntarcticLocation
```

With regard to **relations**, OIL permits expressing binary relations by means of slots. The slot `arrivalPlace` between the concepts `Travel` and `Location` is defined as follows:

```
slot-def arrivalPlace
  domain Travel
  range Location
```

In OIL, we can state that a slot can be applied to two different concepts. The following code defines the slot `departurePlace`, whose domain may be `Flight` or `Ship`.

```
slot-def departurePlace
  domain Flight or Ship
  range Location
```

Besides, slot constraints can use qualified restrictions (that is, we define both the slot range and its cardinality in the same restriction). This feature is useful to express that the range of the slot `departurePlace` is different for the concepts `Flight` and `Ship`, as shown in the following code:

```
slot-constraint departurePlace cardinality 1 Airport
```

```
slot-constraint departurePlace cardinality 1 Port
```

Slots can be organized in hierarchies with the *rdfs:subPropertyOf* primitive. Inverse slots can also be specified with the *inverseRelationOf* primitive. Additionally, mathematical properties such as transitiveness and symmetry can be attached to slots. For example, we can define that the slot `isArrivalPlaceOf` is the inverse of the slot `arrivalPlace`.

```
slot-def isArrivalPlaceOf
  inverse arrivalPlace
```

Ternary and higher arity relations cannot be expressed in OIL directly. They can be represented using reification, as explained when dealing with other languages. To do this, we use a class that represents the relation and one slot for each relation argument whose type corresponds to the argument type. Now we define the relation `connects`. Note that we lose the constraint that cities must be different and that the road section starts in one city and ends in another city.

```
class-def connects
  slot-constraint firstArgument cardinality 1 Location
  slot-constraint secondArgument cardinality 1 Location
  slot-constraint thirdArgument cardinality 1 RoadSection
```

In OIL **functions** are defined as functional slots. These functions must be binary because slots in OIL have only two arguments: one input and one output. For example, the slot departureDate of the concept Travel can be defined as a functional slot because any journey has only a departure date. The definition of this slot would be as follows:

```
slot-def departureDate
  domain Travel
  range Date
  properties functional
```

In OIL, as in other DL languages, formal **axioms** are built using a subset of first order logic. They are usually described as disjoint or exhaustive knowledge. As an example, the axiom that states that trains cannot go from the USA to Europe can be defined with the following disjoint expression presented also in Chapter 1:

```
disjoint
  TrainTravel
  (Travel and (slot-constraint arrivalPlace
                    value-type EuropeanLocation)
          and (slot-constraint departurePlace
                    value-type USALocation))
```

Now we move to the OIL *object level* layer, which is only present in *Instance OIL* and *Heavy OIL*. If we use the XML representation of OIL, **instances** are represented with the same syntax that RDF(S). Thus, the same RDF definitions presented in the RDF(S) section are valid for OIL. Let us see now the plain text representation of our instance of the flight AA7462:

```
instance-of AA7462-08-Feb-2002 AA7462
  related departureDate AA7462-08-Feb-2002 Feb8-2002
  related singleFare AA7462-08-Feb-2002 300USDollars
  related arrivalPlace AA7462-08-Feb-2002 Seattle
```

4.4.4.2 Reasoning mechanisms
OIL has been developed as a kind of "formalization" of frames, using DL to add formal semantics to the frame formalism. Therefore, OIL is based on formal semantics that permits the existence of an inference engine.

As we have already commented in other sections, DL inference engines can be used for many purposes. They can be used to perform **automatic classifications** of ontology concepts in concept taxonomies, taking into account the *subclass-of* primitives and the slot constraints inside concept definitions. They can be used for **constraint checking**, taking into account the consistency of the concept taxonomies defined in the ontology.

We must add that, independently of the inference engine selected to perform reasoning with OIL, multiple **inheritance** is permitted in this language, though **exception handling** is not addressed in it.

Several inference engines can be used to reason with OIL ontologies. Let us focus on two of them: FaCT and RACER.

The FaCT system (*Fast Classification of Terminologies*) (Horrocks et al., 1999) is a DL classifier that includes two reasoners: one for the logic SHF (ALC augmented with transitive roles, functional roles and a role hierarchy) and another for the logic SHIQ (SHF augmented with inverse roles and qualified number restrictions). Both of these reasoners use sound and complete tableaux algorithms. FaCT can be downloaded free[29] and can be run in Lisp. There is a CORBA interface available for it, which allows an easy integration with other systems. For instance, FaCT has been integrated in OILEd and Protégé-2000.

RACER (*Renamed ABox and Concept Expression Reasoner*) (Haarslev and Möller, 2001) also supports the logic SHIQ, and is available in Java, C++ and Lisp. Like FaCT, it can be downloaded free[30] and has been integrated in OilEd.

4.4.5 DAML+OIL

DAML+OIL (Horrocks and van Harmelen, 2001) was developed by a joint committee from the USA and the European Union (mainly OIL developers) in the context of the DARPA project DAML (*DARPA Agent Markup Language*). The main purpose of this language is to allow semantic markup of Web resources.

DAML+OIL has passed through several stages in its development. The first version of the language, called DAML-ONT, was created just as an extension of RDF(S) and provided frame-based KR primitives. It was released in October 2000. The following version, released in December 2000, was called DAML+OIL. This second version moved away from frames to DL, as shown by Bechhofer and colleagues (2001b). The last version of DAML+OIL was released in March 2001. Basically, this last version fixed some problems that were detected in the prior specification and changed some of the primitives of that version. None of these DAML+OIL versions used a layered structure for the language as OIL did.

In Chapter 2, we described the DAML+OIL KR ontology and explained which primitives were equivalent to those of the RDF KR ontology (*rdf:Property, rdf:type*, and *rdf:value*), which were equivalent to those of the RDFS KR ontology (*rdfs:Literal, rdfs:subPropertyOf, rdfs:subClassOf, rdfs:domain, rdfs:range, rdfs:label, rdfs:comment, rdfs:seeAlso* and *rdfs:isDefinedBy*), and which were new (the rest of them). In this section, we will use the prefix that indicates the language to which it belongs (*rdf* for RDF, *rdfs* for RDF Schema and *daml* for DAML+OIL) for all the primitives.

DAML+OIL ontologies are written in XML (no plain text syntax, as in the case of OIL). And they can also be written with the triple notation for RDF. We will use

---

[29] http://www.cs.man.ac.uk/~horrocks/FaCT/
[30] http://www.fh-wedel.de/~mo/racer/index.html

the XML syntax for all the examples in this section so that readers can get a flavor of this syntax.

There are many tools, systems and applications to manage and use DAML+OIL ontologies. Many of them are being adapted to the OWL language, since this language will supersede DAML+OIL.

4.4.5.1 Knowledge representation

DAML+OIL ontologies are based on RDF(S). Therefore, an ontology in DAML+OIL must start with the declaration of the RDF root node. In this node we will include the namespaces for the RDF, RDFS and DAML+OIL KR ontologies. Besides, the namespace *xsd* is usually included for XML Schema datatypes. Please note that *xsd* refers to a different URL than the one used for the same namespace in RDF(S). When DAML+OIL was created RDF(S) did not support XML Schema datatypes. In March 2001, the valid URL for XML Schema datatypes was *http://www.w3.org/2000/10/XMLSchema*. Later, RDF(S) gave support to XML Schema datatypes and that namespace had already changed to *http://www.w3.org/2001/XMLSchema*. However, DAML+OIL has not evolved and existing DAML+OIL ontologies use the old reference for XML Schema datatypes.

```
<rdf:RDF
 xmlns:rdf="http://www.w3.org/1999/02/22-rdf-syntax-ns#"
 xmlns:rdfs="http://www.w3.org/2000/01/rdf-schema#"
 xmlns:xsd="http://www.w3.org/2000/10/XMLSchema#"
 xmlns:daml="http://www.daml.org/2001/03/daml+oil#">
```

As in RDF(S), the order in which definitions appear in DAML+OIL ontologies is not relevant, but DAML+OIL ontologies usually define the header of the ontology first and then the ontology terms.

The header of a DAML+OIL ontology includes: the ontology version (optional), the ontology documentation, which uses the primitive *rdfs:comment*, and the imported ontologies. In our case, we will import ontologies about units ,and datatypes (XML Schema definitions). We will also import the DAML+OIL KR ontology.

```
<daml:Ontology rdf:about="">
 <daml:versionInfo>1.0</daml:versionInfo>
 <rdfs:comment>Sample ontology for travel
       agencies</rdfs:comment>
 <daml:imports
   rdf:resource="http://delicias.dia.fi.upm.es/DAML/units"/>
 <daml:imports
   rdf:resource="http://www.w3.org/2000/10/XMLSchema"/>
 <daml:imports
   rdf:resource="http://www.daml.org/2001/03/daml+oil"/>
</daml:Ontology>
```

As in RDF(S), we will use XML entities to refer to terms from other ontologies rather than use directly the URL of those terms. In the RDF(S) section we indicated how to define entities in XML documents.

Concepts are known as classes in DAML+OIL, and are created with the primitive *daml:Class*. Besides its name, a class might contain its documentation (with *rdfs:comment*) and expressions with the following list of primitives:

- *rdfs:subClassOf* contains class expressions. It allows defining the superclasses of the class.
- *daml:sameClassAs* and *daml:equivalentTo* also contain class expressions. These primitives define necessary and sufficient conditions for the class (i.e., they are used for redefining concepts already defined), and can be used indistinctly.
- *daml:oneOf*, defines a class by enumerating exhaustively all its instances. This is a way to define a class extensionally.
- *daml:intersectionOf*, *daml:unionOf* and *daml:complementOf* define an expression as a conjunction, a disjunction, or a negation of other expressions respectively.

According to the DL terminology, DAML+OIL is a SHIQ language. Sometimes it appears as a SHOIQ language, where the *O* expresses the possibility of defining "nominals" (individuals that are used in *daml:oneOf* expressions). This means that class expressions can be built using the following constructors:

- Conjunction (*daml:intersectionOf*), disjunction (*daml:unionOf*) and negation (*daml:complementOf*).
- Collections of individuals (*daml:oneOf*).
- Property restrictions (*daml:Restriction*). They contain a reference to the property to which the restriction is applied with the primitive *daml:onProperty* and another element for expressing the restriction. The following restrictions can be applied to properties: value restriction (*daml:toClass*), existential restriction (*daml:hasClass*), role fillers (*daml:hasValue*), number restriction (*daml:cardinality*, *daml:maxCardinality*, *daml:minCardinality*) and qualified number restriction (*daml:cardinalityQ*, *daml:maxCardinalityQ*, *daml:minCardinalityQ*).
- Additionally, role expressions can express inverse roles (*daml:inverseOf*), and role hierarchies can be defined (*daml:subPropertyOf*).

The grammar to build class expressions is shown next:

```
class-name |
<daml:intersectionOf>
   class-expr class-expr+
</daml:intersectionOf> |
<daml:unionOf> class-expr class-expr+ </daml:unionOf> |
<daml:complementOf> class-expr </daml:complementOf> |
<daml:oneOf rdf:parseType="daml:collection">
   instance-expr+
</daml:oneOf> |
<daml:Restriction>
   <daml:onProperty> property-name </daml:onProperty>
   restriction-expr
</daml:Restriction>
```

instance-expr represents an instance of a class. It is defined as follows:

```
<daml:Thing rdf:resource="#instanceName"/>
```

restriction-expr represents a restriction on a property when applied to the class. It can be any of the following:

```
<daml:toClass> class-expr </daml:toClass> |
<daml:hasClass> class-expr </daml:hasClass> |
<daml:hasValue> instance-name </daml:hasValue> |
<daml:cardinality> non-neg-integer </daml:cardinality> |
<daml:maxCardinality> non-neg-integer </daml:maxCardinality> |
<daml:minCardinality> non-neg-integer </daml:minCardinality> |
<daml:cardinalityQ> non-neg-integer </daml:cardinalityQ>
<daml:hasClassQ> class-expr </daml:hasClassQ> |
<daml:maxCardinalityQ> non-neg-integer</daml:maxCardinalityQ>
<daml:hasClassQ> class-expr </daml:hasClassQ> |
<daml:minCardinalityQ> non-neg-integer</daml:minCardinalityQ>
<daml:hasClassQ> class-expr </daml:hasClassQ>
```

The definition of the primitive concept `Travel` is shown below. The class expression inside *rdfs:subClassOf* establishes restrictions on the instance attributes of this concept: a travel has exactly an arrival date and a departure date (whose type is `date`, which is a predefined XML Schema datatype), at most, a single fare (whose type is `currencyQuantity`, which is defined in the `units` ontology) and this travel may be made with zero, one or several companies.

```
<daml:Class rdf:ID="Travel">
  <rdfs:comment>A journey from place to
       place</rdfs:comment>
  <rdfs:subClassOf>
    <daml:Restriction>
      <daml:onProperty rdf:resource="#arrivalDate"/>
      <daml:toClass rdf:resource="&xsd;date"/>
      <daml:cardinality>1</daml:cardinality>
    </daml:Restriction>
    <daml:Restriction>
      <daml:onProperty rdf:resource="#departureDate"/>
      <daml:toClass rdf:resource="&xsd;date"/>
      <daml:cardinality>1</daml:cardinality>
    </daml:Restriction>
    <daml:Restriction>
      <daml:onProperty rdf:resource="#companyName"/>
      <daml:toClass rdf:resource="&xsd;string"/>
    </daml:Restriction>
    <daml:Restriction>
      <daml:onProperty rdf:resource="#singleFare"/>
      <daml:toClass
             rdf:resource="&units;currencyQuantity"/>
```

```
      <daml:maxCardinality>1</daml:maxCardinality>
    </daml:Restriction>
  </rdfs:subClassOf>
</daml:Class>
```

The definition of the defined concept `Flight` is shown below. A flight is a type of travel. It has an instance attribute called `flightNumber`, which must have exactly one value of type `integer`. Besides, it has also an attribute called `transportMeans`, whose value is "plane". This value is inherited by all the subclasses and instances of `Flight`.

```
<daml:Class rdf:ID="Flight">
  <rdfs:comment>A journey by plane</rdfs:comment>
  <daml:intersectionOf rdf:parseType="daml:collection">
    <daml:Class rdf:about="#Travel"/>
    <daml:Restriction>
      <daml:onProperty rdf:resource="#flightNumber"/>
      <daml:toClass rdf:resource="&xsd;integer"/>
      <daml:cardinality>1</daml:cardinality>
    </daml:Restriction>
    <daml:Restriction>
      <daml:onProperty rdf:resource="#transportMeans"/>
      <daml:hasValue>
          <xsd:string rdf:value="plane"/>
      </daml:hasValue>
      <daml:cardinality>1</daml:cardinality>
    </daml:Restriction>
  </daml:intersectionOf>
</daml:Class>
```

Class attributes can be represented as we explained in RDF(S). Although this type of definition is valid in RDF(S), DAML+OIL inference engines will not take it into account, since it is not included in the DAML+OIL specification.

Besides, the primitives *daml:equivalentTo* and *daml:sameClassAs* may be used indistinctly for defining equivalences between classes. These expressions are normally used for defining synonyms. For instance, `TravelByAir` could be a synonym of `Flight` in our ontology, as can be seen below:

```
<daml:Class rdf:ID="TravelByAir">
  <daml:sameClassAs rdf:resource="#Flight"/>
</daml:Class>
```

In the previous definitions, we have explored how to represent restrictions on instance attributes in DAML+OIL by expliciting their type and cardinality. We have also explored how to represent restrictions on class attributes expliciting their values. Concept attributes must be defined as properties in the ontology. In

DAML+OIL, there are two types of properties: *daml:ObjectProperty*, whose range is a class, and *daml:DatatypeProperty*, whose range is a datatype.

To define a property we may explicit its domain and range with the primitives *rdfs:domain* and *rdfs:range*. We can also state that a property is a subproperty of other properties with the primitive *rdfs:subPropertyOf*. Finally, we can also express equivalence between properties with *daml:samePropertyAs* or *daml:equivalentTo* indistinctly, and inverse properties with *daml:inverseOf*. Let us now see the attribute definitions `arrivalDate`, `departureDate`, `companyName` and `singleFare` of the concept `Travel`, and the attribute definitions `flightNumber` and `transportMeans` of the concept `Flight`.

```
<daml:DatatypeProperty rdf:ID="arrivalDate">
    <rdfs:domain rdf:resource="#Travel"/>
    <rdfs:range rdf:resource="&xsd;date"/>
</daml:DatatypeProperty>
<daml:DatatypeProperty rdf:ID="departureDate">
    <rdfs:domain rdf:resource="#Travel"/>
    <rdfs:range rdf:resource="&xsd;date"/>
</daml:DatatypeProperty>
<daml:DatatypeProperty rdf:ID="companyName">
    <rdfs:domain rdf:resource="#Travel"/>
    <rdfs:range rdf:resource="&xsd;string"/>
</daml:DatatypeProperty>
<daml:ObjectProperty rdf:ID="singleFare">
    <rdfs:domain rdf:resource="#Travel"/>
    <rdfs:range rdf:resource="&units;currencyQuantity"/>
</daml:ObjectProperty>

<daml:DatatypeProperty rdf:ID="flightNumber">
    <rdfs:domain rdf:resource="#Travel"/>
    <rdfs:range rdf:resource="&xsd;integer"/>
</daml:DatatypeProperty>
<daml:DatatypeProperty rdf:ID="transportMeans">
    <rdfs:domain rdf:resource="#Travel"/>
    <rdfs:range rdf:resource="&xsd;string"/>
</daml:DatatypeProperty>
```

Concept **taxonomies** in DAML+OIL are created with the *rdfs:subClassOf* primitive in the case of primitive concepts, and with the *daml:intersectionOf, daml:unionOf, daml:sameClassAs* or *daml:equivalentTo* primitives in the case of defined concepts. We have already seen some examples when defining the concepts `Travel` and `Flight`.

Disjoint and exhaustive knowledge can be expressed in DAML+OIL. Disjointness between concepts is expressed with the *daml:disjointWith* primitive. We present below the definitions of the concepts `AA7462`, `AA2010` and `AA0488` stating that they are disjoint with each other. Note that due to the symmetry of the *daml:disjointWith* primitive, it would not be necessary to write all the *daml:disjointWith* statements, though it would be enough to write only three (for example, AA7462 *daml:disjointWith* AA2010, AA7462 *daml:disjointWith* AA0488, and AA2010 *daml:disjointWith* AA0488).

```
<daml:Class rdf:ID="AA7462">
  <rdfs:subClassOf
          rdf:resource="#AmericanAirlinesFlight"/>
  <daml:disjointWith rdf:resource="#AA2010"/>
  <daml:disjointWith rdf:resource="#AA0488"/>
</daml:Class>

<daml:Class rdf:ID="AA2010">
  <rdfs:subClassOf
          rdf:resource="#AmericanAirlinesFlight"/>
  <daml:disjointWith rdf:resource="#AA7462"/>
  <daml:disjointWith rdf:resource="#AA0488"/>
</daml:Class>

<daml:Class rdf:ID="AA0488">
  <rdfs:subClassOf
          rdf:resource="#AmericanAirlinesFlight"/>
  <daml:disjointWith rdf:resource="#AA7462"/>
  <daml:disjointWith rdf:resource="#AA2010"/>
</daml:Class>
```

Note that the disjoint decomposition has been represented by explicitly including a *rdfs:subClassOf* statement in each of the concept definitions, which link each concept with the concept AmericanAirlinesFlight.

Partitions are expressed with the *daml:disjointUnionOf* primitive. Let us see now the definition of the partition of the concept Location in EuropeanLocation, AsianLocation, NorthAmericanLocation, SouthAmericanLocation, AfricanLocation, AustralianLocation, and AntarcticLocation.

```
<daml:Class rdf:ID="Location">
  <daml:disjointUnionOf rdf:parseType="daml:collection">
    <daml:Class rdf:resource="#EuropeanLocation"/>
    <daml:Class rdf:resource="#NorthAmericanLocation"/>
    <daml:Class rdf:resource="#SouthAmericanLocation"/>
    <daml:Class rdf:resource="#AsianLocation"/>
    <daml:Class rdf:resource="#AfricanLocation"/>
    <daml:Class rdf:resource="#AustralianLocation"/>
    <daml:Class rdf:resource="#AntarcticLocation"/>
  </daml:disjointUnionOf>
</daml:Class>
```

There are no specific primitives in DAML+OIL to represent exhaustive decompositions of a concept, although they can be represented with the *daml:unionOf* primitive, similarly to the use of *daml:disjointUnionOf*.

We have already presented some binary **relations** for building taxonomies in DAML+OIL. In this language, binary relations are defined with the primitive *daml:ObjectProperty*. It is not compulsory to define explicitly the domain and range of a property in DAML+OIL. Thus, if two different concepts have properties with the same name, the property domain will contain two classes. If the attribute types are different for each class, it is recommended not to define the range of the property in the property definition but to add the restriction about its type to the definition of the corresponding classes. For instance, in the case of the relation `departurePlace` applied to the concept `Ship` and the concept `Flight`, we have the following definitions:

```
<daml:ObjectProperty rdf:ID="departurePlace">
  <rdfs:domain>
    <daml:unionOf>
      <daml:Class rdf:resource="#Flight"/>
      <daml:Class rdf:resource="#Ship"/>
    </daml:unionOf>
  </rdfs:domain>
  <rdfs:range rdf:resource="#Location"/>
</daml:ObjectProperty>

<daml:Class rdf:ID="Flight">
...
  <daml:Restriction>
    <daml:onProperty rdf:resource="#departurePlace"/>
    <daml:toClass rdf:resource="#Airport"/>
    <daml:cardinality>1</daml:cardinality>
  </daml:Restriction>
...
</daml:Class>

<daml:Class rdf:ID="Ship">
...
  <daml:Restriction>
    <daml:onProperty rdf:resource="#departurePlace"/>
    <daml:toClass rdf:resource="#Port"/>
    <daml:cardinality>1</daml:cardinality>
  </daml:Restriction>
...
</daml:Class>
```

The definition of a relation can include some additional mathematical properties. We declare that a relation is transitive (*daml:TransitiveProperty*), that it has just one value when applied to an instance (*daml:UniqueProperty*), or that it is unambiguous (*daml:UnambiguousProperty*). The last two cases define global cardinality restrictions on the property no matter which class they are applied to.

Higher arity relations must be defined as concepts in DAML+OIL, as they are defined in other languages. The corresponding definition for the ternary relation `connects` is as follows:

```
<daml:Class rdf:ID="connects">
  <rdfs:comment>A road connects two different
       cities</rdfs:comment>
</daml:Class>
<daml:ObjectProperty rdf:ID="firstArgument">
  <rdfs:domain rdf:resource="#connects"/>
  <rdfs:range rdf:resource="#Location"/>
</daml:ObjectProperty>
<daml:ObjectProperty rdf:ID="secondArgument">
  <rdfs:domain rdf:resource="#connects"/>
  <rdfs:range rdf:resource="#Location"/>
</daml:ObjectProperty>
<daml:ObjectProperty rdf:ID="thirdArgument">
  <rdfs:domain rdf:resource="#connects"/>
  <rdfs:range rdf:resource="#RoadSection"/>
</daml:ObjectProperty>
```

As in other markup languages, in DAML+OIL we cannot express the constraint that cities are not part of each other and that the road starts in one of the cities and ends in the other one.

Functions are not components of the DAML+OIL knowledge model. However, binary functions may be represented with the *daml:UniqueProperty* primitive previously discussed. Higher arity functions cannot be represented in this language.

Neither are formal **axioms** components of the DAML+OIL knowledge model either. In this case, the same studies carried out on RDF(S) by Maedche and colleagues (2000) could be applied to DAML+OIL since DAML+OIL is built on top of RDF(S).

With regard to **instances**, they are defined using only RDF vocabulary. Thus the definition of our instance of flight AA7462 is similar to the one presented in Section 4.4.3. We have changed the range of the property singleFare, which refers to an instance of the concept CurrencyQuantity in the ontology of units, while in Section 4.4.3 it refers to a literal value (300 US Dollars). Since the attribute *rdf:datatype* was included in RDF(S) after DAML+OIL was created, the value of the attribute departureDate is also expressed differently from that one, as proposed in XML Schema. Claims could also be represented in the same fashion as they were in RDF(S).

```
<AA7462 rdf:ID="AA7462Feb082002" >
  <singleFare rdf:resource="&units;USDollar300"/>
  <departureDate>
    <xsd:date rdf:value="2002-02-08"/>
  </departureDate>
  <arrivalPlace rdf:resource="#Seattle"/>
</AA7462>
```

4.4.5.2 Reasoning mechanisms

Model-theoretic semantics (van Harmelen et al., 2001a) and a KIF axiomatization (Fikes and McGuinness, 2001) are provided for DAML+OIL. Both approaches give meanings to those primitives that are specifically defined in the DAML+OIL KR ontology. Any additional statements, resulting in other RDF triples, are perfectly allowed in this language. However, DAML+OIL is silent on the semantic consequences (or lack thereof) of such additional triples.

Both specifications of the semantics of DAML+OIL permit building inference engines or using existing ones. In fact, there are several inference engines available for DAML+OIL. For instance, FaCT and RACER (described when dealing with OIL description) can be used to reason with DAML+OIL ontologies since they allow reasoning with SHIQ languages.

TRIPLE (Sintek and Decker, 2001) is an inference engine that allows defining the semantics of any RDF-based language by means of rules. Hence it can be used with OIL, DAML+OIL and OWL ontologies[31]. In the case of DAML+OIL ontologies, TRIPLE may also use external classifiers such as FaCT and RACER. This inference engine is available in Java and can be downloaded free[32].

The JTP theorem prover, referenced in the section of Ontolingua and KIF, provides support for reasoning with DAML+OIL ontologies based on the KIF axiomatization of DAML+OIL primitives.

DAML+OIL ontologies can be used in Jess[33]. For example, the DAML+OIL API provided by GRCI[34] allows loading DAML+OIL statements from Jess. This permits writing Jess programs that can reason with domain ontologies written in DAML+OIL.

The DAML Query Language[35] (DQL) also uses DAML+OIL ontologies. DQL is a formal language and protocol for a querying agent and an answering agent to use in conducting a query-answering dialogue.

Finally, all the inference engines available for RDF(S) can be used for DAML+OIL. However, these inference engines do not exploit the semantics of DAML+OIL primitives but take them as if they were other RDF triples without any specific semantics.

---

[31] As TRIPLE does not provide any implementation of the semantics of OIL, it was not presented in the previous section, though it could be used for reasoning with OIL ontologies.
[32] http://triple.semanticweb.org/
[33] http://herzberg.ca.sandia.gov/jess/
[34] http://codip.grci.com/
[35] http://www.daml.org/2003/04/dql/dql

As explained in the OIL section, the use of DL classifiers (such as FaCT or RACER) permits performing **automatic classifications** of the ontology concepts, and detecting inconsistencies in this concept taxonomy.

Independently of the inference engine that we use for reasoning with our DAML+OIL ontologies, multiple **inheritance** is allowed. However, conflicts in multiple inheritance are not yet solved. **Constraint checking** can be performed on the values of properties and their cardinalities.

Finally, many tools can be used currently for authoring DAML+OIL ontologies[36] such as OILEd, OntoEdit, WebODE and DUET, among others. Some of them will be dealt with in detail in Chapter 5. Any other tool capable of working with RDF(S) ontologies can also be used for developing DAML+OIL ontologies provided that the ontology developer uses the DAML+OIL KR primitives. RDF(S) query engines, storage systems and parsers can be used to manage DAML+OIL ontologies since they can be serialized in RDF(S).

4.4.6 OWL

As was commented in the introduction to this chapter, OWL (Dean and Schreiber, 2003) is the result of the work of the W3C Web Ontology (WebOnt) Working Group, which was formed in November 2001. This language derives from and supersedes DAML+OIL. It covers most of DAML+OIL features and renames most of its primitives. As the previous languages, OWL is intended for publishing and sharing ontologies in the Web. By the time of writing this description (April 2003), OWL is a last call W3C Working Draft[37]. The current language specification is quite stable and it is foreseen that it will be promoted to a W3C Recommendation in June 2003.

In Section 2.1.5, we described the OWL KR ontology, and explained that OWL has a layered structure, as OIL had. OWL is divided into three layers: OWL Lite, OWL DL and OWL Full. In this section, we will explain how to build an ontology in OWL DL, and will point out how it differs from OWL Lite.

Like DAML+OIL, OWL is built upon RDF(S). Therefore, some RDF(S) primitives are reused by OWL, and OWL ontologies are written either in XML or with the triples notation for RDF. We will use the XML syntax for all the examples in this section.

As OWL is derived from DAML+OIL it shares many features with that language. The main differences between OWL and DAML+OIL are the following:

- OWL does not include qualified number restrictions (*daml:hasClassQ*, *daml:cardinalityQ*, *daml:maxCardinalityQ*, and *daml:minCardinalityQ*).
- OWL permits defining symmetric properties, which were not considered in DAML+OIL, with the primitive *owl:SymmetricProperty*.

---

[36] http://www.daml.org/tools/

[37] In this section, we describe the status of OWL as of January 2003. Some features of this language may change in the future, since it is still in a development phase.

- OWL does not rename the RDF(S) primitives reused by the language, as happened in DAML+OIL. For instance, *rdfs:subClassOf*, *rdfs:subPropertyOf*, etc.
- In OWL many DAML+OIL primitives have been renamed. For example, the primitive *daml:toClass* has been renamed as *owl:allValuesFrom*. The equivalences between OWL and DAML+OIL primitives was presented in Figure 2.6.
- OWL does not include the primitive *daml:disjointUnionOf*, since it can be effected by combining *owl:unionOf* and *owl:disjointWith*.

Other minor differences exist between both languages and they are explained in detail by Dean and Schreiber (2003).

4.4.6.1 Knowledge representation

An ontology in OWL starts with the declaration of the RDF root node. In this node we must include the namespaces for the RDF, RDFS and OWL KR ontologies. If XML Schema datatypes are used, it may be helpful to include a namespace for XML Schema, which is usually prefixed as *xsd* (and which points to the newest URL of XML Schema, as in RDF(S)).

```
<rdf:RDF
 xmlns:rdf="http://www.w3.org/1999/02/22-rdf-syntax-ns#"
 xmlns:rdfs="http://www.w3.org/2000/01/rdf-schema#"
 xmlns:xsd="http://www.w3.org/2001/XMLSchema#"
 xmlns:owl="http://www.w3.org/2002/07/owl#">
```

As in other languages, the order in which definitions appear in OWL ontologies is not relevant since it is based in RDF(S). However, OWL ontologies usually define the header of the ontology first and then the ontology terms.

The header of an OWL ontology may include: the ontology documentation (*rdfs:comment*); the ontology version (*owl:versionInfo*); and the imported ontologies (*owl:imports*). As we did with our DAML+OIL ontology, we will import ontologies about units and datatypes. It is not necessary (nor recommended) to import the OWL KR ontology. The ontology header may also include information about version control with the primitives *owl:backwardCompatibleWith*, *owl:incompatibleWith*, and *owl:priorVersion*, which were described in Chapter 2. Inside the ontology we can also find definitions of deprecated classes and properties with the *owl:DeprecatedClass* and *owl:DeprecatedProperty* primitives.

```
<owl:Ontology rdf:about="">
 <owl:versionInfo>1.0</owl:versionInfo>
 <rdfs:comment>Sample ontology for travel
       agencies</rdfs:comment>
 <owl:imports
   rdf:resource="http://delicias.dia.fi.upm.es/owl/units"/>
 <owl:imports
   rdf:resource="http://www.w3.org/2001/XMLSchema"/>
</owl:Ontology>
```

Concepts are known as classes in OWL and are created with the primitive *owl:Class*. Besides its name, a class may also contain its documentation (with *rdfs:comment*) and any number of expressions with the following list of primitives:

- *rdfs:subClassOf* contains class expressions. It allows defining the superclasses of the class.
- *owl:disjointWith* asserts that the class cannot share instances with the class expression in this primitive.
- *owl:equivalentClass* also contains class expressions. This primitive defines necessary and sufficient conditions for the class (i.e., it is used for redefining concepts already defined).
- *owl:oneOf* defines a class by enumerating exhaustively all its instances. This is a way to define a class extensionally.
- *owl:intersectionOf*, *owl:unionOf* and *owl:complementOf* define a class expression as a conjunction, a disjunction, or a negation of other class expressions respectively.

The first two primitives (*rdfs:subClassOf* and *owl:disjointWith*) define necessary conditions for the class (they can be used in the definition of primitive concepts), while the rest of primitives define necessary and sufficient conditions for the class (that is, they are used to define defined concepts). In OWL Lite the only primitives that can be used are *rdfs:subClassOf*, *owl:equivalentClass*, and *owl:intersectionOf*. In all the cases they can only be used with class identifiers and property restrictions.

According to the DL terminology, OWL is a SHOIN language. This means that class expressions can be built with the following constructors:

- Conjunction (*owl:intersectionOf*), disjunction (*owl:unionOf*), and negation (*owl:complementOf*) of class expressions.
- Collections of individuals (*owl:oneOf*).
- Property restrictions (*owl:Restriction*). They contain a reference to the property to which the restriction is applied with the primitive *owl:onProperty* and an element for expressing the restriction. The following restrictions can be applied to properties: value restriction (*owl:allValuesFrom*), existential restriction (*owl:someValuesFrom*), role fillers (*owl:hasValue*), and number restriction (*owl:cardinality*, *owl:maxCardinality*, *owl:minCardinality*).
- Besides, role expressions can express inverse roles (*owl:inverseOf*) and role hierarchies (*rdfs:subPropertyOf*).

Therefore the grammar to build class expressions in OWL is very similar to that of DAML+OIL, as shown below. Note that Boolean expressions and enumerations are enclosed in *<owl:Class>..</owl:Class>* tags.

```
class-name |
<owl:Class> boolean-expr </owl:Class> |
<owl:Class>
  <owl:oneOf rdf:parseType="Collection">
     instance-expr+
  </owl:oneOf>
</owl:Class> |
```

```
<owl:Restriction>
   <owl:onProperty> property-name </owl:onProperty>
   restriction-expr
</owl:Restriction>
```

boolean-expr is defined as follows:

```
<owl:intersectionOf>
   class-expr class-expr+
</owl:intersectionOf> |
<owl:unionOf> class-expr class-expr+ </owl:unionOf> |
<owl:complementOf> class-expr </owl:complementOf>
```

instance-expr represents an instance of a class. It is defined as follows:

```
<owl:Thing rdf:resource="#instanceName"/>
```

restriction-expr represents a restriction on a property when applied to the class. It can be any of the following (note that qualified number restrictions cannot be defined in OWL, in contrast with DAML+OIL):

```
<owl:allValuesFrom> class-expr </owl:allValuesFrom> |
<owl:someValuesFrom> class-expr </owl:someValuesFrom> |
<owl:hasValue> instance-name </owl:hasValue> |
<owl:cardinality rdf:datatype="&xsd;nonNegativeInteger">
      non-neg-integer
</owl:cardinality> |
<owl:maxCardinality rdf:datatype="&xsd;nonNegativeInteger">
      non-neg-integer
</owl:maxCardinality> |
<owl:minCardinality rdf:datatype="&xsd;nonNegativeInteger">
      non-neg-integer
</owl:minCardinality>
```

In OWL Lite class expressions can only contain class names and property restrictions. The primitive *owl:hasValue* cannot be used in property restrictions. Besides, the primitives *owl:allValuesFrom* and *owl:someValuesFrom* only contain class identifiers or named datatypes, and cardinality restrictions only take the values 0 or 1. OWL DL does not impose any of these restrictions.

The definition of the primitive concept Travel is shown below. The concept Travel is defined as an intersection of several restrictions using *rdfs:subClassOf*: a travel has exactly one arrival date and one departure date (whose type is date, which is defined as an XML Schema datatype), at most, a single fare (whose type is currencyQuantity, which is defined in the units ontology) and this travel may be made with zero, one, or several companies.

```
<owl:Class rdf:ID="Travel">
  <rdfs:comment>A journey from place to
        place</rdfs:comment>
  <rdfs:subClassOf>
    <owl:Restriction>
      <owl:onProperty rdf:resource="#arrivalDate"/>
      <owl:allValuesFrom rdf:resource="&xsd;date"/>
      <owl:cardinality
            rdf:datatype="&xsd;nonNegativeInteger">
            1
      </owl:cardinality>
    </owl:Restriction>
  </rdfs:subClassOf>
  <rdfs:subClassOf>
    <owl:Restriction>
      <owl:onProperty rdf:resource="#departureDate"/>
      <owl:allValuesFrom rdf:resource="&xsd;date"/>
      <owl:cardinality
            rdf:datatype="&xsd;nonNegativeInteger">
            1
      </owl:cardinality>
    </owl:Restriction>
  </rdfs:subClassOf>
  <rdfs:subClassOf>
    <owl:Restriction>
      <owl:onProperty rdf:resource="#companyName"/>
      <owl:allValuesFrom rdf:resource="&xsd;string"/>
    </owl:Restriction>
  </rdfs:subClassOf>
  <rdfs:subClassOf>
    <owl:Restriction>
      <owl:onProperty rdf:resource="#singleFare"/>
      <owl:allValuesFrom
            rdf:resource="&units;currencyQuantity"/>
      <owl:maxCardinality
            rdf:datatype="&xsd;nonNegativeInteger">
            1
      </owl:maxCardinality>
    </owl:Restriction>
  </rdfs:subClassOf>
</owl:Class>
```

The definition of the defined concept Flight is shown below. A flight is a kind of travel. It has an instance attribute called flightNumber, which must have exactly one value of type integer. Finally, it has also another instance attribute called transportMeans, whose value is "plane". This last restriction cannot be expressed in OWL DL, since *owl:hasValue* cannot be used in this version of the language. As occurred with DAML+OIL, we could have represented this attribute as a class attribute by attaching it directly to the definition of this concept. However, this part of the definition would not have been interpreted by OWL tools.

```
<owl:Class rdf:ID="Flight">
  <rdfs:comment>A journey by plane</rdfs:comment>
  <owl:intersectionOf rdf:parseType="Collection">
    <owl:Class rdf:about="#Travel"/>
    <owl:Restriction>
      <owl:onProperty rdf:resource="#flightNumber"/>
      <owl:allValuesFrom rdf:resource="&xsd;integer"/>
      <owl:cardinality
            rdf:datatype="&xsd;nonNegativeInteger">
        1
      </owl:cardinality>
    </owl:Restriction>
    <owl:Restriction>
      <owl:onProperty rdf:resource="#transportMeans"/>
      <owl:hasValue rdf:datatype="&xsd;string">
        plane
      </owl:hasValue>
      <owl:cardinality
            rdf:datatype="&xsd;nonNegativeInteger">
        1
      </owl:cardinality>
    </owl:Restriction>
  </owl:intersectionOf>
</owl:Class>
```

Equivalence between classes can be defined with the primitive *owl:equivalentClass*. For instance, `TravelByAir` is a synonym of `Flight` in our ontology, as can be seen below:

```
<owl:Class rdf:ID="TravelByAir">
  <owl:equivalentClass rdf:resource="#Flight"/>
</owl:Class>
```

In the previous definitions, we have explored how to represent restrictions on instance attributes in OWL, expliciting their type and cardinality. We have also explored how to represent restrictions on class attributes expliciting their values. Concept attributes must be defined as properties in the ontology. Like in DAML+OIL, in OWL there are two types of properties: *owl:ObjectProperty*, whose range is a class, and *owl:DatatypeProperty*, whose range is a datatype.

To define a property we may explicit its domain and range with the primitives *rdfs:domain* and *rdfs:range*. The primitive *rdfs:range* can refer to a class expression in OWL DL and only to a class identifier or to a named datatype in OWL Lite . We can state that a property is a subproperty of other properties with the primitive *rdfs:subPropertyOf*. Finally, we can express equivalence between properties with *owl:equivalentProperty*, and inverse properties with *owl:inverseOf*. Now we present the attribute definitions `arrivalDate`, `departureDate`, `companyName` and `singleFare` of the concept `Travel`, and the attribute definitions `flightNumber` and `transportMeans` of the concept `Flight`. We can see that these definitions have the same structure than the ones for DAML+OIL.

```
<owl:DatatypeProperty rdf:ID="arrivalDate">
   <rdfs:domain rdf:resource="#Travel"/>
   <rdfs:range rdf:resource="&xsd;date"/>
</owl:DatatypeProperty>
<owl:DatatypeProperty rdf:ID="departureDate">
   <rdfs:domain rdf:resource="#Travel"/>
   <rdfs:range rdf:resource="&xsd;date"/>
</owl:DatatypeProperty>
<owl:DatatypeProperty rdf:ID="companyName">
   <rdfs:domain rdf:resource="#Travel"/>
   <rdfs:range rdf:resource="&xsd;string"/>
</owl:DatatypeProperty>
<owl:ObjectProperty rdf:ID="singleFare">
   <rdfs:domain rdf:resource="#Travel"/>
   <rdfs:range rdf:resource="&units;currencyQuantity"/>
</owl:ObjectProperty>

<owl:DatatypeProperty rdf:ID="flightNumber">
   <rdfs:domain rdf:resource="#Travel"/>
   <rdfs:range rdf:resource="&xsd;integer"/>
</owl:DatatypeProperty>
<owl:DatatypeProperty rdf:ID="transportMeans">
   <rdfs:domain rdf:resource="#Travel"/>
   <rdfs:range rdf:resource="&xsd;string"/>
</owl:DatatypeProperty>
```

We have already seen some examples of how to create concept **taxonomies** in OWL using *rdfs:subclassOf* for primitive concepts, and *owl:intersectionOf*, *owl:unionOf*, or *owl:equivalentClass* for defined concepts. Disjoint knowledge can be expressed with the *owl:disjointWith* primitive. We present below the definitions of the disjoint concepts `AA7462`, `AA2010`, and `AA0488`. Like in DAML+OIL, the *owl:disjointWith* primitive is symmetric; hence, three statements would be enough to state the disjointness between these classes. Note that this knowledge cannot be represented in OWL Lite since the primitive *owl:disjointWith* is not defined for this version of the language.

```
<owl:Class rdf:ID="AA7462">
  <rdfs:subClassOf
          rdf:resource="#AmericanAirlinesFlight"/>
  <owl:disjointWith rdf:resource="#AA2010"/>
  <owl:disjointWith rdf:resource="#AA0488"/>
</owl:Class>
```

```
<owl:Class rdf:ID="AA2010">
  <rdfs:subClassOf
         rdf:resource="#AmericanAirlinesFlight"/>
  <owl:disjointWith rdf:resource="#AA0488"/>
</owl:Class>

<owl:Class rdf:ID="AA0488">
  <rdfs:subClassOf
         rdf:resource="#AmericanAirlinesFlight"/>
</owl:Class>
```

Similarly to DAML+OIL, exhaustive decompositions can be represented with the *owl:unionOf* primitive. Regarding partitions, we commented in the introduction to this language that the DAML+OIL primitive *daml:disjointUnionOf* has not been included in OWL. The reason for this is that partitions can be expressed by combining the *owl:disjointWith* and the *owl:unionOf* primitives, though they result in a much longer and less readable definition. As with disjoint decompositions, exhaustive decompositions and partitions cannot be represented in OWL Lite either. Let us see now the definition of the partition of the concept Location in the concepts NorthAmericanLocation, SouthAmericanLocation, EuropeanLocation, AsianLocation, AfricanLocation, AustralianLocation, and AntarcticLocation. We must define that Location is the union of those seven classes.

```
<owl:Class rdf:ID="Location">
  <owl:unionOf rdf:parseType="Collection">
    <owl:Class rdf:resource="#EuropeanLocation"/>
    <owl:Class rdf:resource="#NorthAmericanLocation"/>
    <owl:Class rdf:resource="#SouthAmericanLocation"/>
    <owl:Class rdf:resource="#AsianLocation"/>
    <owl:Class rdf:resource="#AfricanLocation"/>
    <owl:Class rdf:resource="#AustralianLocation"/>
    <owl:Class rdf:resource="#AntarcticLocation"/>
  </owl:unionOf>
</owl:Class>
```

We must also define the six classes as disjoint with each other. We show below, as an example, the definition of the class EuropeanLocation.

```
<owl:Class rdf:ID="EuropeanLocation">
  <rdfs:subClassOf rdf:resource="#Location"/>
  <owl:disjointWith
       rdf:resource="#NorthAmericanLocation"/>
  <owl:disjointWith
       rdf:resource="#SouthAmericanLocation"/>
  <owl:disjointWith rdf:resource="#AsianLocation"/>
  <owl:disjointWith rdf:resource="#AfricanLocation"/>
```

```
  <owl:disjointWith rdf:resource="#AustralianLocation"/>
  <owl:disjointWith rdf:resource="#AntarcticLocation"/>
</owl:Class>
```

Binary **relations** are defined with the primitive *owl:ObjectProperty*. The global domain and range of a relation can be explicitly defined with the *rdfs:domain* and *rdfs:range* primitives, which can contain any class expression (except for OWL Lite, in which they can only contain class identifiers, or named datatypes for *rdfs:range*). However, as in DAML+OIL, it is not compulsory to define explicitly the global domain and range of a property. Instead, these restrictions can be defined locally inside class definitions with property restrictions, as presented in some of the concept definitions above. Below we present the definition of the relation departurePlace that can be applied to the concept Ship and the concept Flight, and that has different ranges for each of the concepts to which it is applied (Port and Airport respectively):

```
<owl:ObjectProperty rdf:ID="departurePlace">
  <rdfs:domain>
    <owl:Class>
      <owl:unionOf>
        <owl:Class rdf:resource="#Flight"/>
        <owl:Class rdf:resource="#Ship"/>
      </owl:unionOf>
    </owl:Class>
  </rdfs:domain>
  <rdfs:range rdf:resource="#Location"/>
</owl:ObjectProperty>

<owl:Class rdf:ID="Flight">
...
  <owl:Restriction>
    <owl:onProperty rdf:resource="#departurePlace"/>
    <owl:allValuesFrom rdf:resource="#Airport"/>
    <owl:cardinality
        rdf:datatype="&xsd;nonNegativeInteger">
        1
    </owl:cardinality>
  </owl:Restriction>
...
</owl:Class>

<owl:Class rdf:ID="Ship">
...
  <owl:Restriction>
    <owl:onProperty rdf:resource="#departurePlace"/>
    <owl:allValuesFrom rdf:resource="#Port"/>
    <owl:cardinality
        rdf:datatype="&xsd;nonNegativeInteger">
```

```
                1
    </owl:cardinality>
   </owl:Restriction>
...
</owl:Class>
```

Besides, in OWL we can define property hierarchies (with the *rdfs:subPropertyOf* primitive), we can state equivalences between properties (with the *owl:equivalentProperty* primitive), and we can assert the inverse of a property (with the *owl:inverseOf* primitive).

In addition to using *owl:ObjectProperty* to define binary relations, we can provide additional logical information about it with the following primitives:

- *owl:TransitiveProperty*. This primitive states that the relation is transitive.
- *owl:SymmetricProperty*. This primitive states that the relation is symmetric.

We can also state global cardinality restrictions on all kinds of properties (either object properties or datatype properties):

- *owl:FunctionalProperty*. This primitive states that the relation or attribute has only one value when applied to an instance of a concept of this domain. This primitive can be used for object properties (binary relations) and for datatype properties (concept attributes).
- *owl:InverseFunctionalProperty*. This primitive declares that the property is unambiguous, that is, for each instance of its range there is, at most, one instance of its domain that can take it. Consequently, this primitive can be used only with object properties. However, in OWL Full it can also be used with datatype properties.

Concerning higher arity relations, they must be defined as concepts in OWL (like in DAML+OIL). Below we present the definition for the ternary relation `connects`:

```
<owl:Class rdf:ID="connects">
  <rdfs:comment>A road connects two
       cities</rdfs:comment>
</owl:Class>
<owl:ObjectProperty rdf:ID="firstArgument">
  <rdfs:domain rdf:resource="#connects"/>
  <rdfs:range rdf:resource="#Location"/>
</owl:ObjectProperty>
<owl:ObjectProperty rdf:ID="secondArgument">
  <rdfs:domain rdf:resource="#connects"/>
  <rdfs:range rdf:resource="#Location"/>
</owl:ObjectProperty>
<owl:ObjectProperty rdf:ID="thirdArgument">
  <rdfs:domain rdf:resource="#connects"/>
  <rdfs:range rdf:resource="#RoadSection"/>
</owl:ObjectProperty>
```

In OWL we cannot express the constraint that cities are not part of each other and that the road starts in one of the cities and ends in the other.

Functions are not components of the OWL knowledge model, though binary functions can be represented with the *owl:FunctionalProperty* primitive previously discussed. Higher arity functions cannot be represented in this language.

Formal **axioms** are also not components of the OWL knowledge model.

Finally, **instances** are defined using only RDF vocabulary, as occurred in DAML+OIL. In OWL, we must use the attribute *rdf:datatype* to express the value type of datatype properties, as explained in the RDF(S) section. Therefore, the definition of our instance of flight AA7462 is as follows:

```
<AA7462 rdf:ID="AA7462Feb082002" >
  <singleFare rdf:resource="&units;USDollar300"/>
  <departureDate rdf:datatype="&xsd;date">
     2002-02-08
  </departureDate>
  <arrivalPlace rdf:resource="#Seattle"/>
</AA7462>
```

Claims could also be represented in the same way as they were in RDF(S), and we can also assert that two instances are equivalent (with *owl:sameIndividualAs* and *owl:sameAs* indistinctly) or different (with *owl:differentFrom*). In addition, we can express that a set of individuals are all different from each other (with *owl:AllDifferent*). Note that these primitives are needed because OWL does not assume the unique name assumption for identifiers. This means that two terms with different identifiers can represent the same individual. Hence if two terms refer to different individuals we need to explicitly declare that both terms are different. For instance, the following definition states that in our ontology the identifiers Seattle, NewYork and Madrid refer to different individuals:

```
<owl:AllDifferent>
  <owl:distinctMembers rdf:parseType="Collection">
    <City rdf:about="#Seattle"/>
    <City rdf:about="#NewYork"/>
    <City rdf:about="#Madrid"/>
  </owl:distinctMembers>
</owl:AllDifferent>
```

4.4.6.2 Reasoning mechanisms
The model-theoretic semantics of OWL is described by Patel-Schneider and colleagues (2003). This semantics is described in two different ways: as an extension of the RDF(S) model theory and as a direct model-theoretic semantics of OWL. Both of them have the same semantic consequences on OWL ontologies, and

they are based on the DAML+OIL model-theoretic semantics, taking into account the differences between both languages.

Like DAML+OIL, OWL allows including any additional statements (RDF triples) in its ontologies apart from those explicitly defined in the language. However, OWL is silent on the semantic consequences (or lack thereof) of such additional triples.

A set of test cases has been defined by Carroll and De Roo (2003) including entailment tests, non-entailment tests, consistency tests, inconsistency tests, etc. They illustrate the correct usage of the OWL and the formal meaning of its constructs.

Due to its similarities with OIL and DAML+OIL, inference engines used for these languages (FaCT, RACER, TRIPLE, etc.) can be easily adapted for reasoning with it. There are not many inference engines available yet for reasoning with OWL, but we foresee that there will be soon. A reasoning engine already available is Euler[38].

As with other languages, these inference engines will permit performing **automatic classifications** of OWL ontology concepts, and detecting inconsistencies in OWL concept taxonomies.

Furthermore, we can say that multiple **inheritance** is allowed in OWL ontologies (as we have discussed when describing how to create class expressions). In the semantics of OWL, however, there is no explanation on how conflicts in multiple inheritance can be solved. **Constraint checking** can be performed on the values of properties and their cardinalities.

OWL assumes monotonic reasoning, even if class definitions or property definitions are split up in different Web resources. This means that facts and entailments declared explicitly or obtained with inference engines can only be added, never deleted, and that new information cannot negate previous information.

As with DAML+OIL, many tools will be available for authoring OWL ontologies; tools capable of editing RDF(S) ontologies can also be used for developing OWL ontologies provided that the ontology developer uses the OWL KR primitives. In addition, RDF(S) query engines, storage systems, and parsers can be employed to manage OWL ontologies since they can be serialized in RDF(S). Finally, we must add that systems that transform DAML+OIL ontologies into OWL ontologies are already available[39].

4.5 Conclusion

In summary, different ontology languages have different expressiveness and inference mechanisms. KR paradigms underlying all these languages are diverse: frames, description logics, first (and second) order logic, conceptual graphs,

---

[38] http://www.agfa.com/w3c/euler/
[39] http://www.mindswap.org/2002/owl.html

semantic networks, production rules, deductive rules, etc. In many cases, they are even based on combinations of several formalisms.

In this chapter, we have tried to show the most important features of each language: the KR paradigm underlying the language, the components that can be represented, their syntax, the reasoning mechanisms available, how ontologies implemented in each language can be used in other systems, etc. We have tried to illustrate this with examples from the same domain, so that the reader can compare not only different syntaxes, but also different modeling styles with each language.

This section is divided into two. First, we present some conclusions related to the knowledge representation capabilities of all the languages described in this chapter, which are summarized in a table. Then, we discuss about the suitability of these languages for different ontology-based applications and uses.

4.5.1 Knowledge representation

As a summary to this chapter, Table 4.1 shows some results of a comparative study between all the languages described. This comparison does not aim to show an exhaustive list of features of all the languages presented in this chapter, since each language is based on different KR paradigms and has its own distinguishing features. Neither does it aim to establish a score of languages (in the sense of "language X is better than language Y"), as different, and sometimes incompatible, features may be needed for different ontology-based applications. It only aims to help understand better the similarities and differences between languages and the capabilities of each of them.

Cells in the table will be filled using '+' to indicate that it is a supported feature in the language, '-' for non supported features, and 'W' for non supported features that could be supported with some workaround. The contents of this table present the situation of languages as of January 2003. They may change because of language evolution, especially in the cases of RDF(S) and OWL.

An extended version of this study can be found in Corcho and Gómez-Pérez (2000) and Gómez-Pérez and Corcho (2002), with the exception of DAML+OIL and OWL in the first reference, and of OWL in the second one. In Chapter 5, we will provide a table where we will show the relationship between ontology languages and ontology tools, so as to have an idea of which tools we can use to create ontologies in each language, and which tools are able to import ontologies implemented in different languages.

Now we will comment on the main results presented in Table 4.1, trying to highlight the main differences between the languages described in this chapter.

Table 4.1: A summary of ontology language features.

	Ontolingua	LOOM	OKBC	OCML	FLogic	SHOE	XOL	RDF(S)	OIL	DAML+OIL	OWL
CONCEPTS											
Attributes											
Instance attributes	+	+	+	+	+	+	+	+	+	+	+
Class attributes	+	-	+	+	+	-	+	W	-	W	W
Facets											
Type constraints	+	+	+	+	+	+	+	+	+	+	+
Cardinality constraints	+	+	+	+	W	-	+	-	+	+	+
Procedural knowledge	-	+	-	+	-	-	-	-	-	-	-
CONCEPT TAXONOMIES											
Subclass-Of	+	+	+	+	+	+	+	+	+	+	+
Disjoint-Decomposition	+	+	-	+	W	-	-	-	+	+	+
Exhaustive-Decomposition	+	-	-	W	W	-	-	-	W	W	W
Partition	+	+	-	+	W	-	-	-	+	+	W
RELATIONS											
Binary relations	+	+	+	+	+	+	+	+	+	+	+
n-ary relations	+	+	W	+	W	+	W	W	W	W	W
Relation hierarchies	+	+	-	+	W	-	-	+	+	+	+
Integrity constraints	+	+	-	+	+	-	-	-	-	-	-
FUNCTIONS											
Binary functions	+	+	W	+	+	-	W	-	+	+	+
n-ary functions	+	+	-	+	+	-	-	-	-	-	-
OTHER COMPONENTS											
Formal Axioms	+	+	-	+	+	-	-	-	-	-	-
Instances	+	+	+	+	+	+	+	+	+	+	+
Procedures	+	+	-	+	-	-	-	-	-	-	-
Rules	-	+	-	+	-	+	-	-	-	-	-

The main conclusion obtained from the analysis of the table is related to the different expressive power of each language. While some languages permit representing heavyweight ontologies (with formal axioms, functions, rules, procedures, and other rich modeling components), others only permit representing lightweight ontologies (basically, concepts, concept taxonomies, and relations between them). There are relevant differences in expressiveness between traditional languages and ontology markup languages. In fact, most of these components can be represented in traditional languages (such as Ontolingua, LOOM and OCML), while ontology markup languages do not normally provide means to do it. For instance, in the case of formal axioms, ontology markup languages rely on a future "logic layer" that must be built on top of them, and that will provide extra logical features not provided by the languages themselves.

We will now comment briefly on each of the main features presented in the table.

As we have said above, all the ontology languages allow representing concepts and their attributes (aka slots, roles, and properties). Instance **attributes** define concept properties whose value(s) are assigned by each concept instance. They can be defined in all the languages. Class attributes specify properties of the concept itself. There are no specific primitives or keywords to represent them in SHOE, RDF(S), and in the DL-based languages (LOOM, OIL, DAML+OIL, and OWL). This is due to the fact that reasoning with these attributes in description logics is difficult. However, they can be represented in RDF(S), DAML+OIL, and OWL with a workaround, as specified in the table. This workaround consists in defining them as properties whose domain is the class *rdfs:Class*, *daml:Class*, and *owl:Class* respectively, and specifying their value(s) in the concept definition where the class attribute takes a value.

If we deal with **facets** (attribute constraints), we can see that all the languages allow constraining the type of attributes. Regarding cardinality constraints, both minimum and maximum cardinalities can usually be represented, except for SHOE and RDF(S), where they cannot, and FLogic, where minimum cardinalities cannot be represented and maximum cardinalities can only be 1 or N (unspecified). Table 4.1 also shows whether it is possible to attach procedures to attributes or not. Only LOOM and OCML allow representing that kind of knowledge.

Concept taxonomies allow structuring the domain concepts in a hierarchical way. The *subclass of* relationship between concepts is considered in all the languages since it is the basic way to define these hierarchies. More complex knowledge such as partitions, and disjoint and exhaustive concept decompositions cannot be represented in many languages.

Sometimes, the same knowledge can be represented with different modeling components. For example, disjointness in DAML+OIL and FLogic is implemented differently: DAML+OIL provides special KR primitives to represent disjointness, while to represent disjointness in FLogic we must use formal axioms.

Another example is related to partitions. In DAML+OIL, partitions are defined with the primitive *daml:disjointUnionOf.* In OWL, partitions must be defined in two steps: first, expliciting that the concepts in the partition are disjoint; and second, defining the superconcept as the union of all the concepts in the partition.

All languages allow representing binary **relations** between concepts. In many languages, attributes and relations are represented with the same primitives, although they have different ranges: datatypes and concepts respectively. Relations of higher arity must be normally created by reification (representing them as concepts), as we have shown in many examples throughout this chapter.

Relation hierarchies can be represented in the DL-based languages, plus Ontolingua and OCML. In FLogic, these hierarchies can be represented with formal axioms. With regard to more complex constraints, such as general integrity constraints on relations, they can be only expressed by those languages that allow representing formal axioms.

Functions are very similar to relations. In Gruber's definition presented in Chapter 1, a function is a special case of relation where the value of its nth argument is unique for its n-1 preceding arguments. As in the case of relations, there are important differences between languages with respect to the arity of functions. Except for SHOE and RDF(S), binary functions can be defined (either directly or using workarounds) in all the languages. However, n-ary functions cannot be represented in ontology markup languages.

Finally, we will comment on the other ontology components: formal axioms, instances, rules, procedures, etc.

We have already discussed the differences in expressiveness between traditional and markup languages, especially in relation to the definition of **formal axioms**. While this could be considered as an important drawback in ontology markup languages, most of them (except SHOE and XOL) have been designed taking into account that an additional logic layer could be built on top of them.

As for **instances**, all the languages allow creating instances of the concepts and of the relations defined in an ontology. In the case of RDF(S), OIL, DAML+OIL and OWL, instances are represented in RDF.

With regard to **rules**, some languages include them as a useful extension to allow users to perform more inferences with the language. In the case of LOOM and OCML, the chaining mechanism of these rules (backward or forward) can be determined in the rule definition.

We have also dealt with **procedures** and procedural attachments. Procedures can be created in Ontolingua, LOOM and OCML. These three languages are based on Lisp. Hence, procedures in these languages must be defined in Lisp.

4.5.2 Using ontology languages in ontology-based applications

Once we have commented all the features of each language extracted from Table 4.1, we will give some advice on the use of languages for different kinds of ontology-based applications. This advice is based on our experience and on the case studies available from the literature:

In **e-commerce applications**, ontologies are usually used for representing products and services that are offered in e-commerce platforms and are given to users in catalogues they can browse through (Léger et al., 2000). Representational needs are not too complex: basically, we need concepts and attributes, and n-ary relations between concepts. However, reasoning needs are usually higher: if the number of products or services offered in the platform is high, automatic classifications are very useful for organising these products or services automatically (hence, languages based on description logics are extremely helpful), and an efficient query answering is also important in this environment (this is provided by most of the studied languages).

When using **PSMs** and domain ontologies together two languages are strongly recommended, as they provide explicit support for this integration as well as reusable libraries: OCML and FLogic. In fact, both of them are operational modeling languages and solve the issue of PSM prototyping easily. A generic model of parametric design problem solving is provided in OCML (Motta, 1999), and KARL (Fensel, 1995) (a customization of FLogic) has been used for PSM modelization, too.

In the context of the **Semantic Web**, and for **exchanging** ontologies between applications, languages based on XML are easily read and managed since standard libraries for the treatment of XML are available free. However, it is not difficult to adapt traditional languages to XML syntax, which could make use of the same kind of libraries. The main advantage of RDF(S), OIL, DAML+OIL and OWL is the strong support they receive from other communities besides the ontology community, and this means that more tools are available for editing, handling, and documenting the ontologies.

The creation of **upper-level ontologies** requires high expressiveness and mostly there are not great needs for reasoning support. Upper-level ontologies have been generally specified in DL languages such as LOOM or CLASSIC. The Cyc knowledge base is specified in CycL (Lenat and Guha, 1990), which is a language based on frames and first order logic.

In general, languages based on description logics have been widely used in applications that needed **intelligent integration of heterogeneous information sources**. For instance, CLASSIC has been used in OBSERVER (Mena et al., 2000), LOOM in Ariadne (Barish et al., 2000), CARIN is the language used in the PICSEL project (Goasdoué et al., 2000) and OIL has been used in an urban planning process (Stuckenschmidt, 2000). In addition most of them have been used for **information**

retrieval. For example, LOOM has been used in OntoSeek (Guarino et al., 1999). The main reason for this broad use is their inference support.

4.6 Bibliographical Notes and Further Reading

For readers interested in exploring the analysis of the expressive power and reasoning mechanisms of ontology languages, we recommend two papers: Corcho and Gómez-Pérez (2000), and Gómez-Pérez and Corcho (2002). In both, the description of an evaluation framework of ontology languages and the corresponding analysis of ontology languages are dealt with extensively.

For those interested in the understanding of each ontology language, we recommend the following documents:

- for Ontolingua and KIF, Farquhar and colleagues (1997) and Genesereth and Fikes (1992);
- for LOOM, the LOOM reference manual Version 2.0 (Brill, 1993), the tutorial for LOOM Version 2.1 (LOOM Tutorial, 1995), and a retrospective on LOOM (MacGregor, 1999);
- for OKBC, Chaudhri and colleagues (1998);
- for OCML, Motta (1999), which also shows the use of OCML in parametric design problem solving;
- for FLogic, Kifer and colleagues (1995);
- for XOL, Karp and colleagues (1999);
- for SHOE, Luke and Heflin (2000);
- for RDF(S), both Lassila and Swick (1999), Brickley and Guha (2003), and the RDF Primer (Manola and Miller, 2003);
- for OIL, the OIL whitepaper, by Bechhofer and colleagues (2000);
- for DAML+OIL, Horrocks and van Harmelen (2001) and the DAML+OIL walkthrough (van Harmelen et al., 2001b);
- for OWL, the OWL Guide (Smith et al., 2003).

We also provide some URLs for finding updated information about ontology markup languages since most of them are still in a development phase:

- for SHOE, we recommend *http://www.cs.umd.edu/projects/plus/SHOE/*;
- for RDF(S), we recommend visiting the following links: the Dave Beckett's RDF Resource Guide (*http://www.ilrt.bristol.ac.uk/discovery/rdf/resources/*), the FORTH RDF(S) pages (*http://www.ics.forth.gr/proj/isst/RDF/*) and the RDF(S) pages in the W3C site (*http://www.w3c.org/RDF/*);
- for OIL, we recommend visiting *http://www.ontoknowledge.org/oil/*;
- for DAML+OIL, we recommend the DAML home page (*http://www.daml.org*);
- for OWL, we strongly recommend visiting the URL of the W3C Web Ontology (Web-Ont) Working Group (*http://www.w3.org/2001/sw/WebOnt/*), since it will contain the most up-to-date documents about this language.

Tutorials about RDF, RDFS and OWL are also available in *http://www.xfront.com/rdf/*, *http://www.xfront.com/rdf-schema/*, and *http://www.xfront.com/owl/* respectively.

Other markup languages are now being created to provide more functionalities to the Semantic Web. One example is RuleML (*http://www.dfki.uni-kl.de/ruleml/*), which is being constructed as a markup language to define any kind of rules (transformation rules, derivation rules, inference rules, etc.) that can be used in the Web. Not only XML, but also RDF(S) and DAML+OIL versions of RuleML are available (and they will be adapted to OWL). Rules written in this language can be translated to different rule-based systems where they can be executed.

If you are interested in learning more about DL languages we recommend "The Description Logic Handbook", by Baader and colleagues (2003), and the following URL: *http://www.dl.kr.org/*, where you can find many links to resources (workshops, publications, tutorials, systems, etc.) related to the description logics field.

Finally, the deliverable D.1.1 "Technical Roadmap" of the OntoWeb thematic network, funded by the European Commission, contains brief descriptions and references to the most relevant ontology languages. As in other chapters, we also recommend the OntoRoadMap application, created inside the thematic network OntoWeb (*http://babage.dia.fi.upm.es/ontoweb/wp1/OntoRoadMap/index.html*), which allows researchers to browse and update information on ontology languages. We also recommend visiting the Web site of the Special Interest Group on Ontology Language Standards (*http://www.cs.man.ac.uk/~horrocks/OntoWeb/SIG/*) of the thematic network OntoWeb.

Chapter 5

Ontology Tools

To build ontologies is complex and time consuming, and it is even more if ontology developers have to implement them directly in an ontology language, without any kind of tool support. To ease this task, in the mid-1990s the first ontology building environments were created. They provided interfaces that helped users carry out some of the main activities of the ontology development process, such as conceptualization, implementation, consistency checking, and documentation. In the last few years, the number of ontology tools has greatly increased and they have been diversified. Gómez-Pérez (2002) distinguishes the following groups:

- *Ontology development tools*. This group includes tools and integrated suites that can be used to build a new ontology from scratch. In addition to the common edition and browsing functions, these tools usually give support to ontology documentation, ontology export and import to/from different formats and ontology languages, ontology graphical edition, ontology library management, etc.
- *Ontology evaluation tools*. They are used to evaluate the content of ontologies and their related technologies. Ontology content evaluation tries to reduce problems when we need to integrate and use ontologies and ontology-based technology in other information systems.
- *Ontology merge and alignment tools*. These tools are used to solve the problem of merging and aligning different ontologies in the same domain.
- *Ontology-based annotation tools*. With these tools users can insert instances of concepts and of relations in ontologies and maintain (semi)automatically ontology-based markups in Web pages. Most of these tools have appeared recently, in the context of the Semantic Web.
- *Ontology querying tools and inference engines*. These allow querying ontologies easily and performing inferences with them. Normally, they are strongly related to the language used to implement ontologies.

- *Ontology learning tools.* They can derive ontologies (semi)automatically from natural language texts, as well as semi-structured sources and databases, by means of machine learning and natural language analysis techniques.

Some tool suites integrate tools from different groups, and some other isolated tools provide a limited set of functions. But in this chapter we focus only on the first four groups of ontology tools: ontology development, ontology evaluation, ontology merge and alignment, and ontology-based annotation tools. Ontology evaluation tools are described in the context of the ontology tool suites where they are integrated. We do not describe ontology querying tools and inference engines attached to ontology development tools, because they usually depend on the language used to implement ontologies and most of them were described in Chapter 4. Nor do we deal with ontology learning tools, which are out of the scope of this book.

We will start by describing **ontology development tools and tool suites** like KAON (Maedche et al., 2003), OilEd (Bechhofer et al., 2001a), the Ontolingua Server (Farquhar et al., 1997), OntoSaurus (Swartout et al., 1997), Protégé-2000 (Noy et al., 2000), WebODE (Arpírez et al., 2003), and WebOnto (Domingue, 1998). We will try to answer the following basic questions, which normally arise when a new ontology is being built or an existing ontology is to be reused with a tool.

- Which activities of the ontology development process are supported by each tool?
- What is the expressiveness of the underlying knowledge model attached to the tool?
- What kinds of user interface does the tool provide to model ontology terms?
- Does the tool provide an advanced user interface to model formal axioms or complex expressions?
- Does the tool need to be installed locally or not?
- Can it be used with a Web browser?
- Where are the ontologies stored (in databases or files)?
- Does the tool have an inference engine and querying tools?
- Which ontology languages or formats does the tool generate?
- Is the tool able to import ontologies implemented in ontology languages or in other formats?
- Is it possible to migrate an ontology from one tool to another without losing knowledge?
- How can ontology-based applications use ontologies developed with a tool?
- What types of consistency checking and content evaluation does the tool perform?

Different (or even the same) ontology libraries may contain several ontologies that model the same domain. Such ontologies might be modeled following different or the same set of design principles and ontology modeling components. This situation will be specially frequent in the Semantic Web, where applications are not committed to a unique ontology. **Ontology alignment and merge tools** can be used to harmonize existing ontologies in the same domain. For this they first establish links between terms of the original ontologies. With ontology alignment the original ontologies are preserved and with ontology merge a unique ontology is generated from the original ones. With these tools applications could reach consensus on their ontologies both at design and run time.

In this chapter we describe in detail the PROMPT plug-in (Noy and Musen, 2000), which is integrated in Protégé-2000. We also describe briefly Chimaera (McGuinness et al., 2000), the FCA-Merge toolset (Stumme and Maedche, 2001), GLUE (Doan et al., 2002), and the merge module of OBSERVER (Mena et al., 2000). We will try to answer the following questions, which normally arise when an ontologist has to select an ontology alignment or merge tool:

- Which ontology components (i.e., concepts, concept taxonomies, attributes, relations, etc.) can be merged or aligned?
- Does the tool require that the source ontologies be expressed in the same language or format? Does it work with ontologies expressed in different languages? Which ones?
- What is the degree of automatization of the merge and alignment processes supported by the tool? Is it fully automatic or is it totally supervised?
- Are the merge and alignment tools integrated into other ontology development tools or tool suites?

Once the conceptual model of an ontology is built (either by a process of building the ontology from scratch or by merging other ontologies), the process of ontology population usually starts. This process consists in creating a knowledge base containing instances of the ontology concepts and instances of the ontology relations. Ontology development tools and tool suites provide basic support for the ontology population so that ontology developers can create instances with their ontology editors. **Ontology annotation tools** have appeared in the context of the Semantic Web to support the creation of instances of concepts and instances of relations related to the content of Web resources. The ontology annotation tools described in this chapter are: AeroDAML (Kogut and Holmes, 2001), COHSE (Bechhofer et al., 2002), MnM (Vargas-Vera et al., 2001), OntoAnnotate (Handschuh et al., 2001), and the SHOE Knowledge Annotator (Heflin and Hendler, 2001). The following questions may arise when populating ontologies with these tools:

- What types of instances does the annotation tool suggest (instances of concepts, with their attribute values, and/or instances of relations)?
- Where are the annotations stored (in the source page or in an annotation server)?
- In which languages are annotations stored?
- In which languages are ontologies handled?
- What automatization degree does the annotation tool support? Is it manual or automatic? Does it suggest annotations for Web resources?
- Does the tool allow annotating static Web pages?; and dynamic Web pages?; and images?

Most of the tools described in this chapter are in an advanced development stage, and many of their corporate users belong to R&D departments of companies and universities. As there seems to be great activity going on in this area, we recommend consulting tool developers for updated information.

5.1 Ontology Tools Evolution

Ontology tools' technology has improved enormously since the creation of the first environments. If we take into consideration the evolution of ontology development tools since they appeared in the mid-1990s, we can distinguish two groups[1]:

- Tools whose knowledge model maps directly to an ontology language. These tools were developed as ontology editors for a specific language. In this group we have included: the Ontolingua Server (Farquhar et al., 1997), which supports ontology construction with Ontolingua and KIF; OntoSaurus (Swartout et al., 1997) with Loom; WebOnto (Domingue, 1998) with OCML; and OilEd (Bechhofer et al., 2001a) with OIL first, and later with DAML+OIL.

- Integrated tool suites whose main characteristic is that they have an extensible architecture, and whose knowledge model is usually independent of an ontology language. These tools provide a core set of ontology related services and are easily extended with other modules to provide more functions. In this group we have included Protégé-2000 (Noy et al., 2000), WebODE (Arpírez et al., 2003), OntoEdit (Sure et al., 2002a), and KAON (Maedche et al., 2003).

We are going to present how this evolution took place and to highlight the most relevant features of the tools of each group.

As commented above, the main characteristic of the first group of tools is that they have a strong relationship with a specific ontology language. These tools were created to allow editing and browsing ontologies in their corresponding languages and to import and export ontologies from/to some other ontology languages, but they require that users have knowledge of their underlying ontology language.

The **Ontolingua Server** (Farquhar et al., 1997) was the first ontology tool created. It appeared in the mid-1990s, and was built to ease the development of Ontolingua ontologies with a form-based Web interface. Initially the main application inside the Ontolingua Server was the ontology editor. Then other systems were included in the environment, such as a Webster, an equation solver, an OKBC server, the ontology merge tool Chimaera, etc.

In parallel to the development of the Ontolingua Server, **OntoSaurus** (Swartout et al., 1997) was implemented as a Web editor and browser for LOOM ontologies. OntoSaurus consists of two main modules: an ontology server, which uses the knowledge representation (KR) system[2] attached to the LOOM language, and a Web browser, which allows editing and browsing LOOM ontologies with HTML forms.

---

[1] In each group, we have followed a chronological order of appearance. Note that sometimes the most important bibliographic reference of a tool may have been written several years later than its first release.

[2] Levesque (1984) defines a knowledge representation system as a server supporting two kinds of operations: telling the system additional information and asking queries. He also states that, unlike other systems, KR systems use not only explicitly told but also inferred information, in answering questions.

In 1997, **WebOnto** (Domingue, 1998) was released. WebOnto is an ontology editor for OCML ontologies. The main difference with respect to the previous tools lay in that the ontology editor was not based on HTML forms, but on Java applets, but its great advantage over the rest of ontology development tools was its strong support for collaborative ontology edition, which allowed synchronous and asynchronous discussions about the ontologies being built by groups of users.

OilEd (Bechhofer et al., 2001a) was developed in 2001 as an ontology editor for OIL ontologies. With the creation of DAML+OIL, OilEd was adapted to manage DAML+OIL ontologies, and in the near future it will be adapted to manage OWL. Users of OilEd should know how to model ontologies using a DL approach. OilEd provides consistency checking functions and automatic concept classifications by means of the FaCT inference engine, though other DL inference engines such as RACER can also be used.

In recent years a new generation of ontology-engineering environments has been developed. The design rationale for these environments is much more ambitious than that of previous tools. They are built as integrated tool suites that provide technological support to a wide variety of activities of the ontology development process. For this purpose, they have extensible, component-based architectures, where new modules can easily be added to provide more functions to the suite. Besides, the knowledge models underlying these environments are usually language independent and provide translations from and to several languages and formats.

Protégé-2000 (Noy et al., 2000) is an open source, standalone application with an extensible architecture. The core of Protégé-2000 is its ontology editor, which can be extended with plug-ins that add more functions to the environment, such as ontology language import and export (FLogic, Jess, OIL, XML, Prolog), OKBC access, constraints creation and execution (PAL), ontology merge (PROMPT, which is described in Section 5.3.1), etc.

WebODE (Arpírez et al., 2003) is also an extensible ontology-engineering suite based on an application server, whose development started in 1999. The core of WebODE is its ontology access service, which is used by all the services and applications plugged into the server. The WebODE's Ontology Editor, which allows editing and browsing WebODE ontologies, is based on HTML forms and Java applets. The workbench integrates services for ontology language import and export (XML, RDF(S), OIL, DAML+OIL, OWL, CARIN, FLogic, Jess, Prolog), for axiom edition with WAB (WebODE Axiom Builder), for documentation, for evaluation, for evolution, for learning, for merge, and an inference engine. WebODE can interoperate with Protégé-2000.

OntoEdit (Sure et al., 2002a) is an extensible and flexible environment based on a plug-in architecture. Its ontology editor is a standalone application that allows editing and browsing ontologies, and includes functions for collaborative ontology building, inferencing, handling of domain lexicons, etc. This editor exports and imports ontologies in different formats (XML, FLogic, RDF(S), and DAML+OIL). There are two versions of OntoEdit: OntoEdit Free and OntoEdit Professional, each with a different set of functions.

The **KAON** tool suite (Maedche et al., 2003) is an open source extensible ontology engineering environment. The core of this tool suite is the ontology API, which defines its underlying knowledge model based on an extension of RDF(S). The OI-modeler is the ontology editor of the tool suite that provides capabilities for ontology evolution, ontology mapping, ontology generation from databases, etc.

Merge tools are described in Section 5.3; their evolution can be summarized as follows:

In the mid-1990s, research groups at the Universidad del País Vasco, MCC and the University of Georgia began to develop **OBSERVER** (Mena et al., 1996). The research community was already aware of the fact that rather than building "the" ontology for a domain, it was more suitable to align or merge existing ontologies, as described in Section 3.6. OBSERVER could do this, because it merged automatically ontologies of the same domain to access heterogeneous information sources. However, the merge process was carried out by an internal module and, therefore, it was invisible to the user.

Several years later, in the late 1990s, two groups at Stanford University developed two of the most relevant ontology merge tools: Chimaera and the PROMPT plug-in. **Chimaera** (McGuinness et al., 2000) was built by the Knowledge Systems Laboratory (KSL) to aid in the process of ontology merge, and the **PROMPT plug-in** (Noy and Musen, 2000), integrated in Protégé-2000, was built by the Stanford Medical Informatics (SMI). The added value of the latter was that it provided support to the ontology merge method PROMPT, described in Section 3.6.3.

Approximately at the same time, the Institute AIFB of the University of Karlsruhe developed the **FCA-Merge toolset** (Stumme and Maedche, 2001) to support the FCA-Merge method, described in Section 3.6.2.

Finally, in 2002, **GLUE** (Doan et al., 2002) was developed at the University of Washington. GLUE is a system that semi-automatically finds mappings between concepts from two different ontologies.

Ontology-based annotators are described in Section 5.4; their evolution can be summarized as follows:

Several ontology-based annotation initiatives started around 1997: the SHOE project (Luke et al., 1997), the $(KA)^2$ initiative (Benjamins et al., 1999), and the Planet-Onto project (Domingue and Motta, 2000), among others. These can be considered the precursors of the current Semantic Web. All these efforts proved that the manual coding of annotations in Web pages was a hard task and consequently there was a need for tools to ease it.

As a result of the SHOE project we can cite the **SHOE Knowledge Annotator** (Heflin and Hendler, 2001), a basic tool to annotate HTML documents with SHOE, which was the first to appear. This tool has given way to another called **SMORE**, which allows managing RDF(S) and DAML+OIL ontologies and annotations.

The rest of annotators were developed later almost at the same time. All of them are characterized for creating DAML+OIL annotations: **OntoMat-Annotizer** (Handschuh et al., 2001), developed by the Institute AIFB at the University of Karlsruhe, and **OntoAnnotate** (Handschuh et al., 2001), based on the previous one and commercialized by Ontoprise, are standalone applications that allow users to create manually annotations of Web documents.

MnM (Vargas-Vera et al., 2001) was created in 2001 and its second version has been released in April 2003. It is also a standalone application to create annotations manually, but it additionally gives support to semi-automatic and fully automatic document annotation processes by using information extraction modules.

COHSE (Bechhofer et al., 2002) is installed as a sidebar of the Mozilla browser. Its architecture is more complex than that of the other tools, because it is based on ontology and annotation servers. It creates automatically ontology-based annotations in documents and lets users create other annotations, which are stored in the annotation server.

Finally, the **UBOT AeroDAML** tool (Kogut and Holmes, 2001) is available as a Web application to which the users send the file to be annotated, and which returns the annotations found in the document with respect to several top-level and general ontologies.

As we can see from this evolution description, ontology-based annotators are evolving from manual tools that help in the edition of annotations to more complex tools that automate some of the annotation processes.

5.2 Ontology Development Tools and Tool Suites

After the brief historical introduction of ontology tools, we are going to describe in detail each of the most representative ontology development tools and tool suites. Many others have been created to aid in the ontology development process, but we have decided to consider only the most relevant ones (either for historical reasons or because they are widely used).

We are going to use the following structure to describe all the tools and tool suites in this section, so that we can answer the questions commented in the previous section. First, we present some general information about the tool and its developers, about its architecture, and about its knowledge model. Then we deal with the ontology edition and browsing functionalities provided by the ontology editor, with the inference services attached to it, with its documentation options, with its collaborative ontology construction capabilities, and with other functions such as consistency checking, evaluation, ontology libraries, etc. Finally, we describe how we can interoperate with the tool: export and import formats and languages that it supports, other tools with which it can interoperate, and how to integrate ontologies developed with this tool in other information systems.

5.2.1 Language-dependent ontology development tools

In this section we describe the ontology tools of the first group: the Ontolingua Server, OntoSaurus, WebOnto, and OilEd. These tools are characterized by their tight relationship with an ontology language: Ontolingua, LOOM, OCML, and OIL respectively.

5.2.1.1 The Ontolingua Server

The Ontolingua Server[3] (Farquhar et al., 1997) was created in the mid-1990s by the Knowledge Systems Laboratory (KSL) at Stanford University. The main objective of this system was to ease the collaborative building of ontologies in the Ontolingua language and to provide a repository of ontologies. Most of the applications of the Ontolingua Server are available for public use at the URL specified in the footnote.

Architecture

The Ontolingua Server is organized as a set of ontology related Web applications, which are built on top of the Ontolingua KR system. The most important application in the toolset is the ontology editor, which is also described in this section. In addition to the ontology editor, the Ontolingua Server includes a Webster (to obtain term definitions), an OKBC server (to access Ontolingua ontologies through the OKBC protocol), and Chimaera (to analyze, merge and integrate ontologies).

The Ontolingua KR system is implemented in Lisp. Ontologies are stored as Lisp text files and retrieved from the server file system when they are loaded with any of the applications in the toolset. The user interfaces of the ontology editor, the Webster, and Chimaera are based on HTML forms. The OKBC server does not have any user interface but is available from remote clients, as we present later.

Knowledge model

As commented above, Ontolingua is the KR system that the Ontolingua Server uses internally. Thus the KR paradigm underlying the Ontolingua Server is that of the Ontolingua language, described in detail in Chapter 4. As was also explained in Chapter 4, the Ontolingua language consists of a combination of frames and first order logic, and allows representing classes, which are organized in class taxonomies, relations, functions, formal axioms, and instances.

In addition to the features provided by the Ontolingua language, the Ontolingua Server allows assembling Ontolingua ontologies, so that ontologies can be built in a modular way. There are three different possibilities of assembling Ontolingua ontologies (Farquhar et al., 1997):

- Inclusion. An ontology includes and uses definitions from other ontologies. For instance, our travel ontology uses the concepts `Date` and `Time` from an ontology about time. Circular ontology inclusions are allowed.
- Restriction. An ontology imports definitions from another ontology and makes them more specific. For instance, if our travel agency only uses US Dollars and Euros as currencies, the imported concept `CurrencyQuantity` can be restricted to `USDollar` and `Euro` in our travel ontology.
- Polymorphic refinement, A definition from any ontology is redefined in the ontology that imports it. Let us suppose that `departurePlace` has been defined as a relation between the concepts `Travel` and `Location` in a general ontology about traveling. The polymorphic refinement consists in importing this definition to our travel ontology and redefining it as a relation between the concepts `Flight` and `Airport`, and as a relation between the concepts `Ship` and `Port`.

---

[3] http://ontolingua.stanford.edu/

Ontology editor

We now describe the main features of the Ontolingua Server ontology editor, also known as the Ontolingua Server frame-editor or even as the Ontolingua Server. As we said before, the ontology editor is a Web application, based on HTML forms, where users can browse ontologies and ontology libraries, edit ontologies collaboratively, export ontologies to several languages, import ontologies from several languages, etc.

In Figure 5.1 we show a screenshot of the ontology editor for creating the concept Flight of our travel ontology. As the figure shows, the user interface is divided into two frames: the one at the top shows the menu with the editing options available to the user, and the one at the bottom shows the HTML form to create the new class, where we must specify the class name (Flight), and we can optionally specify the natural language (NL) documentation and the superclasses of the concept (in the figure we have declared that Flight is a subclass of Travel).

Once the form is filled, we should send its description to the server to store the Flight definition in Ontolingua. Then the term Flight becomes available in our ontology and we can use it to define other ontology terms (i.e., relations, functions, axioms, and instances) where this term appears.

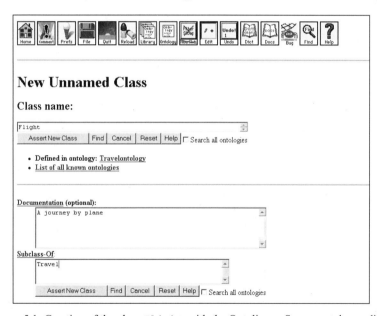

Figure 5.1: Creation of the class Flight with the Ontolingua Server ontology editor.

In Figure 5.2 we show an ontology editor screenshot in which we can see the result of browsing the relation arrivalDate of our travel ontology. This figure is similar to the previous one. In addition to the top frame with the menu, there are two more new frames in it: the one at the middle presents information about the relation browsed such as the name of the ontology where it is defined, a link to the Lisp source code of that ontology, the arity of the relation, etc.; and the one at the bottom presents the translation of the relation to OKBC. The user interfaces for creating and browsing other ontology components are similar to this one.

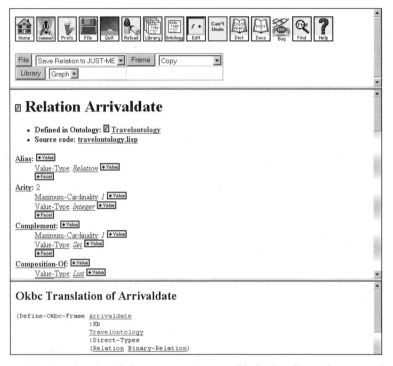

Figure 5.2: Browsing the relation `arrivalDate` with the Ontolingua Server ontology editor.

Besides creating and browsing ontology term definitions, there are many other functions available in the ontology editor. For example, we can browse graphically the class taxonomy of an ontology and the relations between classes, we can move through one term definition to another in the same ontology or in a different one using hyperlinks, etc.

The main drawback of editing an ontology with the Ontolingua ontology editor is that, although ontology developers must fill in forms to create ontology terms, the information to fill them in usually requires a thorough knowledge of KIF and of the Ontolingua language. For example, the KIF expression of an Ontolingua axiom must be written directly in a text box, with no help from the user interface. The same occurs to the expression of a relation constraint such as the one presented for the relation `connects` in Section 1.3.1. Therefore, if the developer does not have a comprehensive knowledge of KIF and the Ontolingua language (what includes knowledge of the Frame Ontology and of the OKBC Ontology), (s)he will not be able to create a medium or complex ontology. We refer to Section 2.1.1 for a description of the Frame Ontology and the OKBC ontology, and to Section 4.3.1 for a description of KIF and the Ontolingua language.

The Ontolingua Server ontology library contains more than 50 ontologies, among which we can find the Frame Ontology and the OKBC Ontology, and also KIF-Extensions, KIF-Lists, KIF-Meta, KIF-Numbers, KIF-Relations, and KIF-Sets, which define several parts of the KIF vocabulary. All these ontologies are imported in every Ontolingua ontology.

Concerning the collaborative construction of ontologies, the Ontolingua Server ontology editor permits managing users and user groups, who can share their ontologies. Users can work in different sessions and with different groups for each session, and then decide which ontologies can be shared with members of each group. However, collaboration is rather limited, since no locking mechanisms for ontology terms nor version management functions exist in the editor.

Interoperability

Once an ontology is available in the Ontolingua Server (either because it has been created with the ontology editor or has been uploaded to the server), there are two modes of using it from an external application. Both choices are shown graphically in Figure 5.3.

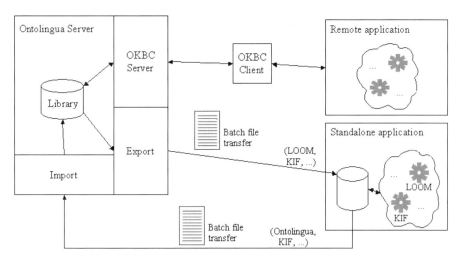

Figure 5.3: Ontolingua-based applications architecture.

The first mode consists in connecting to the OKBC Server (Chaudhri et al., 1998) available in the Ontolingua Server, from a remote client, as shown in the top right corner of the figure. For this purpose, the remote application connected to the OKBC server can use any of the programming languages for which there is an OKBC client binding implemented, namely Java, C, and Lisp. Ontologies are accessed dynamically through the OKBC server by means of the OKBC protocol primitives. These ontologies can be both read and updated as some OKBC protocol primitives allow modifying the ontology being accessed.

The second possibility consists in using the ontology editor to translate the ontology into an implementation language, as shown in the bottom right corner of the figure. The Ontolingua Server can export ontologies to KIF, LOOM, CLIPS

(Giarratano and Riley, 1998), CML[4] (Stanley, 1986), Epikit (Genesereth, 1990), CORBAs IDL (Mowbray and Zahavi, 1995), and Prolog. Once the corresponding file has been generated and stored locally, it can be used by a standalone local application. To reason with ontologies in any of these languages, their corresponding inference engines must be installed in the local machine and the ontologies must be loaded onto them. For instance, if an Ontolingua ontology is translated into KIF, the JTP[5] (Java Theorem Prover) inference engine can be used; if it is translated into LOOM, it can be loaded in the LOOM KR system; etc. If the ontology is modified by the local application, it can be uploaded to the Ontolingua Server with its import translators. Besides Ontolingua ontologies, the Ontolingua Server can import ontologies implemented in KIF, CORBAs IDL, and CML.

The main advantages of building a remote application over translating the ontology into a language and using the generated file in a standalone application are the following:
- Ontologies are accessed and updated dynamically when using the OKBC server. Therefore, if the ontology changes, it does not need to be regenerated in the format used by our local application and reloaded again.
- The use of the OKBC protocol ensures that our application will be able to access other OKBC-aware systems besides Ontolingua, such as LOOM, Protégé-2000, etc.

Although the Ontolingua Server was the first ontology environment to appear, the lack of inference engines for Ontolingua during the 1990s (JTP was available in 2002) made it difficult to work with Ontolingua ontologies in ontology-based applications. Furthermore, the low quality of the Ontolingua Server translations into other languages (Valente et al., 1999; Brilhante, 1999) caused many difficulties when the translated ontologies were used with their corresponding KR systems and inference engines.

5.2.1.2 OntoSaurus
OntoSaurus[6] (Swartout et al., 1997) was developed at the same time as the Ontolingua Server by the Information Sciences Institute (ISI) at the University of Southern California. The objective of OntoSaurus was the development of LOOM ontologies (aka LOOM theories) by means of a Web browser. OntoSaurus is freely available in the aforementioned URL, only with browsing functions, and can also be downloaded and installed locally.

Architecture
OntoSaurus consists of two modules: the ontology server, which uses the LOOM KR system and provides concept classification and instance matching functions; and the Web ontology editor and browser, which generates dynamically HTML pages

---

[4] Compositional Modeling Language. It should not be mistaken for the Conceptual Modeling Language proposed in the CommonKADS methodology (Schreiber et al., 1999).
[5] JTP is implemented in Java and can be downloaded for free at *http://www.ksl.stanford.edu/software/JTP*
[6] http://www.isi.edu/isd/ontosaurus.html. Version 1.9 (March 2002).

(including images and other text documentations) from the LOOM ontologies stored in the ontology server. Both modules and the interfaces between them are implemented in Lisp. The ontology editor is built on top of the Common Lisp Web server CL HTTP (Mallery, 1994).

Ontologies in OntoSaurus are stored as Lisp LOOM files and can be retrieved and parsed whenever a user wants to access them. These ontologies can be accessed with the Web ontology editor and browser, and with remote clients through an OKBC server. The OKBC server for OntoSaurus is not included in its standard installation package; therefore it must be installed and configured using the OKBC server library provided by the KSL[7].

Knowledge model

The LOOM KR system is the core of the OntoSaurus ontology server; therefore LOOM is the underlying language of OntoSaurus. With this description logic language, already described in Chapter 4, we can represent concepts and concept taxonomies, relations between concepts, functions, formal axioms and instances.

As it occurs in the Ontolingua Server, OntoSaurus allows including LOOM ontologies into others. Every ontology in OntoSaurus includes the built-in theory containing the concept *Thing*.

Ontology editor

The OntoSaurus ontology editor is a Web application to edit and browse ontology definitions in LOOM. The ontology edition in OntoSaurus is similar to that of the Ontolingua ontology editor. The ontology developer is presented with HTML forms that must be filled in to create ontology definitions. As in the case of the Ontolingua ontology editor, we should have a good command of the LOOM language if we want to create complex expressions for an ontology term, since the HTML form-based user interface only provides basic functions for creating concepts and their attributes, relations, etc.

Regarding ontology browsing, the OntoSaurus ontology editor provides two functions that use the LOOM inference engine, described in Section 4.3.2; these functions are:

- Concept classifications, which are generated automatically from LOOM concept definitions.
- Instance matching, which is performed to search for instances whose definition matches a query expressed in description logic.

Figure 5.4 shows the OntoSaurus browser presenting the results of using these functions. On the right of the figure we can see the result of browsing the concept Travel from our travel ontology. The browser presents the concept definition in LOOM and a fragment of the concept taxonomy for its child concepts. This concept taxonomy is obtained by means of the concept classification reasoning mechanism. Although it cannot be observed in the figure, the browser also presents information about the parent concepts of the concept being browsed, the relations defined for that concept, its instances, the production rules related to it, etc.

---

[7] http://www.ksl.stanford.edu/software/OKBC/

On the left of the figure we can see the answer to a simple query about the instances of the concept `Travel`; it gives the following results: `AA7462_Feb082002`, `AA7462_Feb092002` and `AA0488_Feb082002`. Thus OntoSaurus not only presents direct instances of that concept, but also instances of its subconcepts (in our case, of its child concepts `AA7462` and `AA0488`).

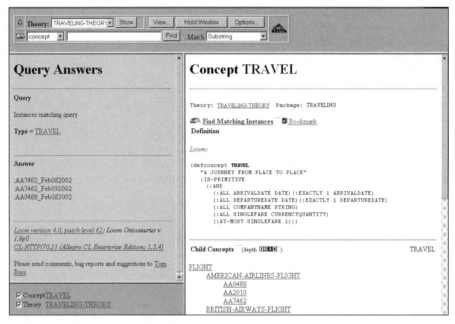

Figure 5.4: Browsing and querying the travel ontology with OntoSaurus.

The public version of the OntoSaurus ontology editor has an ontology library that holds several ontologies. The most relevant are: the *built-in theory*, which defines basic terms of the LOOM KR system and is imported by all the ontologies in the system; *Cyc-SENSUS*, which is a combination of the Cyc and SENSUS upper-level ontologies; *SUMO*, which is a subset of the Suggested Upper Merged Ontology, described in Section 2.2.4; *IDL-Theory*, which describes IDL entities used in the translation of ontologies to CORBA's IDL; *Inspect*, which was used in a knowledge based system for air campaign plan evaluation and critiquing (Valente et al., 1996); and several sample ontologies on the domains of aircrafts, vessels and weather.

As regards the cooperative construction of ontologies, the OntoSaurus ontology editor is able to manage users but not user groups. On the other hand, ontologies can be locked when somebody is editing them and this prevents other people from updating them at the same time.

Interoperability

Ontologies developed with OntoSaurus can be integrated into ontology-based applications in the same way as we can integrate Ontolingua ontologies. They can be downloaded in LOOM, PowerLoom[8], Stella (Chalupsky and MacGregor, 1999), Ontolingua, KIF, CORBAs IDL, and C++. Therefore we can use the inference engines of these languages to reason with the ontologies downloaded. OntoSaurus also imports ontologies implemented in PowerLoom, Stella, and CORBAs IDL.

OntoSaurus ontologies can be accessed and modified from remote clients (implemented in LISP, Java, or C) using the OKBC protocol, provided that the OKBC server is installed and available in the server.

5.2.1.3 WebOnto

WebOnto[9] (Domingue, 1998) was developed by the Knowledge Media Institute (KMi) at the Open University (United Kingdom). It appeared in 1997 as a Web application to browse and develop collaboratively OCML ontologies. WebOnto is freely available to edit and browse ontologies though users must request from the WebOnto developers a user account in order to have edition capabilities.

Architecture

WebOnto consists of two main modules: the ontology server and the ontology editor. Unlike the Ontolingua Server ontology editor and OntoSaurus, the WebOnto's user interface uses Java applets instead of HTML forms. Hence it allows editing and browsing concept taxonomies and relations between concepts with a fully graphical user interface, which is an important added value. Forms are used to edit instances and their attribute values, and text boxes are used to edit complex OCML expressions (rule expressions, operational definitions for relations and functions, etc.).

The WebOnto ontology server uses OCML. Consequently, WebOnto ontologies are stored as OCML files in the server. To access them WebOnto is built on top of the LispWeb HTTP server (Riva and Ramoni, 1996), a specialized HTTP server written in Common Lisp (Steele, 1990).

Knowledge model

WebOnto ontologies are implemented in the OCML language, described in Section 4.3.4. As we commented there, OCML is a kind of "operational Ontolingua" based on a combination of frames and first order logic. Hence it allows representing concepts, concept taxonomies, relations, functions, axioms, and rules.

Like OCML, WebOnto distinguishes between four types of ontologies: domain, task, method, and application ontologies. Besides, all these types of ontologies can include definitions from other ontologies. WebOnto gives support to this ontology inclusion by means of its graphical interface, where ontology inclusion is represented with an ontology library tree.

Ontology editor

Once a new ontology has been created somewhere in the ontology library tree, new terms can be created graphically. With the WebOnto graphical user interface we can define the same ontology components as those in OCML, that is, concepts and their

---

[8] http://www.isi.edu/isd/LOOM/PowerLoom/documentation/documentation.html
[9] http://webonto.open.ac.uk/

attributes, relations between concepts, functions, procedures, rules, axioms, and instances. In Figure 5.5 we can see a fragment of the concept taxonomy of our travel ontology. The left frame shows the names of the terms defined in the ontology. The middle frame contains an icon for each of the ontology components that can be defined in the ontology. The right frame is the graphical edition area where users can drag and drop components from the middle frame and connect them together forming concept taxonomies and establishing relations between them. When a new term is added to the graphical user interface, its name appears in the left frame. Finally, the window at the bottom right of the figure shows the result of inspecting (browsing) the class `Travel`. The window shows the ontology in which the class has been defined, its natural language documentation, its subclasses, and its attributes (slots), including their cardinality and value type.

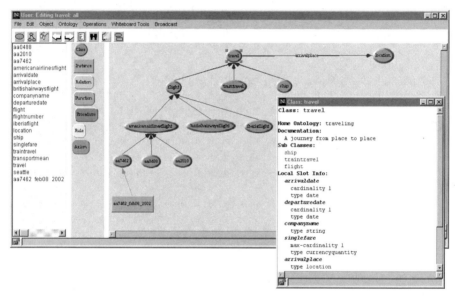

Figure 5.5: Fragment of the concept taxonomy of the travel ontology, and inspection of the concept `Travel` with WebOnto.

Concept instances are created in a similar way as the rest of the components, that is, by dragging and dropping them from the middle frame to the graphical edition area. Once the instances are connected to the concept they belong to, the information about their attributes and their relations is used to fill in the forms dynamically generated from the description of that concept and its superclasses by applying inheritance. Figure 5.6 shows the form that permits creating an instance of the concept `AA7462`. As we can see, to define the instance we fill in the values of the attributes `flightnumber`, `transportmeans`, and `companyname`, and of the relations `arrivalplace`, `singlefare`, `departuredate` and `arrivaldate`. The form also presents the value type and the allowed values of each attribute and relation. In the case of relations, if the user decides to create a new instance as the destination of the relation, the corresponding form will be shown as well, and this will permit creating several instances at the same time.

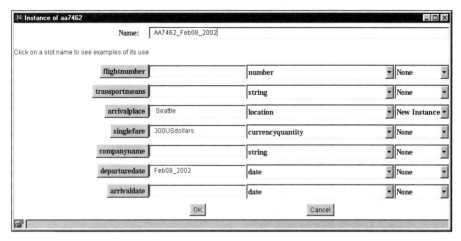

Figure 5.6: Edition of the instance `AA7462_Feb08_2002` with WebOnto.

Not all the edition operations in the ontology can be performed in a graphical manner or with forms. Complex operations such as defining axiom and rule expressions, operational definitions of functions and relations, etc., have to be made directly in OCML with the aid of text boxes displayed by the ontology editor. The edition of these OCML expressions requires that the user should have a comprehensive knowledge of the OCML syntax and its underlying KR ontology.

When editing and browsing ontologies, users can highlight specific fragments such as relevant parts of the concept taxonomy, all the instances of one concept, relations between specific concepts, etc. These highlighted parts are known as diagrams or views and users can create, save and load them at any time.

WebOnto also allows users to assert facts (*tell*), unassert facts (*unassert*), ask for information (*ask* and *setofall*) and evaluate OCML expressions (*evaluate*) on the ontology being edited or browsed. These operations are provided by the OCML KR system. In addition to being able to perform these operations on WebOnto ontologies, users can run application ontologies in WebOnto.

Consistency checking capabilities are also provided by WebOnto because they are supplied by the OCML KR system. Among other capabilities WebOnto allows checking type constraint violations, checking whether the destination value of a relation instance is defined in the ontology or not, etc.

Regarding the collaborative ontology edition features, WebOnto is one of the most advanced ontology tools available. It provides a broadcast/receive functionality that permits synchronous and asynchronous discussions between users about changes or updates on any ontology that they edit or browse. This functionality uses a tool called Tadzebao (Domingue, 1998).

Interoperability
Ontologies developed with WebOnto have been successfully integrated in several ontology-based applications at KMi, such as Planet-Onto (Domingue and Motta, 2000), ScholOnto (Buckingham-Shum et al., 2000), etc., and in other tools, such as the ontology-based annotation tool MnM (Vargas-Vera et al., 2001), described in Section 5.4.2.

WebOnto ontologies can be accessed through the OCML KR system (using Lisp) or through the LispWeb HTTP server (using the HTTP protocol). The source code of the OCML KR system can be downloaded and installed locally.

OCML ontologies can be translated to Ontolingua. Consequently, we can import them into the Ontolingua Server and use them in applications with any of the architectures proposed in Figure 5.3. This would allow, for instance, using the OKBC protocol for accessing an ontology developed with WebOnto and imported in the Ontolingua Server. OCML ontologies can also be translated to/from RDF(S), which ensures that these ontologies can be used by RDF(S) tools.

5.2.1.4 OilEd
OilEd[10] (Bechhofer et al., 2001a) is an ontology editor developed at the University of Manchester, and was initially developed in the context of the European IST project On-To-Knowledge. It was first built as an editor for OIL ontologies, and later adapted to DAML+OIL. In the future, it will be adapted to OWL. The current version (December 2002) is 3.5, and can be downloaded from the URL specified.

Architecture
OilEd is a standalone application implemented in Java designed as a simple ontology editor for DL ontologies (first for OIL, later for DAML+OIL, and in the future for OWL ontologies). The main objective of its design is to reduce the burden of implementing ontologies directly in a DL language. Consequently, OilEd has not many extensibility capabilities: the only extensions that can be made are related to backends; that is, new import and export modules can be added easily to the editor. OilEd ontologies are stored as DAML+OIL files.

OilEd can connect to any DL reasoner that uses the interface described in the DL Implementation Group (DIG) reasoner interface (Bechhofer, 2002). Currently, it can connect to reasoning engines such as FaCT (Horrocks et al., 1999) and RACER (Haarslev and Möller, 2001), to detect inconsistencies in class taxonomies.

Knowledge model
As we have mentioned above, OilEd is an ontology editor for DL ontologies. Its underlying knowledge model has undergone several changes. First, it was adapted from OIL to DAML+OIL and in the future it will be modified to be compliant with OWL. As explained in Chapter 4, DAML+OIL is a SHOIQ language according to the DL terminology. DAML+OIL allows representing classes organized in class taxonomies, properties, property restrictions, and individuals. Disjoint and exhaustive subclass partitions are represented as axioms in OilEd.

---

[10] http://oiled.man.ac.uk/

Term definitions from other ontologies can be included in OilEd ontologies since OilEd provides ontology inclusion functions. Terms from different ontologies are referred to with XML namespaces.

Ontology editor

We now describe the main features of this editor. Unlike the ontology editors described in previous sections and available as Web applications, OilEd is a standalone application that is run from local computers. This affects the look and feel of its user interface and some of the operations that can be performed with it.

Figure 5.7 shows a screenshot of the OilEd ontology editor for the edition of the concept Travel. It shows different tabs for editing ontology components: classes, properties, individuals, and axioms, and two more tabs for editing some ontology general information (*Container* tab) and for editing namespaces (*Namespaces* tab).

On the left of the figure we can see the list of classes of the ontology. For each class we can edit its NL documentation, superclasses, and property restrictions that include cardinality restrictions, existential type restrictions (*has-class*), and universal type restrictions (*to-class*). In addition, we can determine if the class is primitive or defined by selecting *SubclassOf* and *SameClassAs* in the *Properties* box respectively.

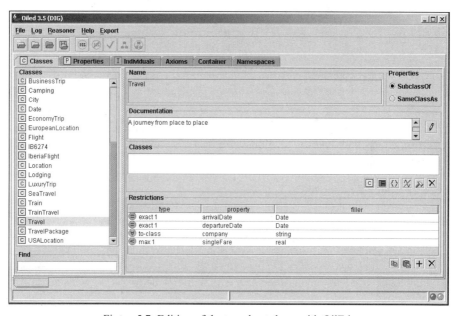

Figure 5.7: Edition of the travel ontology with OilEd.

Unlike other ontology editors, OilEd does not show the ontology class taxonomy during class edition but only a plain list of class names sorted alphabetically. This is because the ontology class taxonomy is not computed by the ontology editor but by the DL reasoners to which it connects. These DL reasoners are also able to detect inconsistencies in the class taxonomy during their process of automatic classification, which are reported to OilEd users. Figure 5.8 shows part of the class taxonomy of our travel ontology as returned by the FaCT classifier.

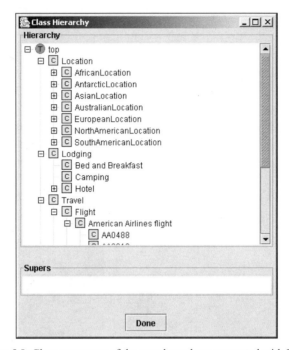

Figure 5.8: Class taxonomy of the travel ontology generated with FaCT.

With regard to properties, we can edit their NL documentation, domain and range, superproperties, and inverse relations. We can also determine whether they are symmetric, transitive, and unique (equivalent to the *daml:UnambiguousProperty* primitive). For the domain and range of properties we can use complex expressions since these are permitted in DL languages.

Concerning individuals, OilEd does not provide advanced functions to create them. For example, it does not check that the information included for an individual is correct with respect to the properties defined for the class to which it belongs. In fact, the creation of individuals is just intended for their use in DAML+OIL expressions, such as *daml:oneOf*, described in Chapter 4. That is, OilEd is not thought to be used as an instance-acquisition tool where ontology instances are easily inserted.

Since OilEd has been designed as a simple tool to edit DL ontologies, it does not have other functions present in other ontology editors such as collaborative ontology edition, graphical class taxonomy edition, etc. For documentation purposes, ontologies can be exported to HTML and class taxonomies can be exported to the dotty format used by the graphical browser GraphViz[11].

---

[11] http://www.research.att.com/sw/tools/graphviz/

Interoperability
Besides exporting ontologies to DAML+OIL, OilEd ontologies can be exported to the RDF(S) and OWL ontology languages. They can also be exported to the XML formats SHIQ and DIG, readable by FaCT and by any DL reasoner supporting DIG respectively (such as FaCT and RACER).

Consequently, OilEd ontologies can be used in standalone applications that can deal with these languages and that may use the inference engines attached to them.

In addition, OilEd can import ontologies implemented in RDF(S), OIL, DAML+OIL, and the SHIQ XML format.

5.2.2 Extensible language-independent ontology development tools and tool suites

In this section we present the following set of integrated tools and tool suites: Protégé-2000, OntoEdit, WebODE and KAON. These tools are characterized by their open architecture, which allows an easy extensibility and integration with other applications, and by their language independent underlying knowledge model (except for KAON).

5.2.2.1 Protégé-2000
Protégé-2000[12] (Noy et al., 2000) is the latest version of the Protégé line of tools, created by the Stanford Medical Informatics (SMI) group at Stanford University. The first Protégé tool was created in 1987 (Musen, 1989); its main aim was to simplify the knowledge acquisition process for expert systems. To achieve this objective, it used the knowledge acquired in previous stages of the process to generate customized forms for acquiring more knowledge. Since then, Protégé has gone through several releases and has focused on different aspects of knowledge acquisition (knowledge bases, problem solving methods, ontologies, etc.), the result of which is Protégé-2000. The history of the Protégé line of tools was described by Gennari and colleagues (2003). It has around 7000 registered users.

Protégé-2000 is oriented to the task of ontology and knowledge-base development. It is freely available for downloading under the Mozilla open-source license. The current version is 1.8 (April 2003).

Architecture
Protégé-2000 is a Java-based standalone application to be installed and run in a local computer. The core of this application is the ontology editor, described further.

Protégé-2000 has an extensible architecture for creating and integrating easily new extensions (aka plug-ins). These extensions usually perform functions not provided by the Protégé-2000 standard distribution (other types of visualization, new import and export formats, etc.), implement applications that use Protégé-2000 ontologies, or allow configuring the ontology editor. Most of these plug-ins are

---

[12] http://protege.stanford.edu/

available in the Protégé Plug-in Library[13], where contributions from many different research groups can be found.

We now describe the three groups of plug-ins that can be developed for Protégé-2000 with actual examples of such types of plug-ins:

- **Tab plug-ins**. These are the most common types in Protégé-2000, and provide functions that are not covered by the standard distribution of the ontology editor. To perform their task, tab plug-ins extend the ontology editor with an additional tab so that users can access its functions from it. The following functions are covered by some of the plug-ins available: ontology graphical visualization (Jambalaya tab and OntoViz tab), ontology merge and versioning (PROMPT tab), management of large on-line knowledge sources (UMLS and WordNet tabs), OKBC ontology access (OKBC tab), constraint building and execution (PAL tab), and inference engines using Jess (Friedman-Hill, 2003), Prolog, FLogic, FaCT, and Algernon[14] (Jess, Prolog, FLORA, OIL, and Algernon tabs respectively).

- **Slot widgets**. These are used to display and edit slot values without the default display and edit facilities. There are also slot widgets for displaying images, video and audio, and for managing dates, for measurement units, for swapping values between slots, etc.

- **Backends**. These enable users to export and import ontologies in different formats: RDF Schema, XML, XML Schema, etc. There is a backend for storing and retrieving ontologies from databases so that not only ontologies can be stored as CLIPS files (the default storage format used by Protégé-2000) but they can also be stored in any database JDBC compatible. Recently a backend to export and import ontologies in XMI[15] has been made available.

Knowledge model

Protégé-2000 knowledge model is based on frames and first order logic. It is OKBC compatible, which means that the main modeling components of Protégé-2000 are classes, slots, facets and instances. Classes are organized in class hierarchies where multiple inheritance is permitted and slots can also be organized in slot hierarchies. The knowledge model allows expressing constraints in the PAL language, which is a subset of KIF, and allows expressing metaclasses, which are classes whose instances are also classes.

Classes in Protégé-2000 can be concrete or abstract. The former may have direct instances while the latter cannot have them; instances of the class must be defined as instances of any of its subclasses in the class taxonomy.

Slots are global to the ontology (two different slots cannot have the same name in an ontology) and can be constrained in the classes to which they are attached. For instance, we can define the global slot age, which refers to the age of a traveler. When attached to the class Young Traveler, the minimum and maximum values for this slot are 16 and 30 years-old respectively, and when applied to the class

---

[13] http://protege.stanford.edu/plugins.html
[14] http://www.cs.utexas.edu/users/qr/algy/
[15] XML Metadata Interchange, used to exchange UML models with XML.

`Adult Traveler`, the minimum and maximum values for this slot are 30 and 65 years-old respectively.

Like in OKBC, Protégé-2000 also distinguishes between two types of slots: template and own slots. The standard facets for template slots in Protégé-2000 are: NL documentation, allowed values, minimum and maximum cardinality, default values, inverse slot and template-slot values. Other facets can be created and attached to the slots to describe them. For instance, in our travel ontology we could add the facet `currency` to the slot `price` to express the currency in which the value of that slot is specified.

Protégé-2000's knowledge model can easily be extended by means of metaclasses. Metaclasses are defined as classes whose instances are also classes. They are used as templates to create other classes in Protégé-2000. This means that the template slots defined at the metaclass are converted into own slots in the classes that are instances of the metaclass. These classes must fill the values for their own slots. For example, in our travel ontology we know that the class `AA7462` has the own slot `company Name` with the value "*American Airlines*". A similar situation appears with the classes `AA2010`, `AA0488`, etc., and their own slot `company Name`. To represent such knowledge in Protégé-2000, we can create a metaclass

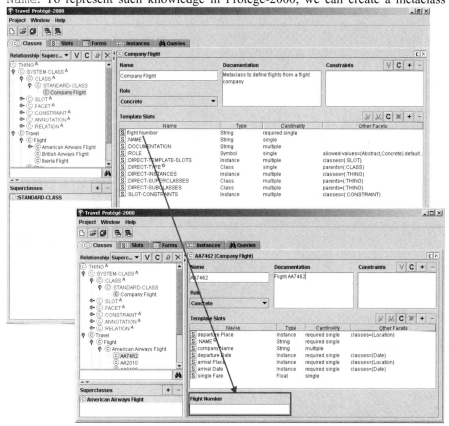

Figure 5.9: Edition of metaclasses with Protégé-2000.

`Company Flight` with the template slot `company Name`, and create the previous classes as instances of that metaclass. These classes will have an own slot `company Name` where we will input its value. Figure 5.9 shows the metaclass `Company Flight` with its template slot `company Name`, and the form for the class `AA7462`, which is an instance of that metaclass and must fill the value of its own slot `company Name`.

Protégé-2000 ontologies can be imported into other Protégé-2000 ontologies in two different ways: (a) by including them as external terms, that is, as terms that have been defined in another ontology and cannot be edited; and (b) by merging them, that is, by copying their definitions in the current ontology so that they can be redefined.

Ontology editor

Protégé-2000's ontology editor browses and edits the ontology's class taxonomy using a tree structure, defines global slots, attaches slots to classes, creates class instances, etc. It provides common search, copy&paste and drag&drop functions, among others, and also different pop-up menus according to the type and features of the ontology component being edited.

In Figure 5.10 we can see a snapshot of the ontology editor for editing the concept `Travel` of our travel ontology. The left frame shows the class taxonomy of the ontology. In this frame we can observe that `Travel` is a subclass of the predefined class *:THING*. In Protégé-2000, all the top classes of a class taxonomy must be subclasses of this predefined class. The main frame shows a form where the ontology developer can fill in the information about the class that we are editing. Besides the class name, we can provide its role (concrete or abstract, depending on

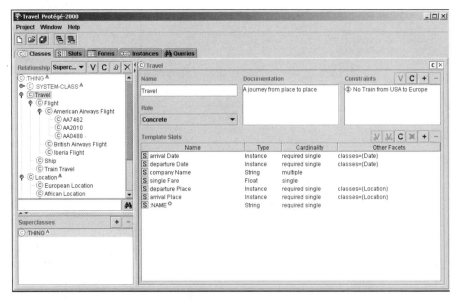

Figure 5.10: Edition of the concept `Travel` with Protégé-2000.

whether we can create direct instances of the class or not), its documentation, its applicable constraints, and its template slots. The "Template Slots" box contains the slots attached to the class and the slots inherited by it through the class taxonomy. As shown in this figure, we have attached the following slots to the class `Travel`: `arrival Date`, `departure Date`, `company Name`, `single Fare`, `arrival Place`, `departure Place`, and `:NAME` (the last slot is used to identify instances of the class `Travel`).

Figure 5.11 is a snapshot of the ontology editor for editing the slot `arrival Date` of our travel ontology. The left frame shows the hierarchy of the slots already defined in the ontology (a slot can be defined as a subslot of another). Besides the domain-dependent slots defined by the ontology developer for a domain ontology there are other predefined slots that are applied to other slots and classes of the standard knowledge model of Protégé-2000 (*:ANNOTATED-INSTANCE*, *:ANNOTATION-TEXT*, etc.). The main frame shows the form to be filled in when we define a domain-dependent slot. It contains fields for its name, NL documentation, value type, minimum and maximum cardinalities, minimum and maximum values for numeric slots, template and default values, and the name of the inverse slot, if any.

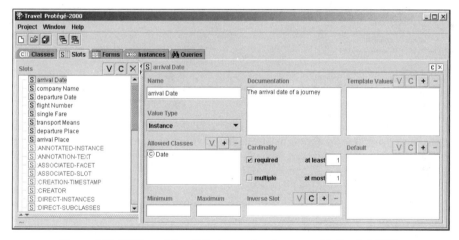

Figure 5.11: Edition of the attribute `arrival Date` with Protégé-2000.

Slots in Protégé-2000 can be used to specify attributes and ad hoc relations between classes, and this distinction is expressed in their slot value type. The former are defined as a simple datatype (*integer*, *float*, *string*, and *Boolean*) or as an enumerated datatype (*symbol*). The latter are defined as *class instances* or *classes*. If we define the slot value type as *any*, it can have any of the previous value types. If the value type of a slot is *Instance* or *Class*, a box appears in the slot definition form to include its destination classes.

When we attach slots to a class (this is performed in the class edition form, such as the one presented in Figure 5.10), we can override some of the features that have been defined globally for them, as we commented in the knowledge model section. The form used to redefine them is similar to that of Figure 5.11.

One of the outstanding features of the Protégé-2000 ontology editor, when compared with other ontology editors, is that we can design the screen layouts used to create instances. Ontology developers can select which kind of forms will be presented, where the form fields will be located for each slot, which slot widgets they want to use for each slot, etc. Figure 5.12 is a screenshot of Protégé-2000 for editing the form corresponding to the instances of the class `Travel`.

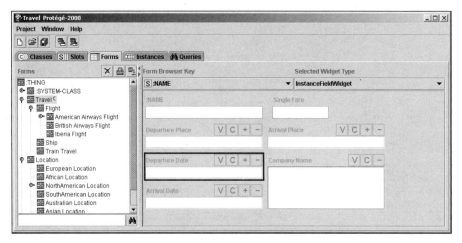

Figure 5.12: Form edition for the instances of the class `Travel` with Protégé-2000.

The Protégé-2000 ontology editor also contains a *Queries* tab. With this tab users can create queries about instances that have or have not a specific value for a slot, about instances whose slot value is greater or lower than a specific number, etc. Queries are stored in a query library and can be combined.

The PAL tab checks which PAL constraints are violated by the ontology instances. Figure 5.10 shows that the PAL constraint "*No train from USA to Europe*" is attached to the class `Travel`. Other inference engines integrated as tab plug-ins in Protégé-2000 are FLORA (a XSB[16] engine for FLogic's ontologies), Prolog, and Jess.

The ontology editor generates different types of ontology documentation: HTML documents and ontology statistics. There are also plug-ins for visualizing ontologies graphically such as the OntoViz and Jambalaya tab plug-ins.

Other tab plug-ins cover other functions. We recommend visiting the Protégé-2000 plug-in library for updated and extra information about them.

An ontology library available for downloading can be found in the Protégé-2000 Web site with ontologies such as the UNSPSC ontology, the Dublin core, etc. Since

---

[16] XSB is a logic programming and deductive database system.

Protégé-2000 can import ontologies in several formats, it can import ontologies from other ontology libraries such as the DAML ontology library[17], the Ontolingua Server ontology library, etc.

Regarding collaborative ontology edition, Protégé-2000 does not support it, though some work is being done in this direction to migrate Protégé-2000 to a multi-user environment.

Interoperability

Once we have created an ontology in Protégé-2000, there are many ways to access Protégé-2000 ontologies from ontology-based applications.

All the ontology terms can be accessed with the Protégé-2000 Java API. Hence it is easy for ontology-based applications to access ontologies as well as use other functions provided by different plug-ins. This API is also available through a CORBA-based server so that remote clients can access Protégé-2000 ontologies.

Protégé-2000 ontologies can be exported and imported with some of the backends provided in the standard release or as plug-ins: RDF(S), XML, XML Schema, and XMI. As explained in other sections, once the corresponding output file has been generated and saved locally, it can be used by any local application capable of managing that format. In the case of XMI, the UML model translated can be used to obtain Java classes from it.

5.2.2.2 WebODE

WebODE[18] (Corcho et al., 2002; Arpírez et al., 2003) is an ontological engineering workbench developed by the Ontology Group at Universidad Politécnica de Madrid (UPM). The current version is 2.0. WebODE is the offspring of the ontology design environment ODE (Blázquez et al., 1998), a standalone ontology tool based on tables and graphs, which allowed users to customize the knowledge model used for conceptualizing their ontologies according to their KR needs. Both ODE and WebODE give support to the ontology building methodology METHONTOLOGY.

Currently, WebODE contains an ontology editor, which integrates most of the ontology services offered by the workbench, an ontology-based knowledge management system (ODEKM), an automatic Semantic Web portal generator (ODESeW), a Web resources annotation tool (ODEAnnotate), and a Semantic Web services editing tool (ODESWS).

Architecture

WebODE has been built as a scalable, extensible, integrated workbench that covers and gives support to most of the activities involved in the ontology development process (conceptualization, reasoning, exchange, etc.) and supplies a comprehensive set of ontology related services that permit interoperation with other information systems.

WebODE is platform-independent as it is completely implemented in Java. To allow scalability and easy extensibility, it is supported by an application server so

---

[17] http://www.daml.org/ontologies/
[18] http://webode.dia.fi.upm.es/

that services can be easily created and integrated in the workbench by means of a management console. One important advantage of using this application server is that we can decide which users or user groups may access each of the services of the workbench.

Figure 5.13 illustrates the services currently available in the WebODE workbench. The core of the WebODE's ontology development services are: the cache, consistency and axiom services, and the ontology access service (ODE API), which defines an API for accessing WebODE ontologies. One of the main advantages of this architecture is that these services can be accessed remotely from any other application or any other instance of the workbench. WebODE ontologies are stored in a relational database so they can manage huge ontologies quite efficiently. WebODE also provides backup management functions for the ontologies stored in the server.

The figure shows that the interoperability services are running on top of the ontology access service. These services import ontologies from XML, XCARIN, RDF(S), DAML+OIL, and OWL; and export ontologies to XML, FLogic, XCARIN, RDF(S), OIL, DAML+OIL, and OWL. Ontologies are also exported to languages that are not specifically created for defining ontologies such as Prolog, Jess, and Java. For instance, the Prolog export service is used as a basis of the WebODE's inference engine.

Other middleware services such as WebPicker, ODEClean, and ODEMerge, which are described further, also use the WebODE ontology access API or the XML export/import services.

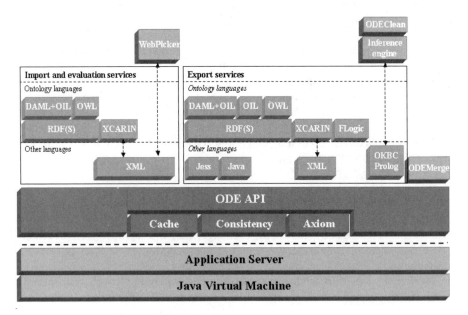

Figure 5.13: WebODE workbench's service architecture.

Knowledge model

Ontologies in WebODE are conceptualized with a very expressive knowledge model (Arpírez et al., 2001). This knowledge model is based on the reference set of intermediate representations of the METHONTOLOGY methodology (Fernández-López et al., 1999), described in Chapter 3. Therefore, the following ontology components are included in the WebODE's knowledge model: concepts and their local attributes (both instance and class attributes, whose type can be any XML Schema datatype); concept groups, which represent sets of disjoint concepts; concept taxonomies, and disjoint and exhaustive class partitions; ad hoc binary relations between concepts, which may be characterized by relation properties (symmetry, transitiveness, etc.); constants; formal axioms, expressed in first order logic; rules; and instances of concepts and relations.

In addition to the previous components, bibliographic references, synonyms, and abbreviations can be attached to any of the aforementioned.

The WebODE's knowledge model allows referring to ontology terms defined in other ontologies by means of imported terms. Imported terms are identified with URIs and these are of two types: those available in another WebODE ontology, either in the same or in a different WebODE server (referred to as *webode://WebODE_host/ontologies/ontology#name*), and those identified by a different type of URI.

WebODE instances are defined inside instance sets. Thus, we can create different instantiations for the same ontology, which are independent from each other. For instance, we can instantiate our travel ontology in different instance sets, one for each travel agency using the ontology.

Ontology editor

The WebODE ontology editor is a Web application built on top of the ontology access service (ODE API). The ontology editor integrates several ontology building services from the workbench: ontology edition, navigation, documentation, merge, reasoning, etc.

Three user interfaces are combined in this ontology editor: an HTML form-based editor for editing all ontology terms except axioms and rules; a graphical user interface, called OntoDesigner, for editing concept taxonomies and relations graphically; and WAB (WebODE Axiom Builder), for editing formal axioms and rules. We now describe them and highlight their most important features.

Figure 5.14 is a screenshot of the HTML interface for editing instance attributes of the concept `Travel` of our travel ontology. The main areas of this interface are:

- The browsing area. To navigate through the whole ontology and to create new elements and modify or delete the existing ones.
- The clipboard. To easily copy and paste information between forms.
- The edition area. It presents HTML forms to insert, delete and update ontology terms (concepts, attributes, relations, etc.), and tables with knowledge about existing terms. Figure 5.14 shows four attributes of the concept `Travel`: `arrival Date`, `company Name`, `departure Date`, and `single Fare`, and an HTML form to create a new instance attribute for this concept.

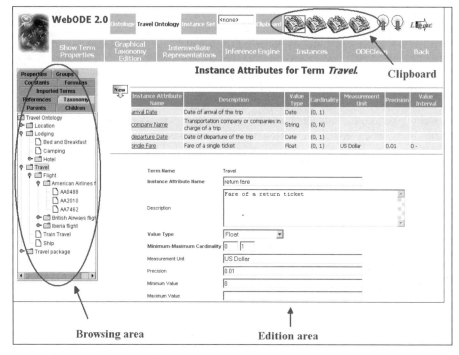

Figure 5.14: Edition of an instance attribute with the WebODE ontology editor.

OntoDesigner eases the construction of concept taxonomies and ad hoc relations between concepts and allows defining views to highlight or customize the visualization of fragments of the ontology for each user.

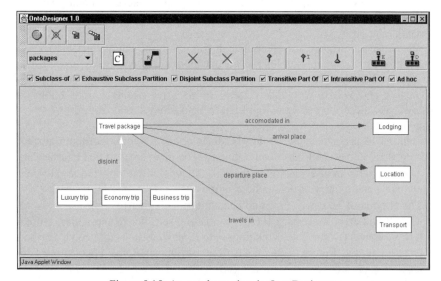

Figure 5.15: An ontology view in OntoDesigner.

Concept taxonomies are created with the following set of predefined relations: *Subclass-Of*, *Disjoint-Subclass-Partition* (*Disjoint-Decomposition*), *Exhaustive-Subclass-Partition* (*Partition*), *Transitive-Part-Of* and *Intransitive-Part-Of*.

Figure 5.15 shows a view of our travel ontology in OntoDesigner, where we have selected the concepts `Travel package`, `Luxury Trip`, `Economy Trip`, `Business Trip`, `Lodging`, `Location`, and `Transport`, and several ad hoc and taxonomic relations between them.

OntoDesigner can be used as part of the ODEClean evaluation module, as will be explained further.

The WebODE Axiom Builder (WAB) (Corcho et al., 2002) is a graphical editor for creating first order logic axioms and rules. In WebODE, formal axioms are used to model sentences that are always true while rules are normally included in the ontology to infer new knowledge. Figure 5.16 shows an axiom in WAB that states that "every train that departs from a European location must arrive in a European location". The buttons below the text box help write logical expressions with quantifiers (universal and existential) and logical connectives (negation, conjunction, disjunction, logical implication, and logical equivalence); and the lists below them are to easily include ontology concepts, their attributes and their ad hoc relations, and ontology constants. Users can also write directly the axiom expression with WAB.

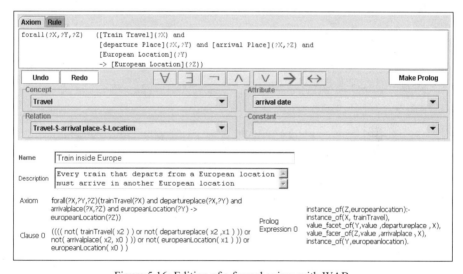

Figure 5.16: Edition of a formal axiom with WAB.

When an axiom is completely written in the text box, WAB checks that it uses the vocabulary contained in the ontology (checks that the concepts appearing in the axiom exist in the ontology, that the relations can be applied to those concepts, etc.). Then WAB transforms the axiom into Horn clauses through a skolemization process. If the axiom cannot be transformed into Horn clauses, WAB warns the user of this. These Horn clauses are then transformed into Prolog using primitives defined in the OKBC knowledge model so that can be used by the Prolog inference engine attached to WebODE, as described below. The Horn clause that corresponds to the axiom is shown on the bottom left of the figure, and the Prolog rule, which uses the OKBC primitives *instance_of* and *value_facet_of*, is shown on the bottom right.

Rules are similarly created with WAB. Figure 5.17 shows a rule that states that "every trip that departs from Europe is arranged by the company Costa Cruises". Rules are also checked, transformed into a Horn clause (shown on the bottom left of the figure), and then into a Prolog rule (shown on the bottom right of the figure).

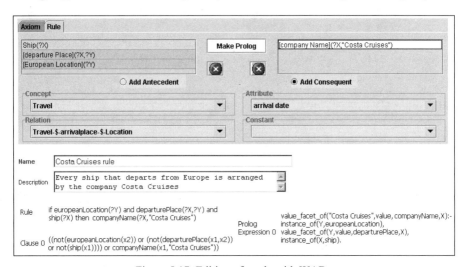

Figure 5.17: Edition of a rule with WAB.

We now describe other ontology building services integrated in the ontology editor: the documentation service, ODEMerge, the OKBC-based Prolog inference engine, and ODEClean.

The WebODE ontology documentation service generates WebODE ontologies in different formats that can be used to document: HTML tables representing the Methontology's intermediate representations described in Section 3.3.5 and HTML concept taxonomies. Figure 5.18 illustrates a fragment of the concept dictionary of our travel ontology, and Figure 5.19 shows the result of one of the HTML documentation formats generated with this service; this figure contains a fragment of the concept taxonomy of the ontology and specifies the attributes of each concept (preceded by a hollow bullet) and the ad hoc relations whose domain (symbol ==>) or range (symbol <==) is each concept.

The WebODE merge service (ODEMerge) performs a supervised merge of concepts, attributes, and relationships from two ontologies built for the same domain. It uses natural language resources to find the mappings between concepts of both ontologies so as to generate the resulting ontology.

Concept name	Class attributes	Instance attributes	Relations
AA7462	--	--	same Flight as
American Airlines Flight	company Name	--	--
British Airways Flight	company Name	--	--
Five-stars Hotel	number of Stars	--	--
Flight	--	--	same Flight as
Location	--	name size	is Arrival Place of is Departure Place of
Lodging	--	price of Standard Room	placed in
Travel	--	arrival Date company Name departure Date return Fare single Fare	arrival Place departure Place
Travel Package	--	budget final Price name number of Days travel Restrictions	travels in accommodated in arrival Place departure Place

Figure 5.18: A fragment of an intermediate representation generated by the WebODE ontology documentation service.

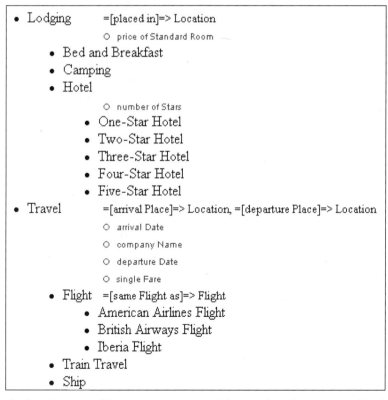

Figure 5.19: A fragment of the concept taxonomy of the travel ontology generated by the WebODE ontology documentation service.

WebODE includes an inference engine that consists of a Prolog implementation of a subset of the OKBC protocol primitives. This engine uses the Ciao Prolog interpreter (Hermenegildo et al., 2000). Since WebODE ontologies can be translated into Prolog, the inference engine obtains an ontology in Prolog from the Prolog export service and loads it into the Prolog interpreter. With this process, the implemented OKBC primitives can build more complex Prolog programs for being executed in the Prolog interpreter for any purpose.

The inference engine can be accessed from the WebODE ontology editor with the user interface shown in Figure 5.20. In the figure, the middle text box shows the results of querying the inference engine of all the subclasses of the concept `Travel` in our ontology. It returns two answers to this query: the first is a list that contains the concepts `Flight`, `Train Travel` and `Ship`[19], which are the direct subclasses of the concept `Travel`; the second answer is also a list that contains all the ontology concepts that are direct and indirect subclasses of the concept `Travel`. As the rest of WebODE services, the inference engine can be executed not only from the user interface of the ontology editor but also by means of its Java API.

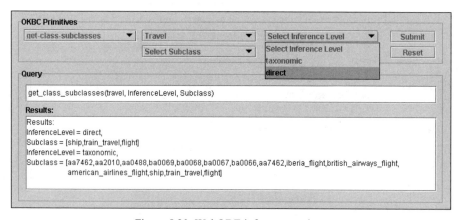

Figure 5.20: WebODE inference engine.

Currently, the WebODE inference engine is used for several purposes: querying ontology terms either with the predefined OKBC primitives or with user-defined Prolog programs; asserting new knowledge with the Prolog expressions generated by WAB; detecting inconsistencies in the ontology; and evaluating the ontology with ODEClean.

ODEClean (Fernández-López and Gómez-Pérez, 2002b) is a service for evaluating concept taxonomies based on the OntoClean method (Welty and Guarino, 2001). As described in Section 3.8.3, this method relies on some philosophical notions such as rigidity, identity, and unity[20]. Users with access to this service can

---

[19] Please note that these concepts appear with their first letter in lowercase because if they started in uppercase they would be considered variables by the Prolog interpreter. This transformation is performed by the Prolog export service.
[20] ODEClean also applies the notion of dependency, explained in Section 2.2.1.

edit the meta-properties of each concept and evaluate ontologies according to this method. Figure 5.21 shows a screenshot of OntoDesigner after evaluating with ODEClean the class taxonomy that was presented in Figure 3.52. The three errors presented in Section 3.8.3 are detected by ODEClean.

ODEClean evaluation axioms are defined declaratively in Prolog instead of being hard-wired in the code of this service and are loaded in the inference engine when this service is invoked. This provides flexibility so that evaluation axioms can be easily changed if the OntoClean method is changed.

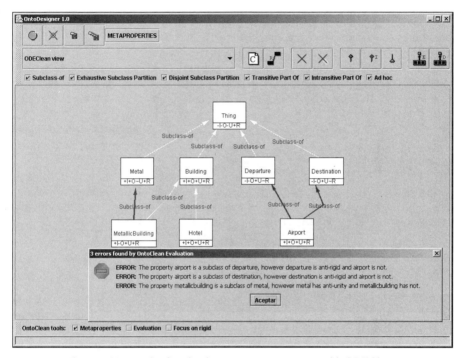

Figure 5.21: Result of evaluating a concept taxonomy with ODEClean.

The WebODE workbench also provides several ontology evaluation functions: the ontology consistency service and the RDF(S), DAML+OIL, and OWL evaluation services.

The ontology consistency service shown in Figure 5.13 provides constraint checking capabilities for the WebODE ontologies and is used by the ontology editor during the ontology building process. It checks type constraints, numerical values constraints, and cardinality constraints, and verifies concept taxonomies (i.e., external instances of an exhaustive decomposition, loops, etc.).

The RDF(S), DAML+OIL, and OWL evaluation services evaluate ontologies according to the evaluation criteria identified by Gómez-Pérez (2001), described in Section 3.8.2. They detect errors in ontologies implemented in these languages and provide suggestions about better design criteria.

Finally, user groups can be created to collaborate in the edition of ontologies. Several users can edit the same ontology without errors by means of synchronization mechanisms.

Interoperability

There are several ways of using WebODE ontologies inside ontology-based applications.

First, they can be accessed from its Java API via a local service or application running on the same computer where the ontology server is installed. This API avoids accessing directly the relational database where ontologies are stored and it includes cache functions to accelerate the access to ontology terms. WebODE ontologies can be accessed not only from inside the local server but also remotely with RMI (Remote Method Invocation) and Web services.

Second, ontology export services available in the workbench permit generating WebODE ontologies in XML and in several other ontology languages such as: RDF(S), OIL, DAML+OIL, OWL, XCARIN and FLogic. Translations into Prolog can be used similarly.

Third, ontologies can be transformed into Protégé-2000. So we can use them inside the Protégé-2000 ontology editor or use the interoperability capabilities provided by this tool.

Finally, WebODE ontologies can be transformed into Java. In this process, concepts are transformed into Java beans, attributes into class variables, ad hoc relations into associations between classes, etc., with their corresponding constructors and methods to access and update class variables, etc. This Java code can be used to create other Java applications, uploaded in rule systems like Jess, etc.

5.2.2.3 OntoEdit

OntoEdit[21] (Sure et al., 2002a) is an ontology engineering environment initially created by the Institute AIFB at the University of Karlsruhe and now is being commercialized by Ontoprise GmbH. The current version is 2.7 (January 2003). Free and professional versions of OntoEdit are available. The free version can be downloaded and installed locally. The professional version is not free but includes quite a few more functions than the free one such as an inference engine, graphical query tools, more export and import modules, graphical rule editors, etc.

Architecture

Like Protégé-2000, OntoEdit is a Java standalone application that can be installed and run in a local computer, though it is not open source. Its architecture is similar to that of Protégé-2000. The OntoEdit ontology editor comprises the core modules of the application and can be extended with plug-ins, based on the OntoMat-Plugin-Framework[22]. OntoEdit ontologies are stored as files (in this case, XML files) although in the professional version they can be stored in any relational database with JDBC support.

---

[21] http://www.ontoprise.de/customercenter/software_downloads/free
[22] http://sourceforge.net/projects/ontomat

The plug-ins available for extending OntoEdit are different according to the version used (free or professional), and can be classified in two groups:

- **Export and import filters**. To export and import ontologies in different languages: RDF(S), OXML[23], DAML+OIL, and FLogic. The professional version also includes an export and import filter for SQL schemas.
- **General plug-ins**. To perform any other functions. The free version of OntoEdit includes plug-ins for managing domain lexicons, for editing instances and expressing disjoint concepts. The professional version includes plug-ins such as graphical rule editors, the inference engine OntoBroker, graphical query tools, and ontology mappings.

Other plug-ins and extensions of OntoEdit are described by Sure and colleagues (2002a, 2002b). Among these, there are extensions to create ontology requirement specifications (OntoKick), to help in the first stages of the ontology development (aka ontology brainstorming process) (Mind2Onto), to provide ontology locking mechanisms, etc. Another plug-in converts OntoEdit standalone architecture to a client/server architecture by means of an ontology server.

Knowledge model

OntoEdit's knowledge model (OXML 2.0) is based on frames. It can represent concepts and their attributes, binary relations between concepts, formal axioms, and instances.

OntoEdit distinguishes two types of concepts: abstract and concrete. Their behavior with respect to their instances is the same as we explained for Protégé-2000: abstract concepts cannot have direct instances while concrete concepts can. Concepts are classified in concept taxonomies, which can use multiple inheritance; and two concepts can be explicitly declared as disjoint.

Attributes and binary relations are defined similarly in the ontology editor and they are local to the concept where they are defined. As a consequence, we can create two different attributes or binary relations with the same name in an ontology provided they are defined in different concepts. The following predefined datatypes are for attributes: *String*, *Integer*, *Double*, and *Boolean*. They can be easily extended to other datatypes. As for relations, the range can be any of the concepts defined in the ontology.

Regarding axioms, ontology developers can decide the formal language with which they want to represent them (FLogic, Prolog, Datalog, first order logic, etc.). FLogic is the default language for representing these formal axioms and is the language used by the inference engine plug-in.

OXML allows specifying the ontologies that an ontology imports with an *imports* statement. However, OntoEdit does not access nor shows the terms from the ontologies imported as other tools do. Imported ontology terms can be referred to with their corresponding URI.

---

[23] OntoEdit's XML-based Ontology representation Language.

Ontology editor

With the OntoEdit's ontology editor, the ontology concept taxonomy can be browsed and edited and relations, instances, etc., can also be edited by means of a tree structure. The OntoEdit's ontology editor provides search and copy&paste functions to ease the edition of concept taxonomies. In Figure 5.22 we show a screenshot of OntoEdit Free for editing the concept `Travel` of our travel ontology. As we can observe, the concept `Travel` is a subclass of the *Root* concept (which is predefined for all OntoEdit ontologies). The concept `Travel` has four attributes: `arrivalDate`, `departureDate`, `companyName`, and `singleFare`; and two relations: `arrivalPlace` and `departurePlace`.

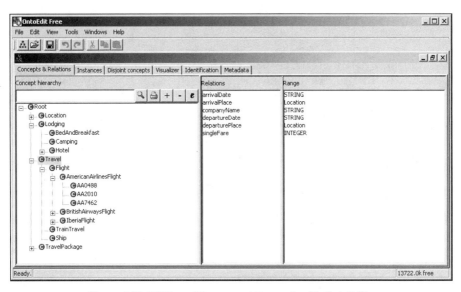

Figure 5.22: Edition of the concept `Travel` with OntoEdit.

In contrast with other editors, all the ontology terms defined in OntoEdit can be described by multilingual labels. These multilingual labels can be used to refer to the different ontology terms in several natural languages (English, German, French, etc.).

OntoEdit permits including bibliographic references (aka information sources) in an ontology. These references cannot be attached to individual ontology term definitions but to the whole ontology. Additional information on ontologies from the Dublin Core metadata is also included: ontology developers, ontology domain, ontology namespace, etc.

Figure 5.23 shows the *Visualization* user interface of the ontology editor to navigate and edit the ontology graphically. With this user interface, ontology developers can easily create concept taxonomies and relations between concepts, add concept instances, and visualize fragments of the ontology, search for ontology terms in the graph, etc.

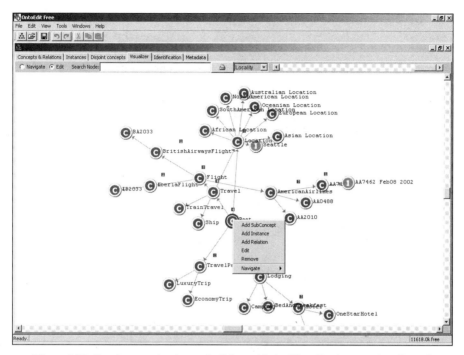

Figure 5.23: Ontology navigation and edition with the Visualization user interface of OntoEdit.

Regarding reasoning services, the OntoEdit Free version does not include any inference support. However, OntoEdit Professional provides two plug-ins: the graphical rule editor for editing FLogic axioms and the inference plug-in, which integrates the Ontobroker inference engine and can be used for purposes such as querying, consistency checking, rule execution, etc. Ontobroker uses FLogic axioms to perform inferences.

Finally, and regarding collaborative ontology building functions, OntoEdit Professional includes, as commented above, facilities for locking fragments of an ontology concept taxonomy. The locking mechanism was explained by Sure and colleagues (2002a) and it is used only with the plug-in that converts OntoEdit into a client-server architecture.

Interoperability

There are two ways of using OntoEdit ontologies inside an ontology-based application. On the one hand, we can export OntoEdit ontologies to several ontology languages (OXML, FLogic, RDF(S), and DAML+OIL) and use them with their corresponding tools and KR systems. In addition to these ontology languages, OntoEdit can also import ontologies from directory structures, where each directory is considered as a concept in the ontology, and from Excel files, where each line is also considered to be a concept. As commented above, OntoEdit professional has an import and export module for SQL schemas. On the other hand, we can use the Java API for ontology access since OntoEdit is a Java application.

5.2.2.4 KAON

The KAON (KArlsruhe ONtology) tool suite[24] (Maedche et al., 2003) is being developed by the Institutes AIFB and FZI at the University of Karlsruhe. We describe the version 1.2.5, released in January 2003. The KAON tool suite can be downloaded free under an open source license from Sourceforge[25].

Architecture
Like the previous tools and platforms, the KAON tool suite is being developed with a flexible and scalable architecture. It is organized in three layers: backends for ontology storage, middleware for the services offered by the tool suite, and client applications that access the ontology middleware and provide end-user applications. The KAON tool suite is completely implemented in Java and can be extended with plug-ins. Figure 5.24 shows the modules implemented for each of these layers:

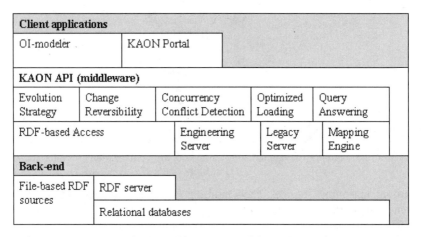

Figure 5.24: KAON tool suite architecture (Maedche et al., 2003) (© 2003 IEEE)

- **Backends**. KAON ontologies can be stored and accessed with three different backends but with the same knowledge model: as RDF(S) files, as RDF(S) models stored in a relational database (with the KAON RDF Server), and as KAON models stored in a relational database (with the KAON Engineering Server). The RDF Server and the Engineering Server run on top of the JBOSS application server[26].
- **Ontology middleware**. The most important KAON services are provided in this layer. One of them is the KAON API for accessing KAON ontologies. Other middleware services are: an ontology evolution service that detects the implications of changes on ontology terms; a change reversibility service that keeps track of ontology changes; a concurrent conflict detection for collaborative ontology engineering; a query answering service; etc.

---

[24] http://kaon.semanticweb.org/
[25] http://sourceforge.net/projects/kaon
[26] http://www.jboss.org/

- **Client applications**. For this tool suite client applications have been already created, such as the OI-modeler, which is an ontology editor for KAON ontologies, and KAON Portal, which allows creating ontology-based Web portals.

Some other modules are being implemented and have not been released yet because they are still in an early development stage. One of these modules is KAON REVERSE, which maps relational databases and ontologies.

Knowledge model

The knowledge model underlying the KAON tool suite (aka KAON Language) is based on an extension of RDF(S). With KAON we can model ontologies with concepts, properties (to express relations and attributes), and instances of concepts and of properties. Concepts are organized in concept taxonomies (with the *subclassOf* relation) and properties are organized in property hierarchies (with the *subPropertyOf* relation). The extensions to RDF(S) are mainly related to properties: we can define their property cardinalities; we can distinguish between relations and attributes depending on whether their range is a concept or a datatype; we can define relations as symmetric or transitive; and finally, we can define the inverse relation of a given one.

The KAON knowledge model also attaches labels, documentation, synonyms and word stems in different natural languages to concepts, properties, and concept instances.

With regard to more complex components, such as formal axioms, these cannot be expressed in KAON. The same applies to the creation of disjoint and exhaustive knowledge in concept taxonomies.

KAON ontologies can include ontology terms from other KAON ontologies. The top concept of any KAON concept taxonomy is the *Root* concept (*http://kaon.semanticweb.org/2001/11/kaon-lexical#Root*). All KAON ontologies include the following: *http://kaon.semanticweb.org/2001/11/kaon-lexical* and *http://kaon.semanticweb.org/2001/11/kaon-root*, which contain concepts such as *LexicalEntry*, *Synonym*, *Documentation*, *Label*, *Stem*, *Language*, and the *Root* concept.

Ontology editor

The KAON ontology editor is called the OI-Modeler. A previous version of an ontology editor for this tool suite was the OntoMat SOEP (Simple Ontology and Metadata Editor Plug-in), which was similar to the OntoEdit ontology editor and is now unsupported.

Figure 5.25 shows the graphical user interface of the OI-Modeler to edit our travel ontology. The figure shows some concepts (represented by boxes), the *subclassOf* relations between them (represented by lines, whose edges get wider next to the concept that is a subclass, and thinner next to the concept that is the superclass), and the properties whose domain is the concept `Travel` (represented by rounded squares). The small icons that appear attached to each symbol are for navigating the ontology. Finally, this user interface makes zooms of the graph, rotates it and shows it with hyperbolic views. It uses the TouchGraph graphical library[27].

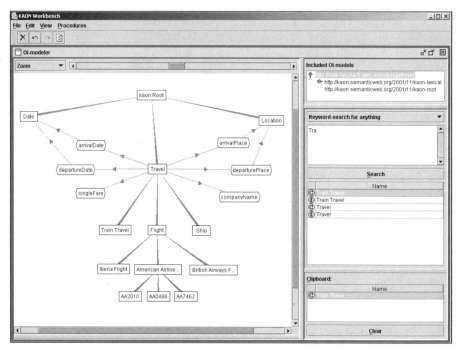

Figure 5.25: Edition of the travel ontology with the KAON OI-Modeler graphical user interface.

On the right of the figure, the user interface shows the ontologies included in the current ontology. It also includes facilities both for searching ontology terms and for executing KAON queries on the ontology, which are based on description logic. The right bottom box contains the clipboard for copying and pasting any ontology term with drag&drop operations.

Together with the graphical user interface, a form-based user interface can be used to browse and edit KAON ontologies. Figure 5.26 shows this user interface for editing the concept Travel. When browsing or editing a concept, we can manage its superconcepts and subconcepts, its properties (that is, the properties whose domain or range is the concept being edited), its labels, documentation, synonyms and word stems in different natural languages, and its instances. The user interface for managing properties allows browsing and editing property hierarchies, property labels, NL documentation, synonyms, and word stems, and property domains and ranges. Finally, the user interface for managing instances allows browsing and

---

[27] http://www.touchgraph.com/

editing the concept to which it belongs, the property instances that can be applied to that instance and its labels, documentation, synonyms, and word stems.

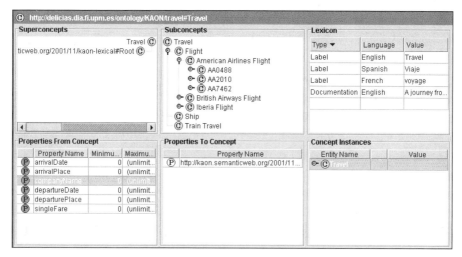

Figure 5.26: Edition of the travel ontology with KAON OI-Modeler.

As we commented in the architecture section, the KAON tool suite gives support to the ontology evolution process. The KAON OI-Modeler can establish the evolution strategy, that is, the ontology evolution parameters to be considered when editing an ontology. For instance, when removing a concept we can choose whether to remove its subclasses, to define its subclasses as subclasses of the *Root* concept, or to connect its subclasses to the superclasses of the removed concept. Every time an edition action is performed on an ontology, the evolution strategy selected is considered. Users may decide whether to create an evolution log, and whether to receive a notification of the evolution details every time they perform such an operation.

KAON includes support for the ontology collaborative edition. The KAON OI-Modeler provides change reversibility options and concurrency conflict detection when several users are updating an ontology at the same time.

Interoperability
Ontology-based applications can use KAON ontologies with different architectures, as detailed below:

On the one hand, ontologies can be accessed and modified with the KAON Java API. KAON ontologies can be stored in files or databases (either with the RDF Server, which enables persisting RDF models in a relational database, or with the KAON engineering server, which enables persisting KAON ontologies in a relational database). The KAON API can also be accessed using Web services with the KAON Web Service (KAON WS). In version 1.2.5, KAON WS is in an early stage of development, so it provides only a few functionalities of the KAON API, though it will be extended with the whole API.

On the other hand, KAON ontologies can be exported to the KAON language (RDF(S) plus extensions) and RDF(S). KAON can also import ontologies written in the KAON language, RDF(S) and the RDF(S) code generated by Protégé-2000.

5.2.3 Some other ontology tools

We have presented the most relevant and important ontology development tools currently available. In fact, many other tools have been developed for ontology building though some of them are not widely known or used; others have been designed specifically for small groups of people or projects, etc. In this section we provide a brief description of some of these lesser known tools (in alphabetical order):

APECKS (Tennison and Shadbolt, 1998) stands for *Adaptive Presentation Environment for Collaborative Knowledge Structuring*. APECKS is a WWW-based ontology editor whose main aim is to support collaborative ontology building. APECKS allows individuals to create personal ontologies that can be compared with others' to prompt discussion about the sources of their differences and similarities.

Apollo[28] (Wolff et al., 2001) is a Java-based open source ontology editor whose underlying KR model is based on the OKBC protocol. Ontologies created with this editor can be stored in different formats using plug-ins. Currently Apollo can export ontologies to CLOS and OCML. The user interface has an open architecture for an easy configuration and allows having different views of the ontologies edited.

CODE4[29] (Skuce and Lethbridge, 1995) is short for *Conceptually Oriented Description Environment*. CODE4 is a general purpose knowledge management system implemented in Smalltalk. One of its main features is that it provides different views (hierarchical, graphical, property matrix) to the same knowledge source. Its underlying knowledge model, CODE4-KR, is based on frames, conceptual graphs, object-orientation, and DL systems. The Web offspring for CODE4 is **IKARUS**[30] (Skuce, 1996), which stands for *Intelligent Knowledge Acquisition and Retrieval Universal System*.

Co4[31] (Alemany, 1998; Euzenat, 1996) stands for *Cooperative Construction of Consensual Knowledge Bases*. This tool supports the protocol Co4 for the cooperative construction of ontologies, described in Section 3.7.

DUET[32] (Kogut et al., 2002) is short for *DAML UML Enhanced Tool*. It is being developed by GRCI International, Inc. DUET differs from other tools in that it is not a standalone application but an add-on of Rational Rose[33] and of ArgoUML[34], which

---

[28] http://apollo.open.ac.uk/

[29] http://www.csi.uottawa.ca/~doug/CODE4.html

[30] http://www.csi.uottawa.ca/~kavanagh/Ikarus/IkarusInfo.html

[31] http://co4.inrialpes.fr/

[32] http://grcinet.grci.com/maria/www/CodipSite/Tools/Tools.html

[33] http://www.rational.com/products/rose/index.jsp

[34] http://argouml.tigris.org/

are not ontology engineering but software engineering tools. DUET imports DAML+OIL ontologies and transforms them into UML class diagrams. It also exports UML class diagrams to DAML+OIL according to a set of mapping functions[35]. Figure 5.27 shows a fragment of the UML class diagram that corresponds to the travel ontology. As can be seen in the figure, properties are represented as UML classes with the stereotype *<<DAMLproperty>>* and the relations *daml:domain*, and *daml:range*. The *Subclass-Of* relationships are represented through specialization relationships in UML.

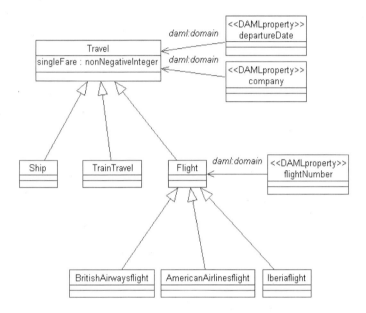

Figure 5.27: Fragment of the UML class diagram of the travel ontology.

The **GKB-Editor**[36] (*Generic Knowledge Base Editor*) is a tool for browsing and editing OKBC knowledge bases (written in Ontolingua, Ocelot, LOOM, Theo, SIPE, etc.). Users can view the knowledge base from various viewpoints and display only the desired portions of the knowledge base. Incremental browsing allows the user to control what is displayed and the level of detail.

Medius Visual Ontology Modeler[37] (VOM) (Kendall et al., 2002) is similar to DUET. It has been developed by SandPiper Software and the KSL at Stanford University. Like DUET, VOM is installed as an add-on of Rational Rose and allows creating ontologies with UML, which can be transformed into XML Schema, RDF and DAML+OIL.

---

[35] http://grcinet.grci.com/maria/wwwlibrary/DUET_Docs/DAML-UML_CoreMapping_V5.htm
[36] http://www.ai.sri.com/~gkb/
[37] http://www.sandsoft.com/products.html

Unicorn[38] is an ontology environment for aggregating relational schemas, XML Schemas, and other data formats into a single ontological model. From this model, queries (in SQL) and transformations between the different formats (in XSLT) are automatically generated. Unicorn also generates database schemas and XML Schemas.

5.3 Ontology Merge Tools

Ontology merge tools help users find similarities and differences between source ontologies to create a resulting merged ontology that includes terms from them. To achieve this purpose, they identify automatically potential correspondences between terms in the source ontologies or provide the environment for the users to find and define these correspondences (Noy and Musen, 2002).

These tools are often known generically as ontology mapping, aligning, and merge tools, because they perform similar operations for the activities of mapping, aligning, and merging, as described in Section 3.6. Among these tools we can cite Chimaera (McGuinness et al., 2000), the FCA-Merge toolset (Stumme and Maedche, 2001), GLUE (Doan et al., 2002), the merge module integrated in OBSERVER (Mena et al., 2000), and the PROMPT plug-in (Noy and Musen, 2000). The FCA-Merge toolset and the PROMPT plug-in give support to the methods with the same name described in Section 3.6.

In this section we give a detailed description of the PROMPT plug-in, which is integrated in Protégé-2000 and gives support to the ontology merge method with the same name. The PROMPT plug-in is perhaps the most complete of all the tools mentioned, hence most of this section will be devoted to explaining how we can merge two ontologies with it. We also describe briefly Chimaera, the FCA-Merge toolset, GLUE, and the merge module integrated in OBSERVER.

5.3.1 The PROMPT plug-in

The ontology merge method PROMPT (Noy and Musen, 2000) was presented in Section 3.6.3. It is a semi-automated method for ontology merge and alignment, and has been implemented as a plug-in for Protégé-2000. Since it gives semi-automated support the plug-in performs some tasks automatically (namely, matching suggestions, updating changes, and finding conflicts in the resulting ontology) and guides the user in performing other tasks for which its intervention is required (namely, selecting the operation to perform). In addition to the ontology merge functions provided by this plug-in, it also adds some version-management ones.

We will illustrate how this plug-in works with an example of how to merge two ontologies on the traveling domain. Let us suppose that we have built two ontologies in Protégé-2000: *Travel Ontology 1* and *Travel Ontology 2*, shown in Figure 5.28. Both ontologies have the same definitions for the class Date. They have also similar definitions for the class Location, concrete in the first ontology and

---

[38] http://www.unicorn.com/

abstract in the second ontology. Its subclasses are defined identically in both ontologies. Furthermore, we have defined the metaclass `TravelType` in both of them. However they have different definitions for the class `Travel` since it has a different number of attributes attached in each ontology, some of them with the same name and others with different names. In addition, the subclasses of the class `Travel` are different in each ontology: in the first ontology we have defined the classes `Flight` (with some more subclasses) and `TrainTravel`, while in the second we have defined the classes `Ship` and `Train Travel`[39], the last one with the subclass `Travel in High-Speed Train`.

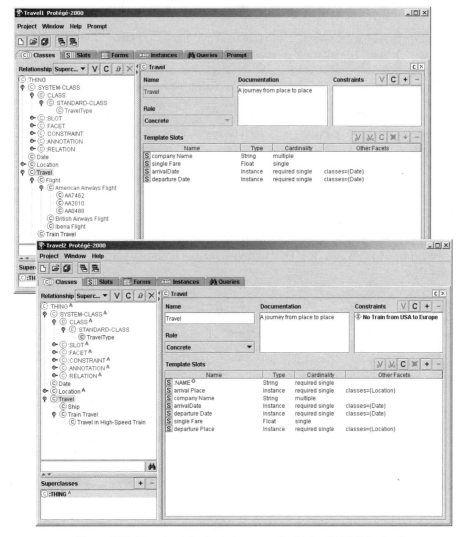

Figure 5.28: Travel ontologies to be merged with the PROMPT plug-in.

---

[39] Note the lexical difference between `TrainTravel` and `Train Travel`.

The cyclic steps involved in the merge process with PROMPT were described in Section 3.6.3. We will see how the PROMPT plug-in gives support to all of them.

As a support to the first step (to make initial suggestions), the PROMPT plug-in creates a list of possible matches based on the similarity of the term names of both ontologies. The list includes the following operations: merging classes and metaclasses; merging slots; merging bindings between a slot and a class; performing a deep copy of a class from one ontology (this includes copying all the parents of a class up to the root of the hierarchy and all the classes and slots to which the class refers); and performing a shallow copy of a class from one ontology (only the class, and not its parents nor the classes and slots it refers to).

Figure 5.29 shows the initial list of matches proposed by the PROMPT plug-in for our example, with a brief explanation of the reason why it suggests the operation selected. For instance, it proposes to merge the class `Travel` from the first ontology and the class `Travel` from the second because they have identical names. It also proposes to merge the classes `TrainTravel` and `Train Travel` although they do not have the same name. The last three suggestions are for copying operations: the first suggests a deep copy of the class `Flight` from the first ontology (copying all its subclasses, as determined by the parameter *subs*), and the other two suggest shallow copies of the classes `Ship` and `Travel in High-Speed Train` from the first and second ontology respectively.

On the right of the figure, we can see the ontology resulting from the merge process, which initially does not contain any domain concepts.

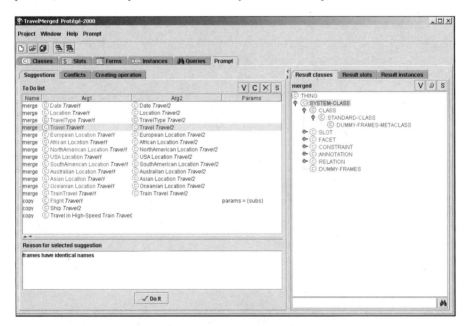

Figure 5.29: List of operations suggested by the PROMPT plug-in.

When the user has selected the operation that (s)he wants to perform, the PROMPT plug-in performs the operation and executes automatically all the changes associated to that type of operation. For instance, if the user decides to merge the term `Travel` from both ontologies, the PROMPT plug-in not only includes that term in the merged ontology but also all the original slots attached to it, as shown in Figure 5.30.

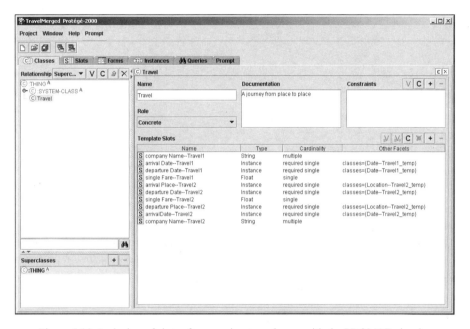

Figure 5.30: Inclusion of slots after merging two classes with the PROMPT plug-in.

When an operation (and all its associated changes) is performed the PROMPT plug-in identifies the conflicts between them. The following conflicts can be identified: name conflicts (more than one frame with the same name); dangling references (a frame refers to another frame that does not exist); redundancy in the class hierarchy (more than one path from a class to a parent other than root); and slot-value restrictions that violate class inheritance.

For example, Figure 5.31 shows that although we have included the slots `arrival Place`, `departure Place`, `arrival Date` and `departure Date` in the merged ontology, the classes defined as their value types (`Location` and `Date`) have not been included yet.

As defined in the PROMPT algorithm, all the steps described can be performed iteratively until we have obtained the final merged ontology.

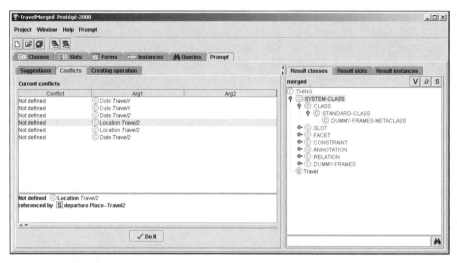

Figure 5.31: Conflicts after two classes are merged with the PROMPT plug-in.

5.3.2 Some other ontology merge tools

We start the brief description of other ontology merge tools with **Chimaera**[40], a tool built on top of the Ontolingua Server. Chimaera allows merging two or more ontologies available in any OKBC-compliant system. It is also able to handle many possible input formats (Ontolingua, KIF, Protégé-2000, DAML+OIL, etc.).

In Chimaera, ontologies to be merged are loaded together into a common one where users perform the operations needed to obtain the merged ontology. Chimaera

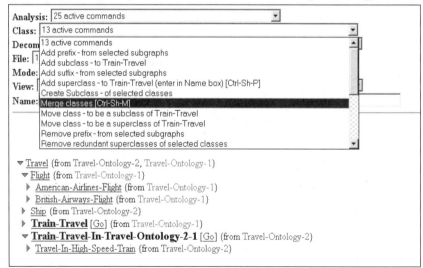

Figure 5.32: List of operations that can be done with two classes in Chimaera.

---

[40] http://www.ksl.stanford.edu/software/chimaera/

gives semi-automatic support for some steps of the ontology merge process such as generating a list of term names that are equivalent in the source ontologies or suggesting potential candidates to be merged. Figure 5.32 shows a screenshot of Chimaera where the user has selected the concepts Train Travel from the first and second ontology to be merged. The list shows the actions that the user can perform with both classes: creating superclasses, creating subclasses, merging both classes, moving classes, etc.

Unlike the PROMPT plug-in, Chimaera does not guide users in the operations that can be performed in each step of the merge process.

The **FCA-Merge toolset** (Stumme and Maedche, 2001) gives support to the FCA-Merge method described in Section 3.6.2. These tools automate the instance extraction step and the FCA-Merge core algorithm. Other steps defined in the method, such as deriving the merged ontology from the concept lattice obtained and setting the relation names, require the interaction of the ontology engineer.

The authors propose to use OntoEdit to edit the merged ontology; however, the toolset is not closely integrated yet.

GLUE (Doan et al., 2002) uses machine learning techniques to find semi-automatic mappings between concepts from two ontologies. Instead of using heuristics to find mappings between ontologies, as the rest of ontology merge tools do, GLUE uses several similarity measures based on probabilistic definitions (frequencies of concept and attribute names, distribution of attribute values, etc.), and applies multiple learning strategies, each of which exploits a different type of information either in the data instances or in the taxonomic structure of the ontologies.

OBSERVER[41] (Mena et al., 2000; Mena and Illarramendi, 2001) is an ontology-based system to access heterogeneous information sources. Ontologies represent the information sources accessed and are related to each other by synonymy, hyponymy, and hypernymy relations. When OBSERVER needs to use several heterogeneous ontologies that describe the same domain, it automatically merges them by carrying out the following steps:

- Adding the ontology name to the name of each term, so that terms with the same name and from different ontologies can be distinguished.
- Dealing with synonymy relations. If two terms are connected with a synonymy relation, only one of them is kept in the ontology. The other term is replaced by its synonym in all the ontology expressions where it appears.
- Dealing with hyponymy relations. If two terms are connected with a hyponymy relation (t_1 is hyponym of t_2), then a *Subclass-Of* relation is established between them (t_1 is a subclass of t_2)[42].
- Dealing with hypernymy relations. If two terms are connected with a hypernymy relation (t_1 is hyperonym of t_2), then a *Subclass-Of* relation is established between them (t_2 is a subclass of t_1).

---

[41] http://siul02.si.ehu.es/~jirgbdat/OBSERVER/
[42] Note that we have not distinguished between the linguistic and the conceptual level of the terms presented, as we did in section 3.5.

5.4 Ontology-based Annotation Tools

Ontology-based annotation tools, aka ontology-based annotators, are primarily designed to allow inserting and maintaining ontology-based markups in Web pages. Most of these tools have appeared recently with the emergence of the Semantic Web. Annotators were first conceived as tools that could be used to alleviate the burden of including ontology-based annotations manually into Web pages. Then many of them have evolved into more complete environments that use Information Extraction (IE) and Machine Learning (ML) techniques to propose semi-automatic annotations for Web documents.

Ontology-based annotators can be seen as the evolution of some instance-acquisition tools and modules, created to allow managing instances in knowledge bases. The main difference between annotators and these traditional instance-acquisition tools and modules is that ontologies are populated on the Web, that is, instances are not stored in a centralized knowledge base but on distributed Web pages. Besides, these annotations are implemented in ontology markup languages such as XML, SHOE, RDF(S), OIL, DAML+OIL, and OWL[43].

Ontology-based document annotation appeared first in pre-Semantic Web applications like the SHOE project (Luke et al., 1997), the $(KA)^2$ initiative (Benjamins et al., 1999), and the Planet-Onto project (Domingue and Motta, 2000), among others.

Besides, annotations have been widely used in the natural language processing field. NL texts are processed and annotated with different linguistic levels (Leech, 1997; EAGLES, 1996):

- Lemma annotation (aka lemmatization). It accompanies every word-token in a text with its lemma.
- Morphosyntactic annotation (aka part of speech annotation, POS tagging or grammatical tagging). It annotates the grammatical class (noun, verb, etc.) of each word-token in a text together with its morphological analysis.
- Syntactic annotation. It annotates higher-level syntactic relationships between categories. These relationships might be determined, for example, by means of a phrase-structure or dependency parse.
- Semantic annotation. It annotates semantic relationships between items in the text and semantic features of words in a text.
- Discourse annotation. It adds discourse tags such as apologies, greetings, etc.

To better understand how these tools work, let us suppose that we are willing to annotate the HTML page shown in Figure 5.33, available at *http://delicias.dia.fi.upm.es/airlinetickets.html*. Let us also suppose that this HTML page belongs to the Web site of a travel agency and summarizes the information about a flight from Madrid to Seattle on February 8, 2003.

---

[43] Strictly speaking, annotations are only stored in XML, SHOE, and RDF, because in RDFS, OIL, DAML+OIL, and OWL, instances are actually stored in RDF.

Flight details

Outbound	Leaving from **Madrid** - Barajas - Spain on Saturday 08 February 2003 at **11:50** Arriving in **Chicago** - O'Hare International - United States of America same day at **14:10** Airline: American Airlines Flight No. AA 7615 Type of aircraft: Airbus Industrie A340 All Series PAX/H
	Leaving from **Chicago** - O'Hare International - United States of America on Saturday 08 February 2003 at **16:48** Arriving in **Seattle** - Seattle/Tacoma International - United States of America same day at **19:23** Airline: American Airlines Flight No. AA 1605 Type of aircraft: non referenced/B

Figure 5.33: HTML document that describes the details of a flight.

According to the travel ontology used throughout this book, we have found the following information for the first stage of the flight shown in the figure:

- "Flight details" represents an instance of the concept Flight. Let us call this instance AA7615_Feb08_2003.

- "Madrid" represents an instance of the concept SpainLocation and the target of the relation departurePlace whose source instance is AA7615_Feb08_2003.

- "Saturday 08 February 2003" represents an instance of the concept Date and the target of the relation departureDate whose source instance is represented by "Madrid".

- "11:50" represents an instance of the concept Time and the target of the relation departureTime whose source instance is represented by "Madrid".

- "Chicago" represents an instance of the concept USALocation and the target of the relation arrivalPlace whose source instance is AA7615_Feb08_2003.

- "same day" represents an instance of the concept Date and the target of the relation arrivalDate whose source instance is AA7615_Feb08_2003, and which is equivalent to the instance "Saturday 08 February 2003".

- "14:10" represents an instance of the concept Time and the target of the relation arrivalTime whose source instance is AA7615_Feb08_2003.

- "American Airlines" is the value of the attribute companyName of the instance AA7615_Feb08_2003.

- "AA7615" is the value of the attribute flightNumber of the instance AA7615_Feb08_2003.

- "Airbus Industrie A340 All Series PAX/H" is the value of the attribute transportMeans of the instance AA7615_Feb08_2003; etc.

From this example we can infer that ontology-based annotators usually manage three types of information:

- **Concept instances** that relate a Web resource to one or several concepts in an ontology. For example, "Flight details" represents an instance of the concept Flight, and is named as AA7615_Feb08_2003. Concept instances do not necessarily have a name.
- **Attribute values** that relate a concept instance with a Web resource, which is the value of one of its attributes. As described in Chapter 4, in ontology markup languages attributes are also known as datatype properties. For example, "American Airlines" is the value of the attribute companyName.
- **Relation instances** that relate two concept instances, which are represented by Web resources. For example, the flight AA7615_Feb08_2003 and the location Madrid are connected by the relation departurePlace.

In this section we present the following annotation tools or environments: COHSE, MnM, OntoAnnotate, OntoMat, SHOE Knowledge Annotator, and UBOT AeroDAML. We will suppose that this page is not generated dynamically, but that it is static HTML, as these tools have not been designed to annotate content to be generated dynamically.

5.4.1 COHSE

COHSE[44] (Bechhofer et al., 2002; Bechhofer and Goble, 2001) stands for Conceptual Open Hypermedia Services Environment. COHSE is an environment that allows annotating Web pages with OIL and DAML+OIL and creating navigation links between annotations. This set of tools is being jointly developed by the Information Management Group (University of Manchester) and the Intelligence, Agents, Multimedia Group (University of Southampton).

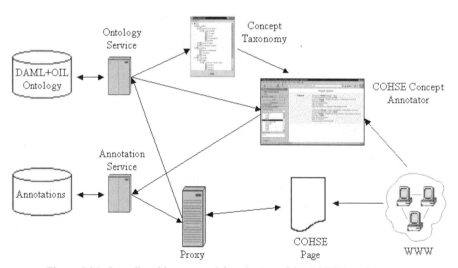

Figure 5.34: Overall architecture and functioning of the COHSE environment.

---

[44] http://cohse.semanticweb.org/

COHSE consists of several interconnected modules, as shown in Figure 5.34. The core modules in this environment are the Ontology Service and the Annotation Service. The Ontology Service stores DAML+OIL ontologies and supplies them to other modules. The Annotation Service stores Web page annotations and provides them to other modules. Both servers can be accessed locally or through a URL so users in different machines can access ontologies and manage annotations simultaneously.

The Ontology Service and the Annotation Service are used by the Mozilla Annotator tool (COHSE Concept Annotator), which is installed as a sidebar in the Mozilla browser[45], as shown in Figure 5.35. With this tool users can select any of the ontologies available in the Ontology Service and browse only the ontology concepts. When a HTML page is opened in the browser users select some text in it, select the ontology concept it belongs to and add a natural language comment to the annotation. This done, the annotation is submitted to the Annotation Service to store it.

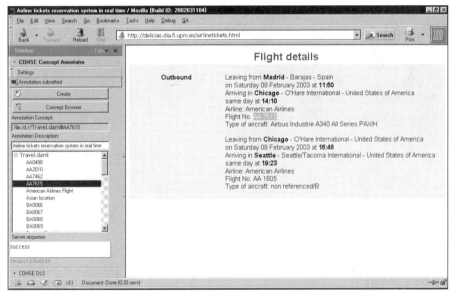

Figure 5.35: Annotation of the instance AA7615_Feb08_2003 with COHSE Concept Annotator.

The annotations created with the COHSE Concept Annotator can be viewed using the COHSE DLS sidebar, as Figure 5.36 illustrates. This sidebar acts as a proxy of COHSE annotations: it retrieves the annotations related to the Web page browsed from the Annotation Service and includes the information about these annotations in the Web browser.

---

[45] http://www.mozilla.org/

COHSE only permits creating annotations of those concepts that are described in an ontology but not of attribute values nor of relation instances. The annotation process is not completely manual since the COHSE DLS tool also proposes annotations for the Web pages browsed according to the ontology selected. In Figure 5.36, COHSE has automatically annotated the words "Flight", "Madrid", "Chicago", and "Seattle". They have small boxes next to them. The rest of the annotations, also marked with small boxes, have been included by a user.

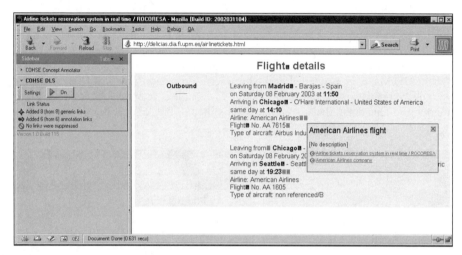

Figure 5.36: Browsing annotations of the instance `AA7615_Feb08_2003` with COHSE DLS Proxy.

Since the annotations created with the COHSE Concept Annotator are stored in the Annotation Service instead of being included in the Web pages, tools must be able to access the Annotation Service in order to retrieve annotations and use them.

5.4.2 MnM

MnM[46] (Vargas-Vera et al., 2001) is a standalone application that integrates a Web browser and an ontology viewer and that permits annotating documents manually, semi-automatically, and automatically. It is being developed by the Knowledge Media Institute at the Open University (United Kingdom), in the context of the AKT[47] Interdisciplinary Research Collaboration.

MnM is an extensible Java application, based on a plug-in architecture, available for download from the aforementioned URL. For the time being it can load ontologies stored in a WebOnto server, described in Section 5.2.1.3, or stored in files or URLs in any of the following ontology languages: RDF(S), DAML+OIL, and OCML. Similarly, the annotations created with this tool can be used to populate existing ontologies or be attached to the original document (XML format, where the tag names are the names of the concepts, of its attributes, and of its relations).

---

[46] http://kmi.open.ac.uk/projects/akt/MnM/index.html
[47] Advanced Knowledge Technologies: http://www.aktors.org/

Figure 5.37 shows our HTML document annotated manually the instance AA7615_Feb08_2003 of our Web page. We have selected the text that represents this instance in the browser window and the concept from which this instance is instance of. As we can see in the figure, we can add the instance name and the values and target concepts for its attributes and relations respectively.

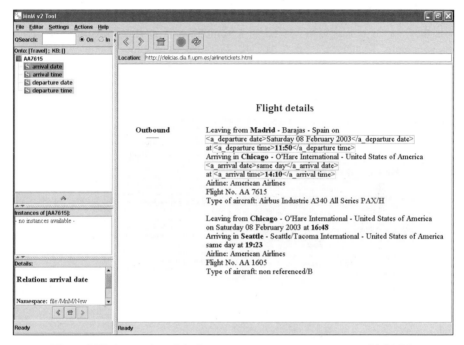

Figure 5.37: Annotation of the instance AA7615_Feb08_2003 with MnM.

Concerning the automatic annotation of documents, MnM uses information extraction engines to detect concept instances appearing in documents. These engines must be trained with a set of text and HTML annotated documents so that they generate the rules used to extract information from other documents. When the module is trained it can be used to detect concept instances, attribute values, and relation instances in other documents. Users may decide to edit the annotations performed by the information extraction module or to leave them as they are generated.

A plug-in for the information extraction engine Amilcare (Ciravegna, 2001) is included in the standard distribution. Other information extraction engines could be added as plug-ins, too.

The annotations generated by this tool can be used in different environments. MnM stores instances in various formats: OCML (so it can be used by any OCML-aware tool or application such as WebOnto, Planet-Onto, etc.), RDF, DAML+OIL, and XML.

5.4.3 OntoMat-Annotizer and OntoAnnotate

OntoMat-Annotizer[48] (Handschuh et al., 2001) is a tool for creating manually DAML+OIL annotations. It is being developed by the Institute AIFB at the University of Karlsruhe. The commercial version of OntoMat-Annotizer is called OntoAnnotate[49] and is distributed by Ontoprise.

Like MnM, OntoMat-Annotizer is a Java standalone application with a plug-in interface for extensions. It includes an ontology browser to explore ontology concepts and instances, and a HTML browser to display documents and its annotated parts. This tool permits dragging and dropping parts of the text into the annotations being created. In the version 0.41 of this tool the annotation process is fully manual and has not any automated support for text annotation.

With this tool, users can create concept instances, with their attributes, and relation instances, as shown in Figure 5.38. On the left part of the user interface, we can see the attributes and relations of the selected instance that can be filled. In the case of the relations, the tool also presents the instances that can be related to the selected instance with that relation.

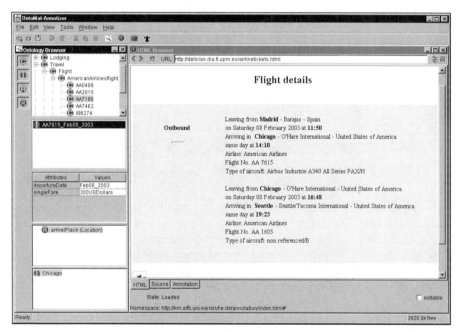

Figure 5.38: Annotation of the instance `AA7615_Feb08_2003` with OntoMat-Annotizer.

OntoMat-Annotizer loads DAML+OIL ontologies. Annotations created with this tool are stored in DAML+OIL, either as separate files or embedded in the HTML

---

[48] http://annotation.semanticweb.org/ontomat.html
[49] http://www.ontoprise.de/com/co_produ_tool2.htm

documents annotated. These annotations can be used by a wide range of applications in the Semantic Web.

5.4.4 SHOE Knowledge Annotator

The SHOE Knowledge Annotator[50] (Heflin and Hendler, 2001) is a tool for creating manual annotations in HTML pages with the SHOE language. It has been developed by the Parallel Understanding Systems Group, at the Department of Computer Science, University of Maryland. This tool has been the basis for the creation of SMORE[51], a more complex tool.

The SHOE Knowledge Annotator is available as a Java applet and as a standalone Java application. Both of them have the same functionalities. Annotations can refer to concepts and relations from one or several ontologies implemented in SHOE, which means that this tool creates annotations of instances of concepts, of their attribute values (attributes are represented in SHOE as relations, as described in Section 4.4.1), and instances of relations.

Figures 5.39 and 5.40 show the user interface of the standalone application. Unlike other tools, the HTML document is not browsed as in common Web browsers: only its source code can be accessed. The upper-left window of both figures contain the concept instances. When one of these instances is selected the upper-right and lower windows are updated with information related to it. The upper-right window contains the names of the ontologies that the instance uses. The lower window contains the claims made by this instance. Two types of claims can be made here:

- Claims of information about the instance. In Figure 5.39, the instance `AA7615_Feb08_2003` claims that it is an instance of the class `AA7615`, that it arrives at Chicago, that its departure date is February 8, 2003, and that its single fare costs 300$.

- Claims of information about other instances. In Figure 5.40, the instance `TravelPrice` not only claims that it is an instance of the class `Travel Agency`, which is located in New York and whose name is "TravelPrice Unlimited", but it also claims that the single fare for the instance `AA7615_Feb08_2003` is 200$ (there is a cheaper negotiated price between this travel agency and the American Airlines flight company).

The SHOE code corresponding to these annotations is embedded in the original HTML document. Figure 5.41 shows part of the resulting code, as presented by the tool. If we save this document and then open it with a standard Web browser, we will find no differences between the original and the annotated documents. An

---

[50] http://www.cs.umd.edu/projects/plus/SHOE/KnowledgeAnnotator.html
[51] http://www.mindswap.org/~aditkal/editor.shtml

important remark should be made at this point: though SHOE can be written either in HTML or XML, the SHOE Knowledge Annotator only creates HTML code.

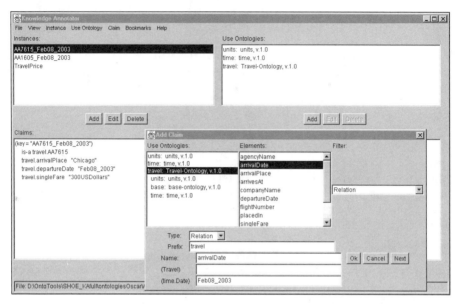

Figure 5.39: Edition of the instance `AA7615_Feb08_2002` with SHOE Knowledge Annotator.

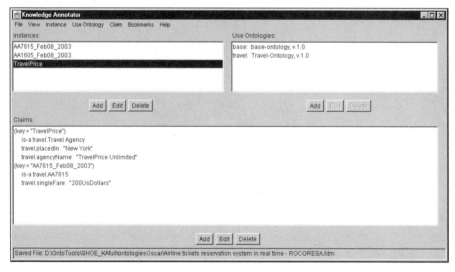

Figure 5.40: Edition of the instance `TravelPrice` and some claims about the instance `AA7615_Feb08_2003` with SHOE Knowledge Annotator.

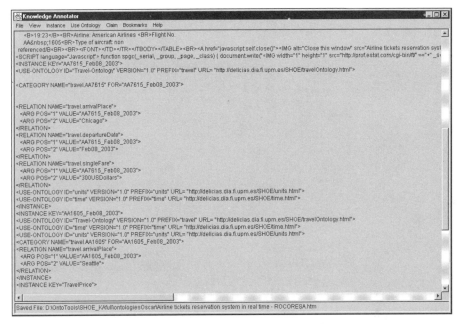

Figure 5.41: Source code of SHOE annotations.

SHOE annotations can be used with any of the KR systems able to manage SHOE ontologies such as Parka or XSB, and with any of the tools available in the SHOE suite such as Exposé, Running SHOE, and Semantic Search. All of them were mentioned in Section 4.4.1.

5.4.5 UBOT AeroDAML

AeroDAML[52] (Kogut and Holmes, 2001) generates automatically DAML+OIL annotations from text documents. It was developed by Lockheed Martin Corporation as part of the UBOT (UML Based Ontology Toolset) project.

AeroDAML is available both as a Web form and as a standalone application. In the Web version, shown in Figure 5.42, users send a text file and AeroDAML sends back the DAML+OIL annotations for that text. These annotations are created according to the DAML+OIL versions of OpenCyc[53], the CIA World Factbook[54], SUMO[55], and AeroDAML[56]. Some of these ontologies were described in Chapter 2.

The automatic annotation feature of AeroDAML is supported by the text-mining system AeroText. This system parses natural language text and extracts those items

---

[52] http://ubot.lockheedmartin.com/ubot/hotdaml/aerodaml.html
[53] http://www.cyc.com/2002/04/08/cyc.daml
[54] http://www.daml.org/2001/12/factbook/factbook-ont
[55] http://reliant.teknowledge.com/DAML/SUMO.daml
[56] http://ubot.lockheedmartin.com/ubot/2002/08/aerodaml-ont.daml

that have any correspondence with the underlying ontology used. The default extraction rules of this text-mining system can also be modified.

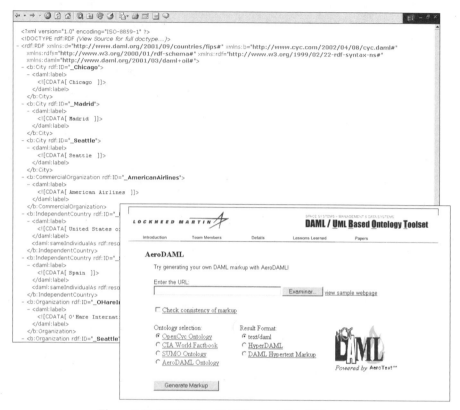

Figure 5.42: UBOT AeroDAML annotation Web server.

AeroDAML generates instances of concepts (proper nouns, common nouns, dates, currency quantities, etc.), attribute values, and instances of properties (a person belongs to an organization, an organization is based in a location, etc.).

Since the annotations created by AeroDAML are provided in DAML+OIL, any DAML+OIL-aware tool can use them as long as they are appended to the corresponding Web page. AeroDAML could also be used as an automatic annotation service to provide DAML+OIL annotations on-line.

5.5 Conclusions

In this chapter we have described the most relevant ontology building (Section 5.2), ontology merge (Section 5.3), and ontology-based annotation tools (Section 5.4). We have divided this section of conclusions according to the three types of ontology tools identified and we will finish with some global conclusions to this chapter.

Concerning **ontology development tools**, we have made a distinction between two groups of tools: those created for editing ontologies in a specific ontology language, and those created as integrated extensible tool suites, most of which are language independent and provide more functions than those strictly related to ontology edition. Finally, we have briefly described some other tools that could be used for ontology building although they have not been created specifically for that purpose nor are they widely used.

In addition to giving general information about tools in each group, we have discussed the following aspects: software architecture, knowledge model, ontology edition and browsing functions (including inference services attached, documentation options, logical expression editors, collaborative ontology construction, etc.), and interoperability choices. Tables 5.1 to 5.5 summarize the contents of Section 5.2, and can give some guidance in the process of deciding which ontology building tool or tool suite to choose to develop an ontology. We present here some conclusions extracted from the analysis of these tables.

Our first comments are related to the contents of Table 5.1, which contains some general information about the tools. We must highlight the fact that most of these tools have been developed by university research groups. As we commented in the introduction to this chapter, ontology technology is already in an advanced development stage and most of their corporate users belong to R&D departments of universities and companies. However, the transfer of this technology is now starting and it is foreseen that it will be adopted by a higher and wider number of users, since new companies are appearing with the aim of commercializing it.

As shown in the table, except for OntoEdit Professional that is distributed under license, the rest of the tools are either open source or offer free access to its functions. Another interesting aspect of tools is that only OntoEdit and WebODE give support to ontology building methodologies (On-To-Knowledge and METHONTOLOGY respectively), though this does not prevent them from being used with other methodologies or with no methodology at all.

Table 5.2 is focused on the technological aspects of the tools, paying special attention to their software architecture (standalone, client-server, n-tier), their extensibility capabilities, the programming language(s) in which they are implemented, and their backends, that is, how they store ontologies (normally in files or in databases).

The architecture and extensibility capabilities of tools are closely related. The first tools that appeared (Ontolingua, OntoSaurus, and WebOnto) have a client/server architecture and, consequently, are difficult to extend though this does not mean that they cannot be extended with other functions. More modern tools such as OilEd, OntoEdit, and Protégé-2000, have a 3-tier architecture, where there is a clear distinction between the backends in charge of ontology storage, the business logic modules in charge of most of the logic of the application, and the frontends, in

Table 5.1: Ontology building tools: general information.

	KAON	OilEd	OntoEdit	Ontolingua	OntoSaurus	Protégé 2000	WebODE	WebOnto
Developers	AIFB-FZI (University of Karlsruhe)	IMG (University of Manchester)	Ontoprise	KSL (Stanford University)	ISI (University of Southern California)	SMI (Stanford University)	Ontology Group (Universidad Politécnica de Madrid)	KMI (Open University)
Version (date)	1.2.5 (Jan2003)	3.5 (Dec2002)	2.6 (Nov2002)	1.0.649 (Nov2001)	1.9 (Mar2002)	1.8 (Apr2003)	2.1 (Mar2003)	2.3 (May2001)
Availability	Open source	Open source	Freeware Licenses	Free access	Open source Free access	Open source	Free access	Free access
Methodological support	No	No	On-To-Knowledge	No	No	No	METHONTOLOGY	No

Table 5.2: Ontology building tools: software architecture.

	KAON	OilEd	OntoEdit	Ontolingua	OntoSaurus	Protégé 2000	WebODE	WebOnto
Application architecture	n-tier	3-tier	3-tier	Client/server	Client/server	3-tier	n-tier	Client/server
Extensibility	Application server	Backends	Plug-ins	--	--	Plug-ins	Application server	--
Ontology storage	Files DBMS	Files	Files	Files	Files	Files DBMS	DBMS	Files
Programming language	Java	Java	Java	Lisp	Lisp	Java	Java	Java + Lisp

Table 5.3: Ontology building tools: knowledge model.

	KAON	OilEd	OntoEdit	Ontolingua	OntoSaurus	Protégé 2000	WebODE	WebOnto
KR formalism	Frames	DL	Frames + FOL	Frames + FOL	DL	Frames + FOL	Frames + FOL	Frames + FOL
Underlying KR language	KAON	DAML+OIL	OXML	Ontolingua	LOOM	--	--	OCML
Formal axiom language	--	--	FLogic	KIF	LOOM	PAL	WAB	OCML

Table 5.4: Ontology building tools: ontology editors.

	KAON	OilEd	OntoEdit	Ontolingua	OntoSaurus	Protégé 2000	WebODE	WebOnto
Front-end	Java Swing	Java Swing	Java Swing	HTML	HTML	Java Swing	HTML and applets	Applets
Graphical concept taxonomy edition	Yes	No	Yes	No	No	Yes	Yes	Yes
Graphical prunes	Yes	No	Yes	No	No	Yes	Yes	Yes
Zooms	Yes	No	Yes	No	No	Yes	No	No
Formal axiom editor	No	Yes	No	No	No	Yes	Yes	No
Collaborative edition	Yes	No	Yes	Yes	Yes	No	Yes	Yes
Inference engine	--	FaCT (built-in) RACER DIG compliant	OntoBroker	JTP	LOOM classifier	PAL (built-in) Jess FaCT Prolog FLORA Algernon	Prolog (built-in) Jess	OCML KR system
Consistency checking	Yes	Yes	Yes	No	Yes	Yes	Yes	Yes
Automatic classification	No	Yes	No	No	Yes	No	No	No

Table 5.5: Ontology building tools: interoperability.

	KAON	OilEd	OntoEdit	Ontolingua	OntoSaurus	Protégé 2000	WebODE	WebOnto
With other tools	KAON-Portal	--	OntoAnnotate OntoMat Semantic Miner	Chimaera OKBC	OKBC	PROMPT OKBC ArgoUML	ODE-KM ODE-SeW ODE-SWS ODEAnnotate Protégé-2000	MnM
Import	KAON RDF(S)	RDF(S) OIL DAML+OIL SHIQ	OXML RDF(S) DAML+OIL FLogic	Ontolingua KIF CML IDL	LOOM PowerLOOM Stella IDL	XML RDF(S) XML Schema XMI	XML RDF(S) DAML+OIL OWL CARIN	OCML RDF(S)
Export	KAON RDF(S)	RDF(S) OIL DAML+OIL OWL SHIQ DIG	OXML RDF(S) DAML+OIL FLogic	Ontolingua KIF LOOM CLIPS CML Epikit Prolog IDL	LOOM PowerLOOM KIF Ontolingua Stella IDL C++	XML RDF(S) XML Schema FLogic CLIPS Java XMI	XML RDF(S) OIL DAML+OIL OWL CARIN FLogic Prolog Jess Java	OCML Ontolingua RDF(S)

charge of all the application user interfaces. These tools are easier to extend than the previous ones. OilEd allows easily changing its backends so that ontologies can be stored in different formats. OntoEdit and Protégé-2000 allow easily extending not only the backends but also the ontology editor user interface by means of plug-ins. The tool suites KAON and WebODE are based on application server architectures, which also provide good extensibility features, multi-user support, access management facilities for users, etc.

Most of the tools store their ontologies in text files. This limits the size of the ontologies that can be built with them. Only KAON, Protégé-2000, and WebODE are able to store their ontologies in databases, and thus to manage larger ontologies. Finally, most of the tools have been developed completely in Java.

Table 5.3 illustrates the ontology tool knowledge model, which determines the components to be used when building ontologies. Most of the tools represent ontologies combining frames and first order logic. However, this does not mean that they can represent the same components with the same amount of information. Only two of these tools, OilEd and OntoSaurus, are based on description logic.

The second row in the table refers to the underlying KR language attached to each tool. OilEd, the Ontolingua Server, OntoSaurus, and WebOnto are associated with ontology languages described in Chapter 4: DAML+OIL, Ontolingua, LOOM, and OCML respectively. The other tools are not associated with any language, although in the cases of KAON and OntoEdit the knowledge models are called KAON and OXML respectively.

The last row contains information about languages in which formal axioms can be expressed. Except for KAON and OilEd, all the tools have some language for defining formal axioms: OntoEdit uses FLogic, the Ontolingua Server uses KIF, OntoSaurus uses LOOM, Protégé-2000 uses the PAL language, WebODE uses the WAB language, and WebOnto uses OCML.

Table 5.4 shows the most relevant information about the ontology editors of each tool or tool suite. First, we start with the characteristics of the ontology editor user interface (whether it is a Web application, based on HTML forms and/or Java applets, or a local application).

Next we discuss their graphical edition and browsing capabilities (graphical concept taxonomy edition, graphical prunes, and zooms). These rows show that, except for OilEd, Ontolingua, and OntoSaurus, all the ontology editors provide graphical means to edit and browse ontologies, where classes are usually represented as nodes in the graphs, and relations are usually represented as edges between nodes. In addition to these graphical edition and browsing functions, the table shows that only OilEd, OntoEdit Professional, Protégé-2000, and WebODE give some support for writing formal axioms and complex expressions. The task of writing these ontology components is usually difficult, and these tools contain specific graphical editors, parsers, and validators.

Several tools support editing ontologies collaboratively by managing users and groups of users, and their corresponding access and write permissions to different sets of ontologies. This permits that several users edit the same ontology simultaneously. The most advanced tool is WebOnto, which permits discussions about parts of the ontology being edited.

Then we present the list of inference engines that can be used with the tool. Some inference engines are integrated, by default, in the ontology editor; others are integrated as plug-ins. Protégé-2000 is the tool that provides more inference engines attached. Normally, these inference engines are used to perform constraint checking on the ontologies being built so that the ontology editors ensure that the ontologies built with them are free of errors. The last comment on the inference capabilities of tools is about automatic classifications. Only OilEd and OntoSaurus are able to create concept classifications automatically with their built-in DL inference engines.

Table 5.5 deals with interoperability choices for all the tools. This is an important aspect since it summarizes how we can use the ontologies developed with each tool and how we can use the ontologies implemented in other languages or tools. The table shows first some of the tools with which each tool can interoperate. It contains knowledge portals such as KAON-Portal and ODESeW; ontology-based annotators such as ODEAnnotate, OntoAnnotate, and MnM; Semantic Web Services building tools, such as ODESWS; UML modeling tools, such as ArgoUML; ontology merge tools, such as Chimaera and PROMPT; etc. In some of these tools we have also included OKBC because any other applications could access their ontologies by means of this protocol.

The table also shows the lists of import and export formats of each tool, which provide a good overview of their interoperability choices. The lists contain ontology languages (Ontolingua, LOOM, RDF(S), DAML+OIL, OWL, etc.), general purpose languages (Prolog, Jess, etc.), and programming languages (C++, Java, etc.). Though at first sight we may think that two tools can interoperate with each other if they share some import/export format, we should be careful about this when deciding whether two tools really interoperate or not. In the translation processes much information can be lost, that is, not translated, and the resulting ontology in the target tool could be different from that of the original tool.

With regard to **ontology merge tools**, they have appeared because many times ontology developers have to reuse several ontologies of the same domain and need to integrate them in one ontology. A wide variety of tools can be used to perform the ontology merge activity, as described in Section 5.3.

On the one hand, ontologists may decide to follow their own ontology merge method and their intuition and use Chimaera to perform the operations of ontology merge. If they require some guidance about the ontology concepts that should be merged, ontologists may rely on GLUE to find mappings between them.

On the other hand, ontologists may decide to follow existing ontology merge methods such as PROMPT or FCA-Merge and use the PROMPT plug-in or the FCA-Merge toolset respectively.

The time spent in the ontology merge process is reduced if ontologists use these tools instead of performing the whole activity manually. Nevertheless, ontology merge is a difficult activity that requires an important interaction with users. For instance, most of the tools deal only with concepts and their attributes, concept taxonomies, and relations between concepts and do not give support to the merge of formal axioms.

Other important aspects are: the integration of these tools into other ontology development platforms (only the PROMPT plug-in and Chimaera are integrated in other tools, Protégé-2000 and Ontolingua respectively); and the limitations related to the ontology languages that they can process.

Ontology-based annotation tools have appeared in the context of pre-Semantic Web and Semantic Web applications. They are usually integrated in other tool suites or they interoperate with other ontology development tools.

COHSE and MnM deserve special attention because they have complex architectures: ontologies and annotations are retrieved and stored in ontology and annotation servers respectively. Many of these tools can also work independently, that is, they load the ontologies to use for annotation and the documents to be annotated and allow users to perform their document annotation operations.

The manual annotation of documents is a high-cost and error-prone task, as has been proven by pre-Semantic Web initiatives such as (KA)^2 (Benjamins et al., 1999), Planet-Onto (Domingue and Motta, 2000). To alleviate this task, an important effort is being currently made in the automation of document annotations. Tools like COHSE, MnM, and AeroDAML have incorporated or are incorporating information extraction, machine learning, and natural language processing modules that minimize the annotation effort.

Finally, it is clear that most of the tools annotate their documents in RDF(S) and DAML+OIL and will migrate to OWL, since these are the markup languages used in the Semantic Web. However, the internal infrastructure of most of them is based on more stable and older languages, such as OCML, SHOE, FLogic, etc.

5.6 Bibliographical Notes and Further Reading

For those interested in ontology tools, there is a Special Interest Group on Enterprise-Standard Ontology Environments on the framework of the European OntoWeb thematic network (IST-2000-29243). Its goal is to support the dialog for the development of quality requirements for enterprise-standard ontology environments and to steer future ontology development towards addressing these requirements. Its URL is *http://delicias.dia.fi.upm.es/ontoweb/sig-tools/index.html*.

Some of the most relevant results of the work performed in the OntoWeb thematic network are the following:

- The deliverable D1.3 "A survey on ontology tools", edited in June 2002, contains descriptions and comparisons of many different kinds of ontology tools, aimed at ontology building, ontology merge and integration, ontology evaluation, and ontology-based annotation. It also gives a broad description of ontology storage and querying tools, focusing specially on RDF(S)-based ontology tools.
- The deliverable D1.5 "A survey on ontology learning methods and techniques" describes methods and tools that can be used to (semi)automatically derive ontologies from natural language texts.

- A series of workshops on ontology tool evaluation (EON2002 and EON2003), where several experiments with ontology tools are being carried out. We recommend reading the proceedings and checking the results of the experiments at the following URLs: *http://km.aifb.uni-karlsruhe.de/eon2002/* and *http://km.aifb.uni-karlsruhe.de/ws/eon2003/* respectively.

At *http://xml.coverpages.org/Denny-OntologyEditorSurveyText20021111.html*, Michael Denny's survey on ontology editors can be found. This survey provides a good overview of ontology editors that was compiled during the summer of 2002 and released at the end of that year.

Several ontology merge tools are described in Section 3 ("Ontology merge and integration tools") of the deliverable D1.3 of OntoWeb, cited above. We also recommend reading about the ontology mapping framework MAFRA (Maedche et al., 2002). To learn more about ontology-based systems and architectures where ontologies are aligned by means of mappings, we recommend reading about KRAFT (Preece et al., 2001) and MOMIS (Bergamaschi et al., 2001).

The following workshops contain topics related to ontology integration: the IJCAI'03 workshops on Ontologies and Distributed Systems (*http://www.cs.vu.nl/~heiner/IJCAI-03/*) and on Information Integration on the Web (*http://www.isi.edu/info-agents/workshops/ijcai03/iiweb.html*), and the ISWC'03 Workshop on Semantic Integration (*http://smi.stanford.edu/si2003/*).

An updated resource about annotations can be found in the following URL: (*http://annotation.semanticweb.org*). For a deep study of annotation tools, we also recommend reading the proceedings of the KCAP'01 workshop of Knowledge Markup and Semantic Annotation (*http://semannot2001.aifb.uni-karlsruhe.de/*) and the ECAI'02 Workshop on Semantic Authoring, Annotation and Knowledge Markup (SAAKM-02) (*http://saakm2002.aifb.uni-karlsruhe.de/index.html*).

The relationships between linguistic and ontology-based annotation are being explored in workshops like the NLPXML-2003 on Language Technology and the Semantic Web, held in conjunction with the EACL2003 conference. Its URL is: *http://www.cs.vassar.edu/~ide/events/NLPXML3.html*. We also recommend publications from Aguado and colleagues (2002, 2003) and Buitelaar and colleagues (2003).

Bibliography

Abecker A, Bernardi A, Hinkelmann K, Kühn O, Sintek M (1998) *Toward a Technology for Organizational Memories.* IEEE Intelligent Systems 13(3):40–48

Adriaans P, Zantinge D (1996) *Data Mining.* Addison-Wesley, Harlow, United Kingdom

Agrawal R, Imielinski T, Swami A (1993) *Mining association rules between sets of items in large databases.* In: Buneman P, Jajodia S (eds) ACM SIGMOD Conference on Management of Data. Washington, DC, pp 207–216

Aguado G, Álvarez-de-Mon I, Gómez-Pérez A, Pareja-Lora A (2003) *OntoTag: XML / RDF(S) / OWL Semantic Web Page Annotation in ContentWeb.* In: Ide N, Romary L, Wilcock G (eds) 3rd Workshop on NLP and XML (NLPXML-2002). Budapest, Hungary

Aguado G, Álvarez-de-Mon I, Gómez-Pérez A, Pareja-Lora A, Plaza-Arteche R (2002) *A Semantic Web Page Linguistic Annotation Model.* In: Ide N, Welty C (eds) Semantic Web Meets Language Resources. Edmonton, Alberta, Canada. AAAI Press. Menlo Park, California.

Aguado G, Bañón A, Bateman J, Bernardos S, Fernández M, Gómez-Pérez A, Nieto E, Olalla A, Plaza R, Sánchez A (1998) *ONTOGENERATION: Reusing domain and linguistic ontologies for Spanish text generation.* ECAI'98 Workshop on Applications of Ontologies and Problem-Solving Methods. Brighton, United Kingdom, pp 1–10

Alemany C (1998) *Étude et réalisation d'une interface d'édition de bases de connaissances au travers du World Wide Web.* CNAM Technical Report. Grenoble, France

Allen J (1984) *Towards a general theory of action and time.* Artificial Intelligence 23:123–154

363

Angele J, Fensel D, Landes D, Studer R (1998) *Developing knowledge-based systems with MIKE*. Journal of Automated Software Engineering 5(4):389–418

Arpírez JC, Corcho O, Fernández-López M, Gómez-Pérez A (2003) *WebODE in a nutshell*. AI Magazine. To be published in 2003

Arpírez JC, Corcho O, Fernández-López M, Gómez-Pérez A (2001) *WebODE: a scalable ontological engineering workbench*. In: Gil Y, Musen M, Shavlik J (eds) First International Conference on Knowledge Capture (KCAP'01). Victoria, Canada. ACM Press (1-58113-380-4), New York, pp 6–13

Arpírez JC, Gómez-Pérez A, Lozano-Tello A, Pinto HS (2000) *Reference Ontology and (ONTO)^{2}Agent: the Ontology Yellow Pages*. Knowledge and Information Systems: An International Journal 2(4):387–412

Arpírez JC, Gómez-Pérez A, Lozano A, Pinto HS (1998) *(ONTO)^{2}Agent: An ontology-based WWW broker to select ontologies*. In: Gómez-Pérez A, Benjamins RV (eds) ECAI'98 Workshop on Applications of Ontologies and Problem-Solving Methods. Brighton, United Kingdom, pp 16–24

Aussenac-Gilles N (1999) *Gediterm, un logiciel de gestion de bases de connaissances terminologiques*. Terminologies Nouvelles 19:111–123

Aussenac-Gilles N, Biébow B, Szulman S (2002) *Modelling the travelling domain from a NLP description with TERMINAE*. In: Angele J, Sure Y (eds) EKAW'02 Workshop on Evaluation of Ontology-based Tools (EON2002), Sigüenza, Spain. CEUR Workshop Proceedings 62:112–128. Amsterdam, The Netherlands (*http://CEUR-WS.org/Vol-62/*)

Aussenac-Gilles N, Biébow B, Szulman S (2000a) *Revisiting Ontology Design: A Methodology Based on Corpus Analysis*. In: Dieng R, Corby O (eds) 12th International Conference in Knowledge Engineering and Knowledge Management (EKAW'00). Juan-Les-Pins, France. (Lecture Notes in Artificial Intelligence LNAI 1937) Springer-Verlag, Berlin, Germany, pp 172–188

Aussenac-Gilles N, Biébow B, Szulman S (2000b) *Corpus analysis for conceptual modelling*. In: Aussenac-Gilles N, Biébow B, Szulman S (eds) EKAW'00 Workshop on Ontologies and Texts. Juan-Les-Pins, France. CEUR Workshop Proceedings 51:1.1–1.8. Amsterdam, The Netherlands (*http://CEUR-WS.org/Vol-51/*)

Baader F, Hollunder B (1991) *KRIS: knowledge representation and inference system*. SIGART Bulletin 2(3):8–14

Baader F, McGuinness D, Nardi D, Patel-Schneider P (2003) *The Description Logic Handbook: Theory, implementation and applications*. Cambridge University Press, Cambridge, United Kingdom

Baclawski K, Kokar MM, Kogut PA, Hart L, Smith J, Holmes III WS, Letkowski J, Aronson ML (2001) *Extending UML to support ontology engineering for the Semantic Web*. In: Gogolla M, Kobryn C (eds) 4th International Conference on the Unified Modeling Language (UML'01). Toronto, Canada. (Lecture Notes in Computer Science LNCS 2185) Springer-Verlag, Berlin, Germany, pp 342–360

Barish G, Knoblock CA, Chen Y-S, Minton S, Philpot A, Shahabi C (2000) *The theaterloc virtual application.* In: Engelmore R, Hirsh H (eds) 12th Annual Conference on Innovative Applications of Artificial Intelligence (IAAI'00). Austin, Texas, pp 980–987

Bateman JA, Fabris G, Magnini B (1995) *The Generalized Upper Model Knowledge Base: Organization and Use.* In: Mars N (ed) Second International Conference on Building and Sharing of Very Large-Scale Knowledge Bases (KBKS '95). University of Twente, Enschede, The Netherlands. IOS Press, Amsterdam, The Netherlands, pp 60–72

Bateman JA, Kasper RT, Moore JD, Whitney RA (1990) *A General Organization of Knowledge for Natural Language Processing: The Penman Upper Model.* Technical Report. USC/Information Sciences Institute, Marina del Rey, California

Bechhofer S (2002) *The DIG Description Logic Interface: DIG/1.0.* Technical Report. *http://potato.cs.man.ac.uk/dig/interface1.0.pdf*

Bechhofer S, Goble C (2001) *Towards Annotation Using DAML+OIL.* In: Handschuh S, Dieng R, Staab S (eds) KCAP'01 Workshop on Knowledge Markup and Semantic Annotation. Victoria, Canada. *http://semannot2001.aifb.uni-karlsruhe.de/schedule_new.html*

Bechhofer S, Carr L, Goble C, Hall W (2002) *Conceptual Open Hypermedia = The Semantic Web?* Technical Report. *http://cohse.semanticweb.org/papers/index.html*

Bechhofer S, Horrocks I, Goble C, Stevens R (2001a) *OilEd: a reasonable ontology editor for the Semantic Web.* In: Baader F, Brewka G, Eiter T (eds) Joint German/Austrian conference on Artificial Intelligence (KI'01). Vienna, Austria. (Lecture Notes in Artificial Intelligence LNAI 2174) Springer-Verlag, Berlin, Germany, pp 396–408

Bechhofer S, Goble C, Horrocks I (2001b) *DAML+OIL is not enough.* In: Decker S, Fensel D, Sheth A, Staab S (eds) First Semantic Web Working Symposium (SWWS'01). Stanford, California, pp 151–159

Bechhofer S, Broekstra J, Decker S, Erdmann M, Fensel D, Goble C, van Harmelen F, Horrocks I, Klein M, McGuinness D, Motta E, Patel-Schneider P, Staab S, Studer R (2000) *An informal description of Standard OIL and Instance OIL.* White paper. *http://www.ontoknowledge.org/oil/downl/oil-whitepaper.pdf*

Beckett D (2003) *RDF/XML Syntax Specification (Revised).* W3C Working Draft. *http://www.w3.org/TR/rdf-syntax-grammar*

Benjamins VR, Gómez-Pérez A (1999) *Overview of knowledge sharing and reuse components: ontologies and problem solving methods.* In: Benjamins VR (ed) IJCAI'99 Workshop on Ontology and Problem Solving Methods: Lessons

Learned and Future Trends. Stockholm, Sweden. CEUR Workshop Proceedings 18:1.1–1.15. Amsterdam, The Netherlands (*http://CEUR-WS.org/Vol-18/*)

Benjamins VR, Fensel D, Decker S, Gómez-Pérez A (1999) *(KA)²: Building ontologies for the Internet: a mid term report*. International Journal of Human Computer Studies 51:687–712

Bergamaschi S, Castano S, Beneventano D, Vincini M (2001) *Semantic Integration of Heterogeneous Information Sources*, Special Issue on Intelligent Information Integration, Data & Knowledge Engineering 36(1):215–24

Bernaras A, Laresgoiti I, Corera J (1996) *Building and reusing ontologies for electrical network applications*. In: Wahlster W (ed) European Conference on Artificial Intelligence (ECAI'96). Budapest, Hungary. John Wiley and Sons, Chichester, United Kingdom, pp 298–302

Berners-Lee T (1999) *Weaving the Web: The Original Design and Ultimate Destiny of the World Wide Web by its Inventor*. HarperCollins Publishers, New York

Biébow B, Szulman S (1999) *TERMINAE: a linguistic-based tool for the building of a domain ontology*. In : Fensel D, Studer R (eds) 11ᵗʰ European Workshop on Knowledge Acquisition, Modeling and Management (EKAW'99). Dagstuhl Castle, Germany. (Lecture Notes in Artificial Intelligence LNAI 1621) Springer-Verlag, Berlin, Germany, pp 49–66

Biron PV, Malhotra A (2001) *XML Schema Part 2: Datatypes*. W3C Recommendation. *http://www.w3.org/TR/xmlschema-2/*

Blázquez M, Fernández-López M, García-Pinar JM, Gómez-Pérez A (1998) *Building Ontologies at the Knowledge Level using the Ontology Design Environment*. In: Gaines BR, Musen MA (eds) 11ᵗʰ International Workshop on Knowledge Acquisition, Modeling and Management (KAW'98). Banff, Canada, SHARE4:1–15

Blum BI (1996) *Beyond Programming*. Oxford University Press, New York

Bodenreider O (2001) *Medical Ontology research*. Technical Report. Lister Hill National Center, National Library of Medicine. Maryland, Washington. *http://etbsun2.nlm.nih.gov:8000/publis-ob-offi/*

Bonner AJ, Kifer M (1995) *Transaction Logic Programming*. Technical Report CSRI-323. University of Toronto. Toronto, Canada. *http://www.cs.toronto.edu/~bonner/transaction-logic.html*

Borgida A, Brachman RJ, McGuinness DL, Resnick LA (1989) *CLASSIC: a structural data model for objects*. In: Clifford J, Lindsay BG, Maier D (eds) ACM SIGMOD International Conference on the Management of Data. Portland, Oregon, pp 58–67

Borgo S, Guarino N, Masolo C (1997) *An Ontological Theory of Physical Objects*. In: Ironi I (ed) 11ᵗʰ International Workshop on Qualitative Reasoning (QR'97). Cortona, Italy, pp 223–231

Borgo S, Guarino N, Masolo C (1996) *A Pointless Theory of Space Based on Strong Connection and Congruence*. In: Carlucci-Aiello L, Doyle J (eds) 5th International Conference on Principles of Knowledge Representation and Reasoning (KR'96). Morgan Kaufmann Publishers, San Francisco, California, pp 220–229

Borst WN (1997) *Construction of Engineering Ontologies*. Centre for Telematica and Information Technology, University of Tweenty. Enschede, The Netherlands

Bourigault D, González I, Gros C (1996) *LEXTER, a Natural Language Tool for Terminology Extraction*. In: Gellerstam M, Järborg J, Malmgren SG, Norén K, Rogström L, Papmehl CR (eds) 7th EURALEX International Congress, Goteborg, Sweden, Part II, pp 771–779

Brachman RJ (1979) *On the Epistemological Status of Semantic Networks*. In Findler NV (ed) Associative Networks: Representation and Use of Knowledge by Computers. Academic Press, London, United Kingdom

Brachman RJ, Fikes RE, Levesque HJ (1983) *Krypton: A Functional Approach to Knowledge Representation*. IEEE Computer 16(10):67–73

Brachman RJ, Schmolze JG (1985) *An overview of the KL-ONE knowledge representation system*. Cognitive Science 9(2):171–216

Bray T, Paoli J, Sperberg-McQueen CM, Maler E (2000) *Extensible Markup Language (XML) 1.0*. W3C Recommendation. *http://www.w3.org/TR/REC-xml*

Brewka G (1987) *The Logic of Inheritance in Frame Systems*. In: McDermott (ed) 10th International Joint Conference on Artificial Intelligence (IJCAI'87), Milan, Italy. Morgan Kaufmann Publishers, San Francisco, California, pp 483–488

Brickley D, Guha RV (2003) *RDF Vocabulary Description Language 1.0: RDF Schema*. W3C Working Draft. *http://www.w3.org/TR/PR-rdf-schema*

Brilhante V (1999) *Using Formal Metadata Descriptions for Automated Ecological Modeling*. In: Cortés U, Sànchez-Marrè M (eds) AAAI'99 Workshop on Environmental Decision Support Systems and Artificial Intelligence (EDSSAI'99). Orlando, Florida, pp 90–98

Brill D (1993) *Loom Reference Manual for Loom Version 2.0*. *http://www.isi.edu/isd/LOOM/documentation/manual/quickguide.html*

Broekstra J, Klein M, Decker S, Fensel D, van Harmelen F, Horrocks I (2001) *Enabling Knowledge Representation on the Web by Extending RDF Schema*. In: Shen VY, Saito N (eds) 10th International World Wide Web Conference (WWW10). Hong Kong, pp 467–478

Buckingham-Shum S, Motta E, Domingue J (2000) *ScholOnto: An Ontology-Based Digital Library Server for Research Documents and Discourse*. International Journal on Digital Libraries 3(3):237–248

Buitelaar P (2001) *Semantic Lexicons: Between Ontology and Terminology*. In: Simov K, Kiryakov A (eds) Ontologies and Lexical Knowledge Bases (OntoLex'00). OntoText Lab., Sofia, Bulgaria, pp 16–24

Buitelaar P, Bryant B, Ide N, Lin J, Pareja-Lora A, Wilcock G (2003) *The Roles of Natural Language and XML*. In: Language and Linguistics, Academia Sinica, Taiwan

Bylander T, Chandrasekaran B (1988) *Generic Tasks in Knowledge-based reasoning: The right level of abstraction for Knowledge Acquisition*. In: Gaines B, Boose J (eds) Knowledge Acquisition of Knowledge Based Systems 1:65–77. Academic Press, London, United Kingdom

Carroll JJ, De Roo J (2003) *OWL Web Ontology Language Test Cases*. W3C Working Draft. *http://www.w3.org/TR/owl-test/*

Casati R, Varzi AC (1999) *Parts And Places: The Structures Of Spatial Representations*. MIT Press, Cambridge, Massachusetts

Chalupsky H, MacGregor, RM (1999) *STELLA - a Lisp-like language for symbolic programming with delivery in Common Lisp, C++ and Java*. In: 1999 Lisp User Group Meeting, Franz Inc., Berkeley, California

Chandrasekaran B, Johnson TR, Benjamins VR (1999) *Ontologies: what are they? why do we need them?* IEEE Intelligent Systems & their applications, Special Issue on Ontologies, 14(1):20–22

Chandrasekaran B, Johnson TR, Smith JW (1992) *Task-structure analysis for knowledge modeling*. Communications of the ACM 35(9):124–137

Chaudhri VK, Farquhar A, Fikes R, Karp PD, Rice JP (1998) *Open Knowledge Base Connectivity 2.0.3.* Technical Report. *http://www.ai.sri.com/~okbc/okbc-2-0-3.pdf*

Chen IA, Markowitz VM (1996) *The Object-Protocol Model (Version 4)*. Technical Report LBNL-32738 (revised). *http://gizmo.lbl.gov/DM_TOOLS/OPM/OPM_4.1/OPM/OPM.html*

Chen PP (1976) *The Entity-Relationship Model: Toward a Unified View of Data*. ACM Transactions on Database Systems 1(1):9–36

Chen W, Kifer M, Warren DS (1993) *Hilog: a foundation for higher-order logic programming*. Journal of Logic Programming 15:187–230

Chikofsky EJ, Cross II JH (1990) *Reverse engineering and design recovery: A taxonomy*. IEEE Software Magazine, 7(1):13–17

Church A (1958) *Ontological Commitment*. The Journal of Philosophy 55:1008–1014

Ciravegna F (2001) *Adaptive Information Extraction from Text by Rule Induction and Generalisation*. In: Nebel B (ed) 17th International Joint Conference on Artificial Intelligence (IJCAI'01). Seattle, Washington. Morgan Kauffmann Publishers, San Francisco, California, pp 1251–1256

Cocchiarella NB (2001) *Logic and Ontology.* Axiomathes 12:117–150. Kluwer Academic Publishers, Dordrecht, The Netherlands

Cocchiarella NB (1991) *Formal Ontology.* In: Burkhardt H, Smith B (eds) Handbook of Metaphysics and Ontology. Philosophia Verlag, Munich, pp 640–647

Conen W, Klapsing R (2001) *Logical Interpretations of RDFS - A Compatibility Guide.* Working paper. November, 2001. *http://nestroy.wi-inf.uni-essen.de/rdf/new_interpretation/*

Conen W, Klapsing R (2000) *A Logical Interpretation of RDF (discussion paper).* Linköping Electronic Articles in Computer and Information Science. Journal of Electronic Transactions on Artificial Intelligence 5(13)

Corcho O, Gómez-Pérez A (2001) *Solving integration problems of e-commerce standards and initiatives through ontological mappings.* In: Gómez-Pérez A, Grüninger M, Stuckenschmidt H, Uschold M (eds) IJCAI'01 Workshop on Ontologies and Information Sharing. Seattle, Washington, pp 131–140. CEUR Workshop Proceedings 47:131–140. Amsterdam, The Netherlands (*http:/ceur-ws.org/Vol-47/*)

Corcho O, Gómez-Pérez A (2000) *A Roadmap to Ontology Specification Languages.* In: Dieng R, Corby O (eds) 12th International Conference in Knowledge Engineering and Knowledge Management (EKAW'00). Juan-Les-Pins, France. (Lecture Notes in Artificial Intelligence LNAI 1937) Springer-Verlag, Berlin, Germany, pp 80–96

Corcho O, Fernández-López M, Gómez-Pérez A, Vicente O (2002) *WebODE: an Integrated Workbench for Ontology Representation, Reasoning and Exchange.* In: Gómez-Pérez A, Benjamins VR (eds) 13th International Conference on Knowledge Engineering and Knowledge Management (EKAW'02). Sigüenza, Spain. (Lecture Notes in Artificial Intelligence LNAI 2473) Springer-Verlag, Berlin, Germany, pp 138–153

Cranefield S, Purvis M (1999) *UML as an ontology modelling language.* In: Fensel D, Knoblock C, Kushmerick N, Rousset MC (eds) IJCAI'99 Workshop on Intelligent Information Integration. Stockholm, Sweden. CEUR Workshop Proceedings 23:5.1–5.8. Amsterdam, The Netherlands (*http://CEUR-WS.org/Vol-23/*)

de Hoog R (1998) *Methodologies for Building Knowledge Based Systems: Achievements and Prospects.* In: Liebowitz J (ed) Handbook of Expert Systems. CRC Press Chapter 1, Boca Raton, Florida

Dean M, Schreiber G (2003) *OWL Web Ontology Language Reference.* W3C Working Draft. *http://www.w3.org/TR/owl-ref/*

Decker S, Erdmann M, Fensel D, Studer R (1999) *Ontobroker: Ontology Based Access to Distributed and Semi-Structured Information.* In: Meersman R, Tari Z, Stevens S (eds) Semantic Issues in Multimedia Systems (DS-8), Rotorua, New Zealand. Kluwer Academic Publisher, Boston, Massachusetts. pp 351–369

Decker S, Brickley D, Saarela J, Angele J (1998) *A Query and Inference Service for RDF*. In: Marchiori M (ed) The Query Languages Workshop (QL'98). Boston, Massachusetts. *http://www.w3.org/TandS/QL/QL98/pp/queryservice.html*

Dieng-Kuntz R, Corby O, Gandon F, Giboin A, Golebiowska J, Matta N, Ribière M (2001) *Méthodes et outils pour la gestion de connaisances. Une approache pluridisciplinaire du Knowledge Management*, 2nd edn, Dunot, Paris, France

Dieng-Kuntz R, Corby O, Giboin A, Ribière M (1998) *Methods and Tools for Corporate Knowledge Management*. In: Gaines BR, Musen M (eds) Eleventh Workshop on Knowledge Acquisition, Modeling and Management (KAW'98), Banff, Canada, KM 3:1–20

Doan A, Madhavan J, Domingos P, Halevy A (2002) *Learning to Map between Ontologies on the Semantic Web*. In: Lassner D (ed) Proceedings of the 11th International World Wide Web Conference (WWW 2002), Honolulu, Hawaii. *http://www2002.org/refereedtrack.html*

Domingue J (1998) *Tadzebao and WebOnto: Discussing, Browsing, and Editing Ontologies on the Web*. In: Gaines BR, Musen MA (eds) 11th International Workshop on Knowledge Acquisition, Modeling and Management (KAW'98). Banff, Canada, KM4:1–20

Domingue J, Motta E (2000) *PlanetOnto: From News Publishing to Integrated Knowledge Management Support*. IEEE Intelligent Systems & their applications 15(3):26–32

Domingue J, Motta E, Watt S (1993) *The Emerging Vital Workbench*. In: Aussenac N, Boy G, Gaines B, Linster M, Ganascia JG, Kodratoff Y (eds) 7th European Workshop on Knowledge Acquisition for Knowledge-Based Systems (EKAW'93). Toulouse and Caylus, France. (Lecture Notes in Computer Science LNCS 723) Springer-Verlag, Berlin, Germany, pp 320–339.

Downs E, Clare P, Coe I (1998) *Structured Analysis and Design Method (SSADM)*. Prentice Hall, New Jersey

Dubuisson O (2000) *ASN.1 - Communication between heterogeneous systems*. Morgan Kaufmann Publishers, San Francisco, California

EAGLES (1996) *EAGLES: Recommendations for the Morphosyntactic Annotation of Corpora*. EAGLES Document EAG--TCWG—MAC/R. University of Birmingham, Birmingham, United Kingdom *http://www.ilc.cnr.it/EAGLES96/annotate/annotate.html*

Enery TMC, Wilson A (2001) *Corpus linguistics: an introduction*. Edinburgh University Press, Edinburgh, United Kingdom

Euzenat J (1996) *Corporate memory through cooperative creation of knowledge bases and hyper-documents*. In: Gaines BR, Musen MA (eds) 10th Knowledge Acquisition for Knowledge-Based Systems Workshop (KAW'96). Banff, Canada. *http://ksi.cpsc.ucalgary.ca/KAW/KAW96/euzenat/euzenat96b.html*

Euzenat J (1995) *Building Consensual Knowledge Bases: Context and Architecture.* In: Mars N (ed) Second International Conference on Building and Sharing of Very Large-Scale Knowledge Bases (KBKS '95). University of Twente, Enschede, The Netherlands. IOS Press, Amsterdam, The Netherlands, pp 143–155

Evett MP, Hendler JA, Spector L (1994) *Parallel Knowledge Representation on the Connection Machine.* Journal of Parallel and Distributed Computing 22:168–184

Farquhar A, Fikes R, Rice J (1997) *The Ontolingua Server: A Tool for Collaborative Ontology Construction.* International Journal of Human Computer Studies 46(6):707–727

Faure D, Poibeau T (2000) *First experiments of using semantic knowledge learned by ASIUM for information extraction task using INTEX.* In: Staab S, Maedche A, Nedellec C, Wiemer-Hastings P (eds) Ontology Learning ECAI-2000 Workshop, pp 7–12

Fellbaum C, Miller GA (1990) *Folk psychology or semantic entailment? A reply to Rips and Conrad.* Psychological Review 97:565–570

Fensel D (2000) *Ontologies: silver bullet for Knowledge Management and Electronic Commerce.* Springer-Verlag, Berlin, Germany. *http://www.cs.vu.nl/~dieter/ftp/spool/silverbullet.pdf*

Fensel D (1995) *The knowledge acquisition and representation language KARL.* Kluwer Academic Publishers, Dordrecht, The Netherlands

Fensel D, van Harmelen F, Horrocks I, McGuinness DL, Patel-Schneider PF (2001) *OIL: An ontology infrastructure for the Semantic Web.* IEEE Intelligent Systems & their applications 16(2):38–44

Fensel D, Angele J, Decker S, Erdmann M, Schnurr HP, Staab S, Studer R, Witt A (1999) *On2broker: Semantic-based access to information sources at the* WWW. In: de Bra P and Leggett J (eds) World Conference on the WWW and Internet (WebNet'99). Honolulu, Hawaii, pp 1.366–1.371

Fernández-López M (1996) *CHEMICALS: ontología de elementos químicos.* Proyecto fin de carrera. Facultad de Informática, Universidad Politécnica de Madrid. Madrid, Spain

Fernández-López M, Gómez-Pérez A (2002a) *Overview and analysis of methodologies for building ontologies.* The Knowledge Engineering Review 17(2):129–156

Fernández-López M, Gómez-Pérez A (2002b) *The integration of OntoClean in WebODE.* In: Angele J, Sure Y (eds) EKAW'02 Workshop on Evaluation of Ontology-based Tools (EON2002), Sigüenza, Spain. CEUR Workshop Proceedings 62:38–52. Amsterdam, The Netherlands. *http://CEUR-WS.org/Vol-62/*

Fernández-López M, Gómez-Pérez A, Rojas-Amaya MD (2000) *Ontologies' crossed life cycles*. In: Dieng R, Corby O (eds) 12th International Conference in Knowledge Engineering and Knowledge Management (EKAW'00). Juan-Les-Pins, France. (Lecture Notes in Artificial Intelligence LNAI 1937) Springer-Verlag, Berlin, Germany, pp 65–79

Fernández-López M, Gómez-Pérez A, Pazos A, Pazos J (1999) *Building a Chemical Ontology Using Methontology and the Ontology Design Environment*. IEEE Intelligent Systems & their applications 4(1):37–46

Fernández-López M, Gómez-Pérez A, Juristo N (1997) *METHONTOLOGY: From Ontological Art Towards Ontological Engineering*. Spring Symposium on Ontological Engineering of AAAI. Stanford University, California, pp 33–40

Fikes R, McGuinness D (2001) *An Axiomatic Semantics for RDF, RDF Schema, and DAML+OIL*. KSL Technical Report KSL-01-01. Stanford, California. *http://www.w3.org/TR/daml+oil-axioms*

Fox MS (1992) *The TOVE Project: A Common-sense Model of the Enterprise*. In: Belli F, Radermacher FJ (eds) Industrial and Engineering Applications of Artificial Intelligence and Expert Systems. (Lecture Notes in Artificial Intelligence LNAI 604) Springer-Verlag, Berlin, Germany, pp 25–34

Friedman-Hill E (2003) *Jess in Action: Java Rule-Based Systems*. Manning Publications Company, Greenwich, Connecticut

Frohn J, Himmeröder R, Kandzia P, Schlepphorst C (2000) *How to Write F-Logic Programs in FLORID - A Tutorial for the Database Language F-Logic*. *http://www.informatik.uni-freiburg.de/~dbis/florid/*

Gambra R (1999) *Historia sencilla de la filosofía*, 24th edn. Rialp, Madrid, Spain

Gangemi A, Guarino N, Oltramari A (2001) *Conceptual analysis of lexical taxonomies: the case of Wordnet top-level*. In: Smith B, Welty C (eds) International Conference on Formal Ontology in Information Systems (FOIS'01). Ogunquit, Maine. ACM Press, New York, pp 3–15

Gangemi A, Pisanelli DM, Steve G (1999) *An Overview of the ONIONS Project: Applying Ontologies to the Integration of Medical Terminologies*. Data & Knowledge Engineering 31(2):183–220

Gangemi A, Pisanelli DM, Steve G (1998) *Some Requirements and Experiences in Engineering Terminological Ontologies over the WWW*. In: Gaines BR, Musen MA (eds) 11th International Workshop on Knowledge Acquisition, Modeling and Management (KAW'98). Banff, Canada, SHARE10:1–20

Genesereth MR (1990) *The Epikit Manual*. Technical Report. Epistemics Inc., Palo Alto, California. *http://logic.stanford.edu/papers/epikit-1.4-manual.ps*

Genesereth MR, Fikes RE (1992) *Knowledge Interchange Format. Version 3.0. Reference Manual*. Technical Report Logic-92-1. Computer Science Department. Stanford University, California. *http://meta2.stanford.edu/kif/Hypertext/kif-manual.html*

Gennari JH, Musen MA, Fergerson RW, Grosso WE, Crubézy M, Eriksson H, Noy NF, Tu SW (2003) *The Evolution of Protégé: An Environment for Knowledge-Based Systems Development*. International Journal of Human-Computer Studies 58(1):89–123

Giarratano JC, Riley G (1998) *Expert Systems: Principles and Programming*, 3rd edn, PWS Publishing, Boston, Massachusetts

Goasdoué F, Lattes V, Rousset M (2000) *The Use of CARIN Language and Algorithms for Information Integration: The PICSEL Project*. International Journal of Cooperative Information Systems (IJCIS) 9(4):383–401

Gómez-Pérez A (2002) *A Survey on Ontology Tools*, OntoWeb deliverable D1.3. *http://ontoweb.aifb.uni-karlsruhe.de/About/Deliverables/D13_v1-0.zip*

Gómez-Pérez A (2001) *Evaluation of Ontologies*. International Journal of Intelligent Systems 16(3):391–409

Gómez-Pérez A (1999) *Evaluation of Taxonomic Knowledge on Ontologies and Knowledge-Based Systems*. In: Gaines BR, Kremer R, Musen MA (eds) 12th Knowledge Acquisition for Knowledge-Based Systems Workshop (KAW'99), Banff, Canada, pp 6.1:1–18

Gómez-Pérez A (1998) *Knowledge Sharing and Reuse*. In: Liebowitz J (ed) Handbook of Expert Systems. CRC Chapter 10, Boca Raton, Florida

Gómez-Pérez A (1996) *A Framework to Verify Knowledge Sharing Technology*. Expert Systems with Application 11(4):519–529

Gómez-Pérez A (1994a) *Some Ideas and Examples to Evaluate Ontologies*. Knowledge Systems Laboratory, Stanford University, California. *http://www-ksl.stanford.edu/KSL_Abstracts/KSL-94-65.html*

Gómez-Pérez A (1994b) *From Knowledge Based Systems to Knowledge Sharing Technology: Evaluation and Assessment*. Knowledge Systems Laboratory, Stanford University, California. *http://www-ksl.stanford.edu/KSL_Abstracts/KSL-94-73.html*

Gómez-Pérez A, Corcho O (2002) *Ontology Languages for the Semantic Web*. IEEE Intelligent Systems & their applications 17(1):54–60

Gómez-Pérez A, Rojas MD (1999) *Ontological Reengineering and Reuse*. In: Fensel D, Studer R (eds) 11th European Workshop on Knowledge Acquisition, Modeling and Management (EKAW'99). Dagstuhl Castle, Germany. (Lecture Notes in Artificial Intelligence LNAI 1621) Springer-Verlag, Berlin, Germany, pp 139–156

Gómez-Pérez A, Juristo N, Montes C, Pazos J (1997) *Ingeniería del Conocimiento: Diseño y Construcción de Sistemas Expertos*. Ceura, Madrid, Spain

Gómez-Pérez A, Fernández-López M, de Vicente A (1996) *Towards a method to conceptualize domain ontologies*. In: van der Vet P (ed) ECAI'96 Workshop on Ontological Engineering. Budapest, Hungary, pp 41–52

Gómez-Pérez A, Juristo N, Pazos J (1995) *Evaluation and assessment of knowledge sharing technology*. In: Mars N (ed) Towards Very Large Knowledge Bases: Knowledge Building and Knowledge Sharing (KBKS'95). University of Twente, Enschede, The Netherlands. IOS Press, Amsterdam, The Netherlands, pp 289–296

Gordijn J, de Bruin H, Akkermans JM (2001) *Scenario methods for viewpoint integration in e-business requirements engineering*. In: Sprague RH Jr (ed) 34th Hawaii International Conference On System Sciences (HICSS-34)-volume 7 p. 7032. Hawaii. IEEE CS Press, Los Alamitos, California. *http://www.cs.vu.nl/~gordijn/h34-1-1.pdf*

Greenwood E (1973) *Metodología de la investigación social* Paidós, Buenos Aires, Argentina

Gruber TR (1993a) *A translation approach to portable ontology specification*. Knowledge Acquisition 5(2):199–220

Gruber TR (1993b) *Toward principles for the design of ontologies used for knowledge sharing*. In: Guarino N, Poli R (eds) International Workshop on Formal Ontology in Conceptual Analysis and Knowledge Representation. Padova, Italy. (Formal Ontology in Conceptual Analysis and Knowledge Representation) Kluwer Academic Publishers, Deventer, The Netherlands. *http://citeseer.nj.nec.com/gruber93toward.html*

Gruber TR (1992) *Ontolingua: A Mechanism to Support Portable Ontologies*. Technical report KSL-91-66, Knowledge Systems Laboratory, Stanford University, Stanford, California. *ftp://ftp.ksl.stanford.edu/pub/KSL_Reports/KSL-91-66.ps*

Gruber TR, Olsen G (1994) *An ontology for Engineering Mathematics*. In: Doyle J, Torasso P, Sandewall E (eds) Fourth International Conference on Principles of Knowledge Representation and Reasoning. Bonn, Germany. Morgan Kaufmann Publishers, San Francisco, California, pp 258–269

Grüninger M, Fox MS (1995) *Methodology for the design and evaluation of ontologies* In Skuce D (ed) IJCAI95 Workshop on Basic Ontological Issues in Knowledge Sharing, pp 6.1–6.10

Guarino N (1998) *Formal Ontology in Information Systems*. In: Guarino N (ed) 1st International Conference on Formal Ontology in Information Systems (FOIS'98). Trento, Italy. IOS Press, Amsterdam, pp 3–15

Guarino N (1994) *The Ontological Level*. In: Casati R, Smith B, White (eds) *Philosophy and the Cognitive Science*. Hölder-Pichler-Tempsky, Vienna, Austria, pp 443–456

Guarino N, Giaretta P (1995) *Ontologies and Knowledge Bases: Towards a Terminological Clarification*. In: Mars N (ed) Towards Very Large Knowledge Bases: Knowledge Building and Knowledge Sharing (KBKS'95). University of Twente, Enschede, The Netherlands. IOS Press, Amsterdam, The Netherlands, pp 25–32

Guarino N, Welty C (2000) *A Formal Ontology of Properties*. In: Dieng R, Corby O (eds) 12th International Conference in Knowledge Engineering and Knowledge Management (EKAW'00). Juan-Les-Pins, France. (Lecture Notes in Artificial Intelligence LNAI 1937) Springer-Verlag, Berlin, Germany, pp 97–112

Guarino N, Masolo C, Vetere G (1999) *OntoSeek: Content-Based Access to the Web*. IEEE Intelligent Systems & their applications 14(3)70–80

Guarino N, Carrara M, Giaretta P (1994) *Formalizing Ontological Commitments*. In: Hayes-Roth B, Korf RE (eds) 12th National Conference on Artificial Intelligence (AAAI'94). Seattle, Washington. AAAI Press, Menlo Park, California, pp 1.560–1.568

Guha RV (1991) *Contexts: A Formalization and Some Applications*. PhD thesis, Computer Science Department, Stanford University, Stanford, California. *http://www-formal.stanford.edu/guha/guha-thesis.ps*

Haarslev V, Möller R (2001) *Description of the RACER System and its Applications*. In: Goble CA, McGuinness DL, Möller R, Patel-Schneider PF (eds) International Workshop on Description Logics (DL'01). Stanford University, California. CEUR Workshop Proceedings 49:132–141. Amsterdam, The Netherlands (*http://CEUR-WS.org/Vol-49/*)

Hahn U., and Schulz S. 2000. *Towards Very Large Terminological Knowledge Bases: A Case Study from Medicine*. Hamilton HJ (ed) Advances in Artificial Intelligence, 13th Biennial Conference of the Canadian Society for Computational Studies of Intelligence (AI 2000), Montréal,, Quebec, Canada. (Lecture Notes in Computer Science LNCS 1822) Springer-Verlag, Berlin, Germany, pp 176–186

Halliday MAK (1985). *An introduction to functional grammar*. Edward Arnold, London, United Kingdom

Handschuh S, Staab S, Mäedche A (2001) *CREAM — Creating relational metadata with a component-based, ontology-driven annotation framework*. In: Gil Y, Musen M, Shavlik J (eds) First International Conference on Knowledge Capture (KCAP'01). Victoria, Canada. ACM Press (1-58113-380-4), New York, pp 76–83

Hayes P (2002) *RDF Model Theory*. W3C Working Draft. *http://www.w3.org/TR/rdf-mt/*

Hearst MA (1992) *Automatic acquisition of hyponyms from large text corpora*. In Zampolli A (ed) Proceedings of the 15th International Conference on Computational Linguistic (COLING-92). Nantes, France, 1992.

Heflin JD (2001) *Towards the Semantic Web: Knowledge Representation in a Dynamic, Distributed Environment*. PhD dissertation, Department of Computer Science, University of Maryland, College Park, Maryland. *http://www.cs.umd.edu/projects/plus/SHOE/pubs/heflin-thesis-orig.pdf*

Heflin JD, Hendler JA (2001) *A Portrait of the Semantic Web in Action.* IEEE Intelligent Systems & their applications 16(2): 54–59

Heflin JD, Hendler JA (2000) *Searching the Web with SHOE.* In: Bollacker K, Giles CL, Lawrence S (eds) AAAI Workshop on Articial Intelligence for Web Search. AAAI Press, Menlo Park, California, pp 35–40

Hermenegildo M, Bueno F, Cabeza D, Carro M, García M, López P, Puebla G (2000) *The Ciao Logic Programming Environment.* In: Lloyd JW, Dahl V, Furbach U, Kerber M, Lau K, Palamidessi C, Pereira LM, Sagiv Y, Stuckey PJ (eds) International Conference on Computational Logic (CL'00). London, United Kingdom. (Lecture Notes in Computer Science LNCS 1861), Springer-Verlag, Berlin, Germany

Hermes H (1973) *Introduction to Mathematical Logic.* Springer-Verlag, Berlin, Germany

Horrocks I (2000) *A Denotational Semantics for OIL-Lite and Standard OIL.* Technical report. *http://www.cs.man.ac.uk/~horrocks/OIL/Semantics/*

Horrocks I, van Harmelen F (eds) (2001) *Reference Description of the DAML+OIL (March 2001) Ontology Markup Language.* Technical report. *http://www.daml.org/2001/03/reference.html*

Horrocks I, Fensel D, Harmelen F, Decker S, Erdmann M, Klein M (2000) *OIL in a Nutshell.* In: Dieng R, Corby O (eds) 12th International Conference in Knowledge Engineering and Knowledge Management (EKAW'00). Juan-Les-Pins, France. (Lecture Notes in Artificial Intelligence LNAI 1937) Springer-Verlag, Berlin, Germany, pp 1–16

Horrocks I, Sattler U, Tobies S (1999) *Practical reasoning for expressive description logics.* In: Ganzinger H, McAllester D, Voronkov A (eds) 6th International Conference on Logic for Programming and Automated Reasoning (LPAR'99). Tbilisi, Georgia. (Lecture Notes in Artificial Intelligence LNAI 1705) Springer-Verlag, Berlin, Germany, pp 161–180

IEEE (1996) *IEEE Standard for Developing Software Life Cycle Processes.* IEEE Computer Society. New York. IEEE Std 1074-1995

IEEE (1990) *IEEE Standard Glossary of Software Engineering Terminology.* IEEE Computer Society. New York. IEEE Std 610.121990

Ikehara S, Miyazaki M, Shirai S, Yokoo A, Nakaiwa H, Ogura K, Ooyatna Y, Hayashi Y (1997) *Goi-Taikei: A Japanese Lexicon.* Iwanami Shoten, Tokyo, Japan

ISO 8879-1986 (1986) *Information processing - Text and Office Systems - Standard Generalized Markup Language (SGML),* 1st edn, International Organization for Standardization, Geneva, Switzerland

KACTUS (1996) *The KACTUS Booklet version 1.0.* Esprit Project 8145 KACTUS. *http://www.swi.psy.uva.nl/projects/NewKACTUS/Reports.html*

Kalfoglou Y, Robertson D (1999a) *Use of Formal Ontologies to Support Error Checking in Specifications*. In: Fensel D, Studer R (eds) 11th European Workshop on Knowledge Acquisition, Modelling and Management (EKAW'99), Dagsthul, Germany. (Lecture Notes in Artificial Intelligence LNAI 1621) Springer-Verlag, Berlin, Germany, pp 207–224

Kalfoglou Y, Robertson D (1999b) *Managing Ontological Constraints*. In: Benjamins VR, Chandrasekaran A, Gómez-Pérez A, Guarino N, Uschold M (eds) IJCAI99 workshop on Ontologies and Problem-Solving Methods (KRR-5), Stockholm, Sweden. CEUR Workshop Proceedings 18:5.1–5.13. Amsterdam, The Netherlands (*http://CEUR-WS.org/Vol-18/*)

Kankaanpää, T (1999) *Design and implementation of a conceptual network and ontology editor*. VTT Information Technology, Research report TTE1-4-99

Karp PD, Paley SM (1995) *Knowledge representation in the large*. In: Mellish CS (ed) 14th International Joint Conference on Artificial Intelligence (IJCAI'95). Montreal, Canada. Morgan Kaufmann Publishers, San Francisco, California, pp 751–758

Karp PD, Chaudhri V, Thomere J (1999) *XOL: An XML-Based Ontology Exchange Language*. Version 0.3. Technical Report. *http://www.ai.sri.com/~pkarp/xol/xol.html*

Karp PD, Myers K, Gruber TR (1995) *The Generic Frame Protocol*. In: Mellish CS (ed) 14th International Joint Conference on Artificial Intelligence (IJCAI'95). Montreal, Canada. Morgan Kaufmann Publishers, San Francisco, California, pp 768–774

Karvounarakis G, Christophides V (2002) *The RQL v1.5 User Manual*. Technical Report, 2002. *http://139.91.183.30:9090/RDF/RQL/Manual.html*

Kendall EF, Dutra ME, McGuinness DL (2002) *Towards A Commercial Ontology Development Environment* (poster). In: Horrocks I, Hendler JA (eds) First International Semantic Web Conference (ISWC'02). Sardinia, Italy.

Kendall KE, Kendall JE (1995) *Systems analysis and design*, 3rd edn, Prentice Hall, New Jersey

Kent RE (1998) *Conceptual Knowledge Markup Language (version 0.2)* *http://www.ontologos.org/CKML/CKML%200.2.html*

Kietz JU, Maedche A, Volz R (2000) *A Method for Semi-Automatic Ontology Acquisition from a Corporate Intranet*. In: Aussenac-Gilles N, Biébow B, Szulman S (eds) EKAW'00 Workshop on Ontologies and Texts. Juan-Les-Pins, France. CEUR Workshop Proceedings 51:4.1–4.14. Amsterdam, The Netherlands (*http://CEUR-WS.org/Vol-51/*)

Kifer M, Lausen G, Wu J (1995) *Logical Foundations of Object-Oriented and Frame-Based Languages*. Journal of the ACM 42(4): 741–843

Klinker G, Bhola C, Dallemagne G, Marques D, McDermott J (1991) *Usable and reusable programming constructs*. Knowledge Acquisition 3:117–136

Knight K, Luck S (1994) *Building a Large Knowledge Base for Machine Translation*. In: Hayes-Roth B, Korf RE (eds) 12th National Conference on Artificial Intelligence (AAAI'94). Seattle, Washington. AAAI Press, Menlo Park, California, pp 1:773–778

Kogut P, Holmes W (2001) *AeroDAML: Applying Information Extraction to Generate DAML Annotation from Web Pages*. In: Handschuh S, Dieng R, Staab S (eds) KCAP'01 Workshop on Semantic Markup and Annotation. Victoria, Canada. *http://semannot2001.aifb.uni-karlsruhe.de/schedule_new.html*

Kogut P, Cranefield S, Hart L, Dutra M, Baclawski K, Kokar M, Smith J (2002) *UML for Ontology Development*. The Knowledge Engineering Review 17(1):61–64

Lassila O, McGuinness D (2001) *The Role of Frame-Based Representation on the Semantic Web*. Technical Report KSL-01-02. Knowledge Systems Laboratory. Stanford University. Stanford, California

Lassila O, Swick R (1999) *Resource Description Framework (RDF) Model and Syntax Specification*. W3C Recommendation. *http://www.w3.org/TR/REC-rdf-syntax/*

Leech G (1997) *Introducing corpus annotation*. In: Garside R, Leech G, McEnery AM (eds) Corpus Annotation: Linguistic Information from Computer Text Corpora. Longman Addison-Wesley, London, United Kingdom, pp 1–18

Léger A, Arbant G, Barrett P, Gitton S, Gómez-Pérez A, Holm R, Lehtola A, Mougenot I, Nistal A, Varvarigou T, Vinesse J (2000) *MKBEEM: Ontology domain modeling support for multilingual services in e-Commerce*. In: Benjamins VR, Gómez-Pérez A, Guarino N, Uschold M (eds) ECAI'00 Workshop on Applications of Ontologies and PSMs. Berlin, Germany, pp 19.1–19.4

Lenat DB, Guha RV (1990) *Building Large Knowledge-based Systems: Representation and Inference in the Cyc Project*. Addison-Wesley, Boston, Massachusetts

Levesque HJ (1984) *Foundations of a functional approach to knowledge representation*. Artificial Intelligence 23(2):155–212

Levesque HJ, Brachman RJ (1985) *A fundamental tradeoff in knowledge representation and reasoning (revised version)*. In Brachman RJ, Levesque HJ (eds) Readings in Knowledge Representation. Morgan Kaufmann Publishers, San Francisco, California, pp 41–70

Levy AY, Rousset MC (1998) *CARIN: A Representation Language Combining Horn rules and Description Logics*. Artificial Intelligence Journal 104(1-2): 165–209

Lloyd JW (1993) *Foundations of Logic Programming*. Springer-Verlag, New York

Loom (1995) *Tutorial for Loom version 2.1*. Information Sciences Institute. University of Southern California. *http://www.isi.edu/isd/LOOM/documentation/tutorial2.1.html*

Lowe, E. J. (1989) *Kinds of Being. A Study of Individuation, Identity and the Logic of Sortal Terms*. Basil Blackwell, Oxford, United Kingdom

Ludäscher B, Yang G, Kifer M (2000) *FLORA: The Secret of Object-Oriented Logic Programming*. *http://www.cs.sunysb.edu/~sbprolog/flora/docs/manual.ps*

Ludäscher B, Himmeröder R, Lausen G, May W, Schlepphorst C (1998) *Managing Semistructured Data with FLORID: A Deductive Object-Oriented Perspective*. Information Systems 23(8):589–612

Luke S, Heflin JD (2000) *SHOE 1.01. Proposed Specification*. Technical Report. Parallel Understanding Systems Group. Department of Computer Science. University of Maryland. *http://www.cs.umd.edu/projects/plus/SHOE/spec1.01.htm*

Luke S, Spector L, Rager D, Hendler JA (1997) *Ontology-based Web Agents*. In: Johnson WL, Jennings N (ed) First International Conference on Autonomous Agents (AA'97), Marina del Rey, California. ACM Press, New York, pp 59–66

MacGregor R (1999) *Retrospective on LOOM*. Technical Report. Information Sciences Institute. University of Southern California. *http://www.isi.edu/isd/LOOM/papers/macgregor/Loom_Retrospective.html*

MacGregor R (1991) *Inside the LOOM clasifier*. SIGART bulletin 2(3):70–76

Maedche A (2002) *Ontology Learning for the Semantic Web*, Kluwer Academic Publishers, Boston, Massachusetts

Maedche A, Staab S (2000a) *Semi-automatic Engineering of Ontologies from Text*. In Chang SK, Obozinski WR (eds) 12th International Conference on Software Engineering and Knowledge Engineering (SEKE'2000). Chicago, Illinois.

Maedche A, Staab S (2000b) *Mining Ontologies from Texts*. In: Dieng R, Corby O (eds) 12th International Conference in Knowledge Engineering and Knowledge Management (EKAW'00). Juan-Les-Pins, France. (Lecture Notes in Artificial Intelligence LNAI 1937) Springer-Verlag, Berlin, Germany, pp 189–202

Maedche A, Volz R (2001) *The Text-To-Onto Ontology Extraction and Maintenance Environment*. In: Kurfess FJ, Hilario M (eds) ICDM Workshop on integrating data mining and knowledge management, San Jose, California, USA.

Maedche A, Motik B, Stojanovic L, Studer R, Volz R (2003) *Ontologies for Enterprise Knowledge Management*. IEEE Intelligent Systems 18(2):26–33

Maedche A, Motik B, Silva N, Volz R (2002) *MAFRA – A Mapping Framework for Distributed Ontologies*. In: Gómez Pérez A, Benjamins R (eds) 13th International Conference on Knowledge Engineering and Knowledge Management (EKAW'02), Sigüenza, Spain. (Lecture Notes in Artificial Intelligence LNAI 2473) Springer-Verlag, Berlin, Germany, pp 235–250

Maedche A, Schnurr HP, Staab S, Studer R (2000) *Representation Language-Neutral Modeling of Ontologies*. In: Frank U (eds) German Workshop "Modellierung 2000". Koblenz, Germany, pp 128–144

Mahesh K (1996) *Ontology development for machine translation: Ideology and Methodology*. Technical Report MCCS-96-292. Computing Research Laboratory, New Mexico State University, Las Cruces, New Mexico. *http://citeseer.nj.nec.com/mahesh96ontology.html*

Mahesh K, Nirenburg S (1995) *Semantic classification for practical natural language processing*. In: Schwartz RP, Kwasnik BH, Beghtol C, Smith PJ, Jacob E (eds) 6ᵗʰ ASIS SIG/CR Classification Research Workshop: An Interdisciplinary Meeting. Chicago, Illinois, pp 79–94

Mallery JC (1994) *A common lisp hypermedia server*. In: Nierstrasz O (ed) First International World Wide Web Conference, Geneva, Switzerland, pp 239–247

Manola F, Miller E (2003) *RDF Primer*. W3C Working Draft. *http://www.w3.org/TR/rdf-primer/*

Marías J (2001) *Historia de la filosofía*, 4ᵗʰ edn, Filosofía y Pensamiento, Alianza Editorial, Madrid, Spain

McCracken DD, Jackson MA (1982) *Life Cycle Concept Considered Harmful*. ACM Software Engineering notes. 7(2):29–32

McDermott, J (1988) *Preliminary Steps Towards a Taxonomy of Problem Solving Methods*. In: Marcus S (ed) Automating knowledge acquisition for expert systems. Kluwer Academic Publishers, Boston, Massachusetts, pp 225–255

McEntire R, Karp PD, Abernethy N, Olken F, Kent RE, Dejongh M, Tarczy-Hornoch P, Benton D, Pathak D, Helt G, Lewis S, Kosky A, Neumann E, Hodnett D, Tolda L, Topaloglou T (1999) *An Evaluation of Ontology Exchange Languages for Bioinformatics*. Technical Report. *ftp://smi.stanford.edu/pub/bio-ontology/OntologyExchange.doc*

McGuinness D, Fikes R, Rice J, Wilder S (2000) *The Chimaera Ontology Environment*. In: Rosenbloom P, Kautz HA, Porter B, Dechter R, Sutton R, Mittal V (eds) 17ᵗʰ National Conference on Artificial Intelligence (AAAI'00). Austin, Texas, pp 1123–1124

Mena E, Illarramendi A (2001) *Ontology-Based Query Processing for Global Information Systems*. Kluwer Academic Publishers, Boston, Massachusetts

Mena E, Illarramendi A, Kashyap V, Sheth AP (2000) *OBSERVER: An Approach for Query Processing in Global Information Systems based on Interoperation across Pre-existing Ontologies*. International Journal on Distributed and Parallel Databases 8(2):223–271

Mena E, Kashyap V, Sheth AP, Illarramendi A (1996) *OBSERVER: An Approach for Query Processing in Global Information Systems based on Interoperation across Pre-existing Ontologies*. In: Litwin W (ed) First IFCIS International

Conference on Cooperative Information Systems (CoopIS'96). Brussels, Belgium, pp 14–25

Michalsky R (1980) *Knowledge Acquisition through conceptual clustering: a theoretical framework and algorithm for partitioning data into conjunctive concepts.* International Journal of Policy Analysis and Information Systems 4(3):219–243

Miller GA (1995) *WordNet: a lexical database for English.* Communications of the ACM 38(11):39–41

Miller GA, Beckwith R, Fellbaum C, Gross D, Miller K (1990) *Introduction to WordNet: An on-line lexical database.* International Journal of Lexicography 3(4):235–244

Mitchell TM, Allen J, Chalasani P, Cheng J, Etzioni O, Ringuette M, Schlimmer JC (1991) *THEO: A framework for self-improving systems.* In: VanLehn K (ed) Architectures for Intelligence, Chapter 12. Laurence Erlbaum, New York, pp 323–355

Miyoshi H, Sugiyama K, Kobayashi M, Ogino T (1996) *An overview of the EDR Electronic Dictionary and the Current Status of its utilization.* In: Tsujii J (ed) 16th International Conference on Computational Linguistics (COLING'96). Copenhagen, Denmark, pp 1090–1093

Mizoguchi R, Vanwelkenhuysen J, Ikeda M (1995) *Task Ontology for reuse of problem solving knowledge.* In: Mars N (ed) Towards Very Large Knowledge Bases: Knowledge Building and Knowledge Sharing (KBKS'95). University of Twente, Enschede, The Netherlands. IOS Press, Amsterdam, The Netherlands, pp 46–57

Mohedano E (2000) *Ontología de parámetros químicos de iones monoatómicos (alcalinos e hidrógeno) en variables físicas y humanas para aplicaciones de medio ambiente.* Final Year Project. Facultad de Informática, Universidad Politécnica de Madrid, Spain

Morik K, Kietz JU (1989) *A Bootstrapping Approach to Conceptual Clustering.* In: Segre AM (ed) Proceedings of the Sixth International Workshop on Machine Learning, Ithaca, New York. Morgan Kaufmann Publishers, San Francisco, California, pp 503–504

Motta E (1999) *Reusable Components for Knowledge Modelling: Principles and Case Studies in Parametric Design.* IOS Press, Amsterdam, The Netherlands

Mowbray TJ, Zahavi R (1995) *The essential CORBA: System Integration Using Distributed Objects.* John Wiley & Sons and Object Management Group, Chichester, United Kingdom

Musen MA (1993) *An overview of knowledge acquisition.* In: David JM, Krivine JP, Simmons R (eds) Second Generation Expert Systems. Springer-Verlag, Berlin, Germany, pp 415–438

Musen MA (1989) *Automated support for building and extending expert models.* Machine Learning 4:347–376

NCITS (1998) *Draft proposed American National standard for Knowledge Interchange Format.* National Committee for Information Technology Standards, Technical Committee T2 (Information Interchange and Interpretation). *http://logic.stanford.edu/kif/dpans.html*

Neches R, Fikes RE, Finin T, Gruber TR, Senator T, Swartout WR (1991) *Enabling technology for knowledge sharing.* AI Magazine 12(3):36–56

Newell A (1982) *The Knowledge Level.* Artificial Intelligence 18(1):87–127

Niles I, Pease RA (2001) *Towards a standard upper ontology.* In: Smith B, Welty C (eds) International Conference on Formal Ontology in Information Systems (FOIS'01). Ogunquit, Maine. ACM Press, New York, pp 2–9

Noy NF, Musen MA (2002) *Evaluating Ontology-Mapping Tools: Requirements and Experience.* In: Angele J, Sure Y (eds) EKAW'02 Workshop on Evaluation of Ontology-based Tools (EON2002). Sigüenza, Spain. CEUR Workshop Proceedings   62:1–114.   Amsterdam,   The   Netherlands (*http://CEUR-WS.org/Vol-62/*)

Noy NF, Musen MA (2001) *Anchor-PROMPT: Using Non-Local Context for Semantic Matching.* In: Gómez-Pérez A, Grüninger M, Stuckenschmidt H, Uschold M (eds) IJCAI'01 Workshop on Ontologies and Information Sharing. Seattle, Washington, pp 63–70

Noy NF, Musen MA (2000) *PROMPT: Algorithm and Tool for Automated Ontology Merging and Alignment.* In: Rosenbloom P, Kautz HA, Porter B, Dechter R, Sutton R, Mittal V (eds) 17th National Conference on Artificial Intelligence (AAAI'00). Austin, Texas, pp 450–455

Noy NF, Musen MA (1999) *SMART: Automated Support for Ontology Merging and Alignment.* In: Gaines BR, Kremer B, Musen MA (eds) 12th Banff Workshop on Knowledge Acquisition, Modeling, and Management. Banff, Alberta, Canada, 4-7:1–20

Noy NF, Fergerson RW, Musen MA (2000) *The knowledge model of Protege-2000: Combining interoperability and flexibility.* In: Dieng R, Corby O (eds) 12th International Conference in Knowledge Engineering and Knowledge Management (EKAW'00). Juan-Les-Pins, France. (Lecture Notes in Artificial Intelligence LNAI 1937) Springer-Verlag, Berlin, Germany, pp 17–32

Object Management Group (1997) *Object Constraint Language specification.* *ftp://ftp.omg.org/pub/docs/ad/97-08-08.pdf*

Ortega y Gasset J (1939) *El tema de nuestro tiempo*, 2nd edn, Colección Austral, Espasa-Calpe, Buenos Aires, Argentina

Park JY, Gennari JH, Musen MA (1998) *Mappings for Reuse in Knowledge-Based Systems.* In: Gaines BR, Musen MA (eds) 11th International Workshop on

Knowledge Acquisition, Modeling and Management (KAW'98). Banff, Canada, pp SHARE16:1–20

Patel-Schneider PF, Hayes P, Horrocks I (2003) *OWL Web Ontology Language Semantics and Abstract Syntax.* W3C Working Draft. *http://www.w3.org/TR/owl-semantics/*

Pease RA, Carrico TM (1997) *JTF-ATD Core Plan Representation: A Progress Report.* In: Farquhar A, Gruninger M, Gómez-Pérez A, Uschold M, van der Vet P (eds) AAAI'97 Spring Symposium on Ontological Engineering. Stanford University, California, pp 95–99

Pease RA, Niles I (2002) *IEEE Standard Upper Ontology: A Progress Report.* The Knowledge Engineering Review 17(1):65–70

Perrière G, Gautier C (1993) *ColiGene: object centered representation for the study of E. coli gene expressivity by sequence analysis.* Biochimie 75(5):415–422

Pinilla Ponz P (1999) *Ontología de minerales. Aplicación a la clase de los silicatos.* Final-Year Project. Facultad de Informática, Universidad Politécnica de Madrid, Spain

Pinto S, Gómez-Pérez A, Martins JP (1999) *Some issues on ontology integration.* In: Benjamins VR (ed) IJCAI'99 Workshop on Ontology and Problem Solving Methods: Lessons Learned and Future Trends. Stockholm, Sweden. CEUR Workshop Proceedings 18:7.1–7.12. Amsterdam, The Netherlands (*http://CEUR-WS.org/Vol-18/*)

Preece A, Hui K, Gray A, Marti P, Bench-Capon T, Cui Z, Jones D (2001) *KRAFT: An Agent Architecture For Knowledge Fusion.* International Journal of Cooperative Information Systems 10(1&2):171–195

Pressmann RS (2000) *Software Engineering. A Practitioner's Approach.* 5th Edition. McGraw-Hill, New York

Quine WO (1961) *From a Logical Point of View, Nine Logico-Philosophical Essays.* Harvard University Press, Cambridge, Massachusetts

Raggett D, Le Hors A, Jacobs I (1999) *HTML 4.01 Specification.* W3C Recommendation. *http://www.w3.org/TR/html401/*

Rechenmann F (1993) *Building and sharing large knowledge bases in molecular genetics.* In: Fuchi K, Yokoi T (eds) Second International Conference on Building and Sharing of Very Large-Scale Knowledge Bases (KBKS '95). Tokyo, Japan. IOS Press, Tokyo, Japan, pp 291–301

Rector AL, Bechhofer S, Goble CA, Horrocks I, Nowlan WA, Solomon WD (1997) *The GRAIL concept modelling language for medical terminology.* Artificial Intelligence in Medicine 9:139–171

Rector AL, Solomon WD, Nowlan WA, Rush TW (1995) *A Terminology Server for Medical Language and Medical Information Systems.* Methods of Information in Medicine 34:147–157

Rice J, Farquhar A (1998) *OKBC: a Rich API on the Cheap*. Technical Report KSL-98-09. Knowledge Systems Laboratory, Stanford University. *ftp://ftp.ksl.stanford.edu/pub/KSL_Reports/KSL-98-29.pdf*

Riva A, Ramoni M (1996) *LispWeb: a Specialised HTTP Server for Distributed AI Applications*. Computer Networks and ISDN Systems 28(7–11):953–961

Rojas MD (1998) *Ontologías de iones monoatómicos en variables físicos del medio ambiente*. Proyecto Fin de Carrera. Facultad de Informática, Universidad Politécnica de Madrid, Madrid, Spain

Rumbaugh J, Jacobson I, Booch G (1998) *The Unified Modeling Language Reference Manual*. Addison-Wesley, Boston, Massachusetts

Russell S, Norvig P (1995) *Artificial Intelligence: A Modern Approach*. Englewood Cliffs, New Jersey

Sagonas K, Swift T, Warren DS (1994) *XSB as an efficient deductive database engine*. In Snodgrass RT, Winslett M (eds) 1994 ACM SIGMOD International Conference on Management of Data (SIGMOD'94), pp 442–453

Schreiber G, Akkermans H, Anjewierden A, de Hoog R, Shadbolt N, van de Velde W, Wielinga B (1999) *Knowledge engineering and management. The CommonKADS Methodology*. MIT press, Cambridge, Massachusetts

Schreiber ATh, Wielinga BJ, Jansweijer W (1995) *The KACTUS View on the 'O' World*. In Skuce D (ed) IJCAI95 Workshop on Basic Ontological Issues in Knowledge Sharing, pp 15.1–15.10

Schreiber ATh, Wielinga BJ, de Hoog R, Akkermans JM, Van de Velde W (1994) *CommonKADS: A comprehensive methodology for KBS development*. IEEE Expert 9(6):28–37

Shadbolt N, Motta E, Rouge A (1993) *Constructing Knowledge-Based Systems*. IEEE Software 10(6):34–39

Simons P (1987) *Parts, a study in Ontology*. Clarendon Press, Oxford, United Kingdom, Chapters 1–3, pp 5–128

Sintek M, Decker S (2001) *TRIPLE - An RDF Query, Inference, and Transformation Language*. In: Seipel D (ed) Deductive Databases and Knowledge Management (DDLP'01). Tokyo, Japan, pp 364–378

Skuce D (1996) *IKARUS: Intelligent knowledge acquisition and retrieval universal system*. Technical Report. *http://www.csi.uottawa.ca/~kavanagh/Ikarus/Ikarus4.html*

Skuce D, Lethbridge TC (1995) *CODE4: A Unified System for Managing Conceptual Knowledge*. International Journal of Human-Computer Studies 42(4):413–451

Smith MK, Welty C, McGuinness DL (2003) *OWL Web Ontology Language Guide*. W3C Working Draft. *http://www.w3.org/TR/owl-guide/*

Sowa JF (1999) *Knowledge Representation: Logical, Philosophical, and Computational Foundations.* Brooks Cole Publishing Co., Pacific Grove, California

Staab S, Schnurr HP, Studer R, Sure Y (2001) *Knowledge Processes and Ontologies.* IEEE Intelligent Systems 16(1):26–34

Staab S, Erdmann M, Maedche A, Decker S (2000) *An Extensible Approach for Modeling Ontologies in RDF(S).* In: Constantopoulos P (ed) ECDL 2000 Workshop on the Semantic Web, Lisbon, Portugal, pp 11–22

Stanley MT (1986) *CML: a knowledge representation language with application to requirements modeling.* MS thesis. University of Toronto, Toronto, Canada.

Steele GL (1990) *Common Lisp the Language, 2nd edn,* Digital Press, Woburn, Massachusetts

Steels L (1993) *Corporate Knowledge Management.* In: Cuena (ed) Knowledge oriented software design: extended papers from the IFIP TC 12 Workshop on Artificial Intelligence from the Information Processing Perspective, AIFIPP, Madrid, Spain. Published in 1993 in IFIP Transactions: Computer Science and Technology. North Holland, Amsterdam, The Netherlands, pp 91–116

Steels L (1990) *Components of expertise.* AI Magazine 11(2):28–49

Steve G, Gangemi A, Pisanelli DM (1998) *Integrating Medical Terminologies with ONIONS Methodology.* In: Kangassalo H, Charrel JP (eds) Information Modeling and Knowledge Bases VIII. IOS Press, Amsterdam, The Netherlands. *http://ontology.ip.rm.cnr.it/Papers/onions97.pdf*

Stuckenschmidt H (2000) *Using OIL for Intelligent Information Integration.* In Benjamins VR, Gómez-Pérez A, Guarino N (eds) ECAI'00 Workshop on Applications of Ontologies and Problem Solving Methods. Berlin, Germany, pp 9.1–9.10

Studer R, Benjamins VR, Fensel D (1998) *Knowledge Engineering: Principles and Methods.* IEEE Transactions on Data and Knowledge Engineering 25(1-2):161–197

Stumme G, Maedche A (2001) *FCA-MERGE: Bottom-Up Merging of Ontologies.* Bernhard Nebel (ed) Proceedings of the Seventeenth International Joint Conference on Artificial Intelligence (IJCAI 2001). Seattle, Washington. Morgan Kaufmann Publishers, San Francisco, California, pp 225–234

Sure Y, Erdmann M, Angele J, Staab S, Studer R, Wenke D (2002a) *OntoEdit: Collaborative Ontology Engineering for the Semantic Web.* In: Horrocks I, Hendler JA (eds) First International Semantic Web Conference (ISWC'02). Sardinia, Italy. (Lecture Notes in Computer Science LNCS 2342) Springer-Verlag, Berlin, Germany, pp 221–235

Sure Y, Staab S, Angele J (2002b) *OntoEdit: Guiding Ontology Development by Methodology and Inferencing.* In: Meersman R, Tari Z (eds) Confederated International Conferences CoopIS, DOA and ODBASE 2002, University of

California, Irvine. (Lecture Notes in Computer Science LNCS 2519) Springer-Verlag, Berlin, Germany, pp 1205–1222

Swartout W, Gil Y (1995) *Expect: Explicit representations for flexible acquisition.* In: Gaines B, Musen MA (eds) 9th Knowledge Acquisition for Knowledge-Based Systems Workshop (KAW'95). Banff, Canada. *http://www.isi.edu/expect/link/papers/swartout-gil-kaw95.pdf*

Swartout B, Ramesh P, Knight K, Russ T (1997) *Toward Distributed Use of Large-Scale Ontologies.* In: Farquhar A, Gruninger M, Gómez-Pérez A, Uschold M, van der Vet P (eds) AAAI'97 Spring Symposium on Ontological Engineering. Stanford University, California, pp 138–148

Tennison J, Shadbolt, NR (1998) *APECKS: a Tool to Support Living Ontologies.* In: Gaines BR, Musen MA (eds) 11th Knowledge Acquisition for Knowledge-Based Systems Workshop (KAW'98). Banff, Canada, pp KM7:1–20

Terpstra P, van Heijst G, Wielinga B, Shadtbolt N (1993) *Knowledge acquisition support through generalised directive models.* In: David JM, Krivine JP, Simmons R (eds). Second Generation Expert Systems, pp 428–455. Springer-Verlag, Berlin, Germany

Thalheim B (2000) *Entity-relationship modeling. Foundations of Database Technology.* Springer-Verlag, Berlin, Germany

Thompson H, Beech D, Maloney M, Mendelsohn N (2001) *XML Schema Part 1: Structures.* W3C Recommendation. *http://www.w3.org/TR/xmlschema-1/*

Tijerino YA, Mizoguchi R (1993) *MULTIS II: enabling end-users to design problem-solving engines via two-level task ontologies.* In: Aussenac N, Boy G, Gaines B, Linster M, Ganascia JG, Kodratoff Y (eds) 7th European Workshop on Knowledge Acquisition for Knowledge-Based Systems (EKAW'93). Toulouse and Caylus, France. (Lecture Notes in Computer Science LNCS 723) Springer-Verlag, Berlin, Germany, pp 340–359.

Ullman JD (1988) *Principles of database and knowledge-based systems.* Journal of Automated Reasoning 4:397–424.

Uschold M (1996) *Building Ontologies: Towards A Unified Methodology.* In: Watson I (ed) 16th Annual Conference of the British Computer Society Specialist Group on Expert Systems. Cambridge, United Kingdom. *http://citeseer.nj.nec.com/uschold96building.html*

Uschold M, Grüninger M (1996) *Ontologies: Principles, Methods and Applications.* Knowledge Engineering Review 11(2):93–155

Uschold M, Jasper R (1999) *A Framework for Understanding and Classifying Ontology Applications.* In: Benjamins VR (ed) IJCAI'99 Workshop on Ontology and Problem Solving Methods: Lessons Learned and Future Trends. Stockholm, Sweden. CEUR Workshop Proceedings 18:11.1–11.12. Amsterdam, The Netherlands (*http://CEUR-WS.org/Vol-18/*)

Uschold M, King M (1995) *Towards a Methodology for Building Ontologies*. In: Skuce D (eds) IJCAI'95 Workshop on Basic Ontological Issues in Knowledge Sharing. Montreal, Canada, pp 6.1–6.10

Uschold M, King M, Moralee S, Zorgios Y (1998) *The Enterprise Ontology*. The Knowledge Engineering Review 13(1):31–89

Valente A, Russ T, MacGregor R, Swartout W (1999) *Building and (Re)Using an Ontology of Air Campaign Planning*. IEEE Intelligent Systems & their applications 14(1):27–36

Valente A, Gil Y, Swartout WR (1996) *INSPECT: an Intelligent System for Air Campaign Plan Evaluation based on EXPECT*. ISI Technical memo, University of Southern California

van Harmelen F, Patel-Schneider PF, Horrocks I (2001a) *A Model-Theoretic Semantics for DAML+OIL (March 2001)*. Technical Report. *http://www.daml.org/2001/03/model-theoretic-semantics.html*

van Harmelen F, Patel-Schneider PF, Horrocks I (2001b) *Annotated DAML+OIL (March 2001) Markup Language*. Technical Report. *http://www.daml.org/2001/03/daml+oil-walkthru.html*

van Heijst G, Schreiber ATh, Wielinga BJ (1997) *Using explicit ontologies in KBS development*. International Journal of Human-Computer Studies 45:183–292

van Heijst G, van der Spek R, Kruizinga E (1996) *Organizing Corporate Memories*. In: Gaines BR, Musen M (eds) Tenth Knowledge Acquisition for Knowledge-Based Systems Workshop (KAW'96). Banff, Canada, pp 42.1–42.17

Vargas-Vera M, Motta E, Domingue J, Buckingham-Shum S, Lanzoni M (2001) *Knowledge Extraction by using an Ontology-based Annotation Tool*. In: Handschuh S, Dieng R, Staab S (eds) KCAP'01 Workshop on Semantic Markup and Annotation. Victoria, Canada. *http://semannot2001.aifb.uni-karlsruhe.de/schedule_new.html*

Vossen P (ed) (1999) *EuroWordNet General Document. Version 3*. *http://www.hum.uva.nl/ewn/*

Vossen P (ed) (1998) *EuroWordNet: A Multilingual Database with Lexical Semantic Networks*. Kluwer Academic Publishers, Dordrecht, The Netherlands

Warmer JB, Kleppe AG (1998) *The Object Constraint Language: Precise Modeling With UML*. Addison-Wesley, Boston, Massachusetts

Waterman DA (1986) *A Guide to Expert Systems*. Addison-Wesley, Boston, Massachusetts

Welty C, Guarino N (2001) *Supporting Ontological Analysis of Taxonomic Relationships*. Data and Knowledge Engineering 39(1):51–74

Weyhrauch RW (1980) *Prolegomena to a theory of mechanized formal reasoning*. Artificial Intelligence 13(1-2):133–170

Wielinga BJ, Schreiber ATh, Breuker JA (1992) *KADS: a modeling approach to knowledge engineering*. Knowledge Acquisition 4:1–162

Wilkins DE (1999) *Using the SIPE-2 Planning System: A Manual for Version 6.1*. SRI International Artificial Intelligence Center, Menlo Park, California. *http://www.ai.sri.com/~sipe/manual.pdf*

Wolff A, Koss M, Zdrahal Z (2001) *Knowledge Modelling of Hypertension Guidelines*. In: Patel V, Rogers R, Haux R (eds) Tenth World Congress on Health and Medical Informatics (MEDINFO'01). London, United Kingdom. IOS Press Studies in Health Technology and Informatics 84, Amsterdam, The Netherlands, p 302

Index

396

Index of figures

Index of tables